WHITE LAMA

White Lama

THE LIFE OF TANTRIC YOGI

THEOS BERNARD,

TIBET'S LOST EMISSARY

TO THE NEW WORLD

DOUGLAS VEENHOF

HARMONY BOOKS

New York

Published in the United States by Harmony Books, an imprint of the
Crown Publishing Group, a division of Random House, Inc., New York.
www.crownpublishing.com

Harmony Books is a registered trademark and the Harmony Books
colophon is a trademark of Random House, Inc.

Library of Congress Cataloging-in-Publication Data
Veenhof, Douglas.
White Lama: the life of tantric yogi Theos Bernard, Tibet's lost emissary
to the New World / Douglas Veenhof.
Includes bibliographical references and index.
I. Bernard, Theos, b. 1908.   2. Yogis—United States—Biography.
3. Scholars—United States—Biography.   I. Title.
BI32.Y6V365 2011
294.3'923092—dc22
[B]   2010039977

ISBN 978-0-385-51432-3
eISBN 978-0-307-72082-5

Book design by Jennifer Daddio / Bookmark Design & Media Inc.
Jacket design by Nupoor Gordon
Jacket photograph courtesy of the Phoebe A. Hearst Museum of Anthropology,
University of California at Berkeley

1   3   5   7   9   10   8   6   4   2

First Edition

For

JAMES DONALDSON

especially

The real yogi is your unfabricated innate nature.

"Yogi" means to realize the wisdom of pure awareness.

That is how you truly obtain the name yogi. . . .

Tibetan yogis of future generations, keep this in your hearts.

—PADMASAMBHAVA, EIGHTH CENTURY,
The Lotus-Born

CONTENTS

WHITE LAMA

INTRODUCTION

IT IS ESTIMATED that today there are more than eighteen hundred Tibetan Buddhist centers in Europe and the United States, and that nearly eighteen million people in North America alone practice some form of Yoga at studios, gyms, or clinics. With the ubiquity now of these twenty-five-hundred-year-old spiritual practices in the West, it can be hard to imagine that less than a hundred years ago its practitioners were known here only by their caricatures as demon worshipers and contortionists, and if a student wanted to take up a serious practice of Yoga or Tibetan Buddhism, he would have to travel around the world on a difficult journey to their Asian sanctuaries and then spend months trying to penetrate their secret societies.

In 1936, a graduate student at Columbia University named Theos Bernard decided to do just that and went to India for a year of field research on Tantric Yoga. His goal was to collect copies of the fast-disappearing Tantric scriptures and then master their practices under a qualified guru so that he could learn for himself whether these ancient spiritual technologies were still relevant for the modern mind. The exciting twists of his quest led to an invitation from the government of Tibet to make the first-ever spiritual pilgrimage by a Westerner to the forbidden city of

Lhasa, and he returned home to New York after his fifteen-month trip with what a London newspaper proclaimed in a banner headline to be "The Greatest Adventure Story of the Year." He was christened the "White Lama" by the press and became one of the pioneering teachers of both Yoga and Tibetan Buddhism in the West. But then, after a decade in the celebrity spotlight, Theos Bernard suddenly vanished from the cultural landscape.

Like nearly all of the tens of millions of people today who make some use of the practices he helped introduce to the West, I had never heard the name of Theos Bernard until a summer evening in June 2003. I was standing that evening under the stars in a sandy wash that runs out of the Dragoon Mountains in southeastern Arizona waiting with about a dozen others around an arrangement of logs set to be lit for a ritual fire *puja* to mark the end of Geshe Michael Roach's Great Retreat. Out of the night we saw approaching the flashlights of Geshe Michael (the first Westerner in the six-hundred-year history of Tibet's Sera monastery to earn the *geshe* degree, the pinnacle of scholarship) and the five students who all had been living in silent retreat the last three years, three months, and three days. Geshe Michael, dressed in red and yellow monastic robes, stepped over the boundary they had not crossed in all that time, and looked at the small group of faces, illuminated by a hissing lantern, that awaited him in the outside world. When he spotted me he crooked his finger to summon me to him. The first words he whispered after leaving his retreat were, "I have a project for you." He wanted me to do a little journalistic research, he said. Some lawyer from Arizona named Bernard had gone to Lhasa, Tibet, in the 1930s and brought back a big library of Tibetan Buddhist scriptures. He wanted me to find out what I could about him.

A week later Geshe Michael showed me a worn copy of *Hatha Yoga: The Report of a Personal Experience* by Theos Bernard. The retreatants had all been practicing Yoga along with their four long daily sessions of meditation, and one of the few books Geshe Michael allowed into his retreat was this one. First published in 1944 by Columbia University Press, the slim volume was filled with Bernard's personal advice about the arcane practices of Hatha Yoga and illustrated by thirty-six photographs of the author demonstrating with perfect form the poses and practices he describes.

This yogi, Theos Bernard, was, as the introduction to the book revealed, also the Arizona lawyer who went to Lhasa. Geshe Michael was intrigued: Who was this man? How had he gotten an invitation to Lhasa, and how, at a time when there were almost no Yoga teachers in America, had he learned to demonstrate the asanas and mudras with such perfect alignment? A brief editorial note at the beginning of the edition Geshe Michael owned only compounded the mystery about the author. The publisher regretted to inform his readers that Theos Bernard had disappeared without a trace while returning from a monastery in the Himalayas in 1947. "Good luck," Geshe Michael said. "Let me know what you come up with."

It has taken seven years to follow to the end the trail that Geshe Michael set me on with those first clues. Theos Bernard, this forgotten figure, left a huge trove of biographical materials to work through, and at least nine archives around the United States preserve altogether many thousands of pages of his personal journal, letters, photographs, lecture notes, business ledgers, and organizational papers. What emerged from all this material was a fascinating, complex, and sometimes contradictory portrait of a man who was not only a pioneering scholar/adept of both Hatha Yoga and Tibetan Buddhism but also for a decade a huge celebrity—Indiana Jones and Carlos Castaneda rolled into one.

Theos trained as an anthropologist at Columbia University with Margaret Mead and Ruth Benedict, but he got his master's degree there in philosophy and wrote a thesis titled "Tantric Ritual." He was already an accomplished yogi when in the fall of 1936, at the age of twenty-seven, he went to India for a year of research on Yoga and Hindu Tantra for his doctorate. He intended to employ the new techniques of anthropological field research to learn the philosophy and practices of the few remaining Tantric yogis, and then undertake a traditional apprenticeship with a Tantric master and become, as he put it, "a spiritual guinea pig." He would experiment on himself to test whether these antique practices could promise the same transformation in the mind of a modern man as in the great *mahasiddhas* of a thousand years ago.

He was unable to find in India, however, the Tantric master who could teach him both the philosophy and the practices, and he was advised that he must go to Tibet, where the medieval Tantric lineages still thrived.

Tibet, though, had sealed its borders to foreigners 250 years earlier, and aside from a British military incursion in 1904 and the visits of two subsequent British political delegations, only a handful of Western trespassers had managed with disguises and subterfuge to make it to Lhasa. But Theos was determined, and he moved to a Himalayan border town, where he learned the Tibetan language and customs and then overwhelmed every Tibetan official he met with his sincere interest in their religion. It all resulted in an invitation from the highest officials of the Tibetan government to be the first Westerner ever to visit the forbidden city of Lhasa as a Buddhist pilgrim.

Theos spent two and half months in the summer of 1937 living with one of the wealthiest families in Tibet and was given open access to Lhasa's most sacred and secret shrines and temples. He received Tantric initiation from the highest lama in Tibet and was sent home with fifty muleloads of the finest-quality Tibetan Buddhist scriptures and ritual art to support his mission of introducing Tibetan Buddhism in the West. The head of the Tibetan government and the head of the Sakya lineage of Tibetan Buddhism each wrote a letter for Theos to deliver to the president of the United States, Franklin Delano Roosevelt, requesting that he assist Theos in building the first Tibetan Buddhist monastery in America.

One of the first things everyone wanted to know when he returned was what was so special about Theos Bernard that had persuaded the Tibetans to invite him to Lhasa for a pilgrimage when everyone else who made the attempt was still being arrested at the border. The incredible explanation Theos offered was that Tibetans recognized him as an incarnation of Padmasambhava, the great eighth-century saint who introduced Tantra to Tibet and helped build the first monastery there, and they had sent him back to America with everything he needed to be the first White Lama.

The endless newspaper and magazine articles profiling the White Lama created an aura of instant celebrity around him. Within months of his return to the United States, he had an agent and two book contracts. His editor at Scribner's was none other than Maxwell Perkins, the living legend who discovered and brought to print F. Scott Fitzgerald, Ernest Hemingway, and Thomas Wolfe. Hemingway himself asked Perkins for advance copies of Theos' *Penthouse of the Gods* to send to his children.

Theos was featured four times in eighteen months in the *Family Circle*—one of the largest-circulation magazines of the day—and upstaged Errol Flynn, Bette Davis, and Dorothy Lamour on the cover with photos twice the size of theirs. Inside the magazine, long articles profiling him introduced the readership of three million housewives to the mysteries of Tibet and the theories and practices of the subtle body in Tantric Yoga.

While he was in Tibet, Theos shot ten thousand still photographs and eighteen thousand feet of movie film, a collection that was being called the greatest photographic record of Tibet in existence. He edited those into an illustrated lecture and took it on a tour that crossed the United States four times in six months, with capacity crowds filling venues ranging from New York's Town Hall to the Sioux City Knife and Fork Club to see it.

With his celebrity appearances, Theos intended to sow the seeds of Tibetan Buddhism and Tantric Yoga broadly in American popular culture. But he also wished to sow those seeds deeply. Trained as both a philosopher and an anthropologist at Columbia, Theos wanted to cut through the cultural jargon and accretions of "twilight language" that obscured the essence of Yoga and Tantra and employ a skeptical, scientific approach to investigate these ancient spiritual traditions and adapt what worked to the demands of contemporary life.

To do that, he created two visionary institutions. The first was the American Institute of Yoga, a groundbreaking center for practicing in a rigorous and comprehensive curriculum the complete path of Hatha Yoga along with the philosophy of Tibetan Buddhism. The second, called the Academy of Tibetan Literature, established a center near Santa Barbara, California, where Tibetan lamas would be employed to translate the entire Tibetan canon of Buddhist scriptures and a small group of hard-core American students would dedicate years to the study and practice of Tantra.

World War II and his second divorce delayed the full development of his plans for these new centers, and in 1946 he returned to India to continue his studies with Tibetan lamas. After leaving a monastery in a remote Himalayan valley in the fall of 1947, Theos Bernard, at the age of thirty-eight, disappeared without a trace. The young institutions he founded could not survive his untimely death, and after the last news reports about his disappearance, the White Lama, despite his decade of fame, vanished for fifty years from our collective memory.

Most of the thousands of fine Tibetan texts Theos brought home with him were sold to university libraries after his death by his father, but the treasury of Tibetan art that Theos hauled out of Tibet and all his personal papers gathered dust while they passed from his estate to his father's estate and then to his father's housekeeper's estate. Not until 1999, when appraisers were called in to estimate the value of some of the Tibetan artifacts found in the housekeeper's estate for tax purposes, did it become known what an astonishing collection had survived them all. The appraisers rolled up the doors on four self-storage units in Upland, California, and found piled there 119 cardboard boxes and 18 large trunks filled with 750 high-quality pieces of ritual art, the artifacts of a now vanished Tibetan culture.

Among the piles were forty boxes of Theos Bernard's personal papers, a biographer's dream, that included detailed journals of his historic experiences in Tibet, long letters to his two wives and his last love, notes and transcripts of the groundbreaking lectures he delivered to his Yoga groups, organizational papers for the institutions he founded, and drafts of his five published books and unpublished works as well. It all added up to more than thirty shelf-feet of documents when it was all fumigated, organized, and indexed by the Bancroft Library at the University of California. Because of the sheer volume of documents the work was not completed and the documents made available to the public until 2007, four years after Geshe Michael Roach launched me on my research. But it is only now, after the digestion of all those files, that I can finally tell Geshe Michael what I uncovered about this lawyer from Arizona who mastered Hatha Yoga with no apparent teachers and who was sent home from his pilgrimage to Lhasa with the mission to introduce Tibetan Buddhism in America. This is the untold story of Theos Bernard, the White Lama.

Chapter 1

OUT OF A CLEAR SKY

HE WAS BORN Theos Casimir Hamati Bernard on December 10, 1908, at his parents' home in Los Angeles, and although his birth records fail to record the kind of miraculous events that accompanied the eighth-century birth of Padmasambhava, it is clear that Theos arrived to a most unusual turn-of-the-century American family and that his early life in America's Wild West prepared him well for his odyssey across the Tibetan Plateau.

His mother was named Aura, and Theos means "god" in Greek. As his first wife, Viola, pointed out, "Somebody named Aura with a son named Theos is expecting great things, like first white lamas."

The year before Theos' birth, Aura took a long leave of absence from her job as postmaster in Tombstone, Arizona, and, as a friend recollected, went to New York to study Theosophy. It was there, the friend supposed, that she met Theos' father, Glen Agassiz Bernard, who, although only twenty-three years old, had been studying Hindu Tantra for almost a decade.

By the spring of 1908 Glen and Aura were married and living in Los Angeles. The marriage, though, didn't last much past the signing of the birth certificate in December. Glen is said to have abandoned the family shortly after Theos' birth and gone off to India to continue his studies of esoteric Tantric philosophy, and Aura soon left Los Angeles and returned with the infant Theos to her hometown, the Old West legend, Tombstone, Arizona.

Aura had moved as a young girl with her family to the booming mining town of Tombstone in 1884, just six years after prospector Ed Schieffelin discovered a rich ledge of silver in the remote, dusty hills of southeastern Arizona Territory. The town took its name from the mining claim that Schieffelin filed, which he called "Tombstone" in mocking tribute to the soldiers and settlers who had predicted that he would find nothing more among the area's waterless hills and raiding Apaches than his grave.

The silver ore in the area was rich and close to the surface, fueling rumors throughout the West of another bonanza on the scale of the Comstock Lode discovered near Virginia City, Nevada, twenty years earlier. Miners flooded to the area, and within two years of its incorporation as a village, Tombstone, with its ten thousand souls, was one of the largest and most sophisticated towns between New Orleans and San Francisco.

The year after moving to Tombstone, Aura's father died and she went to live at age seven with relatives in Detroit. She was still so homesick after a year, however, that she was sent home to her mother, who by then had married W. A. Harwood, one of the most prominent men in the area.

Harwood was a lumber dealer and the first mayor of Tombstone, which was getting a reputation already as one of the deadliest towns in the West. The boom attracted more men than the mines could employ, and a shiftless crowd of unemployed and growingly desperate and well-armed men loafed on the streets and in the thriving saloons. "Some of the boys will have to be boxed up and sent home yet if they don't behave themselves," wrote Tombstone diarist George Parsons. "Too much loose pistol practice. Bradshaw killed Waters because Waters resented with his fist being teased about a shirt. . . . Men killed every few days, besides numerous pullings and firings of pistols and fist fights."

It was during this period that the gunfight at the O.K. Corral made Tombstone the lawless icon of the Old West. Doc Holliday and the brothers Virgil, Morgan, and Wyatt Earp drew first and shot down the

McLaury brothers and Billy Clanton. Boothill Cemetery was filling fast, and at one point in 1882, President Chester A. Arthur, sensing that the area was spiraling toward anarchy, considered imposing martial law and sending in federal troops to keep order.

For all that, Aura's mother and stepfather provided her and her two brothers and a sister a cultured and sheltered childhood among the scorpions, snakes, bordellos, and saloons. All four children were baptized on the same day, February 17, 1895, when a circuit preacher came to St. Paul's Episcopal Church in Tombstone, and for Aura, who was sixteen at the time, the event marked a blossoming spiritual awareness. She became an active, lifelong member of St. Paul's, ran the Sunday school, and even conducted services in the absence of the circuit preacher.

But Aura's search for spiritual inspiration roamed far beyond the stained-glass windows and walnut pews of St. Paul's. Her father, when he was young, had spent several years in India, and the tales of his adventures there ignited Aura's early interest in the exotic Far East. She investigated the Baha'i faith, the emerging religion whose message that humanity is a single race and should be reconciled in one global society spurred her to attend one of its first conferences in America. Aura's friend Mary Price, who was the principal at the Tombstone elementary school, recalled, "She read the most unusual books in the world. She used to give me a book review once in a while, and it was all on Eastern Philosophy."

At age nineteen, Aura landed what would have been one of the choicest jobs in Tombstone. Through the political connections of her stepfather, W. A. Harwood, Aura received an appointment from President McKinley to be postmaster of Tombstone. She became the youngest woman postmaster in the United States, but the town welcomed her as the manager of one of its most important social hubs. Aura was a good writer and was almost daily asked to pen letters for the many Chinese in the community or write eulogies for departed loved ones. Aura was a much-loved town icon and served as postmaster for ten years until she resigned in February 1908, shortly before her marriage in Los Angeles to Theos' father, Glen Bernard.

With Glen's departure for India so soon after Theos' birth, Aura wasted little time in getting out of California. She took Theos back to

Tombstone, moved in with her parents, and had Theos baptized at St. Paul's when he was six months old. With the grandparents now available to babysit, Aura quickly got a job as a postal clerk from the new postmaster—her brother Francis—who had succeeded her.

No one knows exactly how long Glen stayed in India on his first trip, but census data show he had returned and was renting a room in Ventura, California, by the time Theos was seventeen months old. He stayed in touch with Aura, though their relationship during this period is confusing. The only surviving letter, written by Aura to Glen when Theos was probably three years old, suggests that they were, in fact, still in love and making plans to see each other. "I always want to know you have love for me," she wrote to him, "for your life is dear, very dear to me—and Glen when the sale does take place and you can get away, can we not plan for you to get something in San Francisco? I do not know just when I can go . . . but will write and tell you." She filled Glen in on the details of his growing son's everyday cuteness as if Father were merely away on a business trip. "Little Theos has taken a little cold and had fever again. He seems better today. I ask him, 'where's Papa?' and he waves his little hand and says 'Bye Bye.'" Aura thanked Glen in the letter for a money order he sent, and then, despite the affectionate prologue, asked him to sign some court documents she mailed to him, presumably regarding divorce.

The Tombstone to which Aura and the infant Theos returned in 1909 saw its fortunes still plunging through one of the most desperate periods in the frequent boom-and-bust oscillations of a mining town. In the previous decade, silver had dropped in value and the growing interest in gold and copper siphoned professionals from the old camp. Businessmen followed the miners out of town and in many cases dismantled their wood-frame buildings and took them with them. The community shrank to a population of 649, and Tombstone would have become another of Arizona's ghost towns had it not been the county seat.

With the uncertainty of the times, Aura decided that—regardless of her feelings for Glen—Theos needed a stepfather, and in 1913 she married Jonathan Gordon, a Scottish mining engineer. Gordon, as the family called him, was educated at the University of Edinburgh and Kings College London, and was the only registered mining chemical metallurgical engineer in Arizona. After the wedding, Aura and Theos moved into the small adobe miner's house Gordon rented for $10 a month on Third Street, just a half block from St. Paul's.

About that time, the fortunes of Tombstone veered again toward prosperity. The Phelps-Dodge Company bought the major mining properties in Tombstone near the end of 1913 and began to invest heavily in them. By the spring of 1914, all the vacant houses were filled again, and the mines were running around the clock. In the summer of 1914, the Great War erupted in Europe, and an order from the Allies for twenty-five million shell casings brought record payrolls to the Tombstone mines.

The delayed American entry into the war in the spring of 1917 also brought patriotic fervor to Tombstone. Nine-year-old Theos was among the chorus of schoolchildren that led the singing of patriotic hymns at the weekly downtown rallies in support of the Red Cross and Liberty Bonds. The Gordons also did their part for the war effort by observing the mandates for wheatless Mondays and Wednesdays, meatless Tuesdays, and porkless Saturdays.

By the time the war ended in 1919, Aura and Gordon had three more children, all boys. Gordon was described by a grandson as a "fascinating man, strict, a tyrant." He was fluent in Latin, Greek, French, and Spanish and kept records on everything. Bookshelves lined the living room walls, and Gordon wrote freely in the margins of his many chemistry books arguing with the authors.

One of Theos' school friends, Daniel Hughes, remembered Jonathan Gordon as "a very intelligent, well-educated man, but very impractical. He never made any money." Aura's friend Mary Price observed, "He was a good mining man, and he could have sold his mines for a good price, but he wouldn't sell them because they weren't offering enough. He'd let them starve before he'd sell." Another friend of the family recalled that the Gordons were so poor that when she asked Theos what he wanted for graduation, he replied, "A pair of socks."

In the Gordon household, however, there was a rich, nourishing climate for the boys' developing minds. As a chemist and engineer, Gordon taught his sons to take a scientific approach to life, to make judgments based on evidence, and to keep a mind open to surprise. "Don't reject something that you don't understand until you have a basis for doing so," he taught them. As a result, the house was an occasional "battlefield of debate," as Theos' stepbrother Dugald recalled.

To balance their scientific ideology, Aura insisted her sons learn the arts as well. Theos played piano and Dugald clarinet. There were also a zither and a violin in the house. Aura was a charter member of the Tombstone Woman's Club, was active in its poetry group, and stocked alongside Gordon's chemistry texts on the living room bookshelves an eclectic library of Eastern philosophy.

Theos recalled after the return from his historic trip to Lhasa in 1937 that his youth in the arid hills and vast desert basins of Arizona prepared him well for his fifteen-hundred-mile journey on horseback across the Tibetan Plateau, where suffocating dust storms blocked the sun for hours and a day's travel brought him to sleep on the dirt floor of a mud-block hovel "without even a cowboy saddle for a pillow." In the Gordon household, discipline, hard work, and a spirit of adventure were cardinal virtues, and everyday danger was part of a boy's training.

For young Theos and his gang, exploration of the miles of abandoned mine tunnels under the town was a favorite outing. Whenever they bought candles at the mercantile, the clerk lectured them about the dangers of cave-ins and gas pockets, and they promised with fingers crossed behind their backs to stay out of the old mines.

When Theos and each of his half brothers reached the age of eight they started spending their summers working Gordon's own mines. From the porch of their adobe house in Tombstone, the boys could look across twelve miles of desert basin to the abrupt granite crags of the Dragoon Mountains and the sheer faces of a formation known as Sheepshead Rock. Gordon's mines, the San Juan Group, were located in a high basin behind Sheepshead Rock at a cooler altitude of six thousand feet. A primitive road over the mountains took them most of the way to the claim, but supplies had to be hauled the last mile up a trail by Gordon's string of burros.

The San Juan mining camp, with its bunkhouses, blacksmith shop, and grub shack for the Chinese cook, was built in a cluster of juniper trees under the looming east wall of Sheepshead Rock. A path led to a stream course that flowed during the summer rains down a solid granite sluice and plunged into deep pools. After a hot day of work, the boys shinnied down the limbs of a tall pine to descend a cliff face to reach their favorite swimming hole.

While still young and small, the boys were assigned to pull chain, build monuments, drive stakes, and hold field targets for surveying claim boundaries. As they grew older, stronger, and more experienced, they chopped wood, carried water, loaded ore cars, and eventually set off dynamite charges.

Just a generation after the gunfight at the O.K. Corral, a still-dusty and rugged Tombstone provided Theos and his brothers with an all-American boyhood. Prohibition had closed the grand saloons, and the bordellos of the Great White Way were razed to build a new high school. All four brothers were Boy Scouts, and both Theos and Dugald earned the twenty-one merit badges required to be an Eagle Scout, the highest rank in Scouting.

Outside his family, Theos' gang included his two inseparable friends Daniel Hughes and Billy Fowler, classmates through grammar school, high school, and the University of Arizona. People in Tombstone called them the "Three Musketeers," and their small clique accounted for a full third of Tombstone High's senior class. Theos lettered in every sport available at Tombstone High, but favored running and swimming. As Daniel Hughes remembered, "He was a good athlete, he liked the girls, and he liked excitement." But even while pursuing the typical interests of a young man with promise, Theos already showed a contemplative nature. As Hughes put it, "Theos didn't go to church that much, but he was always thinking about religion."

Theos graduated from Tombstone High in May 1926 and in the fall entered the College of Liberal Arts and Sciences at the University of Arizona in Tucson. He lived on campus in South Hall and washed dishes at the Copper Kettle restaurant near the university in exchange for meals. Aura insisted that everyone in the family contribute what they could for his expenses—even nine-year-old Dugald pitched in when he was able to save a dollar from his paper route.

Theos got straight C's his first term at the university and was midway through an uneventful second term when, on a cold and rainy spring day in 1927, fate intervened to change the course of his life and set him on the path of Yoga. Freshmen who neglected to wear their beanies were subject to hazing, and "a fight with the sophomores," as Daniel Hughes called it, resulted in Theos being thrown into Memorial Fountain. He returned to his room in South Hall for a change of clothes, but the next day he developed a severe cold that quickly turned into strep throat or scarlet fever. He allowed the infection to go untreated, and it quickly worsened to a case of rheumatic fever, which damaged the valves of his heart.

Theos finally checked into the campus infirmary, and a doctor—termed "incompetent" by Aura in a letter to the dean—gave him experimental and highly toxic Mercurochrome injections, thought to stimulate white blood cell defenses against the infection. In his 1939 book, *Heaven Lies Within Us*, Theos wrote:

> I overheard the doctor speaking to my nurse. He said, "He will not live."... In the meanwhile, they would keep me sufficiently doped with morphine, so that the agony itself would not rob me of my last breath.... Every joint of my body was swollen. Indeed, all of my body had become so sensitive to pain that not even the sheets were allowed to touch me. A wall of pillows was built all around me, and the sheets were stretched tight above me. The attendants could not enter the room without causing me pain.

Theos pleaded with his mother to take him home to die in his own bed, and Aura, believing that the Mercurochrome treatments were making him sicker, ignored the doctors' dire protests and arranged a car to take Theos back to Tombstone. The pain of the rattles and jolts of the car over the dusty and corrugated seventy-eight-mile gravel road to Tombstone was excruciating, and once Theos was home, it was days before he could raise his head and take any food except what he could suck through a glass tube.

Theos was in bed for three months, but he slowly began to recover, and when he was strong enough to hold a book, he pored through his mother's library of Eastern philosophy and made plans for the future. Expecting that his damaged heart valves would force Theos to adapt a career to his physical limitations, Aura encouraged him to follow the path of her brother Francis, a successful lawyer, and they planned that after another year of studying liberal arts he would enter the Law College at the University of Arizona.

As the summer grew hotter in Tombstone and Theos grew stronger, Aura allowed him to finish his convalescence with his brothers at the cooler elevation of the San Juan mine. While his brothers and Gordon worked the mine, Theos spent endless undistracted hours in the bunk-house reading the books of Eastern wisdom from his mother's library. He realized quickly, though, that what he needed was not to fill his head with novel ideas but to learn a practical program for regaining the strength of his body. The damage to his heart and the atrophy of his muscles after weeks in bed made getting back into shape through running, swimming, or climbing unthinkable. His modest goal was to become strong enough again to finish his education and keep up the schedule required for work in an office.

One of the books Theos brought to the mine was *The Story of Oriental Philosophy* by L. Adams Beck, a biographer and writer of "Oriental fantasies" popular in the 1920s. "Open the treasure house of Eastern philosophy," the jacket proclaimed. "Learn the teachings of Buddha, Confucius, Lao Tsu, Shankara, Mencius, Patanjali and others. With this book you can understand the mysterious and ancient wisdom of the East." Inside, Theos found hope of a new method to recover his strength: "Infinite energy is at the disposal of any man if he knows how to get it. And this is a part of the science of Yoga."

Inspired by that promise, Theos read over the summer everything he could find on the subject. But however inspiring the books of the time about the endless benefits of practicing Yoga, Theos found none that could actually instruct him on how to do the practices. Indeed, all the books stressed the dangers of attempting to practice without the direct supervision of a teacher, and considering the weakened condition of his heart, Theos took the warnings seriously.

Theos recovered sufficiently to return to the University of Arizona for the fall term of 1927, but he was not a good student, getting mostly C's and D's in his classes. His health, though, seems not to have been the issue. Daniel Hughes, who with Theos lived in Cochise Hall, offered another explanation: "He seldom lived in a room alone. He was a Don Juan with the ladies and out to have all the fun he could."

One night Hughes and Theos went out to a movie and procured an illegal bottle of liquor. "Theos couldn't drink," Hughes said. "After one or two drinks he would start raising Cain." Theos decided to go to his fourth-floor room by climbing the fire escape and the others called up to him, "Come down from there, you'll fall!"

Theos yelled back, "You think I'll fall? Watch me!" and he hung by his knees from the fourth-floor fire escape ladder for several minutes. The fun apparently continued through the summer school session of 1928. Theos took Economics 31 by correspondence but failed to complete the course and got an F.

In the fall of 1929, after two years with indifferent results in the university's College of Liberal Arts and Sciences, Theos took the next step on his career plan and entered the College of Law. At the time, a bachelor's degree was not required for admission to the College of Law, and it was common for students to study liberal arts for a couple of years before specializing. A former registrar at the university remarked about Theos' admission to the Law College, "In those days they graded much harder," and Theos' barely passing grades actually marked him as an average student.

The missing inspiration for Theos' studies may have been supplied that fall by the crash of the stock market, signaling the start of the Great Depression. College has always seemed a good alternative to unemployment lines, and by his second semester in law school, Theos got B's in three classes—Contracts, Torts, and Property Rights in Land—and an A in Agency. Theos finished law school in three years, with his final year on a scholarship, and was awarded a Bachelor of Laws degree on June 3, 1931.

After graduating, Theos went to Los Angeles, the city of his birth, and spent the summer (and likely the fall) working as a clerk for a federal court judge. And although he rarely talked about it and never mentioned it in his memoirs, it was probably then, at age twenty-two, that he met his father, Glen Bernard, for the first time. Their meeting, as Viola Bernard recounted years later, had "a great deal to do with deflecting his path from law to what it became."

Glen's main activity at the time of his first meeting with Theos continued to be what it had been when he abandoned his son twenty-two years earlier to go to India: his research into the many aspects of Yoga practice. Glen supported his research with a variety of jobs in Los Angeles. He worked in the movie industry as an electrician and then got some training as a chemist, working for a time making cosmetics. Glen's interest in chemistry, however, stemmed from his studies of Ayurveda (the ancient Indian system of medicine) and Tantric alchemy (processes for transforming normally toxic mercury into compounds to be ingested as an aid to enlightenment). Glen described his occupation for the 1930 census as "salesman of home medical supplies"—meaning, perhaps, that he was selling the Ayurvedic and homeopathic remedies he compounded. He had been married to a hairdresser for a time around 1920, but when Theos met him he was single again and renting an $18-a-month house in Los Angeles.

Glen Bernard's passion for esoteric Hindu philosophy came out of an unlikely background. He was born in the small farming town of Humeston, Iowa, in 1884, and while still a teenager was introduced to Sylvais Hamati, one of the first teachers of Tantra in the United States, by his older half brother, Peter Perry Baker.

Perry, as he called himself, had been sent by his family when he was thirteen to live with a relative and to apprentice in the building trades in booming Lincoln, Nebraska, and Hamati, a highly educated man of Syrian and Bengali descent, lived across the street. Hamati was one of only about eight hundred East Indians living in the United States at that time, and he spoke fluent English. Rather than apprentice in the building trades, Perry began an intensive course of Vedic studies with his neighbor that included ethics, psychology, philosophy, religion, and natural philosophy, and he continued over the next twelve years to live and travel with Hamati as his disciple.

When Perry was seventeen, he left Lincoln with Hamati and moved to California. Perry's family had also left Iowa and moved to California for a time, and it was probably there that he introduced his nine-year-old half brother, Glen, to Hamati. Glen moved back to Iowa with his family when he was twelve. It is unknown exactly when and how intensively Glen began his studies with Hamati, but by the time Glen was twenty-two, Hamati had left the United States (presumably to return to India). It seems likely that the reason for Glen's trip to India immediately after Theos was born two years later was to visit his guru in Bengal. Before he left his new family, Glen and Aura paid homage to him by naming their son Theos Casimir Hamati Bernard.

Glen made a second trip to India in 1926 at age forty-three. By this time Glen was well connected in the shadowy world of Hindu Tantra, and he stayed for eight months. Those connections may have been the fruit of his trip to visit Hamati seventeen years earlier, or resulted from introductions provided by his half brother, Perry, or even from the well-known Indian yogi Paramahansa Yogananda, who would become famous as the founder of the Self-Realization Fellowship and the author of *Autobiography of a Yogi*.

Yogananda came to the United States in 1920 as India's delegate to an international religious conference in Boston and then spent the next four years teaching on the East Coast. Glen met and perhaps studied with Yogananda there and contributed to financing the national teaching tour Yogananda set out on in 1924 by purchasing from the swami a large, full-headed tiger skin—the meditation rug of high yogis—which Glen kept until his death in 1976.

Glen had also studied in the United States during the 1920s with Yogananda's disciple, Swami Dhirananda, and with Hatha Yogi Wassan (author of the 1927 book *Secrets of the Himalayan Mountain Masters and Ladder to Cosmic Consciousness*), and with Sukumar Chatterji, whose lectures in San Francisco on Pranayama, Ayurvedic medicine, and the various schools of Indian philosophy Glen preserved in hundreds of pages of lecture notes.

However it was arranged, Glen was able on his 1926 trip to Calcutta to consult with one of the best available authorities on the subject of Bengali Tantra, Atal Behari Ghosh. Ghosh was the unidentified collaborator of Sir John Woodroffe on several of the books that first brought a serious study of Tantra to the West. He was the Sanskrit scholar of the pair, and the pseudonym Arthur Avalon—under which Woodroffe published several of his best-known works, such as *The Serpent Power* and *Shakti and Shakta*—appears to be essentially a composite identity for the two of them.

The surviving correspondence between Glen and Atal Behari Ghosh reveals a close, mentoring friendship. Ghosh sent invitations to parties at his house and briefed Glen on Woodroffe, who had returned to teach at Oxford and was having health problems. But more important, after Glen returned to California from India, Ghosh continued to give him detailed instructions and advice on Tantric Yoga practices. He told Glen that he realized practicing concentration in "a country like yours, where everyone seems to be boiling over," was difficult and suggested that to control the mind in meditation he should try fixing his gaze on the tip of his nose or on a speck of light while repeating his mantras. "As for Pranayama," he told him, "never exert yourself more than you can do with ease and comfort." Ghosh admitted his English was "not what it ought to be" and his translations of the Tantras were defective because of that. He hoped Americans would "evolve a language more fit for the expression of spiritual ideas than English is."

By 1931, when Theos met his father for the first time, Glen Bernard had quietly become one of the best-educated native-born Yoga scholars in America. His nearest rival, in fact, was probably his half brother Perry, who had in the previous decades become famous under the name Dr. Pierre Arnold Bernard and founded a posh center for the study of Vedic philosophy and "physical culture" on a country estate in Nyack, New York, called the Clarkstown Country Club. In stark contrast, however, to his half brother's huckstering showmanship at the Clarkstown Country Club, Glen approached Yoga with a dour intellectualism.

Glen's desire to have everything "on a rational basis" was understandable, Ghosh wrote to him, but he would "have to take certain things on trust to start with . . . Reasonableness will dawn before you as you progress." He would, as he continued his practices, "experience what is now beyond your 'conscious' mind's understanding . . . These are material manifestations of unconscious powers."

In the reunion with his father, Theos at last found the teacher he longed for since his introduction to Yoga in the books of his mother four years earlier. Glen instructed his student in a comprehensive series of Hatha Yoga practices to work on, and then advised him to return to the University of Arizona—even though Theos had just finished his law degree—to study philosophy. In February 1932, Theos enrolled for two more years of study in the College of Liberal Arts and Sciences, but with a dramatic change in course from the business-oriented curriculum of his freshman and sophomore years. He registered for the spring semester as a philosophy major and began by taking Logic and Elementary Psychology, earning a B in both.

It was undoubtedly Glen's influence behind Theos' sudden interest in philosophy and psychology, but curiously, after his historic trip to Lhasa made him a celebrity, Theos found it necessary to completely conceal his father's role in shaping him as a yogi. He created instead a fictional Indian guru whom he described in great detail, but during his entire life—even when it was demanded for his academic writings—he refused to name him.

The story Theos tells in his 1939 memoir, *Heaven Lies Within Us*, about meeting his guru is, like much of his autobiographical writings, a mélange of verifiable fact and pure invention. Here he writes that after he discovered the promise of Yoga during his recovery at his family's mine in the Dragoon Mountains, and after studying all the books on Yoga he could find and cautiously developing the elementary practices they described, he despaired that he might never find a teacher to take him further.

> How was such a teacher to be found, of all places, in Arizona? I had often read in my books of Eastern teachings that when a student was ready the teacher was sure to appear. . . . Then, one day, out of a clear sky, I was summoned by one who had just arrived from India. He proved to be my first spiritual teacher or Guru.

Theos states that a member of his family had told the guru about his heart condition and interest in Yoga and asked the guru to contact him during an overnight stop on his travels through Tucson. They met, Theos said, after dinner at the guru's rooming house and talked through the night until dawn.

The guru, in this account, outlined the entire path of Yoga, promised a list of books on Tantric philosophy, and advised Theos to adhere strictly to his vegetarian diet and "forego acquiring the collegiate habit of smoking and indulgence in intoxicants." Most important, the guru gave Theos four practices as the foundation for his yogic path. Before they parted at dawn, Theos wrote, the guru had one more instruction for him. As is the case with most of the practices of Tantra, which require a vow of secrecy, Theos was instructed: "I must never tell anyone about my practices. I should keep my every effort wholly to myself. Silence is Power."

Ironically, after he became famous, Theos wrote at great length about his practices, and his detailed description of his experiments on himself is perhaps his greatest legacy to today's Yoga practitioners. The one thing he refused ever to tell, however, is usually the first thing that teachers of Buddhism or Yoga philosophy tell their students: the lineage of their teachers. In all of the many pages of his writing about this period, Theos refers to his teacher—who all evidence suggests had to be his father, Glen—only as "the Guru."

THE ANONYMOUS GURU, Theos wrote in *Heaven Lies Within Us*, also instructed him to read the masters of both Eastern and Western philosophy, and after the spring term at the University of Arizona in Tucson, Theos returned for the summer of 1932 to Los Angeles, where he took two summer school classes at the University of Southern California: Survey of English Literature and Shakespeare. He undoubtedly also spent as much time as he could cultivating his budding relationship with Glen.

Theos returned to Tucson for the fall term and followed another of the guru's injunctions—to prepare himself to be financially independent—by getting certified to practice law before the Arizona Supreme Court and the U.S. District Court in Arizona. He went to work as a part-time clerk for judge Alfred M. Sames, who had risen to the federal bench after serving as a superior court judge in Tombstone. Theos got the job doing research in the law library through his old friend Daniel Hughes, who worked for Judge Sames as a court interpreter.

Continuing his studies as a philosophy major, Theos took classes in the literature of the Bible, the history of philosophy, elementary Greek, the philosophy of religion, philosophical literature, abnormal psychology, and Roman literature. And along with the full load at school and his part-time job, Theos applied himself to his Yoga practice, which, during this period, as his guru instructed, he kept entirely secret.

The guru instructed Theos that of the four foundational practices he gave him, he should start by mastering Padmasana, the lotus pose. This well-known posture, in which one sits with a straight back and each foot up on the opposite thigh, is considered one of the most stable and powerful poses for meditation, and it was the first pose to learn, the guru told him, if he expected to make any progress in Yoga. Theos was able to get in long hours of practice by sitting in lotus while reading his university assignments.

At the same time, Theos applied himself to Sirshasana, or headstand. He was given no instruction on how to actually get into a headstand, but he was told that once he was able to get up, he should start by holding the pose for only a minute, and when that was comfortable add a few seconds each day. The guru instructed him to always stay within the safe limits of his capacity and stop when his breathing became labored and he began to sweat. Regular practice would gradually increase his capacity until he reached the point where he could remain on his head for three hours straight on thirty consecutive days. He could then consider this practice perfected. Theos was quickly able to reach the point "where half an hour on my head three times a day was the most resting and relaxing thing I could do." He was then able to eventually extend each session to an hour, for a total of three hours each day.

During his years in school Theos maintained a steady correspondence with his guru.

> I wrote often, and no doubt at tiring length. . . . Never would he explain my problem. At best he would say that I was on the right path. It was not his method to teach me; rather it was to stimulate me to teach myself.

If, in the course of his reading, Theos came across a practice he wanted to learn, the guru invariably refused, saying the time for that would come later. "Enthusiasm must be directed," he wrote. "The perfection of one practice was the perfection of all."

Another of the four foundational practices given to Theos by his guru was Uddiyana, or inter-abdominal control, as Theos termed it. The practice calls for hollowing out the abdomen by exhaling the breath and then raising the viscera and diaphragm, bringing the belly button nearly to the backbone. Theos was advised to practice every morning and evening, with increasing sets of rapid contractions until he reached fifteen hundred a day and then continue that for six months. Uddiyana brings the nerves and muscles of the organs under conscious control and the stomach and intestines "lose their lethargy and act with increased vigor," as Theos described it.

The ultimate development of Uddiyana is Nauli, the fourth foundational practice Theos learned. The practice of Nauli draws the abdomen in as far as possible while one stands hunched forward with hands on thighs. With the side muscles fully contracted, the two muscles of the abdominal wall, the recti, are isolated and pushed forward. A sort of rolling motion is then performed, giving the abdomen the appearance of undulating ocean swells.

After Theos had developed Uddiyana and Nauli to the prescribed standards and maintained the practices for six months, the guru wrote that he was now prepared to begin the purification practices. "It was of the greatest importance that one be clean, even to his veins, arteries, and nerves," Theos wrote of that time. The first stage of his training focused on expelling the body's numerous secretions. The bowels should be kept free of all feces and gases, the throat and stomach must be free from excess *kapha*, or phlegm, the acid of the stomach must be reduced to a minimum, and one should perspire a little each day to keep the pores of the skin open.

The six yogic processes of purification Theos learned are called the Shatkarmas: Dhauti, Basti, Neti, Nauli, Trataka, and Kapalabhati. For the time being, Theos concentrated on two of the six practices: Dhauti and Neti. Dhauti is a process for cleansing and massaging the mucous membranes of the throat, esophagus, and stomach that he practiced by swallowing a wetted four-inch-wide, twenty-two-and-a-half-foot-long piece of surgical gauze. Dhauti is recommended for removing excess phlegm, bile, and other impurities of the stomach to prevent coughs, asthma, leprosy, and twenty kinds of diseases caused by excess mucus. Theos was advised to do this practice every morning while doing headstand.

Concealing what would naturally seem bizarre behavior to the uninitiated led to some embarrassing moments.

> Again and again I let the door bell ring and ring. Sometimes, too, the phone would ring with a dogged persistence, due to the fact that the person ringing knew that I was invariably at home at this time. I let him imagine that I was in the tub. Or the person must have been perplexed at my voice, as I tried to talk to him over the phone with about fifteen feet of cloth within me and the rest dangling from my mouth.

The other practice Theos perfected at this time was Neti, a process of cleansing the nasal passages and sinuses and removing all phlegm from the head. As Theos described it, a thin thread is used in the beginning and inserted through one of the nostrils. Aided by vigorous inhalations, the thread passes back into the throat, where it can be reached and drawn out through the mouth. The thread is then slowly pulled back and forth through the nose and mouth. After a few minutes of this, the same operation is performed on the other nostril.

Theos also added a daily cleaning of his ears, teeth, and tongue to his growing practice schedule. The guru instructed him that washing the root of the tongue was necessary for learning the control needed to swallow the tongue, a practice known as Kechari Mudra. The guru wouldn't yet reveal the precise purpose of the practice but promised it would be very important for Theos' future development.

Making use of every available minute, Theos practiced Kechari Mudra while walking around campus, and more awkward encounters were inevitable. With his tongue swallowed into his throat, his mouth would fill with saliva, and his first reaction when surprised by a friend was always a mystifying contortion in his mouth and gulping of saliva. "It was difficult to explain away, except by the remark that I had been daydreaming," Theos recounted in *Heaven Lies Within Us*. "I was continually in a position where I had to make excuses for myself which never sounded quite plausible."

One of the results of his practice was that Theos' resting respiration rate slowed to three or four breaths per minute and his pulse rate dropped to twelve beats per minute. A recurrence in those days of the dangerous symptoms of rheumatic fever was common, and during Theos' frequent checkups, the doctors grew alarmed by his slow heart and breathing rates and ordered him to rest in bed. But they couldn't deny all the other evidence that Theos had, as he told them, never felt better in his life, and they sent him on his way with the usual warnings about not overtaxing himself.

Theos was no longer able to spend summers with his half brothers at the family's San Juan mine, but he tried to get back during school breaks. Theos had shown his half brothers a few of the basic asanas he was working on, and one day he was standing with them in the shadows of the junipers at the mining camp when, as Dugald recalled, Theos drew a circle around them in the dust. They could all easily do a headstand there in that circle, Theos told them; what was the difference between doing it there and in the same size circle on top of the towering Sheepshead Rock? The difference was only in their minds, he told them. It was the fear that they would fall. Theos then led them up to the top of the formation, where he demonstrated his conquest of fear with a headstand on the sheer summit of Sheepshead Rock. For his whole life Dugald kept a photograph of that performance, as well as a series of photos showing Theos doing a headstand on the back of one of their placid mining camp burros.

Although Theos revealed at least these acrobatic aspects of his Yoga practice to his family, he kept it entirely secret at school. By the time he graduated, Theos had mastered all the practices given him by the guru, but even his good friend Daniel Hughes knew nothing about it.

FOR THE SUMMER and fall terms of 1933, Theos focused on philosophy, psychology, and literature classes, and with these he came within two credits of the requirements to add a bachelor of arts degree to the bachelor of laws degree he already held. He arranged to get the last two credits needed in philosophy by examination, allowing him to graduate in May without having to attend classes during the spring term of 1934.

He continued his part-time work in the law library of Judge Sames and picked up some additional work as a bill collector, a business in which, at the depths of the Great Depression, there was always an opening. The manager of a downtown collection agency remembered that Theos came in to discuss an overdue bill one day, and although Theos didn't pay the overdue amount, the manager was seduced by his charisma and not only hired him on the spot but also gave him his choice of accounts to go after.

"He was anxious to get out of Tucson," the manager recalled. "He was a student at the time, but . . . he wanted to get it over with. His interests were elsewhere."

He also remembered, "Theos loved girls. . . . I don't know if it was he that went after the girls, or if they would throw themselves at him. I tended to think it was the latter. I'd see Theos saying good-bye to the girls on the street at the entrance of the building before coming up to the office."

One day that winter, Theos was at his other job in Judge Sames' law library when fate again seemed to take charge of his life. Daniel Hughes was also working in the library at the time and years later remembered that as the day Theos first got the idea of going to New York. Hughes was leafing through the July 1933 issue of *Fortune* magazine when he encountered a three-column feature about Theos' uncle Pierre Arnold Bernard.

The laudatory piece began:

Dr. Pierre A. Bernard no longer wears the robes and the title of the Omnipotent Oom, a name which irreverent reporters gave him. Today his clothes are those of a prosperous, solid businessman and his titles: president of the State Bank of Pearl River, New York, (deposits; $619,000), treasurer of the Rockland County Chamber of Commerce, president of the Rockland County Title Mortgage and Guaranty Co., president of the Biophile Realty Holding Co. He also controls and operates the Clarkstown Country Club. Years ago the tabloids had a pressman's holiday with lurid reports of scandalous goings on at the club. But the last time the newspapers had occasion to mention Dr. Bernard was two years ago when he became a bank president.

Hughes showed the piece to Theos, who was instantly intrigued. Theos had undoubtedly heard some slighting references about his uncle and his country club approach to Yoga from Glen, but this article put an entirely different spin on his career and profiled P. A. Bernard's career path from Tantric guru to business maven in glowing terms. Curiously, the piece mentioned the fact that a member of P. A. Bernard's group, the heiress Mrs. Jacob Wertheim, had built a half-million-dollar house adjacent to his Clarkstown Country Club. Her name would have meant nothing to Theos when he read that, but less than six months later he was married to Mrs. Wertheim's second daughter.

Perhaps sensing that his life was about to change forever, Theos wrote to his uncle, and a reply came with an invitation to visit him in New York along with the money for the trip.

Chapter 2

THE PHILOSOPHER'S DANCE

THE EASTER PARTY on the lawn of his uncle's Clarkstown Country Club was for Theos a young man's version of a debut ball. Not only was he presented to the daughters of some of the arbiters of New York society, but he also was encouraged for the first time to bring his secret Yoga practice out to a welcoming community.

Cut into the stone pediment above the gate Theos walked through that day was the inscription "Here the Philosopher May Dance and the Fool Wear a Thinking Cap." The Reverend Charles Francis Potter, the well-known founder of the Humanist Society, described the club as "one of the rare spots on earth where a group of healthy and happy people makes a play-time pursuit of the deepest philosophies of life."

Located in Nyack, twenty-five miles up the Hudson Valley from Manhattan, the club's emerald lawns and stately half-Tudor lodges offered an elegant setting for the smartly fashioned artists, intellectuals, businessmen, and heiresses who collected around Theos' uncle Pierre Bernard and his wife, Blanche DeVries. They were all drawn to hear the "Loving Guru" expound on his multifaceted, commonsense approach to healthy living based on Hatha Yoga and Tantra.

When Theos was introduced to the group on April 1, 1934, the Clarkstown Country Club was at its peak, with almost four hundred members. At various times in the previous decade the group included such eminent personalities as Mrs. William K. Vanderbilt, second wife of the railroad mogul; Sir Paul Dukes, the former chief of British spies in Russia; conductor Leopold Stokowski; author Francis Yeats-Brown; cosmetics company founder Helena Rubinstein; actress Helen Hayes; and, most important for Theos, Emma Wertheim, widow of the cigar magnate Jacob Wertheim. As the article in *Fortune* had mentioned, Mrs. Wertheim had in 1930 built a thirty-three-room mansion adjacent to the Clarkstown Country Club grounds so that her two young daughters, Diane and Viola, could more easily continue their studies at the club without having to commute from Manhattan.

The Clarkstown Country Club did not intend to duplicate the lavish appointments of the other resorts its affluent members helped finance, but its amenities did include six fine tennis courts, indoor and outdoor swimming pools, two gymnasiums, sports fields, a myriad of gardens, billiard and card rooms, a powerful rooftop telescope, artists' studios, and a fifty-foot cabin cruiser for trips on the Hudson. There was also a small theater company and a library of more than seven thousand volumes that included what was called the finest collection of Sanskrit manuscripts and translations in the United States.

The essence of the club, however, was to be found in the Open Forum, a series with more than 150 lectures a year by leading philosophers, physicians, theologians, and psychologists exemplifying the group's maxim that "philosophy should be the rule, guide, and governor of our lives."

It was all presided over by the club's founder, Pierre Arnold Bernard, or P.A., as he was called—"a phenomenal rascal-master . . . as well-versed in the ways of the world as of the spirit," as Alan Watts, the well-known popularizier of Eastern philosophy, described him in his autobiography. P.A. was a compelling mix of showman and prophet who could lecture for hours on a vast range of topics such as the comparison of Shankara Vedic philosophy with the Gnostic heresies of the early Christians without referring to a single note. At age fifty-eight, when Theos met him, he could still turn a somersault without putting his hands on the ground and could still stop his breath and pulse long enough to be declared dead, only to then sit up and light another of the twenty-five cigars he smoked every day.

Bernard's wife, Blanche DeVries, was a lithe, graciously handsome woman, sixteen years younger than he, who could, again according to Watts, "go through the most astonishing Hatha Yoga contortions I have ever seen." She was a charming, cultivated woman and an accomplished dancer. She had a flair for interior decorating and used her knowledge of costuming and lighting to produce professional effects with the club's theater company and the extravaganza of its annual circus, to which all of Nyack was invited.

Performing under the club's big top—said to be the largest privately owned tent in the United States—acrobats, jugglers, wire walkers, and clowns dazzled the townsfolk, but the highlight of the circus was the performance of the club's four elephants, featuring Old Mom, the ninety-year-old pachyderm legend who carried the entire membership of the Nyack Village Board on her back in local parades. Their act was so polished that the Ringling Circus paid Bernard $1,000 to feature the elephants in the troupe's performances at Madison Square Garden. For all their fame, however, the elephants had to share a garage on the grounds of the country club with Bernard's collection of vintage Stanley Steamers, which he drove on occasion down to Manhattan to pick up particularly important clients.

Also popular with the Nyack villagers was Bernard's championship semipro baseball team. At the depth of the Depression, P.A. helped relieve unemployment in Nyack by hiring 198 men to work alongside the elephants in building a 3,500-seat stadium, which opened in 1933 complete with a public address system and lights for what was claimed to be the country's first night baseball games.

Baseball and circus acts may seem to have little to do with the Clarkstown Country Club's pursuit of philosophy as the "rule, guide, and governor of our lives," but that sort of egalitarian outreach had succeeded in integrating the club and P.A. into the mainstream of Nyack civic affairs, and by the time Theos met him, his uncle was content to describe himself as "a curious combination of the business man and the religious scholar." Public acceptance—or even tolerance—of P.A. and his activities was a recent development, however, and probably had much to do with the current hard times and the amount of money his group injected into the community. For most of the previous three decades, Pierre Arnold Bernard had been first vilified and then lampooned in the newspapers of both coasts as "Oom the Omnipotent" and his Tantra groups branded a "national danger." Theos' choice a few months after meeting his uncle to ground his own study of Tantra in the legitimacy of university academics probably had much to do with the cautionary example of P.A.'s groundbreaking but notorious introduction of Tantra to America.

The "father of Tantra in America," as Pierre Arnold Bernard has rightly been called, was born in an Iowa farm town in 1875 with the name Peter Perry Baker. Hounded by prosecutors and yellow journalists for his promotion of what they termed "mystic religious rites," he became so assiduous at disguising his past that newspapers for fifty years reported he was born with the name Peter Coon, an alias he used for an early court case. His parents divorced when he was three, and Perry, as he was called, lived with his grandparents for a few years until his mother, Kittie, married a widowed farmer, John C. Bernard. When Perry was nine this marriage produced a half brother, Theos' father, Glen Bernard.

Perry had little formal education, but his grandfather and uncle were both doctors and from them he learned some natural history, philosophy, and the basics of medicine. In 1888, when he was thirteen, Peter moved to Lincoln, Nebraska, to live with a relative, and it was there that he met the Syrian-Bengali Tantric scholar Sylvais Hamati, who lived across the street. This was just five years after Ralph Waldo Emerson's widow hosted in her Concord parlor the first lectures by a Hindu in America, and five years before Swami Vivekananda roused an interfaith fervor and received numerous standing ovations at the World's Parliament of Religions in Chicago in 1893 with his quotations from the Bhagavad Gita.

As he would later recount, Perry studied five hours a day for twelve years with Hamati, and as Hamati's main disciple, Perry was quite likely the first American trained in Hatha Yoga by an Indian guru. He read what was available of Sanskrit literature that had been translated into English, but he never learned to read Sanskrit and, contrary to his later claims that he studied in Kashmir and Bengal, he never traveled to India.

Perry and Hamati moved to California in 1891, and by 1900 Perry was calling himself Dr. Pierre Bernard and had become well known for his treatment of nervous disorders. He earned some fame by demonstrating to a group of forty physicians and newspaper photographers in San Francisco that he could voluntarily stop his pulse and respiration long enough to be declared dead, and in 1904 Bernard founded the Bacchante Academy, a clinic where he taught a mélange of self-hypnosis, Yoga, and "Brahmanism." One newspaper reported that he could sew his lips closed without apparent pain and slice a finger so deeply with a knife that blood spurted and then, by thought alone, instantly stop the flow. Bernard claimed in his account of this period that he trained seventy-two physicians (charging $100 each) in the use of "mental suggestion" in medicine.

Dr. Bernard left San Francisco after the great earthquake of 1906 and went to Seattle, where, with Hamati and three others, he founded the Tantrik Order in America, probably the first group of Western students of Tantra ever organized. The group published that same year *Vira Sadhana: International Journal of the Tantrik Order*, an anthology quoting Western scholars and writers from Schopenhauer to Rudyard Kipling attesting that Tantra is a "divine science." The text is illustrated with mystical drawings such as the one on the inside front cover showing a human heart being sliced by a knife with the words "Tantrik Doctrine Initiation" engraved on its blade.

To establish the credentials of Dr. Bernard, *Vira Sadhana* published an interview with Swami Ram Tirath, a professor of Sanskrit literature, science, and mathematics at the University of Lahore whom Mahatma Gandhi once described as "one of the greatest souls not only of India but of the whole world." During his visit to America, between 1902 and 1904, Swami Ram likely became another teacher for Dr. Bernard, and he stated in *Vira Sadhana* that he believed the Tantrik Order had adapted Tantra perfectly for Americans and that in his opinion the primate of the order, Pierre Bernard, possessed "a perfect understanding of Tantrik doctrine, principles, and practice." Also, he was "more energetic, and his knowledge just as extensive," as the mere hundred or so Tantric high priests who survived in India.

For most people outside the Tantrik Order, however, that endorsement meant only that Dr. Bernard was well qualified to expound a depraved tradition. The prevailing attitude among Western Orientalists at the time was that Indian civilization had been in a long decline from the golden age of the Vedas—which rivaled ancient Greece and Rome in achievements—to the degenerate modern era of Hindu superstition, the worst of which survived in the perverse rituals of the Tantras.

As scholar Hugh Urban points outs in his study of Tantra and Western esotericism, Tantra first caught the attention of the West in the early nineteenth-century reports of Christian missionaries, who discovered, as the Baptist William Ward put it, "a most shocking mode of worship" with rites focused on a naked woman that were "too abominable to enter the ears of man and impossible to be revealed to a Christian public."

In India as well, Tantricas were notorious for making the defiance of prevailing mores a foundation of their theology. This iconoclastic attitude is most clearly displayed in the rites of the Kaula School's "Five M's," five substances or activities that all begin with the Sanskrit letter *M* and are normally taboo for orthodox Vedic priests. In these rites, among a circle of initiates, wine, fish, meat, and parched grain are ritually consumed, and sexual union is practiced—either symbolically with iconic substitutes (in the right-hand schools) or with the actual objects (in the left-hand schools).

Dr. Bernard's Tantrik Order, it can be assumed from the clues they left, practiced the left-hand path. The group advertised in the classifieds of a San Francisco newspaper: "Kaula Ritė, Chakra Ring for full Initiate with 7 M's, begins Midnight October 8th; Siva festival following." It is unknown what substances the Tantrik Order might have used for their innovation of the sixth and seventh of the M's, but it appears that the sexual practices were a prominent feature of their instruction.

Dr. Bernard was an early proponent of the idea that Western sexual repression corrupted the spirit. In *Vira Sadhana* he wrote, "In this day and age, when matters pertaining to the sexes are generally avoided, and we are taught that the sexual appetite is an animal craving that should be subdued and concealed it is not surprising that the great majority of persons are blind to the vast importance of the sexual nature. They fail to realize that not only is it the cause of our individual existence, but that it is the well-spring of human life and happiness."

From Seattle Bernard moved on to New York City, and it was there that he first attracted the harangues of tabloid journalism. As Hugh Urban explains, it was through the ensuing decade of sensational headlines pillorying Pierre Arnold Bernard that Tantra was forever branded as a cult of esoteric sexual practices in the American imagination.

At the Oriental Sanctum, which he opened in 1910 on West Seventy-fourth Street, Dr. Bernard taught Hatha Yoga downstairs and evidently conducted secret rituals of the Tantrik Order upstairs. It wasn't long before the group's activities were noticed by a zealous prosecutor and Bernard was jailed. The *New York Times* headlines declared he was arrested as a kidnapper, but the charges filed were "seduction under promise to marry." The judge thought the charges serious enough to require a $15,000 bond, and the press had a field day with the details revealed in the testimony about the Oriental Sanctum's operation. The articles stated Bernard told his followers he was the "reincarnation of the Supreme Being, Oom the Omnipotent," and "I am a god, but I have condescended to put on the habit of a man that I may perform the duties of a Yogi and reveal true religion to the elect of America."

"All priests," Bernard said on the witness stand, "have Nautch girls. In my sacred capacity I cannot marry, but our Nautch girls serve us as wives. It is the duty of the priests to give her all the world's best goods. She is looked upon as sacred."

Front-page stories with titillating headlines appeared in New York and California newspapers for days with tragic portrayals of the girls they said Oom the Omnipotent had kidnapped to serve as "sex slaves" in his Oriental Sanctum. The charges, however, were dropped before the case went to trial. The press reported that Bernard held such telepathic power over the girls that at the preliminary hearing they were reduced to tears on the stand and refused to testify. The case was dismissed and the women left town.

Bernard's next move was to a residential neighborhood on upper Broadway, where he opened the New York Sanskrit College. Complaints from neighbors about noise again drew the attention of the press, which found material for more salacious articles in interviews with the neighbors. "What my wife and I have seen through the windows of that place is scandalous," said one. "We saw men and women in various stages of dishabille. Women's screams mingled with wild Oriental music." The janitor reported that well-dressed women would commonly arrive in taxicabs at midnight and stay till the early hours of the morning.

By this time Bernard had met Blanche DeVries, and it was probably she who introduced him to a clique of wealthy, prominent women interested in the esoteric. They all realized they needed a place in the country where nosy neighbors could not look in the windows and the arrivals and departures of the well-to-do would not draw the attention of gossip columnists. Most prominent among this group of well-heeled acolytes was Mrs. William K. Vanderbilt, second wife of the railroad magnate. She put up the bulk of the $100,000 needed to buy one of the premier Nyack properties fronting the Hudson, a seventy-eight-acre estate with a century-old three-story Georgian mansion said to have been built by a French pirate. They called it the Braeburn Club, and P.A. and Blanche soon had its more than one hundred members dressed alike in bloomers and sandals for their outdoor exercises in classes on "physical culture." The club quickly outgrew the riverfront estate, and in 1922 Mrs. Vanderbilt again put up the money to buy a 256-acre estate in upper Nyack, which they named the Clarkstown Country Club. The yellow press followed the move with lurid headlines such as this one in the *San Francisco Chronicle*: "Country Club Specializes in Sex Worship: Initiates, Known As Tantrik Yoga, Hold Wild Orgies in Nyack New York: Dr. Bernard Is Head: Mrs. W. K. Vanderbilt Spent $200,000 Financing Oom the Omnipotent."

Reacting to the rumors, Nyack townspeople demanded the police take action. A squad of the newly formed New York State Police arrived on horseback one evening and burst into the lecture hall, where they found P.A. on a dais at the front of the room in a headstand telling two dozen seated guests in dinner jackets and evening gowns that the inverted pose would reverse the flow of the circulatory system and bring new life to tired tissues. Before the sergeant in command could finish reading the charges, P.A. tumbled down to his feet and interrupted him: "Whether you realize it or not, you are in the midst of a group of ladies and gentlemen at a private gathering on private property. Get out, or I'll slap you with a damage suit." The abashed troopers left in disarray and never returned. When given the chance later to describe the activities at the club, Bernard replied, "This ain't no love cult here. Just a bunch of people in love with beauty and books."

As Theos discovered on his first visit to the Clarkstown Country Club on that Easter Sunday of 1934, despite the lurid rumors a distinct atmosphere of rectitude suffused the CCC. No intoxicants were allowed on the grounds, and all residents, no matter their social station, were expected to attend to themselves and even make their own beds. As P.A. once lectured:

> Some folk like to spout a lot of Sanskrit terms like Prana, Pranayama, and Karma and what not, as if there were some virtue in foreign words, but it would do their souls a power more good to be on a course of household drudgery, scrubbing floors and so forth... because the first step towards merging with Brahm or God or the Infinite or the Universal Spirit or whatever you like to call it is a sympathetic understanding of one's fellow men.

It was probably that egalitarian, pragmatic approach to metaphysics that attracted Emma Wertheim's daughter Viola to the Clarkstown Country Club. She was introduced to the Yoga classes of Blanche DeVries by her older sister, Diane, and joined the club while still a teenager. After graduating at age sixteen from the Ethical Culture High School, the prestigious prep school on Central Park, Viola spent successive years at Smith College, Barnard, and then Johns Hopkins. She then took five years off from college and lived at the Clarkstown Country Club with her mother and sister before, at age twenty-four, returning to school to complete a bachelor of science degree at New York University. She had an apartment in New York and in the spring of 1934 was just finishing her second year of medical school at Cornell University, where she was one of only four women in her class.

Viola was the youngest child of Jacob Wertheim and his second wife, Emma Stern. Jacob, a self-made millionaire, was the owner of the United

Cigar Company and a member of the board of directors of General Motors. He was a socially progressive businessman who believed that 7 percent was a fair return on capital in an industrial enterprise and the rest of the profits should be split among employees. The Wertheim family was as well connected as they were wealthy. Viola's oldest half brother, Albert Wertheim, married a daughter of Henry Morgenthau, who earlier in 1934 had been appointed Franklin Roosevelt's secretary of the treasury. Her other half brother, Maurice Wertheim, was a Manhattan banker, director of the Theatre Guild, and for a time the publisher of the liberal weekly the *Nation*. He became best known, however, as one of the largest private collectors of Impressionist and Postimpressionist paintings and sculpture, and he displayed in his houses what are now considered monuments of modern art by Degas, Manet, Monet, Van Gogh, Gauguin, Picasso, Seurat, Renoir, Cézanne, Toulouse-Lautrec, Matisse, and Pissarro.

Jacob died when Viola was thirteen and left the family a $9 million estate. At age fifteen Viola received a $20,000 annual allowance from the interest on her $750,000 trust fund. Viola's mother moved to Nyack after Jacob's death so that her two daughters could be fully involved with the Clarkstown Country Club and adjacent to the club grounds she built Sky Island, a thirty-three-room Tudor-style mansion with turrets, octagonal rooms, winding staircases, and a six-car garage.

On Easter weekend of 1934, Viola decided to take a break from her medical textbooks and go out to Nyack to attend the CCC holiday picnic. At the buffet table's silver chafing dishes, she was introduced to Pierre Bernard's nephew from Arizona, and she was instantly attracted by the frontier gentility of the tall, handsome young lawyer with the unique name of Theos. As was his habit, Theos responded to her glances, and judging from the pace of their courtship, they must have decided before Theos left the next week to return to Tucson that they were destined to be together. Only six weeks later he was back in New York.

In the meantime, while in Tucson he concluded the remaining work in Philosophy 120 for the final two credits required to add a B.A. to the law degree he already had, and on May 30 he attended his graduation ceremony, culminating nearly eight years at the University of Arizona. Theos moved to New York by the last week of June, and it wasn't long before he and Viola spent their first night together and "baptized that certain lounge," as they later reminisced. Just five weeks after Theos moved to New York they were married.

Viola wrote a letter to her brother Maurice the week before the wedding to dispel any gossip that the haste was due to pregnancy. She explained that they were so completely sure of themselves that "to waste this leisure of the summer together by waiting any longer would be very wrong as it would mean all our first adjustments in marriage would have to be made while we were working."

She wanted a small, informal wedding, and explained to Maurice that she was too tired from the year's work at school to make the social effort necessary for the pageantry of something grander; most people were out of town for the summer anyway. She also wanted to avoid the kind of society-page publicity and attendant theatrics that accompanied her older sister's wedding, which included a special train that took two hundred guests from New York to the wedding at the family's summer home in New Jersey. And recalling the sort of press that followed Oom the Omnipotent, Viola was anxious that their wedding might be overshadowed with stories about the family relationship of Theos and P.A. and how that might relate to their brief courtship.

Viola would have been especially eager just then to avoid drawing attention to her history with P.A., because she was beginning to have doubts about him. It was slowly dawning on her, Theos wrote in a long letter to his father, Glen, "that P.A. is doing everything to keep her around for her money . . . She just turned over $25,000 to him, so you see her loyalty— even though she is suspicious—she hates to believe it."

Viola had been studying with P.A. for ten years but, as Theos put it, "has never got anywhere with Yoga—and says she has never seen anyone here who has." But now, P.A. told her, she was ready at last to hear the secrets of Yoga. "She has faith in him—feels he has something . . . so she doesn't know whether she is missing the opportunity of a lifetime . . . or not."

One opportunity that Viola and Theos both were certain they didn't want to miss was the chance to continue their university training, and the news that Theos had registered for the fall term at Columbia prompted a loud harangue from P.A. that a Ph.D. was a worthless credential for a true philosopher. Viola too should abandon medical school, he instructed, and they should buy a piece of land from him at the club. He was mollified at last when they promised to reconsider their plans for school during the quiet leisure of their honeymoon and put off a final decision until after they returned in mid-September.

Perhaps sensing that Theos could be groomed as his successor, P.A., when asked about Theos' background in Arizona, presented him to the Wertheims in the best possible light. Although P.A. and his half brother, Glen (Theos' father), had been feuding for a decade over P.A.'s approach to purveying Yoga to the rich and for years had refused even to speak to each other, P. A. nevertheless told Viola's mother that Theos' father was "a man of excellent character—very studious—well read—and had an excellent mind." Theos' mother, Aura, P.A. said, "was well educated and also of strong character."

Viola as well had to sell her family on the suitability of this unknown man from Arizona who had suddenly become her fiancé and embroidered the facts about the standing of his family. She told them that "Theos' people ... have been a family of mining interests and lawyers" and that Theos himself had considerable zinc holdings in Arizona, which, though not producing with the current state of the economy, would give him the means for financial independence when the economy turned around. In the meantime, they would go fifty-fifty on expenses and live simply. Viola made it clear to Maurice that she would not tolerate the hiring of private detectives to investigate Theos.

What no investigator likely would have uncovered, however, and what Theos was most concerned about concealing—even from Viola herself at this point—was not his family's humble life in Tombstone but the true nature of his relationship with his father. Although Theos had probably met Glen for the first time just four years earlier, Glen had since then become the most important influence in his life, his secret teacher of the secret practices of Hatha Yoga. And in what would be a deception he maintained his entire life, Theos decided it was important to hide the fact that it was Glen rather than some Indian swami who was the transmitter of the Hatha Yoga practices at which he was already so advanced. Even years later during his academic career at Columbia, his perceived need to conceal the fact that his primary guru was his father would require elaborate stratagems, and his motivations for the deception require a great deal of historical context to understand. But in this instance, it seems that the point of the deception was to hide Glen and Theos' guru-disciple relationship from P.A. If he knew the truth, they feared, P.A. might see the marriage as threatening the defection of Viola and her thousands of dollars in sponsorship to his feuding half brother, Glen, and he might therefore try to scuttle the wedding.

In a long letter to Glen two weeks before his wedding, Theos wrote that even Viola "need not know who you are—but if she likes you & [P.A.] does attack you—then it [will] all be revealed to her." Glen had sent Theos a list of Sanskrit names he could assume when playing the role of Theos' guru. Theos replied, "They are grand—can't pronounce them—but that is all right. However V. has heard and seen so darn much humbug connected with this stuff that she might become skeptical again. . . . She has heard of you—as my teacher—(not an Indian) so consider a . . . name adaptable to this Caucasian race. Suit yourself."

It was all part of the drama of "marrying this girl with all her dough," Theos wrote. "I do like this girl and do not want P.A. causing us any trouble. She will be one with whom I can always work—broke or rich—so she is a treasure—her money helps—but her character means more. . . . Glad I have such a fine companion—she does it all for me."

THEOS AND VIOLA BERNARD were married without fanfare on August 3, 1934, at the School for Ethical Culture and left immediately on a six-week honeymoon in the new convertible Cadillac club sedan given to them as a wedding gift by Viola's mother. Their first destination was a resort in New Mexico, where they could "rest up and get acquainted," as Theos put it. Then they drove to Tombstone, where Viola met Theos' family for the first time. After that they continued their tour of the West with stops at the Grand Canyon, Yosemite, and San Francisco before stopping for a few days in Los Angeles, where Viola was introduced to Glen Bernard—whether in the role of father or that of guru is not clear. They shipped the car back to New York and on September 2 caught a cruise liner from the

Long Beach pier for a relaxing voyage back to New York through the Panama Canal.

On their return to New York, they had one more wedding obligation on the schedule before settling into their apartment on West 57th Street: a big reception at Sky Island for their Nyack friends. While in Nyack they also had to tell P.A. that they had thought it over, as they had promised, and decided to continue with their plans for school. Viola was in the third of her four years at Cornell Medical School; Theos, who had had plans to go to Harvard before he met Viola, enrolled in the Department of Philosophy at Columbia.

In 1934, when Theos entered the august Department of Philosophy, there were no India specialists on the faculty to guide his interest in the academic study of Hatha Yoga and Tantra, and the department offered only a few courses that touched on Eastern philosophy. The field of comparative religion, which might have interested him, did not emerge as a discipline of its own until the 1950s, and throughout his first years at Columbia Theos debated whether the department of philosophy or of anthropology was best suited for the clear direction he saw for his own studies.

The Columbia philosophy department at the time was dominated by the presence of F. J. E. Woodbridge and John Dewey, two of the founders of the movement known as American naturalism. Naturalism's rejection of the supernatural and its reliance on the scientific method as the only valid means of acquiring knowledge of the world were certainly more accommodating of Theos' interest in Yoga philosophy than the hyperintellectualism that characterized most other Western philosophy of the time. But the third-person speculations of Western philosophy couldn't offer a program of actual practices for attaining metaphysical knowledge directly, and Theos never found among the faculty the wisdom of a guru or even, it appears, a mentor.

Columbia's anthropology program—the first in the United States—was founded in 1899 by the "father of American anthropology," Franz Boas, and was still in 1934 the preeminent anthropology department in the country. Boas taught and inspired a generation of anthropologists, most notably Ruth Benedict and Margaret Mead, to take up the crusade of cultural relativism against the still-dominant nineteenth-century idea that the superiority of Western culture resulted from its production by a more highly evolved race. Boas and his students at Columbia pioneered the participant observation method of ethnographic fieldwork, in which the researcher lives with his subjects, studies their language, and collaborates with them in collecting data. Using that method, both Ruth Benedict and Margaret Mead produced cultural studies that were published as popular mass-market books. Benedict's *Patterns of Culture,* in which she compared personality traits of the Zuni Indians of New Mexico, the Dobu of New Guinea, and the Kwakiutl of coastal Alaska, and Mead's study of adolescence, *Coming of Age in Samoa,* both sold hundreds of thousands of copies over the years and could be found on drugstore shelves as well as at university bookstores.

Through the influence and popularity of their work, cultural relativism became an intellectual rallying cry against fascist propaganda about racial superiority, but even with Benedict and Mead on the faculty, Theos found nothing creative or life-changing in anthropology's crusade. What he wanted to do most was to use anthropology's participant observation methodology to study Tantric philosophy. As he wrote the following year in his master's thesis, titled "Tantrik Ritual":

> What is much needed at the present time is for someone who is willing to work with one of those teachers, who are so rapidly passing away, to first familiarize himself with the literature . . . then go and devote several years of his life to the practice of its method. . . . It does not purport to be able to help anyone through mere instruction alone.

The question for Theos at Columbia was whether anthropology or philosophy would give him the greatest latitude for his own independent line of investigation. As he wrote in a letter to Viola during the summer of 1935 when he was away in New Mexico doing ethnographic field research:

> Regardless of which direction I go—anthro or philo—I will always feel that they are both so unnecessary and inconsequential that it will be difficult for me to hold on to the end. So the question boils itself down to this—which is the easiest way to get a Ph.D. and which will

give the best excuse to go to India and study that which I am interested in. In every case the answer is just about philosophy. But I do hate to bother with what I have to go through in getting the degree.

He ended up taking almost as many anthropology courses as philosophy, but with no professors in either department able to guide him in his desired course of study, Theos turned to the best authority he knew on the subject of Yoga philosophy: his father. At the Christmas break, the first holiday vacation of his studies at Columbia—and his marriage—Theos took the train to visit Glen in Los Angeles. While there, he proposed the idea of sending Glen to India to lay the groundwork for his own research there, which would commence after he finished the year and a half of classes still required for his master's degree. In the meantime, Theos and Viola would pay Glen a stipend of $100 a month to live in India, collect manuscripts, and make connections in the twilight world of Hatha Yoga and Tantra so that Theos would not have to spend the better part of the year he planned to be there in uncovering them.

Glen took some time to think it over and in a letter two months later he accepted the proposal, saying a long stay in India would

enable me to develop more tangibly a lifelong hope, that of sowing the seed of Yoga in this soil and nourishing it until it will survive of its own strength. It has been and still is my belief that if true Yoga is once established on this continent that it will make such strides here as it has only made in its first inception in the land of its birth.

The spiritual elements of true Yoga, Glen believed, were still unknown in the West, and he concluded his letter with a skewer undoubtedly intended for his half brother, P.A., and his country club approach:

What we know as Yoga in the West is so vulgarized as to make the sound of the term itself rasp one's nerves. It seems that wherever Western[ers] ... have intruded they have reduced every spiritual element to the lowest possible [point].

By the spring of 1935, Glen had put his few belongings in storage and moved to Calcutta. Theos and Viola, meanwhile, were making plans to spend the first full summer of their marriage two thousand miles apart. Viola registered for summer classes in obstetrics and gynecology at Cornell, and Theos took a summer job with the federal government's Indian Bureau to explain to the elders of the Southwest tribes the radically new approach of the Indian Reorganization Act of 1934.

As a lawyer and anthropology student, Theos was particularly well qualified to present to the elders this "Indian New Deal," which marked a reversal of the government's disastrous policy, begun in 1887, to assimilate natives into the American mainstream as small, independent farmers, whatever the cost to the Indians.

Under the previous policy, tribal lands were divided into 160-acre parcels and deeded to individual tribal members, with the remaining unassigned land opened for homesteading by white settlers. By 1932, as a result of homesteading and the sale of the individual Indian parcels, whites had taken over two-thirds of the original 138 million acres of reservation lands.

The assimilation policy also encouraged or forced Indian children to live off the reservations far from their families at distant Indian boarding schools, where they got an education in a trade and military drills and were punished for speaking their native language. "Kill the Indian and save the man" was the goal stated by the founder of the first off-reservation school, Captain Richard H. Pratt. "It is a great mistake to think that the Indian is born an inevitable savage. He is born a blank, like all the rest of us. Left in the surroundings of savagery, he grows to possess a savage language, superstition, and life.... Transfer the savage-born infant to the surroundings of civilization, and he will grow to possess a civilized language and habit," he told a conference of educators.

By the 1930s, however, Boas' campaign for cultural relativism and the Lost Generation's disillusionment with modernity after the carnage of World War I turned the rationalizing notion of Manifest Destiny into a romantic longing for, as the new head of the Indian Agency, John Collier, termed it, a "Red Atlantis." Collier saw modernity as "a disaster that was defeating man's perfectibility" and, as his son once recalled, "saw the Indian as the last remnant of natural perfection, a model that must be preserved for human rejuvenation." Collier's initiative, the Indian Reorganization Act, attempted to reverse the splintering of reservations and encouraged the writing of tribal constitutions and election of councils that would, it was hoped, preserve traditional ways.

Theos' vaguely defined job was to inform the tribes about the new philosophy, persuade them to adopt the changes, and, perhaps most important, glean some information about their existing social structures. His vast territory took in all the tribes of northern New Mexico and Arizona, and given a choice, he decided to begin his mission at Taos Pueblo. The pueblo at Taos was the least studied and the most traditional group in his territory, and he was warned by Washington to expect a great deal of resistance. For one thing, he was told, only the elders of the clans—most of who were past sixty—were admitted into the council kiva, and they would be getting advice on how to preserve their fathers' way of life from a university student.

But despite the low expectations, after their first all-day discussions through a translator, the elders agreed to cooperate and invited Theos to live at the pueblo in a little house near the hospital. Once there, Theos soon fell into the peaceful rhythms of the village. "Everything is so restful—no rush or buzz," he wrote to Viola. "The evening comes and the men return from the fields, have a bit to eat, then go up on their roofs and watch the day fade away. . . . They just sit and meditate. Something a few of the white race should learn and those that know about it should try once in a while."

Theos typed two- or three-page letters to Viola almost daily. She, however, didn't have the long silent evenings to fill up, and sometimes it would be a week or longer between her letters, but the correspondence led to an intimacy they hadn't achieved so far in nine months as married students.

"You have told me more this summer through your messages than you could have whispered in my ears in a year's time in NYC," he wrote to her. "You have opened up your subjective self—that which is deep within . . . and this is what I have wanted you to do—I want to live in you as you live in me."

Their first long separation also brought up the question they were never able in their marriage to find the answer to—how to reconcile the divergent demands of their two careers. "After we finish up these jobs that were started before we met—our activities are going to have to be with one another or one of us is going to give up a career," Theos wrote to her.

Midway through the summer, Theos' supervisor came out from Washington and the two of them took a grand two-week driving tour of all the pueblos between the Rio Grande in New Mexico and the Grand Canyon in Arizona—from Sandia and Zuni and the reservations of the White Mountain and San Carolos Apaches to the Navajo and Hopi mesas—"all of the Southwest Indians except the Papago, who I am already familiar with," Theos wrote. They covered twenty-five hundred miles of back roads, introducing themselves to the elders, consulting with archeologists, and photographing secret dances at every stop. Theos wrote to Viola that his supervisor told him to expect

> all the old fogies to think that I am doing everything wrong, but not to be bothered about it for I am the first person in this country to ever try such an experiment and that I have everything to gain and nothing to lose and therefore stay with it. . . . If I can find a new way of securing information then I will have made a real contribution to the field. . . . This will be the first time that anthropology has been used for a practical purpose and it is his feeling and that of several others that if it is to stand up as a science that it will have to produce something that can be used and that I am making the first effort.

When Theos returned from his memorable odyssey, waiting in Santa Fe to greet him was Viola. She had just finished her summer term and exams, and they spent the last week of July together touring the idyllic pueblos around Santa Fe before she returned to New York to start a two-month assignment delivering babies at the Free Maternity Clinic.

Theos' next visitor was John Collier, the idealistic head of the federal Indian Agency. Collier was satisfied with Theos' work at Taos and suggested he move next to Acoma, the picturesque adobe village at the top of a 360-foot sandstone mesa with the claim of being the oldest continuously inhabited settlement in the United States.

It had been Theos' hope from the beginning to split the summer between Taos Pueblo and Acoma, and just as in Taos, his country charm and sincere wish to understand the native worldview eventually broke down the elders' well-practiced distrust of government agents. Council meetings commonly lasted ten hours, and Theos joked that he was asked to be brief while the interpreter elaborated his one-minute remarks into a ten-minute oration.

Theos traveled widely across the entire Acoma reservation to map its boundaries and was struck by the stark grandeur of the area. "So far every corner of the reservation has been a paradise of color and beauty—and every little valley is cultivated—it is a thrill to rise up over a mesa and start to drop down into a hidden valley and find it flourishing with crops," he wrote to Viola.

At one outlying pueblo the leaders suspiciously asked why Collier had sent him. Theos replied that there was a great danger the traditions that had helped their fathers survive the difficult years of reservation life would disappear forever, and he was there to help them preserve them for their children. That response melted the last of their distrust, and the elders spent the next three hours telling Theos about the intricacies of their clan structures. They told him about clans that were by then extinct and of six existing clans that had never before been reported by researchers. Theos knew that if he could have six months more with them, he could get "to the middle of their whole social-religious structure." But the end of August had arrived and it was time for him to leave. The elders asked him to come back to finish his work, offered him a place to live on the mesa at Acoma, and even hinted that he might be allowed into the kivas to witness secret ceremonies.

Theos considered different scenarios for completing a full ethnographic study—returning the following summer or even taking an entire year off from school—and just at that point the Indian Agency made a tantalizing job offer that would allow him to remain and continue the work at $3,800 a year plus expenses. But all those attractive propositions had to be weighed against his plan for a year's research in India and the fact that Glen was already there laying the groundwork for him. Despite the fascinating summer he'd had, he turned down the offer. He was still certain of his future, and as he wrote to Viola:

In a few years I am going to want to spend all of my time in talking, writing, and practicing my own philosophical beliefs which are of Eastern origin so there will be no room for the training that I have received in anthropology....I want to get a group of my own and help them along the road in so far as I can. If I push one further than myself, I will have done more than a good job in this life regardless whether anyone ever hears about it or not....That is what I am after in this lifetime and it is the only thing that makes me feel that I am doing something that justifies my existence.

Those plans for the future also seemed to include inducing Pierre Bernard and Blanche DeVries to open a center in California where he would do his teaching. Theos and DeVries, as he and Viola called her, had struck up a close friendship in the year since they met, and Viola persuaded her to take a vacation out West and join Theos for a trip at the end of his job driving from New Mexico to California and then back east. DeVries arrived in Santa Fe on August 31 and they set out together for Los Angeles with stops along the way at Zion, Bryce Canyon, and the north rim of the Grand Canyon. They then spent several days in Los Angeles before heading to Yosemite, San Francisco, and Lake Tahoe. Before leaving California, Theos wrote to Viola, "The stay in L.A. was absolutely perfect. DeVries has caught the spirit that I had hoped she would and hope that truly you and P.A. also will....I want to have my little group and plant the seeds of Yoga. DeVries sees what I'm talking about so maybe I can forget [it] for awhile and follow."

Theos dropped DeVries in Chicago to visit friends, and then drove on to Washington, D.C., to report to his bosses on the summer's work before pulling into New York on the closing day of registration for the fall term at Columbia. He chose a schedule of nothing but anthropology classes, while Viola, with almost no time off after a demanding summer, faced her last year of medical school.

By that time Glen had been in Calcutta for six months. "Heat. Dirty. Tropical. Hot month ahead," he wrote to them. "India is a lousy place with good stuff so scarce it must be looked for with a fine toothed comb....Lots of ignorance and superstition." He had begun his research by scouring the Imperial Library, "the best in Asia," and visiting swamis at area temples, "no good for practical Yoga, but good for philosophy and metaphors."

After half a year in Calcutta, Glen concluded that "so few now know yoga—[it's] almost a thing of the past. Yoga can better be done in the States—[you] can find pundits there to help with the literature necessary for the path." He thought that Kashmir and Assam might be better because, being at the fringe of the empire, the Tantricas there might have escaped British subjugation. Travel, however, was more expensive than when he had been there ten years before, and he thought he would stay in Calcutta until he had definite leads in other places. He had been initiated into several new Tantric chakras, or circles, leading him to believe that he was in closer touch with the foremost Tantric families than any other Westerner he knew.

Glen met several times in Calcutta with that period's most important Western scholar of Tibetan Buddhism, his friend W. Y. Evans-Wentz. His landmark book, *The Tibetan Book of the Dead,* came out in 1927, and Oxford University Press was just then releasing his book *Tibetan Yoga and Secret Doctrines.* Evans-Wentz suggested that Theos use his anthropological skills to do an ethnographic study of the fifty thousand members of the Lepcha group in Sikkim. They had been little studied, and it would put Theos right in the middle of Tibetan Tantricas in the Himalayan foothills, where he could carry on that aspect of his research. But otherwise, Glen advised Theos against going to Sikkim and Tibet because there were "few there that could help with philosophy and metaphysics and they know no English and [you would] waste time to learn their language."

In the spring of 1936, after ten months in Calcutta, Glen made some contacts that led him on an excursion into the jungle two hundred miles west, where he met two reclusive Tantric alchemists. One was in his fifties and the other over seventy. Neither spoke English, and they wanted Glen to translate the elder yogi's writings. Glen spent almost three months with the Tantricas in their isolated jungle compound at Bhurkunda, which lay about fifteen miles north of the city of Ranchi, the home of Yogananda's famous boys' school and a place that Sir John Woodroffe visited for Tantric research in earlier decades with his collaborator and Glen's Indian mentor,

Atal Behari Ghosh. Also staying at the jungle compound was a sixty-five-year-old man whom Glen described in a letter to Theos as "a real Hatha Yogi [who] knows it and practices it." The yogi practiced through the night, between 11:00 p.m. and 7:00 a.m. This yogi didn't speak English either, and although Glen wrote that he wasn't learning anything entirely new from him, what the yogi was able to communicate was somehow "clarifying." He demonstrated the control of the autonomic body that can be attained through Hatha Yoga by consciously opening the pyloric valve, between the stomach and duodenum, and passing three quarts of water in fifteen minutes. He had mastered eighty-four asanas, and Glen hoped that Theos and Viola would come to Ranchi to film him when they arrived in India.

Glen started his three-month retreat there with a course of Kriya purification practices, such as the Dhauti and Neti practices he had taught Theos at the beginning of his training. The Kriyas were designed to clean excess phlegm from his system before he undertook the next course, Pranayama, some details of which, Glen said, he was glad to have straightened out before he taught them to Theos and Viola. His diet during the retreat consisted of only a few glasses of milk and ghee each day.

The elder swami was gone most of the first month Glen was in camp but then returned to confer Tantric initiations and transmit to Glen the secret processes of Tantric alchemy. The swami demonstrated the method of creating alchemical compounds of mercury, which by itself forms an insoluble poison salt that lodges in the brain and causes insanity or death. To balance and control the energy of mercury, it is compounded with sulfur to produce Kajjali, the base from which most other alchemical substances are created. The most famous of all alchemical compounds adds gold to the mercury sulfide formula, producing Makaradwaja, said to provide endurance, energy, increased immune function, and longevity. The field of alchemy should interest Theos, Glen wrote, because the compounds could beautify, rejuvenate, reverse decay, and even bring the near dead back to life; most important, though, they were purported to accelerate the progress of deep Yoga practices.

Despite having found at last the kind of Yoga practitioners he had vainly sought in Calcutta, after a month in the jungle camp Glen began to complain in his letters to Theos and Viola about the insects and the "low class of living among Hindus." The climate had changed in India since Yoga was developed there two thousand years ago, he said, and now "Yoga can better be practiced in the Southwest and California than in India." But despite the hardships, he concluded, he was happy to do everything possible to prepare the way for their visit.

WHILE GLEN WAS ENDURING the rigors of the Bihar jungle, Theos was negotiating the topic for his master's thesis with the philosophy department at Columbia. His thesis advisor, Herbert W. Schneider, was another of the department's naturalists, and although the professor knew little about the subject, he was supportive and agreed to let Theos write a summary of his two years of independent research on Tantric ritual.

Since 1906, when Pierre Bernard's Tantrik Order in America published *Vira Sadhana*, Western scholars had learned a great deal more about Tantra, mainly through the investigations and writings of the enigmatic Sir John Woodroffe. Woodroffe had a brilliant legal career in India that culminated with his appointments as chief justice of the Calcutta High Court and standing counsel to the government of India, but it was his shadow life for which he is remembered. Between 1913 and his death in 1936, at a time when Tantra was still maligned by Orientalists, Woodroffe collaborated with gurus and Bengali scholars—principally, it appears, Glen's friend Atal Behari Ghosh—to translate and explain a series of Tantric scriptures that made it clear they belonged to a highly sophisticated philosophical system of their own.

Under the pseudonym Arthur Avalon, Woodroffe published in 1919 his most influential book, *The Serpent Power*, the still-popular work that introduced the chakra system and Kundalini Yoga to the Western world. Theos relied on that difficult work and two other of Avalon's studies as the principal sources for his research. Woodroffe died while Theos was writing his thesis. Woodroffe's Tantric guru and Ghosh had also died by that point, leading Theos to lament on the first page of his thesis, "With them goes this knowledge, for the younger people who are rapidly becoming Europeanized [and] no longer see its value."

Outlining his participant observation approach for rescuing Tantra from oblivion, Theos wrote: "One of the first tasks of the student in this field today must be to gather together those manuscripts which are left so that the future may have them.... [O]ne who has an intellectual understanding of the scriptures [must then] put himself... through the various ritual stages so as to gain by experience an estimate of the truth of the teachings." Theos implicitly volunteers for the mission and then sets out to prove he is qualified with a hundred-page précis of the Tantric path to liberation, which he titled "Introduction to Tantrik Ritual."

Hindu Tantra flourished around the tenth century, but it can be traced back at least to the beginning of the first millennium CE, when its radically new approach to spiritual practice swept through Buddhist, Hindu, and Jain communities across all of India. Tradition states that the original sixty-four Tantras were dialogues between Shiva and his earthly spouse, Devi, that were tailored specifically for our present dark age, called the Kali Yuga, during which people have only a weak aspiration to the divine and are easily seduced by the allure of conventional success and fleeting pleasures.

These scriptures dealt with everything from the creation and destruction of the universe through the duties of kings and the consecration of wells to the practice of meditation and yoga. As Theos put it, they were "the encyclopedias of knowledge of their time," but most important, they were practical guides to spiritual practice. Tantra rejected the Vedic precept that a yogi must renounce the world in order to free himself from it. In Tantra, the human body is the vehicle for liberation, which is attained by reversing the process that created the body—and all mind and matter as well—out of the pure potentiality of supreme consciousness.

In the Hindu Tantras, ultimate reality has two aspects: the passive Shiva principle, which contains all things but is beyond manifestation, and the active Shakti principle, which brings all things into being and is therefore considered the Mother of the Universe.

In the human body, Theos wrote, this primordial Shakti power has two aspects of its own, the dynamic *prana* and the dormant Kundalini. *Prana*, as he described it here, is analogous to kinetic energy in physics and is the force that holds the subtle energetic body and the gross physical body together. Kundalini, on the other hand, is analogous to potential energy, such as that stored in the head of water behind a dam, and is represented in the Tantras by a sleeping snake coiled three and a half times at the base of the spine.

The dynamic energy of *prana* flows through seventy-two thousand channels or *nadis* of the subtle body. The three most important channels run a half-inch in front of the spine and are called Ida, Pingala, and Sushumna in Sanskrit. Theos explained that Ida, the channel just to the left of the spine, carries the lunar, feminine *prana;* Pingala, the right channel, carries the solar, masculine *prana.* Sushumna, the central channel, is the "royal road," the *nadi* that connects the vast potential energy of sleeping Shakti at the base of the spine to the twelve-petaled lotus at the crown of the head, where Shiva consciousness resides in the body.

Tantric Yoga, as Theos described it, seeks to unite the individual consciousness with the supreme consciousness of Shiva. One of the main practices employed to do that is Pranayama, exercises that control the inhalation, exhalation, and suspension of the breath for the purpose of redirecting the flow of *prana* in the subtle body. *Prana* usually flows predominantly in the left and right channels, Ida and Pingala, which are responsible for the craving and aggression that normally dominate the mind. Through Pranayama, *prana* can be redirected from the troublesome side channels to the central channel to awaken the "sleeping princess" of Kundalini. The awakened Kundalini then rises and pierces the knots at the five chakras in the central channel that normally prevent *prana* from ascending there and unites with the formless Shiva consciousness to attain *mukti,* liberation, which is experienced as infinite bliss beyond space and time.

Theos emphasized that all these experiences of the subtle body can be observed and verified as predictable signs in the gross physical body. When Kundalini is aroused, an intense heat is felt throughout the body, but as she ascends in the central channel, first the legs will grow cold and then each part of the body will become corpse-like after the Kundalini has risen past it. When she has united with Shiva, the body is still and rigid, and the only remaining trace of warmth is at the crown of the head.

The first time one is able to raise Kundalini to the highest center, Theos stated, the experience will be brief, "for its natural tendency is to return." Final success depends on the strength of the yogi, for the Kundalini must be held in union with Shiva at the crown chakra for three days and three nights to attain "great power."

Theos used the bulk of the thesis to describe how the practices of Hatha Yoga tone and purify the subtle body to bring on Kundalini arousal, its ascent, and the unimaginable bliss of union with ultimate Shiva consciousness. Those detailed practices of Hatha Yoga were the subject of his doctoral dissertation a few years later.

The esoteric nature of Theos' research must have raised some eyebrows at Columbia. A classmate recalled that at one of his final exams Theos was challenged by Professor Ralph Linton, one of anthropology's premier theorists and the successor to Boas as department chairman, who said that if it was true Theos could levitate, he need only prove it by raising the table and he would pass the course without having to take the test. At that point, Theos might have wished he had followed the wisdom of his guru's original advice to keep his studies entirely secret.

Over the winter, Theos and Viola finalized their plans for the near future. Theos would take the next two years off from school and do research for his Ph.D. in India. Viola would join him for the first part of the trip and be back to start her first internship in January. Theos received his master's degree on June 2, 1936, and within a few days, having packed for a long trip across the world, set out first to visit his family in Tombstone. He planned to spend a few weeks there helping to negotiate the sale of the San Juan mine while Viola finished her last few weeks of medical school. They would meet up in San Francisco and catch a ship sailing July 30 across the Pacific.

It took more than a few weeks, but the negotiations on the sale of the mine went smoothly. However, the delayed arrival of the buying company's engineer postponed the final closing on the deal, and while they waited, Theos and his sixty-eight-year-old stepfather, Jonathan Gordon, traveled almost two thousand miles through Arizona looking at vanadium and molybdenum mines that Gordon was considering buying with the proceeds of the San Juan sale. They hiked in with camping gear to sites in the remote desert ranges and slept every night under the stars. In one of his daily letters to Viola, Theos rhapsodized:

I only wish you had slept out under the sky with me last night—a moon which you have never witnessed lighted . . . a diffused mackerel sky. When I look up into the heavens, watching the clouds banking high, waiting for a bolt of lightning to open them up so that their contents can drench us below—it pictures exactly my own situation— daily I am filling up with love—and it will only take the tone of your voice or the warmth of your breath to release all there is being stored within for you. . . . I do love you ever so much and I must come out with it.

Theos invited his mother and brothers to make the trip to San Francisco with him for a final bon voyage at the pier. Aura wanted to visit relatives along the way, and they left after sunset on July 10 to drive across the desert from Tucson to Los Angeles.

Viola met them all in San Francisco on July 29, the day before their departure, and the next day at noon, with a blast of its horn, the ship eased out into the bay while Theos and Viola waved and blew kisses from the rail of the first deck. The boys watched from the pier until the stern of the *Asama Maru*, the fastest ship on the San Francisco–Yokohama run, finally vanished over the horizon, but Theos and Viola had long since disappeared into their stateroom to open a bottle of champagne and unpack their books for the first leg of their six-week voyage to India.

Chapter 3

THE PAGEANT OF INDIA

THEOS AND VIOLA'S PASSAGE to Calcutta included a three-day stop in Japan—with glimpses of Tokyo, Mt. Fuji, and the temples of Kyoto—and an eleven-day dash through China, which at the moment was graced with a lull in the decades of warfare that demolished the feudal order of the emperors.

For the three months that Theos and Viola traveled together in Asia, it was Viola who took charge of the itinerary, and in the pace she set she seemed determined to see every monument to the grandeur of the East's fading empires before they disappeared. In China they flew from Shanghai to Peking and then caught an amphibious mail plane up the Yangtze River, snapping roll after roll of photographs with their Leica 35 mm camera at the Great Wall, Forbidden City, Summer Palace, Temple of Heaven, Ming tombs, and Yangtze gorges.

Their onward passage from Hong Kong was over rough seas produced by a typhoon in the Bay of Bengal, and two weeks of seasickness was mercifully interrupted by port calls in Singapore, Pagan, and then Rangoon, where they were awed by a 250-foot-long reclining Buddha and barefoot monks carrying alms bowls back to massive gilded pagodas.

At noon on September 13, 1936, they disembarked at Calcutta's piers on the Hooghly River, one of the busiest ports in the world, and rolled in a gleaming taxi down a broad boulevard to the British sector of the "City of Palaces." Calcutta had been, until the move of the imperial seat to Delhi twenty-five years earlier, the capital of British India and had been regarded as second only to London in its grandeur. But beyond the marble architecture of the British sector lay "Black Town," a throbbing, squalid city of more than a million Hindus and Muslims, and out their taxi window Theos and Viola watched the passing carnival of sweating men pulling brightly painted rickshaws, ancient bullock carts loaded with the latest machinery, cows wandering between garbage piles, and naked sadhus walking with stately, unperturbed focus through the chaos.

They checked into the Grand Hotel and then went immediately to the American Express office, where they found a large package of mail awaiting them. They discovered, however, that the recent letters they had sent to "Ted"—the code name they used whenever referring to Glen on this trip—were still unclaimed. When they returned to the hotel after dinner, Viola was introduced to the everyday frustrations of travel in India. She left instructions at the desk for tea to be brought up the next morning and answered the door at eleven that night to find a man with coffee and toast. She wrote in her diary, "Pushed bells—nothing happened—why—no servant!" A servant, she figured, would buffer those logistical annoyances, and the next morning Viola hired a young man named Hosseine to live and travel with them at the rate of $1.05 a day plus expenses.

On the second day after their arrival in Calcutta, they finally heard from Glen. Theos and Glen got together the next morning to talk over plans, and afterward Theos met Viola for lunch at Firpo's, Calcutta's best Italian food. When Theos told her about Glen's idea of doing a Yoga retreat with his Tantric alchemy teachers in the jungle near Ranchi, Viola, as she described in her diary, "blew up." What she had in mind for her seven and a half weeks in the country was an itinerary planned around the dozens of letters of introduction she carried with her from their friend Dr. S. L. Joshi, teacher of Indian philosophy at Dartmouth College and secretary of the Clarkstown Country Club. Joshi was highly regarded by his colleagues in India and his letters offered an open door to hospital directors, university chancellors, Yoga researchers, and the prime ministers of

India's two wealthiest princely states. Traveling between those appointments and skimming the tourist highlights of the 1.8 million square miles of British India would keep them traveling fast and leave no time for a long retreat in the jungle.

Caught between the stubborn insistence of his wife and his father, Theos decided it would be prudent to accede to Viola's plan for the weeks she would be with him in India. Glen would travel with them and they would try to track down yogis at places on Viola's itinerary, but clearly the eighteen months of Glen's research in the Calcutta area would be of little use to them on their journey.

They spent a total of four days filled with appointments and errands in Calcutta, and Glen showed immediately that he would be a cantankerous travel companion. He had spent a year and a half preparing for Theos and Viola's visit, and now his advice was being dismissed. At dinner one night he lashed out. The best use of Viola's medical training, he told her, was to make a physiological study of Yoga. But her new interest in psychiatry was interfering with that and was motivated only by her wish to avoid the hard work necessary to carry out his plan for her. Theos, he lectured, was even lazier. His master's thesis was merely based on the research of others and his choice of studying in the philosophy department was just a way to avoid the trials of fieldwork. They had a long, heated talk, and Theos confessed that he was tempted at times to give up academics altogether and go into photography.

As a concession to Glen, they decided that before setting off on their excursion across India they would make a side trip north to the hill station of Darjeeling, the edge of Tibetan cultural influence in the Himalayas. Despite his advice to Theos a year earlier that it would be a waste of time to visit the Tibetan enclaves in the north because no one up there spoke English well enough to explain Tibetan philosophy to them, Glen had wanted to visit Darjeeling but found it too expensive to get there. But now that the train tickets didn't have to come out of his small monthly stipend, Glen suggested that they follow up on a recommendation from his friend, the Tibet scholar W. Y. Evans-Wentz, and start their Indian odyssey with a visit to a well-connected Sikkimese schoolmaster in Darjeeling. As it would turn out, this one introduction that Glen provided would be worth more to Theos and his research than all the contacts Glen so patiently developed during eighteen months in Calcutta put together.

Theos, Viola, and Glen caught the night train north to Siliguri and arrived in a pouring rain. After breakfast at the station, they hired a driver who drove them in his Ford up a narrow road that ascended nearly seven thousand feet in steep switchbacks to the terraced streets of Darjeeling. Built on a ridge with panoramic vistas of the glacier-clad Himalayas, the town's picturesque tin-roofed bungalows and health spas provided the British Raj a temperate summer sanctuary from torrid Calcutta, and resident British tea planters created a lively society in the private clubs and a cultured atmosphere for the town's famous boarding schools.

The Bernards checked into the Mt. Everest Hotel, and, as Viola noted in her travel diary, the hotel's staff of men looked on while a hearty, all-woman crew of porters carried the group's heavy suitcases on their backs up long flights of stairs.

Viola had endured a sleepless night on the train and spent the afternoon sick in bed at the hotel with chills, fever, joint pains, and a pulse rate that hit 130. While she rested, Theos and Glen went out to track down Jinarosa, the schoolmaster whom Evans-Wentz suggested they should meet. They hired two rickshaws—which for the steep roads of Darjeeling required two men to pull and two men to push—and after a few inquiries were directed through steep alleys to the well-known Jinarosa's house. A man who spoke polished English greeted them warmly at the door, and although Jinarosa was away for the day, he invited them in. The man introduced himself as Jinarosa's cousin and explained that he was visiting from the neighboring principality of Sikkim, where he served as judicial secretary to His Highness the maharaja. When the man heard that Theos wished to do research on Tantra for his doctoral degree, he told them that he had met the Tibet explorer and author Alexandra David-Neel during her stay in Sikkim two decades earlier, and he knew the lama David-Neel had studied with for two years, the renowned Lachen Gomchen. Jinarosa, the cousin said, could arrange for Theos to study with the Lachen Gomchen as part of his research. David-Neel had written extensively in her books about the Lachen Gomchen's mastery of esoteric Tantric practices and his reputation for mystical powers, and Theos, having read her book *Initiations and Initiates in Tibet* just weeks earlier on the sea voyage to Calcutta, was thrilled with the prospect of meeting the great lama. They should see Jinarosa at his school the next day, the cousin said, and he would surely help them.

Viola was still sick the next day but insisted on joining Theos and Glen for their appointment with Jinarosa at the Young Men's Buddhist Association school, where he was director. The cousin was there and introduced the Bernards to Jinarosa, a fully ordained monk, and to his friend, a highly regarded Tibetan scholar, the iconoclastic monk Gendun Chopel. They all casually talked over Theos' plan to research Tantra, and Jinarosa told them that without a doubt the Lachen Gomchen was the greatest Tantric master in the area and Theos should study with him. The Lachen Gomchen had earlier in his life spent five years in absolute solitude in a cave in the high mountains near the Tibet border, but meeting him now would be easier because he had in recent years come down from his cave to spend winters at a house in the village of Lachen. They all agreed Theos should return in November to study with the Lachen Gomchen.

With almost two years of earnest deliberations about where and with whom Theos should study so effortlessly wrapped up by an afternoon's tea, Theos, Viola, and Glen left Darjeeling the next day and drove with a giddy sense of relief down to Siliguri, where they caught the night train back to Calcutta. Viola was still sick but on her feet, and they spent three more days before departing Calcutta navigating the teeming streets, with a long list of errands to the post office, American Express, the bank, the Kodak lab, and most important, the Thomas Cook office, where agents labored over timetables for all of India's train system to put together a seven-week itinerary that would take them from Calcutta in the east to Rajasthan in the west and from Kashmir in the north to Ceylon in the south. Their last hurried stop was at the army-navy store to buy bedding and two thermos bottles for the many nights ahead on second-class sleeper trains, a mode of travel they chose as a way of getting a close-up view of India's middle class. The garrulous shopkeeper reluctantly released them with their bundles and a final blessing when they heard Hosseine tapping the horn in their waiting taxi. They were running late and now had to dash to Calcutta's Howrah Station, with Hosseine leaning out the window shouting "Howrah! Howrah! Howrah!" to clear a way through the congested streets.

They loaded their luggage through the open window of their compartment and boarded just moments before the train pulled away from the platform, leaving them gasping as they collapsed in their seats to begin their six-thousand-mile journey across the length and breadth of British India, the most astonishing pageant of religions, races, cultures, and tongues ever assembled within a single border.

They awoke at sunrise in Benares, a city of a quarter million inhabitants perpetually inundated by a million pilgrims who came to purify themselves in the holy water of the Ganges or to escape the cycle of rebirth altogether by dying next to it. A hive of temples, hallowed niches, and narrow alleys with a five-thousand-year history crowded its banks, and shortly after they arrived, Theos and Viola hired a boatman to row out onto the broad, placid river for a panoramic view of it all. At the city's fabled ghats—the terraces of stone stairs fronting the river—thousands of devout Hindus waded into the slow edge of the current and hoisted urns of sacred Ganges water for the morning's bathing ritual. At the burning ghats, their boatman drifted in close and Theos shot movie footage of human bodies aflame or smoldering in cremation fires that varied drastically in size.

Theos took the spectacle in with a researcher's detachment and noted in a magazine article on his return, "A thin man burns in seven hours and a fat one in four. The selling of wood is a racket at Benares, and only the wealthy can afford to buy enough wood for pyres of the proper size. So in most cases, after the usual pitiful stock of fuel has burned out, the corpse is thrown into the stream to be swept down to the waiting crocodiles below the town."

In the afternoon Theos and Glen drove through the rain to visit Sarnath, the place where in 530 BCE Gautama Buddha first turned the Wheel of Dharma, and the next afternoon they caught a train for Agra, the capital for three generations of Mughal sovereigns. There Theos, eager to get familiar with the new movie camera, shot some 16 mm footage of the Taj Mahal and the red sandstone Agra Fort, and then they hired a driver to take them thirty miles west to Fatehpur Sikri, the grand, pristinely preserved capital of the Mughal emperor Akbar. Built in 1571, this masterpiece of Mughal architecture was abandoned after only fourteen years of occupation, because, it is said, the water in the wells was brackish.

After two nights in Agra, their itinerary led them on a series of night trains to Gwalior and Delhi and then to India's northern tip. From the rail terminus at Jammu they hired a car to drive across the Pir Panjal range to Srinagar in the beautiful Vale of Kashmir. They spent four days there among the lotus-filled lakes with their ornately carved wooden house-boats, majestic mountain vistas, and rich traditions of both Hindu and Buddhist Tantric masters. It was then on to Peshawar, from where they made a day trip to the Afghan border. Theos shot some film of a camel caravan at the legendary Khyber Pass, and from there they began the long trip to the south of India. Along the way they toured the opulent palaces of Rajasthan's maharajas, shared a compartment with a man who gave Theos a lesson on wrapping a turban, and had dinner at a station with an Englishman who had that afternoon shot a tiger.

Five days after leaving Peshawar, they arrived in Bombay, and they checked in immediately at one of the finest hotels in India, the Taj Mahal, where, besides a panoramic view of the Arabian Sea and the Gateway of India, they had, as Viola noted, "orange juice, good coffee & bells to punch." They spent the afternoon sending cables and reading the mail they picked up at the American Express office, among which was the happy news that Viola had passed the National Board exam, a requirement for her medical license. Viola was "full of joy and glee," she noted in her diary, and decked herself out for the champagne celebration that Theos promised, but her "two jungle men grumped through a silent dank dinner."

The dismal mood was rampant in the city that night. Fighting between Muslims and Hindus had broken out over the construction of a temple next to a mosque in the Byculla district. It was a common and deliberate provocation; Muslims regarded the music from a nearby temple as pollution of the prayers uttered during the austere services at their mosque. Police were able to break up attempts to set fire to both the temple and the mosque, but the incident set in motion each group's political apparatus, which could instantly mobilize a force of hired thugs (professionally known as *goondas*) to wage battle in the streets. Sixty-one people were killed over the four days of the riots; many were victims of a newly developed ambush technique in which *goondas* struck unsuspecting passersby with knives from a doorway or narrow lane, then disappeared into the crowd.

This was already the fourth communal riot of the year in India, and as Viola noted in a letter, the riots were "rather unfortunate as not only was most of the city proper closed to traffic—shops closed, etc—... but also a curfew was proclaimed so that dinner engagements could not be made."

Most of the letters of introduction from S. L. Joshi that Viola carried were addressed to well-placed people in southern India, and from this point of their trip on, Theos and Viola seemed determined to make use of every one of them. Over the four days of their stay in Bombay, despite the inconvenience of the riots, they managed appointments with a half dozen leading Sanskrit scholars and researchers doing laboratory studies on the physiology of Yoga practice.

Dr. Vasant G. Rele, author of *The Mysterious Kundalini*, theorized that the Kundalini experience was associated with glandular secretions and scoffed at the classical image of a serpent coiled at the base of the spine. Swami Kuvalayananda briefed them on the X-ray experiments and barometric measurements done on Dhauti and Nauli practitioners at his institute but confessed that, because it had only been operating for twelve years, he couldn't answer their questions about the neurological basis for the bliss of a rising Kundalini. Yogendra Mastamani contended that respiration was really an internal rather than external activity, which was proven, he said, by a yogi he knew who could blow a horn with his mouth while water circulated continuously through his nose. He recommended that Theos meet a yogi in Madras who had perfected Pranayama and was said to be able to walk on water.

Theos would later write in an account about his interviews with Indian researchers,

> I had been instructed many years ago to study everything and accept nothing. . . . So I merely asked endless questions and listened with a receptive mind to another set of settled answers. The one thing most apparent during my investigations was that every one with whom I talked had the ultimate answer. The others, surely, must have been in

the wrong. Thus I continued filling my basket with plucked finalities from the tottering trees of prejudice.

Joshi's letters also led to some social engagements. They were invited to tea and political discussions with the head of King Edward Memorial Hospital and his wife, both of whom had spent time in jail for their advocacy of India's Congress Party and its challenge to British rule. Immediately after that, they were picked up by the wife of a solicitor at the Bombay High Court in her Cadillac for drinks and sandwiches on the lawn of the Lady Wellington Club. Theos and Viola returned to the Taj Mahal before curfew and in its grand dining room had dinner for the first time in Bombay without Glen, and so, as Viola noted, "had champagne and a swell time."

Viola's travel diary makes frequent references to Glen's irascibility during their journey together. As Viola was packing for their departure from Bombay and Theos was out on errands, Glen came into the room and started a harangue about Indian yogis. He was convinced after their interviews with the Yoga researchers that "he was the only one who really knows anything, not even his guru got it completely right."

Just at that moment, porters arrived to take their trunks to the station and Hosseine burst in to announce that he was too sick to continue with them. Hosseine brought with him, however, two candidates for a replacement. Glen's rant was shelved for the time, but his dour mood persisted until he finally left India three months later.

On October 19, with British troops having temporarily quelled the riots, the Bernards and their new servant, Ami, made it to the station and caught an 11:00 p.m. train out of Bombay. They spent the next five days working their way south toward Mysore, where they hoped to catch a glimpse of the last few days of the year's most colorful religious festival, Dasara. Along the way they toured a cave monastery sculpted over the course of eight hundred years into the solid rock walls of a hidden ravine near Ajanta, and had tea with the dewan, or prime minister, of the richest man in the world, His Highness the nizam of Hyderabad, the progressive ruler of India's largest princely state.

From Hyderabad they traveled another twelve hours south to Bangalore, and at stops along the way, the train began to fill with finely dressed holiday travelers headed to the Mysore Dasara festival. When they arrived at their hotel in Bangalore, they found waiting at the desk a reply to the most important of Joshi's letters of introduction. The letter invited them to be the guests of the dewan of Mysore, Sir Mirza Ismael, at Staff Quarters in Mysore for the climax of the ten-day Dasara spectacle. Glen stayed at the hotel in Bangalore, while Theos and Viola went immediately back to the railway station. They had to wait, however, for several overcrowded trains to pass before they found room among the holiday crowds going to Mysore.

They had telegraphed ahead of their arrival and were met at the Mysore station by a member of the maharaja's staff and taken to their quarters in a palace car. During the festival there were no hotel rooms available in Mysore, and the maharaja, Krishnaraja Wodeyar IV, had thoughtfully provided accommodations for a few of his out-of-town guests in sumptuous private tents. The interior of Theos and Viola's tent was divided by screens into three rooms that were elegantly furnished with tapestries, paintings, a dressing table, a desk with stationery, a bathtub, and thick carpets, all illumined by electric lights.

The regal opulence was a reminder of the fact that under the British there were two Indias: the India of the provinces, such as Bengal, Bombay, and Madras, which were ruled directly by the British government in Delhi; and the India of its 565 hereditary princes, whose vassal states still accounted for a third of India's land area and a quarter of her population. The princes had individual treaties with the British monarchy allowing some degree of local autonomy, and each state maintained its own laws, languages, holidays, and family of hereditary sovereigns.

The ten-day Dasara festival in Mysore, one of the wealthiest and most important of the princely states, had been celebrated with legendary pomp since the first Raja Wodeyar ascended the throne of Mysore in 1610 CE. The festival commemorates the victory of truth over evil and on each day a different goddess is honored. On the ninth day everyone venerates Lakshmi, the goddess of wealth, by celebrating the tools of their trade. As Theos noted, "The maharaja offers homage to his throne, street sweepers bow before their baskets and brooms, and children make offerings to their toys and schoolbooks." On the evening of the ninth day of the festival a formal reception, the Great Durbar, is staged at the Mysore Palace during which the elites of South India and foreign dignitaries are presented to pay tribute to His Highness.

Upon arriving at their quarters, Theos and Viola were handed an engraved, gold-embossed invitation from His Highness to the evening's durbar. Full formal dress was stipulated, and officers were requested to wear their dress uniforms and all their medals. They unpacked their best outfits, which for Theos was a dinner jacket and for Viola was her Bergdorf wedding reception dress, and sent them out with their new servant, Ami, for an urgent cleaning and pressing.

They found a list of guests attending the durbar and saw that their names were the only ones on the list without their degrees, titles, or some qualifying piece of biography appended. The clerk at staff headquarters had been rather dismissive of them until later in the day when, "all agog now," as Viola put it in her diary, he deferentially presented them with a second invitation, this one to a small dinner party at the dewan's residence following the evening's durbar.

Ami made it back from the cleaners with their clothes, and they finished dressing just as the palace car arrived. When they stepped out of the car onto the reception carpet at the end of the palace drive, their eyes fell upon an incandescent fantasy. Every feature of the Amba Vilas Palace, with its five-story tower and gilded dome, was luminously outlined against a pitch-black sky by strings of thousands upon thousands of twinkling electric lights.

As they approached the great entrance, the details of this mass of gorgeously carved and colored pillars, arches, balustrades, and screens revealed themselves. "All of it looked like something out of 'The Thousand and One Nights,'" Theos wrote. "There are doors of rosewood, ivory, and silver, and all the marble architraves are inlaid with what is called Agra work—floral arabesques made of shavings of semiprecious stones. People this setting with scores of turbaned dignitaries in silk and jewels, British officers in dress uniforms, and gaily dressed European guests, and you will understand why I was more than a little dazzled by the display."

But before they could make their entrance, two attendants of the court approached Theos and officiously informed him that his coat was "a trifle short" for the occasion. Theos blithely brushed them off by looking back over his shoulder and stating matter-of-factly that that was the way the coat happened to be cut. Unable to gauge the rank of the American, and knowing there were other protocols farther up the line, the attendants allowed them to pass.

The durbar hall was at the top of a grand staircase, and as Theos and Viola began their ascent, another set of attendants shadowed them and then admonished Theos once more that his coat was too short. Theos replied with finality that they were guests of the dewan and continued up the staircase with Viola on his arm, leaving the nonplused attendants staring at each other. A red carpet led them into the immense durbar hall, whose every detail competed for attention. Crystal chandeliers illumined murals with heroic narratives, and projecting balconies looked over the vast court, with marbled floors patterned with inlaid lapis lazuli, garnet, jacinth, and other gems. At the far end of the court, between green and gold fluted columns, stood the maharaja's massive jeweled throne. Made of fig wood and ivory and overlaid with designs in silver and a full ton of gold, the royal seat was reached by climbing nine golden steps. On either side of the throne, rows of gilded chairs were set, with one side reserved for Indian dignitaries and the other for Europeans.

A fanfare of trumpets announced his arrival, and, preceded by an honor guard whipping silk banners in a spiral, the bejeweled Krishnaraja Wodeyar IV glided into the hall accompanied by the British resident, the king of England's influential delegate to the court. The maharaja bowed to the throne and strewed flower petals over it, and then immediately after he mounted the throne, the Europeans formed a line to present themselves to him. The moment Theos and Viola joined the line, a senior official of the court stepped up beside Theos and with a reproving assay of his coat and then his collar stated flatly, "You have no white tie. You must have a white tie in order to pass before His Highness." Theos looked about, and it was true—he was the only gentleman without tails and a white tie. The official assured them it was a regrettable formality, but one they dared not breach, and showed them to seats at the farthest end of the line of gilded chairs.

Theos and Viola sat feeling the sidelong glances of those better attired until the last in line took a seat beside them and, after some introductory ceremony, the entertainment began. There were acrobats, clowns, wrestlers, stilt walkers, dancing girls, four people rolling inside a hoop, a pyramid built with dozens of men, boxing, and a cavalry review, all accompanied by the music of the royal brass band. After the show, the women formed a line to receive a bouquet from His Highness' own hand, and Viola joined it. At the conclusion, two powerful spotlights followed His Highness as he rose and paid a final glittering obeisance to the throne and then retired on the arm of an attendant.

The evening, which had begun for Theos with the enchantment of a twentieth-century fairy tale, ended up providing the trip's greatest embarrassment when he was evicted from the maharaja's reception line. Theos later wrote about the lesson he learned from the incident: "I had come to India . . . to learn its teachings and not primarily to see its sights. Being an American, the last thing that ever entered my mind was to carry a 'white tie' with me. . . . In the practice of Yoga, one must always be prepared outwardly, as well as inwardly, to meet the world in which one lives. So I learned that even a Yogi needs a 'white tie.'"

The day after the celebrations ended, while their servant, Ami, was trying to get a reservation for them on the crowded trains out of Mysore, Theos and Viola tried to track down T. Krishnamacharya, the director of the Mysore palace Yoga school and the one yogi, of all they tried to meet in India, who would have the greatest influence on the kind of physical Yoga that in later decades became so popular in the West. At a time when the asana component of Yoga—the physical postures that are all most Westerners now know of Yoga—had fallen into such obscurity in India that he had to go to Nepal to find a Tibetan guru who could teach them, T. Krishnamacharya innovated a series of dynamic and eclectic routines with roots in asana, Pranayama, Indian wrestling, and British gymnastics. Three of T. Krishnamacharya's students at the Mysore school—Pattabhi Jois, Indra Devi, and B. K. S. Iyengar—later taught widely to Westerners, and the teachers they trained in turn trained the majority of teachers now practicing in the West.

Ami was successful in getting a precious train reservation out of Mysore for that afternoon, and Theos and Viola felt it prudent to leave the city while they could, even though it meant they would miss meeting T. Krishnamacharya. When they got back to Bangalore, squeezed into a six-seat compartment with nineteen others, they met up with Glen and learned that he had gone to Mysore the day before and actually met T. Krishnamacharya. The yogi told Glen that if he would return another time, he would demonstrate stopping his heart and breath, feats of Yoga that interested both Glen and Theos much more than the gymnastic asanas.

Theos, Viola, and Glen left Bangalore on another train that night and in the morning reached Madras on India's southeastern coast. It was the beginning of Viola's last week in India and the two days they spent in Madras were a busy round of appointments, all-day heat, and heavy rain. Viola's letter of introduction there was to a woman who had, as a girl, gone on a hunger strike to get an education. The woman later became the first female medical doctor in Madras and then the first female member of the Madras legislature. They visited an orphanage she founded, a juvenile court, the Victoria College for Girls, and a boys' home all in one day. Theos and Glen tried to find the yogi who, as they had been told in Bombay, could walk on water, but he was away and no one could say where he had gone or when he would return.

After two days in Madras, they caught a night train and arrived finally at the Dhanushkodi Pier, the southern tip of India, where they caught a ferry for a three-and-a-half-hour crossing of the Palk Strait to Ceylon. The frenetic six weeks of Theos' travel with Viola in India were over, and all that remained of their time together was a relaxing few days at a hotel in Colombo. Their six-thousand-mile odyssey had produced a feast of exotic experiences, and they had met, as Theos would write, "all sorts of persons, ranging from Rajas to Beggars, Kavirajas to Magicians, Scholars to Students, Saints to Saddus," but his interviews with scholars and yogis had produced little of use so far for his doctoral research. Based on his investigation to that point, Theos would later summarize his conclusions about the state of Yoga in India:

Only remnants of true Yoga are accessible today to the seeker. Even in India, the home of Yoga, supreme ignorance prevails about Yoga in general, a criticism which does not exclude the educated circles.

It was easy enough to find those who could demonstrate all of Yoga's exoteric teachings. But those who possessed its esoteric knowledge were always far removed from the main highways, and known only to small groups of friends whose high regard for their noble pursuit in this life kept them from revealing to the public where they lived.

Theos' quest for the esoteric knowledge of Yoga would lead him on the next leg of his journey back north to Darjeeling, but before that he had five days left with Viola before her departure for home. Now taking a true holiday at an oceanfront hotel, they passed the days with dancing elephants and visits to spice gardens and filled their nights with champagne cocktails and floor shows in the hotel ballroom. In the final days there were gifts to buy for friends at home and tickets and visas to arrange, the inescapable signs that Viola was soon leaving for New York.

On November 4 they spent their last few hours together having drinks and writing letters aboard the *Katori Maru*, the ship that would carry Viola to Egypt on her route home. At 7:00 p.m. the ship's horn blasted its command for final farewells, and with a last kiss Theos and Viola parted, expecting it would be two years before they saw each other again. Viola noted their parting with these last words in her travel diary: "Theos gone in launch. Finis."

Chapter 4

KALIMPONG

VIOLA'S RETURN TO AMERICA took her through the Suez Canal, and twelve days out of Colombo she reached Port Said at its northern end, where she caught a plane across the Mediterranean to Naples. There she met up with P.A.'s wife, Blanche DeVries, who was taking a break from the Clarkstown Country Club and had sailed across the Atlantic for a short vacation. The two of them traveled together through Italy for a few days before heading north to Paris, where they feasted on the pleasures of the city with Viola's half brother Maurice, who had come, no doubt, on one of his frequent trips to buy Impressionist art. After a few days in Paris, they all returned to New York aboard the *Queen Mary* and docked at the Manhattan Cruise Terminal on November 30, which left Viola with the month of December to prepare for the start of her internship at the Jersey City Hospital.

Theos and Glen, meanwhile, began their long trip on the gritty trains from Colombo back north to Calcutta. Along the way they made a stop in Madras for one more attempt to find the water-walking yogi, Sri Parama-hamsa Sachidananda Yogeeswarar, and this time found him at home. They were graciously received by a vigorous man in his early seventies who had a large stomach on a lean frame and long white hair that flowed into an uncut beard. "Every syllable he spoke was clipped with vitality and sparkled as they could only in one who is clean within," Theos wrote of him. "They glistened with a radiance of inner wealth in the understanding of life. His entire existence had been devoted to his spiritual development."

Theos was surprised to discover during their discussion that in many aspects of Hatha Yoga his own skills exceeded those of the great yogi. But Yogeeswarar had mastered the art of Pranayama—controlling the breath to move the winds in the subtle body—and he taught Theos and Glen another variation of that practice, perfection of which, it is said, can lead to buoyancy of the physical body. He offered as proof of his achievement photographs of himself sitting rather than walking on water while lecturing to a group of disciples. Three years later Theos wrote a book about his Yoga research in India, titled *Heaven Lies Within Us*, that included a compendium of advice on Pranayama practices, which he described as "virtually the Key to Yoga." And although Yogeeswarar provided the best demonstration of Pranayama of all the yogis Theos met in India, he was, like the rest, unable or unwilling to explain how and why it worked.

The journey from Colombo back to Calcutta took ten days, and to save money Theos and Glen slept every night on the hard benches of overcrowded third-class carriages. By day the trains were rolling bazaars, with a new set of ragged vendors boarding at every local stop. Chai wallahs, fruit wallahs, biscuit wallahs, and shoe-shine wallahs hawked their wares in a melodious patter as they followed one another down the pitching aisles.

Day or night, Indian trains abhor a vacuum. One night Theos got up from the hard bench on which he was attempting to sleep in order to urinate through the hole in the carriage floor that served as a privy, and returned to find someone stretched out and already asleep in his place. Another night he woke with a stiff neck and merely sat up to reach for a pillow. When he put his head back down, it landed in someone's lap. Theos made his point by putting the pillow on the man's lap, and the man got up and left. A short while later, Theos was awakened by a tug on his shirt and opened his eyes to see that the offended traveler had returned with the stationmaster and train conductor to inquire with a whining voice why Theos had been so unjust as to deny the poor man an open place.

Theos and Glen gratefully arrived in Calcutta to find the city celebrating a three-day holiday with fireworks and loud processions bearing images of the celebrated deities to cast into the river at the Hooghly ghats. Soon after their arrival they arranged a visit to a large, successful health center run by the brothers of Glen's friend Paramahansa Yogananda, the yogi who was becoming a popular teacher in the United States. The Yogananda brothers focused their approach to Yoga on "muscle control and coordination," as Theos termed it, and they staged for Theos and Glen a private performance of stunts that featured a motorcycle running over a man lying on a bed of nails and a man supporting the weight of a nine-foot-tall elephant on his chest.

Despite such edifying entertainment, within a few days of their arrival in Calcutta Theos and Glen were both eager to get out of the city, and they set out on another train journey—this one covering a thousand miles across Bihar in less than a week. With Viola on her way back to America, they would have been free at last to undertake the retreat with the Tantric alchemists in the jungle camp near Ranchi that Glen had proposed when Theos and Viola first arrived in India. Viola had vociferously vetoed that idea in favor of the train excursion across India, and it is striking that Theos and Glen, now that they could schedule their research as they wanted, didn't immediately throw themselves into the kind of experiential retreat they had been so eager to do at the beginning of the trip. Theos wrote in a letter to Viola that they did go to the Tantricas' camp near Ranchi on their journey across Bihar, but he mentions it as only one of several destinations visited during the week. All he wrote of the Tantricas' jungle camp was, "Then too I have been around to a couple other Tantric retreats that have proved quite interesting and illuminating."

It seems likely that the reason the trip to the Tantricas' jungle camp was so brief was because Theos had firmly decided by this time that he would spend the winter studying Buddhist Tantra with Tibetan teachers near Darjeeling rather than persuing the Hindu Tantras he had surveyed in his master's thesis at Columbia. He recognized that both Hindu and Buddhist Tantra had arisen from a common Tantric lineage about two thousand years ago in northern India. Tantra proliferated rapidly among Hindus, Buddhists, and Jains, and within a few centuries Tantra was a major part of the curriculum taught at the great Buddhist universities of Nalanda and Vikramashila in northern India. Beginning in the eighth century, Tibetan kings made a concerted effort to bring Buddhist scholars and adepts to their kingdom across the Himalayas for the purpose of translating the Buddhist scriptures from Sanskrit into a written Tibetan language created just for the purpose.

Around 775 CE, India's great Tantric adept Padmasambhava was invited to Tibet by King Trisong Detsen to subdue hostile local spirits menacing the construction of Tibet's first Buddhist monastery. He succeeded, and by the time Nalanda and Vikramashila were destroyed in the twelfth century by conquering Muslim armies, the entire canon of Mahayana scriptures, about half of which were Tantras, had been safely brought to Tibet.

Hindus as well as Buddhists were persecuted by the Muslim occupiers, and the Hindu Tantricas were forced underground to practice in secret clans. Over the centuries many of their practices were lost as the holders of the oral tradition died and their foundational texts—hand-copied on palm leaves or birch bark—rotted in the monsoon climate or were devoured by termites. Theos realized that there was still a vast repository of Tantra that was widely practiced in reclusive Tibet, and he concluded that "everything indicated that the north was my goal."

It took a few more weeks in Calcutta to tie up the loose ends of Glen's year and a half of research in the area, and in that time the incessant frustrations of the city began to wear on Theos as they had long worn on Glen. "Nothing is done right in this blasted place and it gets worse everyday," he wrote to Viola. By the first week of December they were more than ready to "clear out of this God-forsaken place" for the winter, and by the eighth of the month they were back among the sublime vistas and jolly smiles of the Tibetans in Darjeeling.

The change in Theos' disposition was instantaneous. "It is impossible to look thru the azure blue of the Himalayan valleys and catch a fleeting glimpse of those majestic ranges of the distant north shoving their noses up into the heavens and not be effected," he wrote to Viola. "I tell you it does things to you—you want to run, fly, jump, and love all at the same time."

Their plan in returning to Darjeeling was to take Jinarosa up on his offer for an introduction to Sikkim's famous Tantric adept, the Lachen Gomchen. The Gomchen, or Great Hermit, had gained renown as a sorcerer after spending five years in a cave in the mountains, during which time he saw no one and subsisted on scraps left at his door by the area's herdsmen. The French explorer Alexandra David-Neel spent two winters studying with the Gomchen at his hermitage between 1914 and 1916 and wrote of him, "Demons obey him and he works miracles. They say he can kill men at a distance and fly through air."

The Oxford adventurer William McGovern was also introduced to the Gomchen during his clandestine approach to the Tibet border and wrote in his 1924 book, *To Lhasa in Disguise:* "The Lachen lama is particularly famous all over Sikkim for his regulation of rain and snow. Even villages in the south dominated by other temples send petitions to him with huge gifts, asking that rain be stopped or made to fall, as is desirable."

Theos was excited to personally investigate those claims but realized immediately after reaching Darjeeling that it was essential to learn the Tibetan language in order to get the most out of the teachers and scriptures he might uncover that winter. And since the Lachen Gomchen spoke no English, he decided that he would make a short initial visit to Lachen and then return to Kalimpong and spend the winter studying the Tibetan language. He would then be better prepared to return to the Gomchen in the spring for more serious instruction.

The village of Lachen is located about fifty miles into the mountains from Gangtok, Sikkim's capital. Sikkim was still at the time a small, independent principality ruled by a maharaja and located strategically between Nepal in the west, Tibet in the north and east, Bhutan in the southeast, and West Bengal in the south. Although the entire country covered only seventy miles from north to south and forty miles from east to west, the elevation in that short distance jumps abruptly from only eight hundred feet to over twenty-eight thousand feet above sea level.

Sikkim was ruled at the time of Theos' visit by His Highness Sri Sri

Sri Sri Sri Maharaja Tashi Namgyal, the eleventh Chogyal. The Lamas of Tibet introduced Buddhism to the monsoon side of the Himalayas and placed the first Chogyal (which means "Divine Ruler") on the throne to rule the aboriginal Lepchas in 1642, and ever since, the Chogyals required propping up by the armies of either the Tibetans, Bhutanese, or British against the aggression of the neighboring Nepalese. Sikkim had existed as a British protectorate since British forces were called in to roust the Nepalese in 1816, and a British resident—or political officer, as he was called there—was appointed in 1899 to oversee His Majesty's affairs in both Sikkim and southern Tibet.

British officials were keenly aware that Sikkim's Himalayan passes were the gateway to Tibet, and sought to influence the succession of the royal line, which sometimes turned on intrigues of operatic complexity. The royal lineage was marked by abdications and premature deaths, and the present maharaja had come to power in 1914 at age twenty-one after the previous Divine Ruler, his half brother Sidkeong Tulku, died suddenly after reigning for less than a year. The suspicion is widely held that the Oxford-educated and zealous reformer Sidkeong Tulku was poisoned by his stepmother, the maharani (perhaps with British complicity), so that she could bring her own son, Tashi Namgyal, to the throne.

Theos' new friend Jinarosa was related to the royal family, and three of his cousins served as private secretary, judicial secretary, and treasurer to His Highness. Within a week of arriving in the north, Theos and Glen drove in a "Baby Austin" (the hardy British-built version of the Model T Ford that was favored for the steep, narrow roads of the area) to a meeting with Jinarosa's cousins in Gangtok. The cousins offered to arrange an introduction to the Lachen Gomchen, and Theos and Glen spent the next two weeks in Gangtok waiting to see if he would respond to a request from the maharaja's office to come down to Gangtok to visit them. Runners were also sent to two other lamas with a request to come to the city immediately.

Gangtok was nestled among rice terraces at six thousand feet, and in December winter clouds cloaked the peaks, bringing snow that could close the higher trails at any time and prevent travel to or from Lachen. After a week with no reply, another runner was sent to the Lachen Gomchen pointing out that Theos and Glen had come all the way from America to see him, and since they didn't know the trails, he should come the last distance to make it easier for them. But as Theos noted, "These holy men need not move for anyone."

Theos and Glen spent the two weeks in Gangtok as guests at the town's dak bungalow, part of the empire-wide system of cottages maintained by the British at regular intervals along main routes for use by traveling officials and the relay of mail runners. The chowkidar, or caretaker, at the Gangtok bungalow spoke only a few words of English, but Theos described him as one of the most comical characters he had met in all his travels. "He is continually talking, telling me all sorts of things, and then after a good old laugh, we part with the satisfaction that we are sure the other party has comprehended what we were trying to convey."

In the morning, the chowkidar would dash into the sitting room with a handful of coals on a piece of tin to start a fire in the stove. He would blow with puffed cheeks on the embers and then dash out again, leaving the door of the stove wide open. He would be gone so long that Theos was certain he had forgotten what he was doing, and in the meantime the smoldering fire filled the room with smoke, stinging their eyes. The chowkidar would return with an armload of wood and then rearrange the coals with his bare hands, put his face into the stove, and resume blowing. After an hour of fussing and coughing, he had a fire going.

Throughout it all, the chowkidar ran around barefooted and in pants cut off at his knees. "You should see the foot on the little fellow," Theos quipped in a letter. "If Rodin has this foot on his Thinker he would have the perfect man. It is just one great big hunk of muscle. You feel that it could play soccer with iron balls."

Having planned to be in Gangtok for just the brief time needed to get an appointment with the Lachen Gomchen, Theos left all his books with the bulk of his luggage in Darjeeling. The days of waiting at the dak bungalow with nothing to study were a sharp contrast to the frenetic pace of travel with Viola and provided some welcome time for reflection. From the porch of the bungalow—with its enchanting vistas of the maharaja's palace and the terraced markets cut from the blue-misted slopes of the deep Ranipuli Valley—the glaciered massif of Kanchenjunga, the third-highest peak on earth, loomed in the west as a backdrop to his contented reveries.

"There is hardly any life that is richer than that of meditation and reflection, if we were only strong enough to live such a continual existence," he wrote to Viola. "There seems to be a very subtle glow of warmth [that] overcomes the personality when a thought strikes a c[h]ord in harmony with nature. I suppose that this is the only way we have of being able to judge the truth of our mental efforts on things that are still too subtle for scientific proof."

While they waited for a reply from the Lachen Gomchen, December 25 arrived, but Theos saw no evidence that anyone in Gangtok had ever heard of a custom called Christmas. The chowkidar served the same stew as on every other day, and, as always, it came with a cup of *tungba*, the native brew of fermented millet drunk hot from bamboo mugs through a bamboo straw. After every swallow the chowkidar was on hand to fill the mug to the brim again with hot water, ensuring that, even if the beverage lost potency, the mug was never emptied.

The postmaster in Darjeeling knew that Theos was still in Gangtok and forwarded to him on Christmas Day the best of all possible gifts, a letter from Viola. It had been three weeks since the last one and, as he wrote in his reply to her, "it meant the difference between a Christmas with life in it and one that was in name only." His letters to her were much more regular than hers to him. Every night before bed he typed additions to a letter he sent out twice a week when the mail left Gangtok.

Along with accounts of the day's events, every one of the three-to-four-page single-spaced letters included long sections proclaiming his love for her. "There is nothing more beautiful nor more effecting than a glimpse of Kanchenjunga," he wrote in reply to her Christmas letter, "but even that fails to a degree when I cannot put my arm around you and look on with you. It is such sights and experiences as this which are welding our inner consciousness together that they may exist as one eternally. Do you have any idea of how much you are missed?"

Neither the Lachen Gomchen nor a messenger from him arrived in Gangtok, and by the first week of January, Theos and Glen decided they would have to risk the weather and go to him. They set out for Lachen with four horses and three Nepali attendants and covered the fifty miles in four stages.

Sikkim's dramatic changes in elevation and the drenching it receives from 118 inches of monsoon rain annually create a succession of garden-like habitats, "everything from the grandeur of the tropics to the splendor of the frozen north," as Theos described it to Viola. "One passes over endless swinging bridges which span the gorges cut by the foaming rapids far below, reflecting through jungles of ferns and orchids. . . . I assure you that the only trip that can compete with this one for beauty is the return from this paradise."

A heavy snow had fallen at Lachen, but the sun was out when they arrived and the accumulation was quickly melting through to the ground. The village was built on a bench at an altitude of eighty-eight hundred feet, from which pine-clad slopes rose to a nineteen-thousand-foot peak. Above the village stood the humble monastery that his disciples had built for the Gomchen as a winter residence. He lived there only during the cold seasons of his later years and preferred still to spend most of the year at his cave hermitage near the village of Thangu, another four thousand feet higher.

Theos guessed the Gomchen to be in his eighties, but observed that his mind still "sparkles as a fountain ever flowing under the sun of understanding." Theos and Glen were unable to find a translator in Gangtok to come with them, but luckily, Karmala, the only person in Lachen who knew English, was home. Theos wrote to Viola that the Gomchen was most cordial and eager to help with his research, and they spent hours together over the next couple of days discussing different aspects of Tantra. Nevertheless, Theos concluded from his visit that he had spent enough time making contacts with great yogis, and that he would be unable to make any more progress until he could read the Tantric scriptures for himself, "for these people are not prone to talk—this Tantric teaching is far more esoteric than writers have ever [led] us to believe."

Theos and Glen made the downhill return trip in three days to Gangtok, where they had "another enlightening interview" with a well-known lama who had come from western Sikkim to meet them. But Theos was ready to go deeper than he could get in the interviews he had had so far.

Summing up all his meetings with yogis and lamas since reaching India three months earlier, Theos wrote, "I have heard a great deal, but I have seen nothing demonstrated except for some fine personalities." He was nonetheless optimistic. "From the present contacts, and with a knowledge of the language and some understanding of their literature I feel that I am going to be able to gain a deeper insight into things of this land than anyone else has been able to do in the past with very few exceptions." Jinarosa recommended that Theos undertake his language studies with a well-known teacher in Kalimpong, a picturesque village cradled in the Indian foothills twenty miles east of Darjeeling, and on January 10 Theos and Glen moved there to find him.

Kalimpong was the busiest Himalayan market town handling commerce between Tibet and the rest of the world. In 1904 the British sent a military force under the command of Colonel Francis Younghusband on a bloody march to Lhasa to demand the ratification of a treaty with Britain that, among other things, opened trade between Tibet and British India. Tibetan traders quickly realized that the treaty offered access to the port of Calcutta, and in Kalimpong mule trains unloaded Tibet's wool export and picked up the bright array of Western consumer goods that supplied the demand in the Lhasa bazaar for British broadcloth, kerosene, hardware, sugar, soap, matches, trilby hats, and cosmetics by Coty and Dior. At Kalimpong the loads were transferred to or from some wheeled vehicle—often oxcarts—that traveled on the steep road out of the foothills to Siliguri, the terminus of the rail line to Calcutta.

The Calcutta-Kalimpong-Lhasa trade route was so much better than any other into Tibet that even the neighboring Chinese used it for much of their commerce and travel. They preferred sending their more valuable commodities such as brick tea, brocades, and porcelain on the long voyage through the South China Sea and around the Malay Peninsula to the Bay of Bengal instead of risking the months of hard and hazardous travel with pack animals across the brigand-infested wastes of northwest China and eastern Tibet.

Kalimpong was also the most important point of social contact between isolated Tibet and the modern world, and, just as in their trading operations, Tibetans in Kalimpong were both importers of foreign culture and exporters of their own. Lhasa's noble families trained with the British military and sent their children to elite boarding schools, such as St. Paul's in Darjeeling, which was founded in 1823 and known as the Eton of India. At the same time, eminent lamas from Tibet's biggest monasteries would stop for months to acclimate and teach at tiny local monasteries before going on to Buddhist pilgrimage sites in the humid lowlands of India.

All in all, with its mild climate, its sublime views of the five snow-capped peaks of Kanchenjunga, and its streets a lively mix of Tibetans, Lepchas, Bhutanese, Nepalis, Bengalis, and their shouted languages, Kalimpong was a place that Theos grew to love, as he later wrote, "more than any other place that I have ever lived on this earth."

Theos and Glen got rooms at the Himalayan Hotel, a large two-story stone house with wide verandas and a manicured garden owned by the legendary David Macdonald. Born of a Sikkimese mother and a Scottish father, Macdonald spoke eight languages and accompanied the 1904 Younghusband Expedition on its invasion of Tibet as an interpreter. The treaty that Younghusband forced Lhasa officials to sign, the Anglo-Tibetan Convention, allowed the British to open three trade marts in Tibet, and Macdonald served as the British trade agent in Yatung and Gyantse for twenty years until his retirement in 1925. He was a short, stout man who raised three daughters in Tibet and was well known for his kindness. After his retirement from the British service, Macdonald and his family turned their spacious house in Kalimpong into a hotel that hosted British functionaries as well as a succession of Everest expeditions—beginning with George Mallory and Andrew Irvine—and mystic travelers such as Alexandra David-Neel. By the mid-1930s, management of the hotel had been taken over by Macdonald's daughter Annie and her husband, Frank Perry, who had served for years with Macdonald in Gyantse as a captain of the military contingent there.

Immediately after settling in at the Himalayan Hotel, Theos arranged a meeting with Gyegyen Tharchin, the language teacher recommended by Jinarosa. "He was a smallish man, with a figure inclined to plumpness," Theos wrote of him. "He had a little fat face with a tiny moustache, [but] . . . what is more important is that . . . he had a full knowledge of the literature of his country and he had been in Lhasa many times. . . . He was exceptionally competent."

Tharchin was already a very busy man. Not only was he writing a Tibetan dictionary, but he was also the editor, publisher, and principal reporter of the only Tibetan-language newspaper in existence, the monthly *Yulchog Sosoi Sargyur Melong,* which Tharchin translated at the time as *Mirror of the New Vicissitudes in Every Corner of the Universe,* but later translators called simply the *Tibet Mirror.*

Tharchin began publishing the paper in 1925 by sending fifty copies to friends in Lhasa, but soon even His Holiness the 13th Dalai Lama had a subscription. Circulation remained small, but copies were passed among a coterie of progressive aristocrats and intellectuals, and the paper had an outsized importance as the only medium through which Tibetans learned about the fast-changing world outside their borders. The *Tibet Mirror* covered current events, such as the Olympics and diplomacy in Europe; profiled world leaders as diverse as Adolf Hitler and Mahatma Gandhi; explained basic science, such as how alignments within the solar system cause eclipses; and reported on the Kalimpong wool market as well as international gold and silver prices. The *Tibet Mirror* also carried advertisements for new products such as the folding bellows cameras and gramophones that were popular with the Lhasa nobility.

The fact that the only Tibetan-language newspaper was published outside the borders of Tibet reflected the fact that inside Tibet almost every printer was fully occupied producing either Buddhist scriptures and their commentaries or biographies of great lamas. Tibetan printers also had not yet discovered moveable type (employed by Gutenberg to print Bibles in Germany five hundred years earlier) but instead used millenia-old techniques relying on laboriously carved wooden printing blocks.

Tharchin was one of the small number of Tibetans who had converted to Christianity. He was born in Lahoul, a district in India's northwest Himalayas, and was baptized at age three by a group of Moravian missionaries who had settled there. He remained a devoted Christian his entire life, and it was probably this exposure to foreign ideals that influenced Tharchin to become an advocate of progressive reform in Tibet. His house in Kalimpong served as a salon for Tibetan nationalists, dissident intellectuals, reformers, and scholar-monks who sought to coax isolated Tibet into the twentieth century.

Despite the fact that he already had a busy schedule, Tharchin welcomed the chance to do a favor for his friend Jinarosa as well as the opportunity for some extra income and agreed to teach Theos two classes a day, before and after his normal workday. For the months he lived in Kalimpong, Theos' day began at 5:00 a.m, when he awoke in a cold room for Yoga practice, which now consisted entirely of Kriya purification and Pranayama breathing practices. He then reviewed his last Tibetan-language lesson before walking the mile to Tharchin's house to begin class at seven. As part of his Kriya purification practices, Theos kept to a strict diet while living in Kalimpong. When he returned from the morning class, he ate a small bowl of mush and then squatted in the corner to do his new vocabulary and grammar exercises until lunch, his one full meal of the day. He ran errands while digesting lunch and then returned to his Tibetan studies again until teatime, when he had a cup of milk. At five he set off for his afternoon class with Tharchin, after which he had, in lieu of dinner, another cup of milk. He then set to work on his new Tibetan exercises until he ended the day sometime after midnight with another long, diary-like letter to Viola. The disciplined schedule paid off. After he learned the characters of the Tibetan alphabet, his vocabulary grew quickly, and by the end of the second week he knew three hundred words and could carry on a simple conversation.

By this time Glen had been in India almost two years and was more than ready to return home. "It would be absolutely wrong to have him remain, for he is about at the point where he is going to kill every Hindu in India," Theos wrote to Viola. "If he met one in his dreams he would throw himself completely out of bed trying to get at him." Yet despite Glen's weariness, Theos could only admire his father's endurance and dedication. "I really marvel at what he has dug up in this country under the conditions he has worked," Theos wrote. "Thru actions, he more than expresses his sincerity in this field."

Theos cabled Viola for $500 to cover the cost of a ticket on a ship home for Glen with stops in Egypt, Paris, and London. Theos also proposed to Viola that they continue to support Glen for the rest of his life with the $100-a-month stipend they paid him while he was in India. Theos needed him to work full-time, he said, collating some information they collected on the Wheel of Life, which Theos thought he might use for his doctoral dissertation. It would also allow Glen to continue with his Tantric alchemy laboratory experiments and, as Theos wrote, "finish up this work on mercury, which is needed for our future practice."

Viola was already supporting the rest of Theos' family in Tombstone. She had been sending $250 a month to Aura through the school year, but Theos suggested they reduce that to $200 a month for the summer so that his three half brothers would be encouraged to get jobs and learn to support themselves.

Maintaining Theos in India, with the cost of film, travel, and Tibetan manuscripts, while supporting the rest of his family as well consumed a large share of the income Viola received from her trust fund, and they both looked for ways to limit their expenses. Viola thought of changing her legal residence to New Jersey during her internship there to reduce their taxes, leading Theos to write to her, "The way you say 'I'll not be costing us much' breaks my heart. It seems as though I am the one who is doing the costing and I hardly know what I can do about it."

Within three weeks of the start of her internship at Jersey City Medical Center, Viola was already physically and emotionally worn out, and Theos' messages of intended support were unlikely to have buoyed her spirits. "Do tell me all about your activities there, even though I have a contempt for Western Medicine, I am interested in you and want to know what you are doing in the field."

But although he disdained the career Viola was exhausting herself to learn, Theos' nightly letters were filled with his love for her and how they would craft a happy future together. The whole point of his learning Tibetan and collecting manuscripts on this trip was to be able to have a "sedentary life of reading, writing and translating" with Viola at home.

I do not like this idea of being separated from you, and it is my purpose not to let it happen again even if it means that I have to stay home and keep a house warm that you are unwilling to do. You can go out and practice medicine or anything else that you wish, but by God I am going to hang around four walls waiting to see you at the end of that busy day of yours. When one's work is in one place and his love in another—he is sitting in the middle of nowhere.... If I cannot talk you into living with me so that I can carry on my work, I will have to give into your line of activities and attend to mine in the next life.

And yet the very next day Theos would write to her about all the advantages of doing his doctoral work at Oxford rather than Columbia, which would require another two or more years of separation. Theos summed up his uncertain vision of the future: "I wonder if there is any way of telling what on earth I will be doing five years from now.... It will be something very much unforeseen, but most regular in its sequence of development. Hell, I bet that I do not even die regularly—probably alone someplace, mad as hell at myself for being there."

AT THARCHIN'S HOUSE, Theos met some of the progressive monks and intellectuals of Tibet, who dropped in whenever they passed through Kalimpong. One day, Tharchin introduced him to Geshe Ngawang Wangyal, a Kalmyk-Mongolian who eighteen years later, in 1955, would be the first Tibetan lama to move to the United States.

Theos met Geshe Wangyal at Tharchin's house on the morning of Losar, the Tibetan New Year, which, following the lunar calendar of 1937, was celebrated during the second week of February. Geshe Wangyal insisted Theos come to his house to continue the celebration with more tea, and there Theos met several other lamas just arrived from Lhasa with whom he could practice his halting Tibetan. They all went off to another house for still more tea, and by the end of the parties, Geshe Wangyal had given Theos a survey of the scriptures studied in the twenty years of the *geshe* program at Gelugpa monasteries and advised him about where he might be able to locate some of them.

Geshe Wangyal was unable, however, to give Theos much information about Tantric texts. At Gelugpa monasteries (of the four branches of

Tibetan Buddhism, Gelugpa is the branch of the Dalai Lamas), Tantra is studied at a separate Tantric college only by the small percentage of highly qualified monks who earn the *geshe* degree, which is roughly equivalent to a Ph.D. Geshe Wangyal had finished his *geshe* debates in Lhasa earlier that year and so had not yet entered the Tantric college.

But of the people Theos met at Tharchin's house, the most important for him at that time was a yogi from India who had come to Kalimpong the month before to learn Tibetan in advance of his own trip across the mountains. The yogi, whom Theos never named, spoke fluent English and could recite long passages of English literature from memory. Theos sensed immediately that this was "a Yogi who is a Yogi," an approving phrase (like "true Yoga") that he used to distinguish the genuine article from pretenders going by the same name. The yogi replied to Theos' first questions about esoteric practices with the pat response of a disciplined Tantrica: the answers are secret. But when Theos inquired whether he had a particular Tibetan Yoga text, he answered that he did, and after a few questions to appraise Theos' level of understanding, he said he would bring it the next day.

The yogi showed up with the text in the morning as promised, and Theos assumed that they would have Tharchin translate parts of it for them. But when Tharchin picked up the text, the yogi grabbed it from him and said he could not allow Tharchin to see it. That provoked Theos, who told the yogi he was just like the rest of the "Yogi Racketeers" in India, and a heated argument followed, with Tharchin shouting that he didn't care about Tantra anyway, it was all tommyrot, and if the yogi felt it was that important, he should go back to his cave and stay there. It ended with Tharchin throwing the yogi out of his house and telling him never to come back.

Theos and the yogi both left at that point, and Theos apologized to him for his role in the fight. The mollified yogi invited Theos to his room, and along the way Theos decided he would strategically reveal the extent of his own knowledge of Tantra, "which did seem to amaze him a bit," Theos wrote to Viola, "for he had never known a European to be able to do anything about these things but write—and write wrongly."

After several long conversations, Theos judged the yogi to be a master of Kechari, Nauli, Neti, Dhauti, Basti, and Vajroli, along with endless asanas, but the yogi no longer practiced any of these because he had already achieved their purpose of cleansing and strengthening the body. Now his practice was mainly Pranayama (the practice of moving subtle energy through the subtle nervous system by control of the breath), and although he could suspend breathing for two hours, he was still far from his goal of twelve days on a single breath, and so considered himself a beginner.

However, even though the yogi was an advanced practitioner, he could not explain the principles involved, and so was unable to instruct Theos in the finer points of Pranayama and their esoteric significance. "They fight with such persistence that in the end they arrive somehow," Theos wrote, "but they . . . are not able to lead others."

ONE AFTERNOON IN LATE FEBRUARY, Theos was looking through a Calcutta newspaper in the dining room of the Himalayan Hotel when he saw a notice that Sir Francis Younghusband would be a featured speaker at an upcoming conference in Calcutta celebrating the centenary of the birth of Sri Ramakrishna, the Indian saint who taught that all religions are only varied paths leading to the common goal of communion with God. Knowing that David Macdonald had been in Lhasa with Younghusband in 1904, Theos proposed that Macdonald come to the conference as his guest, and Macdonald "lit up like a child," as Theos wrote, at the thought of a reunion. They both dropped everything and left immediately for Calcutta. Knowing that a wider introduction among the small circle of Lhasa veterans would boost his own chances of getting there, Theos told Viola, "I am playing my cards in an effort to win my way into Lhasa, I must play a diplomatic game of friendship . . . if I am going to win my invitation."

Almost immediately upon their arrival in Calcutta, they discovered that Younghusband was staying at the same hotel, the Great Eastern, and Macdonald introduced Theos to the renowned explorer and mystic. Younghusband, now in his seventies, was the founder of the World Congress of Faiths, a new organization aimed at helping members of all religions, as he said, "awaken a wider consciousness, . . . the central source of all spiritual loveliness, till what had begun as human would flower as divine."

The source of Younghusband's own mystic rapture can be traced to the second day of the march back to India after his invasion of Lhasa and his forcing on the Tibetans a treaty so severe that even the British Foreign Office shortly repudiated its harsh terms. He had gone alone to a mountainside and, as he described the experience in his book *Vital Religion*, gave himself up to all the emotions of the epochal events he had directed.

> Every anxiety was over—I was full of goodwill as my former foes were converted into stalwart friends. But now there grew up in me something infinitely greater than mere elation and goodwill. . . . I was beside myself with untellable joy. The whole world was ablaze with the same ineffable bliss that was burning within me. I felt in touch with the flaming heart of the world. What was glowing in all creation and in every single human being was a joy far beyond mere goodness as the glory of the sun is beyond the glow of a candle. . . . Never again could I think evil. Never again could I bear enmity. Joy had begotten love.

The power of that realization remained with him for the rest of his life, and it was his mission now, through the World Congress of Faiths, to bring all religions to acknowledge their unity in the mystic joy at the heart of their teachings. Theos and Sir Francis had a long, pleasant initial talk, and Theos found him "very charming—hard to meet in the beginning, but with a good sense of humor once you know him and can get underneath those eyes brows that hide him."

Also staying in Calcutta for a few days before his ship departed for China was Ngagchen Rinpoche, a special envoy to the Lhasa government from the exiled Panchen Lama, the reincarnate lama whose importance in Tibet was second only to that of the Dalai Lama. The Panchen Lama had been in exile in China thirteen years already over a dispute with the 13th Dalai Lama, ostensibly over the size of tax contributions to fund a much-needed modernization of the army. Their feud actually dated back more than thirty years to 1904, when the Panchen Lama refused to depart

Tibet for Mongolia with the Dalai Lama ahead of the invading British but instead went to India and had discussions about using British troops to establish his independence from the Lhasa government. In 1909, when the Dalai Lama was forced to flee invaders again—this time an incursion by the Chinese—the Panchen Lama accepted an invitation from the Chinese *amban,* or imperial resident, to take up residence in Lhasa. He was treated there to many of the prerogatives reserved for the Dalai Lama, such as staying in the Dalai Lama's palaces and parading through Lhasa with the *amban* in the Dalai Lama's palanquin during the Butter Sculpture Festival.

In the 1920s, when the 13th Dalai Lama made an attempt to modernize and expand the Tibetan army to meet the perennial threat from the Chinese on the eastern border, the government's only way of paying the cost of imported weapons was to raise taxes on estate holders. The size of the Panchen Lama's landholdings was second only to the central government's, and in early 1924, when some of his officials were jailed over his refusal to pay the assessment for a full quarter of the modernization bill, the Panchen Lama—claiming it was impossible to raise such a large sum—slipped out of the country with his entourage to China. He had remained in exile ever since, and with his frequent threats to return to his home monastery of Tashilhunpo under the protection of five hundred well-equipped Chinese troops, he remained a long-standing affront to the central government's authority.

The British were eager to help negotiate a settlement between the Lhasa government and the Panchen Lama that would not result in an increase of Chinese influence in Tibet, and they saw the opportunity for a rapprochement after the death of the 13th Dalai Lama in December 1933. At the very time Theos was in Calcutta, in fact, the British had a political delegation in Lhasa trying to mediate a deal. The Tibetan government offered concessions, and Ngagchen Rinpoche was returning to China with the hope of convincing the Panchen Lama that now was the time to return to Tibet on the government's terms, meaning, among other things, without the sizable armed force the Panchen Lama considered necessary for his personal safety.

Theos had met Ngagchen Rinpoche for the first time a few weeks earlier at Tharchin's house and had heard repeatedly of the lama's reputation as being one of the great scholars of Tibet and an authority on Tantra. It was because of his stature, Theos wrote, that Ngagchen Rinpoche commanded a $1,000-a-month retainer plus expenses from the Chinese, purportedly for translation work.

When Theos realized that Tibetan Buddhists were not represented at the weeklong congress of religions, he used his connection with Younghusband to arrange a slot on the program for Ngagchen Rinpoche. On a short taxi ride to the conference hall, Theos not only delivered the invitation to the lama but also audaciously handed him the text of a speech he had penned for him as well. Ngagchen Rinpoche looked over the text and then went on to deliver a long oration without notes, which David Macdonald translated.

Theos considered the address the highlight of the conference, upstaging even Younghusband in his estimation. To celebrate, he invited Ngagchen Rinpoche to join Macdonald and him for dinner in the Great Eastern Hotel dining room. The envoy inquired whether they could also invite Younghusband, with whom he had shaken hands during the 1904 treaty meetings in Lhasa. Younghusband was delighted to join them and brought with him two guests of his own, Charles and Anne Lindbergh, who were neighbors in England and happened to be in India as part of a tour to promote the development of air travel in Asia.

The Lindberghs had been for the previous decade perhaps the greatest celebrities the world had ever known. At age twenty-five, on May 20, 1927, Charles Lindbergh became a folk hero to millions around the world for his daring, first-ever nonstop flight across the Atlantic in his single-engine *Spirit of St. Louis*. As A. Scott Berg details in his biography of Lindbergh, a confluence of new technologies—including radio, telephones, the synchronization of sound in movies, and a system for sending news photos and voices across submarine telegraph cables—created the nascent infrastructure for the media, and for the first time in history all the wired outposts of civilization could almost simultaneously witness an epic event thousands of miles away.

Millions of people around the world tuned to live bulletins after the *Spirit of St. Louis* was sighted over Ireland, confirming it had safely completed the harrowing fifteen-hour leg across the North Atlantic. A crowd of 150,000 rushed the plane when Lindbergh touched down at Le Bourget airfield near Paris, creating a news story of its own. The hero wanted to linger in Europe for a while, but the U.S. ambassador informed him that a battleship was waiting to return him to America. When he reached New York, he was cheered by more than four million people at a ticker-tape parade led by ten thousand soldiers and sailors.

Lindbergh became the first superstar created by the new media. His activities on that single day in New York were captured by almost seven and a half million feet of newsreel film, far eclipsing the entire film library on the previous greatest celebrity, the Prince of Wales.

Lindbergh's wide-ranging curiosity and aptitude led him in the early 1930s to collaborate at the Rockefeller Institute on the invention of a perfusion pump, which for the first time allowed human organs to be kept alive outside the body so they could be surgically repaired. His work brought him to speculate about inducing "artificial hibernation," reducing the respiration and pulse rates of an animal to produce changes in consciousness, and he surveyed the available research on sleep, hypnosis, and anesthesia, as well as the British Library's collection of Indian mysticism and Yoga.

As they talked through dinner, Theos and Lindbergh recognized they had other things in common as well. Both were good-looking, fit, and bold dreamers whose ambition was leavened with that sunny and ingenuous charm seemingly bred into small-town American stars of the time. Over the next few days, Theos and Charles had lunch together three more times. Lindbergh was interested in Pranayama and its applications for high-altitude flight, and Pranayama was a subject on which Theos could claim to be one of a handful of Western authorities. They talked for hours, and Lindbergh insisted that Theos collaborate with him on some experiments at the Rockefeller Institute when they were both in New York. Theos wrote to Viola, "He is as keen as a child in all of my work here. It is amazing his interest."

On the morning of his fifth day in Calcutta, Theos took Charles to his favorite booksellers and helped him fill out his library on Yoga before they ambled off to a luncheon hosted by Ngagchen Rinpoche at the finest restaurant in Calcutta's Chinatown. The prime minister, resplendent in his golden silk robes, presided regally over the thirty-course feast, at which again they were joined by Younghusband and Macdonald. Afterward Theos and Charles strolled back "through the narrow, dark, dingy, filthy alleys of China Town" to the Great Eastern Hotel and spent the rest of the day talking about the practical applications of Yoga and meditation.

During the week in Calcutta, Theos was also able to have a number of private interviews with Ngagchen Rinpoche. They spent hours together discussing Tibetan Tantra, and the lama offered to write to the Panchen Lama's home monastery, Tashilhunpo, and have delivered to Kalimpong some of the books Theos was interested in. He said he would also bring some rare texts from eastern Tibet for Theos when he returned from China in September.

Ngagchen Rinpoche was eager as well to help Theos find sets of the Kangyur and Tengyur, the comprehensive Tibetan canon of Lord Buddha's discourses and the collection of commentaries on them. Theos was aware of only two sets of the 108-volume Kangyur and 225-volume Tengyur in the United States at the time, one at the Library of Congress and the other in the private library of the artist, mystic, and Tibet explorer Nicholas Roerich.

As it happened, Ngagchen Rinpoche had received as a gift while in Lhasa a complete set of the Kangyur that was printed from the same wood blocks used to produce an edition for the 13th Dalai Lama. He had the collection with him, and because he wanted to help Theos find a good set to bring to the United States, Ngagchen Rinpoche said he would consider selling it to him.

The negotiations on the price of the set provided Theos a tutorial for his later dealings. He began by offering gifts—a wristwatch for Ngagchen Rinpoche and a pen and pencil set to his secretary-treasurer—which he presented atop a white silk scarf while kneeling before them. Theos pleaded from many angles and was able to bring the price down from 1,800 rupees to 1,200. Considering that the set was printed on high-quality paper and already sewn up in waterproofed yak skins for shipping, and that twenty-five mules had been hired to haul the 108 volumes on the thirty-day trip from Lhasa to Kalimpong, the price was an extraordinary deal. Ngagchen Rinpoche, however, was so thrilled by the prospect that the set would go to America that he reduced the price still further, to 1,000 rupees. Theos immediately cabled Viola to wire $500 to cover the purchase and shipping to New York.

At their parting, Ngagchen Rinpoche invited Theos to visit the Panchen Lama's home monastery of Tashilhunpo in Tibet's second-largest city, Shigatse, but reminded him that the trip would require, in addition to a British travel permit, permission from the government in Lhasa, something very few Westerners had ever received.

Theos was confident, however, that by deploying the influence of his new friends Macdonald, Younghusband, and Ngagchen Rinpoche, he would at least be able to get a permit from the British to visit Gyantse (the British trade mart in southern Tibet), and he wrapped up his trip to Calcutta with the purchase of a dozen wristwatches and some pens to offer as gifts along the way.

On the evening of March 5, 1937, Theos and Macdonald caught the evening train for the journey back to Kalimpong and immediately upon arriving at the Himalayan Hotel heard the news that the yearlong diplomatic mission to Lhasa of Britain's Sikkim political officer, Basil Gould, had just returned home without achieving the hoped-for reconciliation between the Tibetan government and the Panchen Lama. The official photographer for the mission, F. Spencer Chapman, had checked into the Himalayan Hotel while Theos was in Calcutta, and when Chapman met Theos and discovered their mutual interest in both Tibet and photography, he invited Theos to return to Calcutta with him to help cut and title the thousands of feet of movie film he had shot in Lhasa. Since Tharchin, as it happened, was also away for the week, Theos readily accepted and returned to Calcutta just four days after having left the city.

After viewing the ten thousand feet of 32 mm black-and-white film and another ten thousand feet of 16 mm color film, Theos had praise for the exposure and other technical qualities but thought, "He has not made the most of his opportunity. The pictures ... did give you reality, but above all they gave me greater confidence in my photographic ability." Theos offered a preview of his approach to the subject, writing to Viola, "I feel sorry for the film—he has one of the finest chances ... to do something very much worth while in this field, but I fear that it will never come to pass unless someone gets a hold of him and puts some showmanship and imagination into it."

Theos was forced to stay in Calcutta a few days longer than he planned because at brunch he bit into a piece of toast and lost his front tooth crown. The repair work was "one hell of a mess but between it and the cement it does fill up the hole." Theos thought the bushy beard that he grew over the winter helped conceal it, and he would wait until he left India to have it properly fixed. "This is good enough for this part of the world," he concluded, undoubtedly reluctant to ask Viola to wire still more money.

When he got back to Kalimpong again it was nearly the middle of March and spring had erupted. "All the trees of the jungle are breaking forth with new buds, the evening landscape is lighted up by fireflies, [and] . . . from the moment there is a beam of light to the last sun beam of the day, the atmosphere is filled with one constant ring of singing birds—it is wonderful," he wrote to Viola. After two months of chilly predawn and after-midnight sessions of practice and study, Theos could not restrain his ebullience at the change of seasons. "I tell you every hour is a revived inspiration for life. You do not want to escape the sheer joy of living, not even by a moment's reflection. At all times you want to be at an all time high of conscious feeling."

Theos now brought his language exercises outdoors and memorized his vocabulary assignment while sitting for hours amid the colorful blossoms that covered every slope. Ageratum grew like alfalfa at home, the fragrance of the sweet peas was intoxicating, and there were endless varieties of orchids, but his favorite was the wild lilacs that grew in the tea gardens. Theos found his outdoor studies a refuge from the occasional guests with whom he had to share the Himalayan Hotel. He could keep up a repartee until they went off for a whiskey and soda, but invariably he regretted the waste of time. One benefit of his four-month residency at the hotel, however, was simply having an address where letters, cables, and his subscriptions to the *New York Times* and *Reader's Digest* could catch up with him. Theos and Viola's constant mail stream made his a familiar name to forwarding postmasters and telegraphers across India, and in mid-April a cable was finally delivered at the hotel that had been sent to Theos the previous October announcing that the deadline was nearing for submissions to the Asia Photographic Contest. The cable was addressed only to "Bernard, Bombay," and although it took six months, it found him in Kalimpong.

Theos' routine now had him rising at four in the morning to take a nine-mile walk before his seven o'clock class with Tharchin, and it found him still up at midnight working on a letter to Viola after finishing the exercises from his evening class. On this schedule he was able, by the third week of March, to memorize thirty-five new words in an hour, and to claim a vocabulary of a thousand words. There are at least two unique difficulties in learning the Tibetan language, and both had Theos "breaking a sweat from the effort . . . of concentration needed." First of all, the language employs a separate honorific vocabulary of nouns and verbs to express the actions of a lama or someone of high social rank. "I can talk and understand a conversation between one class perfectly, yet if the same thing is said to one of a different class, it is absolutely all new. There isn't even one word that resembles the former," he wrote to Viola. Another unusual difficulty is that, in the printed language, Tibetan does not use spaces to separate words. All the characters of a sentence are strung together, and a single letter could be a prefix, a suffix, or a word in itself. "There are about ten million little rules which govern the hundred million possible combinations," he wrote.

Theos estimated that he should have a good reading knowledge of the language within a year, and after that he would make a career out of translating the essential Tibetan scriptures, "for it looks as thou[gh] I am almost doomed to handle this end of the philosophic culture for the Western World . . . I am going to strive to make a beginning, for I feel that I have a more complete background for that sort of thing than anyone working in the field today."

Along with working through the available Tibetan grammars with Tharchin, Theos also began to translate the first of the Buddhist texts he was collecting. He had acquired block-printed folio biographies of the Buddhist Tantric masters Padmasambhava, Tilopa, Naropa, Marpa, and Milarepa, and he set as a goal completing the biography of Padmasambhava before he returned to America. He was already, in late March, half finished with that and was trying to locate a seven-volume set of Padma-sambhava's *Complete Esoteric Tantric Works* that was referred to in the biography to tackle next.

Theos realized that his work would only open the way for a later generation of students. "It is next to impossible to find any material on such figures in our country—in fact for most of them there is nothing that has been translated into English. . . . I know that my greatest difficulty has been in finding out what existed and was worth while; so with this as a starter, others will be able to strike to the heart of things much more quickly."

Another obstacle for future scholars was the difficulty in finding Tibetan dictionaries and grammar texts, and Theos intended to return home with as many as possible. He felt fortunate to find a single copy of Sarat Chandra Das' authoritative 1902 Tibetan-English dictionary—which even Tharchin, who had the best collection of language books in the area, did not have. He was also able to find a copy of the very first Tibetan-English dictionary, written by the Hungarian scholar Alexander Csoma de Koros in 1834, allowing him to track mistakes in current translations to their source, since, as he wrote, "Koros made the first [mistakes] and everyone since then has simply copied him."

Despite Theos' dedication to learning Tibetan and translating Buddhist texts, he regarded those only as the means that would reveal the secrets to develop his "other work," the inner development resulting from Yoga practice. Theos' aim in his practice was to test the theories of the Yoga scriptures on himself so that he could pass on only what he knew to work, and already he could say, "I have tasted of enough to prove to me that what they are talking about all exists and is not a lot of hokum of religious fanatics."

He focused for weeks on the Kriya purification practices, and by the end of March he wrote Viola that he would be glad when he was finished with that regimen because "right now I could not feel much lower. There is not a place in the old body that does not ache nor could I feel any more let down; however this is the reaction that should be taking place so I see no need to be concerned except to say that I do not like it." As part of the Kriya practice he reduced his diet to nothing but liquids and lost twenty pounds from his already lean frame, but he wrote, "I feel so clean that I am afraid to take a breath for fear that I will pollute myself."

The purification practices were aimed at cleaning the channels of his body's subtle nervous system so that he could move the inner winds with his Pranayama breathing practices. Theos could by this point suspend breathing for a full six minutes of *kumbhaka,* and he wrote to Viola, "My imagination cannot conceive of any joy that would surpass the experience of going into kumbhaka and remaining there time on end. The experience and after effect is incommunicable." In another letter he wrote he had gained "somewhat of the consciousness which we are seeking, . . . the inner essence of man . . . , Kundalini to be exact."

Now that Theos had proven the truth of the yogi's path to himself, he was eager for Viola to experience it with him, for, as he told her, she would never have faith in his undertakings until she tasted for herself the results that Yoga promised. In his letters, Theos speculated about their future together. As soon as he was finished with his doctorate and she was finished with her medical internships, Theos would be happy to settle down and have children, "for the good of posterity." But until Viola was finished with her training—which would eventually include another five years of postgraduate study in psychoanalysis—he might as well stay in India or Oxford, because he would see little of her anyway: "If you are going to be hidden away in a psychiatric maze, I see no need of twiddling my fingers in N.Y. so that I can see you when some nut does not need your time."

When she finished her internships, he saw them working together to bring the medicine of the West and the metaphysics of the East together through the channel of physiological Yoga. He was trying to find copies of the three-thousand-year-old *Charaka Samhita* and *Sushruta Samhita,* two ancient treatises of Ayurvedic medicine whose physiological principles he considered to be the foundation of Yoga. He had little faith in Western medicine, however, because it had no such basis in a comprehensive philosophy, and Viola's training and ability to heal others would be limited, he told her, until they combined their approaches in a single scientifically based philosophy of health and happiness.

Theos realized that all those plans would have to wait until he finished his doctoral degree—at either Oxford or Columbia—and then he

would bring Tharchin and a a Tantric lama to America to staff a translation institute he would direct. What he had in mind was something very
similar to his uncle's Clarkstown Country Club, with a program of weekend lectures and a full schedule of writing and translation projects. But it
seemed unlikely that the CCC would be the place for his program. The
club was embroiled in controversy, and Theos doubted the group could
survive until he was ready to launch his institute. The many hints in
Theos and Viola's correspondence suggest that, at the least, P.A. was dividing allegiances at the club by openly consorting with another woman,
and Viola had just taken the heartrending step of resigning her membership so as not to be smeared by the association if there was another long
bout of interest in the yellow press.

Her application for a psychiatric residency at Bloomingdale Hospital,
her first choice, was rejected, and as she told Theos, "I've gotten a pretty
good tip... that it was due to recognition of club connection. I'm too
damn busy and perhaps discouraged, to try and fix it."

Theos supported her break from the club but regretted they wouldn't
be able to make use of the facility when he returned. "If that P.A. wasn't
such an utter fool there are a million and one things that could be done
with that environment... for he has a perfect set up, and I... envy him
the things that he is trying his best to destroy," he wrote to Viola. However, if the CCC did fall apart, Theos concluded that he and Viola would
partner with DeVries and start their own club, an intellectual paradise in
which students "would not have to stagnate in the rut of some narrow
scholarly pursuit."

In the near term Theos thought it important to give the field of Tibetan Buddhist studies all the publicity possible, and he proposed a series
of articles for the *New York Times* on his purchase of the Kangyur, which he
hoped would "get students interested so that this work can be carried on
for all time. If I can do no more than inspire others to push forward the
work, I will feel that I have made a worth while contribution," he wrote to
Viola.

His schemes for introducing Tibetan Buddhism to the public went so
far as to consider building a Tibetan monastery for the Hall of Religions
at the 1939 New York World's Fair. He would have DeVries manage it

and "make the whole thing pay" by selling prayer wheels, souvenirs, and Tibetan tea, and Theos would find a huge audience there for his color films and lectures.

But before any of that, Theos had to focus on getting permission to enter Tibet. His latest plan was to apply to the British for permission to spend the entire summer at the trade mart of Gyantse in southern Tibet. He would take all his books with him and set up shop near Gyantse's large monastery, from where he could readily arrange visits of eminent lamas from the three great monasteries near Lhasa. Additionally, by staying in Gyantse all summer, he would avoid India's summer monsoon and be forced to speak only Tibetan.

The decision about granting a travel permit to Gyantse would be made by the Sikkim political officer, Basil Gould. Theos felt confident about the power of his connections with Gould, but permission to travel beyond Gyantse to Lhasa would have to come directly from the highest officials of the Tibetan government. This, he believed, he was unlikely to get, especially with the current anxiety in the capital over the still-unresolved situation with the Panchen Lama. Nonetheless, Theos took any opportunity to cultivate friendships with visiting Tibetans.

Theos accompanied the Macdonalds one evening to a dinner hosted by Rai Bahadur Norbu Dhondup Dzasa, a Tibetan employed by the British as trade agent at Yatung, the second British trade mart in southern Tibet. It was at this occasion that Theos first met Tsarong Lhacham (Pema Dolkar), senior wife of Dasang Dadul Tsarong, head of one of the most prominent noble families in Lhasa. After a traditional Tibetan feast of noodle soup and some thirty side dishes, they visited Norbu's shrine room and Theos charmed Tsarong Lhacham, who spoke no English, by discussing various scriptures with her in her native Tibetan and then reading to her from a Tibetan text.

The following day, the Macdonalds reciprocated with a dinner invitation to the entire group, and after a banquet of Indian curries, Theos led the guests out to the garden, where he shot portraits and color movie footage of them. Tsarong Lhacham was returning to Lhasa soon, and the day after the Macdonalds' dinner, Theos and David Macdonald called on her to bid her farewell. After tea Theos presented her with a basket of parting gifts that included a complete set of Yardley soap, powders, lotions, cleansing cream, base cream, and nail polish, a customary gesture that pleased her immensely.

A few days later, Theos was invited to tea at the home of Raja Dorje, a Bhutanese noble, and there again was Tsarong Lhacham. She had set out for home but been forced to return to Kalimpong after finding the passes closed by a spring snowstorm. They all played a set of badminton on the lawn and, as Theos wrote to Viola, it was "most touching to see them playing this little game in their native dress and with a grace that would put any New York deb to shame."

After the match, Raja Dorje told Theos that he was going to Gangtok to see Gould on some matter and would inquire about the status of Theos' request to visit Gyantse. Tsarong Lhacham added graciously that she would do what she could for Theos in Lhasa. Hearing that, Theos conceived a coordinated strategy for influencing the Tibetan government. He sent letters requesting permission for travel to Lhasa to Tibet's regent, the prime minister, and the four members of the Kashag (the government's executive cabinet), all of whom would have to agree to the request. Accompanying the letters were gifts, the customary Tibetan inducements without which his letters would probably never be opened. Theos sent a Parker Vacumatic pen and pencil set to each of them and added a blotting pad for the prime minister and a Parker desk set for the regent. To Tsarong Lhacham Theos sent a large framed portrait that he had taken of her in Macdonald's garden.

Tharchin had already aroused curiosity in Lhasa with an article about the American yogi in the *Tibet Mirror,* and so, Theos calculated, he should be a subject of conversation before the gifts and letters arrived, which would then give Tsarong Lhacham the opportunity to offer her firsthand appraisal of him. David Macdonald also wrote a letter promoting Theos to one of the Kashag members that he knew, and Theos had tea scheduled with the wife of another official later in the week.

As for permission from the British for the trip to Gyantse, Theos was still waiting for a response to his request from Gould, who was at the time preoccupied with other matters. The Sikkim political officer had returned to Gangtok with a serious illness in early March after his disappointing mission to Lhasa, and it was understandable that he had not immediately responded to Theos' letter, despite the entreaties of his powerful friends. Also, British permission to enter Tibet was still rarely granted, and the policy implications of granting exceptions were thoroughly scrutinized. While waiting to hear from Gould, Theos learned that the wife of the doctor stationed at Gyantse had just arrived at Kalimpong after an eighteen-month separation from her husband. Gould would not allow even her to go all the way to Gyantse, but required her to reside in a half-way village at which her husband could visit her periodically.

On May 1 Theos heard that Gould would be in Kalimpong the next morning and wanted to conduct an interview in person. Theos reported that they "hit it off like old lovers after a twenty-year absence. But I must confess that I have had an unusual build up before the appointment, for everyone about the place has been speaking to him about me and lifting me sky high; so perhaps his curiosity was up." Theos summed up Gould as "a man of about fifty-five standing a little over six feet of which every inch is ego and his entire life has been an effort to express it." However, showing some diplomacy of his own, Theos admitted, "Since this trait runs so high in the Bernard clan, I fully understand it and know when to let the other fellow have the show."

When Gould suggested that Theos write him a formal letter of request so he could send it on with his recommendation for approval to the government of India, Theos had the letter ready in his pocket, and Gould responded by writing out a cable to headquarters and turning it over to Theos to send. With that concluded, they had a long conversation about their common interest in the Tibetan language. Gould had "a fair understanding" of the language, which he had polished somewhat during his year in Lhasa, and he was preparing to publish a book on the subject. He invited Theos to come to Gangtok a few days before his scheduled departure for Tibet and stay with him while they reviewed Gould's manuscript together. They agreed that Theos would leave Kalimpong for Gangtok the following Tuesday and they would work together until the end of the week, at which time Gould would fly to England and Theos would ride to Gyantse.

The few remaining days before Theos' departure were filled with orchestrating nearly a complete village full of merchants and craftsman to deliver his orders on time. A weaver had a heavy blanket for the high, cold passes still on her loom; another was knitting heavy socks; someone else a turtleneck sweater. One group was procuring the paper for his mailing envelopes, and when it arrived they would deliver it to another enterprise that would make the envelopes. A cobbler was finishing up thick-soled, ankle-high shoes for the paths too rocky for the tennis shoes Theos planned to wear most of the time, and the regimental tailor was still sewing the jodhpurs Theos preferred for walking and riding, even if they did make him look like a British major on holiday.

At the shops in Darjeeling, Theos outfitted himself with new bed linen and bath towels and bought a big slab of bacon and several cans of boiled ham so he could "have a respectable breakfast for a while." And to ensure he could stomach whatever meat might be served after that ran out, he packed several jars of French mustard. To carry it all, the carpenters were making pack boxes for the five mules needed to get them to Gyantse.

The most worrisome detail, however, was getting enough movie film for the trip. The Kodak office in Calcutta was having trouble getting supplies from the United States and would let him have only a few reels at a time of the thirty-six he ordered. Theos cabled every Kodak distributor in India and was able to come up with only one extra reel of color movie film. At last the Bombay office notified him that they had just received a shipment from London and were sending fifty reels that should arrive the day before he left. This gave him a total of six thousand feet of movie film, half of which was color—an excessive amount, he realized, for a trip to Gyantse, but he wanted extra on hand if he should suddenly get permission to continue to Lhasa. The investment in movie film alone ran to over $1,000, and an extra mule was required for the load. Film for his still cameras was easier to find, and to go along with the 35 mm Leica he added a Contax purchased for $30 from Gould, who had taken a dozen of them to Lhasa. He could now keep one camera loaded with color film and the other with black-and-white.

With the advice of Frank Perry, Theos outfitted two pack strings. He would travel with one from Gangtok and meet the other at Phari, about a hundred miles up the trail in Tibet. During the years he was stationed in Gyantse with Macdonald, Captain Perry had traveled the trail between

Kalimpong and Gyantse countless times, and he made sure that Theos left with everything he might possibly need. He lent Theos a saddle and bridle, a sleeping bag, and even his tiffin box. The load in every cargo box had to be carefully planned so that some essential would be available at a particular point without having to unpack the entire box. Also, each box had to weigh the same so as to balance on either side of a mule, and the pair could not be so much as a few pounds overweight. Frank offered the wisdom of his experience throughout and for a solid week worked from 6:00 a.m to 11:00 p.m. to make sure Theos would be ready on time.

At last on May 11, 1937 the day to depart Kalimpong arrived. Theos had been up with the last-minute details until after two and rose again at five. Promptly at seven Frank rapped on the door for a final check before the mules arrived to be loaded. It was a gala morning, with Frank filming the entire process of loading the pack boxes on the mules and then they staged a send-off with Theos and Tharchin leading the way. As soon as the camera stopped rolling, Theos sent Tharchin and his two Tibetan attendants on to Gangtok with the pack string while he jumped into an Austin. Theos would drive the first leg of the journey and arrive in Gangtok ahead of them in order to spend the few days planned with Gould. Geshe Ngawang Wangyal came to say good-bye, and the two of them enjoyed the irony that the monk was headed off to the even more alien world of London the following morning. A farewell cable arrived from Viola just as Theos was loading up the Austin, and Frank sent him off with a running handshake as the car pulled out of the compound.

The drive up the valley along the snarling Tista River was hot and dusty, and the driver pulled over several times to pump up a leaking tire. They finally had to stop to patch the tube, and Theos stood watching for an hour as the driver made inept attempts to apply a patch with fingers smeared with grease. The driver waggled his head, totally mystified about why it wouldn't stick, and finally Theos took the tube from him and did the job himself, from the patching to the mounting of the tire back on the car. The driver made up for lost time by careening along the innumerable curves in the road and at last got Theos to Gangtok, where spring was just beginning to throw a splash of color across the hillsides a full month after its eruption in Kalimpong.

He arrived at the residency in time for tea and found the trappings of luxury an amusing contrast to his preparations for crossing the desolate wastes of Tibet. A dinner jacket was provided for the evenings, and Theos noted that with his well-trimmed beard and smart dress he would attract interest even at a New York theater. He began the next morning at five with a canter on a horse from the residency's stables and spent the rest of the day with Gould and his proposed book on the Tibetan language.

Gould wanted Theos' opinion on everything and over their three days together showed him a full set of confidential reports from Lhasa and even his own diary of the Lhasa mission to get his suggestions for extracting sections for publication. This may have been the inspiration for Theos to start his own journal of his journey to Tibet, for it was on this day that he typed the first entry in what would become a saga of more than seven hundred pages. Theos had already planned to take detailed field notes and write long letters to Viola and was prepared for the journal project by having brought with him a portable Underwood typewriter and several reams of onionskin.

Gould also inadvertently inspired Theos to greater ambition with his photography. He showed Theos all the photos of the year in Lhasa and boasted that his was the only color movie film of Tibet. Having already seen that footage with Chapman in Calcutta, Theos was careful not to reveal that he was also bringing several thousand feet of color movie film and planned to do a better job than Gould's mission had done.

"My only hope is that I return with a deeper insight into Tibetan Consciousness than did this last party," Theos wrote to Viola. "They have hundreds upon hundreds of pictures portraying all of the physical realities of Hidden Tibet, but nowhere . . . what fills the life of these people, . . . what occupies their minds, their emotions." If he could capture that essence in his images, Theos concluded, popular demand at home to see them would require a private secretary and press agent to arrange a lecture tour across America.

Theos joked that the few days of luxury with Gould could spoil him for the hardships of Tibet, but even with a few days of feasting, the six-foot Theos started the trip weighing only 140 pounds, more than thirty pounds less than he had weighed upon his arrival in Kalimpong. After their final sumptuous dinner together, Theos and Gould retired to the drawing room for a discussion on the value of studying the classics, leaving Theos to confess how much Greek and Latin he had forgotten. Their conversation eventually turned to the history of Buddhism, and Gould defended the prevailing opinion among British scholars of the time that Tibetan Buddhism was a degenerate branch of Buddhism that had hybridized with Tibet's indigenous shamanism after it was introduced there.

They broke up the discussion about eleven, and Theos retired to his room to finish packing for his five o'clock departure the next morning. Even Gould could do nothing about the fact that the first dak bungalow out of Gangtok was fully booked, meaning Theos would have to begin his journey with a double stage, trudging twenty-three miles uphill to the second. Heavy rain had drenched Gangtok earlier in the week, which meant fresh snow and a cold march through the clouds blanketing Natu La, the 14,200-foot pass that divided Tibet from the known world and Theos Bernard from his unimagined future and unremembered past.

Chapter 5

GYANTSE

THE BANQUETS AT THE RESIDENCY contained some contaminated food, and on the morning of his departure for Tibet Theos woke at 4:00 a.m. with the queasy symptoms of bacterial dysentery. When he tried to swallow the breakfast the cooks had risen early to make for him, it immediately came back out, and he staggered outside for some fresh air. There he found Tharchin, outfitted in sporty golf knickers and a loud tweed jacket, supervising the loading of the transport mules, and Theos looked on bravely as he tried to stay out of the nauseating drift of smoke from the cigarette Tharchin drew on through the end of his fist.

Gould was emphatic that Theos' six-week permit for Gyantse would be impossible to extend. Betting nonetheless that when it expired the British would agree to let him stay longer, Theos tripled the size of the transport—from the initial five mules to fifteen—to haul the necessary books and supplies to make use of more time if it was granted. After seeing the transport mules off, Theos and Tharchin rode to the residency for a last farewell with Gould, and finally at nine o'clock—already four hours behind schedule—they set off on their double stage to the night's camp at Changu.

The trail wound around the mountainside for the first several miles as immense, menacing clouds sped past them and collected halfway up the ascending valley in a billowy, white tempest. They reached the first bungalow at Karponang by one-thirty, and, feeling feverish and weak, Theos told the attendants to wake him in an hour and collapsed on a cot. They set off again immediately after awakening him, in hail and heavy rain on the remaining twelve miles to Changu. Each ascending mile grew colder, and Theos, exhausted and dripping in his Abercrombie and Fitch watch-pocket raincoat, dozed in the saddle. When his head periodically snapped up, his eyes reluctantly opened on a dreamscape ablaze with seventy-foot-high blooming rhododendron trees and delicate pink and red flowers forcing their way through the remnants of the winter's snow.

Of the two "boys" who managed the pack mules and insisted on acting as personal servants, thirty-two-year-old Norphel dressed in native clothes and earrings, while twenty-three-year-old Lhare preferred the European trends. Both, however, were "strong, good-natured fellows, patient and loyal as they make them." The two attendants had raced ahead with the transport during the last hour, and when Theos stumbled through the door of the Changu cabin, they had his bedroll unpacked and waiting. They immediately put him to bed and covered him with a *puksha* (a fur-lined Tibetan robe) and a doubled Tibetan blanket, but still Theos shivered with alternating chills and fever through much of the night before finally dropping off to sleep.

A heavy snow had fallen in the night, and the next morning Theos, still unable to face breakfast, walked out the door to see more rain, sleet, and snow being wrung from the black clouds that boiled up the gorge. He got back on his wet horse, and, wrapped in the *puksha* and thick felt Gilgit knee boots, set off for the next bungalow beyond the still-looming pass.

The last miles to the pass were all above the timberline, and the party waded through the mud and slush of melting snow under a downpour. When, soaked to the skin, they at last reached the narrow ridge of Natu La, Tharchin and the boys yelped and whooped in a joyous chorus, for through the scattering clouds, a blue sky stretched over their sacred homeland, Tibet. They each balanced a stone at the top of the pass' tall rock cairn and mumbled mantras to be borne off with the blessings from the colorful strings of prayer flags fluttering at the ridge top.

For Theos, although he couldn't yet explain it, the vista of the Tibetan valley that opened below him seemed familiar but just beyond memory. The kingdom that lay ahead, where masters still made a daily practice of thousand-year-old Tantric traditions, felt like his sacred homeland too and he sensed some budding opportunity with his return there to provide a link between those masters and the modern world of the West he was born to.

With their first steps across the unguarded border, the weather and the trail quickly improved, and soon after descending into Tibet's Chumbi Valley the wooden dak bungalow that was their destination for the night came into view. The boys brought Theos a bowl of Van Camp's tomato soup mixed with some local yak milk, and, grateful for that bit of nourishment, he settled in for the evening with a candle beside his typewriter to catch up on his journal.

Theos decided to add to the normal day's stage on the third day of their itinerary an ambitious side trip to the only Kagyu monastery in the lower Chumbi Valley. Since its introduction from India in the eighth century Buddhism in Tibet had developed four main schools: Nyingma, Kagyu, Sakya, and Gelug. All four Tibetan schools share the same Middle Way philosophical view about the ultimate nature of reality and agree on the basic outline of the path to enlightenment, but each school traces its lineage to a different Indian or Tibetan master and emphasizes different Tantric practices. The abbot at the area's Kagyu monastery was known as a master of a collection of Tantric practices called the Six Yogas of Naropa, and Theos was eager to meet him.

The boys had already fed the animals and packed before Theos woke at four, and they left the dak bungalow in darkness following the light of a lantern. About five miles before the next bungalow at Yatung, a steep and narrow trail turned off the main route for the high ridge on which the Kagyu monastery was perched. Theos had still been unable to keep anything but liquids in his stomach since leaving Gangtok, but although he felt weak, he was determined to push on. Tharchin had sent word ahead of their visit, and when Theos finally lurched through the monastery gates he was met by a welcoming party of monks in reddish brown robes and shaved heads.

The senior monk escorted the group through a courtyard entrance lined with prayer wheels to a magnificent shrine room, dominated by a forty-foot-high Buddha. Theos was dehydrated and his mouth felt as if it were stuffed with cotton, but he collected himself and threw an offering scarf into the hands of the enormous image. The next instant, however, he felt the panic of imminent nausea and rushed to the nearest door. The door opened not to the outdoors, however, but onto the landing of a shaky staircase which he felt compelled to climb. With a mystified entourage at his heels, he reached the top, and there a narrow hallway led to a small shrine with an extraordinary image of Guru Rinpoche—Padmasambhava, as he is known in Sanskrit—the great eighth-century Tantric master whose biography Theos was translating.

A chair and a table were hurriedly brought to the shrine, and Theos, feeling wobbly, was happy to sit. The head lama, whom Theos guessed to be about seventy-five, swept into the room adorned in a golden robe, drooping mustache, long sparse goatee, and twenty feet of gray hair wound into a shoulder-width cylindrical coil on top of his head. The great lama's glowing face was split from ear to ear with a toothless smile as Theos offered the lama the honorific greeting of a white silk *kata* scarf, but then, Theos could hold out no longer, and he ran for the hall. Just as he bent over and began heaving, scurrying feet brought a pan to hold under his chin. The purge was just what Theos needed, and he returned to the shrine, where he was helped to lie down on a pair of embroidered cushions covered with a snow leopard skin (the traditional seat of great Tibetan yogis). Theos immediately fell into a deep sleep and woke feeling miraculously refreshed three hours later to the voices of Tharchin and the head lama, still in deep conversation.

Theos rolled the blanket into a pillow and, propping himself on an elbow, joined from his bed an illuminating discussion that filled the rest of the day. From it Theos got a better picture of the scope of Padmasambhava's Tantric works and was introduced to the teachings of the Kagyu founder, Tilopa, through his Tantric lineage of Naropa, Marpa, and Milarepa. When Theos asked how to find a teacher to prepare him for Tantric initiation, the lama replied with the response Theos always got to that question: when he was ready, the answer would come.

By late afternoon Theos realized they would have to make a hasty departure from the monastery or darkness would overtake them while still on the steep, descending trail to their stop that night at the British trade mart village of Yatung. They arrived at the Yatung bungalow just at nightfall and with Theos "bleeding at both ends," as he put it in his journal. With that, it was an easy decision to stay the next day in Yantung and hope the dysentery would run its course. Tharchin had a number of Tibetan friends in the village, and when word spread of his arrival, the steady stream of visitors to the bungalow required the pouring of endless cups of butter tea, a staple of Tibetan hospitality. The potation of yak butter, salt, and freshly boiled, black brick tea was prepared by agitating the mix in a slim wooden churn for a couple of minutes. The frothy brew was then poured into a kettle and kept warm over a fire, ready to be served at any time throughout the day. As Theos would discover at nearly every stop over the next months in Tibet, hospitality also required that the cup be topped off again almost as soon the first sip was taken. Whether it was the salutary effects of the Tibetan tea, the day of rest, or a purification the day before at the Kagyu shrine to Padmasambhava, Theos recovered fully from the bout of dysentery before leaving Yatung and during the rest of his time in Tibet never again had so much as a headache.

At Yatung they had to send the transport mules that had carried them over Natu La back to Gangtok and arrange for fresh animals with the village headman. From here on into Tibet, they had to swap their pack animals for those of a different owner at least at the end of every day, and many stretches required changes at a midday station or even more frequently. As Tibet historian Melvyn Goldstein notes, the feudal obligation of Tibetan villagers to provide animals for official travelers was one of the backbones of the central government's administration of the country. The major travel routes of Tibet were divided into stations located a half day's walk apart, allowing a peasant to walk with his animals to the next station and return with them in a single day. The central government issued passports, called *lamyiks*, to travelers that authorized the holder to demand transport and riding animals, sometimes numbering in the hundreds, from the village headman when he arrived at a station. Holders of these permits could also get basic food and shelter at minimal cost. But without the *lamyik,* travel was impossible. As generations of foreign adventurers had found, villagers could be beaten, mutilated, and have their property confiscated for aiding an undocumented traveler, and interlopers were shunned as if they carried plague.

Theos and his party, with their string of fifteen fresh mules, left Yatung before sunrise of their fourth day out, and they soon encountered long pack trains carrying wool down from central Tibet. Travel was slow on the congested trail, and they frequently had to stop and regroup after some of their animals yielded the narrow trail by fleeing straight up the mountain. By late morning they reached the upper end of the Chumbi Valley, and the trail climbed steeply through a vast garden of rhododendrons and high, swaying pines over the valley's lip to a suddenly expansive view across a grass-covered tableland. They had arrived at the southern edge of the Tibetan Plateau, a million square miles of steppe, mountains, and brackish lakes averaging over 14,700 feet in elevation. "You can see why they call this the top of the world," Theos wrote to Viola, "for you no longer feel that the clouds are forming overhead—they are rising on the horizon beside you."

Through the rarefied atmosphere, everything appeared crystal clear. The mellow brown hills dotted with nomads' tents and herds of grazing yaks, the immensity of the landscape, even the clouds of blowing dust— all seemed created to revive human wonder. At one point along the way they saw on a distant hillside herds of kyang, the wild ass of the steppe. Each herd consisted of one stallion and a harem of ten to fifty mares. During the autumn rut, it was said, the mares would sometimes surround a caravan, and, with their neighing, seduce the pack mules to gallop off after them, disappearing over a ridge along with their loads.

On their fifth day out of Gangtok, they reached the bungalow at Phari, a crossroads of trade whose highest point was dominated by a medieval-looking *jong,* or fortress, built with enormously thick and windowless walls sloping inward to a height of 150 feet. The village spreading out from its base was reputed by foreign travelers to be the filthiest place on earth, and Theos had to concur. The Phari villagers, he wrote, "all draped in rags, worn threadbare with dirt and grease accumulated by their grandparents," were "by far the dirtiest, greasiest specimens" he had ever seen. But Theos marveled, they seemed unmistakably content. From the roof of any of the decrepit houses of the village, the 24,000-foot Chumolhari, the Mountain of the Goddess Lady, towered only ten miles away on the border of Tibet and Bhutan, its north face a sheer 9,000-foot wall. As Theos wrote in his journal, "It is quite enough to awaken the dormant awe in any lost and weary soul. . . . It does to the consciousness what the addition of wings would do to a racing car."

All the rest of the way to Gyantse they had to cover more than twenty-five miles a day—and this with the delays arising from the change of transport animals required now at midway stations. They sent word ahead to the next station detailing their requirements, but it was impossible to know what ragtag medley of donkeys, yaks, or worn-out horses would be brought to the corral for them. When the owners arrived at the station with their animals, the first thing they did was complain that all the loads were too heavy. Then, resorting to some local game of chance, they assigned the loads between themselves. But even the lightest of the loads occasioned routine grumbling, which, Theos learned, was all part of the transaction, dramatizing how they deserved a little extra fee for the overage. They also had to deal on this part of the trail with daily sandstorms, and they adopted a schedule of leaving under moonlight at midnight in order to be hunkered down in some dirt hovel by noon, when the scouring, dust-laden clouds nearly extinguished all daylight.

At midmorning of their seventh day out they reached the sheltered station bungalow at Dochen Lake. The younger of Theos' attendants, Lhare, had been born in Kangmar, a village they would reach the next day, and he was overjoyed at the prospect of seeing his mother for the first time in several years. Having swapped the loads from the morning's donkeys to the afternoon's yaks, the group was just about to leave the Dochen Lake stable when the chowkidar of the bungalow called Tharchin back. A message had just arrived with the news that Lhare's mother had died. Tharchin decided that, rather than breaking the news immediately to the sensitive young man and have him ride the next miles nursing his grief, it would be kinder to wait until they were closer to Kangmar. At lunch the following day, only a few hours from home, Tharchin employed what Theos described as "the typical elusive fashion of the East" to suggest to

Lhare that there was every possibility of his mother's passing away before he arrived at her home that afternoon. The boy understood and, alone with "a silent deep sorrow," rode out ahead of the group to Kangmar.

The village lay at the end of a barren valley beneath a wasting red sandstone cliff. Lhare, despite his sadness, decided that his duty at that moment was with the living, and he was waiting at the bungalow with a hot cup of tea when the rest of the group arrived. "How they can nurse their own feelings and think of you is a trait to be admired among any group of people," Theos noted in his journal.

Lhare did not see his mother's face when he arrived at her house, for, according to custom, her corpse had been bound into a fetal ball with her head between her knees. Shortly after death, a high lama was called in to pluck a hair from the top of her head, releasing the spirit through that pore and preventing it from escaping through other openings of the body. Now her spirit was in the Bardo, the state between death and rebirth, where it would remain as a kind of dreaming consciousness for forty-nine days before taking rebirth in another body—as a hell being, a craving ghost, an animal, a human, or either of two types of celestial gods, depending on the karma she had created in her previous lives. During this period, the family of the dead would go to the local monastery with gifts and ask the monks to offer prayers to guide the Bardo-being to a favorable rebirth. For the entire next year the family would remain in mourning until, on the first anniversary of the death, they threw a party for the village at which they were exhorted to get on with their lives. By this time, after all, the dead had already been reborn.

Lhare's family had not yet decided on the day to carry the corpse to the sky burial ground, where it would be flayed and its ribbons of flesh and ground bones fed to the gathered vultures. Theos and Tharchin decided after a long discussion that, although they would like to witness that, they should travel on in the morning to Gyantse in order to arrive in time for the start of Saka Dawa, one of the year's great religious festivals. Lhare, being the eldest son, would stay behind, take care of the final ceremonies, and join them later.

They started before dawn the next morning on the final twenty-nine-mile leg to Gyantse, and by midafternoon they emerged from a deep canyon onto the alluvial fan above the vast Gyantse Plain. The broad valley was surrounded on all sides by barren mountains, but in shocking contrast to the arid waste they had been crossing for days, the entire valley floor was green.

They trotted down a verdant lane between fields of wheat shoots just breaking the earth and tidy farmhouses set among groves of trees. Irrigation water overfilled its ditches and flowed from breaches down the lane for their horses to splash through. A few miles farther, through the distant haze, the imposing fortress walls of Gyantse Jong came into view, dominating the area from a solitary crag rising almost five hundred feet above the Nyang River plain. "Endless thoughts rush thru my mind as we approach our destination where so few are permitted to come," Theos wrote to Viola. "Why have I been allowed . . . what am I going to be able to take away with me with which I will always be able to live?"

Theos and Tharchin rode down a boulevard of cottonwoods to the dak bungalow where they would be staying, and after stabling their ponies, went to announce their arrival to the British commanding officer, Captain Gordon Cable. Captain Cable had been thoroughly briefed on Theos' plans and movements and promptly announced that Theos was not to leave the bungalow without first informing him of his intentions. The captain would then notify Theos if his plan satisfied all rules and regulations and the wishes of the Tibetan trade agent.

Theos had heard that a Theosophist named Henry Carpenter—who had received his permit no less through the intercession of his friend Lord Reading, the former viceroy of India—had been confined to the bungalow during his entire stay at Gyantse, and Theos realized that to be likewise quarantined would entirely defeat his purpose in coming. It was essential, he saw, to make an ally of the Tibetan trade agent—who was also the abbot of Gyantse's five-hundred-year-old Palkhor Chode monastery—and Theos requested an immediate appointment with him.

Cable approved their visit to the monastery, and after the opening courtesies during which Theos offered a *kata* to the abbot and the abbot inquired about the hardships of their journey, the abbot asked Theos about the purpose of their visit to Gyantse. The thing he most desired, Theos told the abbot, was to learn everything possible about their monasteries and the teachings of the different schools of Tibetan Buddhism. They had a cordial two-hour visit, at the end of which the abbot said he was very happy that a foreigner would take such an interest in their teachings. It was divine intention, he was certain, that Theos should come so far with such sincere appreciation and understanding of their teachings on the eve of the most auspicious day of the year. The abbot invited Theos to come to the monastery in the morning to celebrate Saka Dawa, the single day commemorating Lord Buddha's birth, enlightenment, and departure from his body. The day also marked the start of a two-week festival, during which time the karmic results of any good or evil deed were said to be multiplied a hundred thousand times.

The next morning, Theos and Tharchin returned to the monastery at sunrise, and, just inside the gate, Theos gave a turn to another device for multiplying karma—a huge prayer wheel, ten feet high and eight feet in diameter, containing several million repetitions of the sacred *Om mani padme hum* mantra printed on thin paper. A single revolution of the prayer wheel was said to have the same effect as saying the mantra all those millions of times and bestowed a powerful blessing for the practice of a path that would transform a person's impure body, speech, and mind into the pure, exalted body, speech, and mind of a Buddha.

The monastery's fifteen hundred monks were seated in a large courtyard in front of the main assembly hall, with the higher lamas forming two opposing lines in the center. It was an assembly unique among Tibetan monasteries in that at Palkhor Chode members of the Sakya and Nyingma schools practiced in the same facility as the predominant Gelugpas. An attendant led Theos and Tharchin up a flight of stairs to the private room of the abbot, a long balcony chamber overlooking the lines of devout monks they had just passed through. The abbot greeted them, and they were shown to large Tibetan floor cushions as tea was set immediately before them with plates of sweets, cookies, and nuts.

As soon as the monks moved into the temple, the abbot led Theos down to join them. At the entrance was an empty throne reserved for the Dalai Lama, and Theos shocked his host by showing a Tibetan's customary respect for the god-king in prostrating himself three times before it.

"Apparently this was the first time in history that the people had ever known, let alone seen, one of the Western world express a sincerity of devotion to their way of life," Theos wrote that night in his journal.

From here they went into the main temple, where three thousand candles flickered in two rows running completely around the dimly lit sanctuary. The abbot said that the monks were offering a thousand of those candles and reciting a scripture for Theos' long life and happiness. As the chanters droned, the abbot led Theos in a clockwise circle around the temple walls—all of which were covered with frescoes of great lamas of the lineage—until, at the head of the room, they reached a three-story statue of the seated Buddha studded all over with precious stones.

"The environment would instill religious devotion in any soul," Theos wrote in his journal. "Even the most hardened heathen would want to bow or do something. That is the feeling that it gives you, that you must do something, you know not what and you know not why, but something deep within is moved that perhaps you never realized existed before."

Theos made three devotional prostrations before the massive statue, and that simple act of respect for Lord Buddha and Tibetan customs seemed to follow the Saka Dawa formula for multiplying karmic effects, as it was responsible for everything that followed. As Theos told Viola in his letter that night, "You never in your life saw a more awed group of people. . . . It opened everything they possessed for me." The abbot offered Theos, as he wrote, "the highest honor that could ever be given to an outsider, and that is to be accepted as one of their own followers."

The abbot proved that acceptance by leading Theos and Tharchin to a heavy revolving door concealed behind one of the room's large statues. He opened the huge iron lock on the door and led them down a long, dark passageway to the temple's secret inner shrines. At the first chapel, Theos offered *katas* to golden deities adorned with priceless gems, which glittered in a single beam of sunlight that entered the room through a high skylight. The walls were filled with paintings of Tantric deities embracing their consorts, and as a lamp was held to each, the abbot presented Theos to them as if making introductions to dignitaries at a grand reception.

"Never before has a foreigner ever stepped across these thresholds so far as I am able to discover from the Lamas themselves and by general reputation amongst the people," Theos wrote in his journal. "To date, there are no records of any white man ever entering such chambers. Even Waddell, Sir Charles Bell, and David Macdonald, who perhaps have enjoyed the most intimate relationship with the Tibetans of any Europeans, fail to relate any such experience or opportunity."

It was afternoon before they came out into the sunlight again to visit—still within the walls of the monastery compound—one of Tibet's outstanding architectural achievements, the Gyantse Kumbum: a wedding-cake-shaped, hundred-foot-tall octagonal stupa of nine tiers and seventy-five chapels. As they wound their way up the narrowing passages of its tiers, they stepped into the spectral dusk cloaking each chapel to glimpse polychrome sculptures and paintings of the whole phantasmagoric pantheon of Tibetan Tantric deities: male and female archetypes of wrath and compassion, or bliss and wisdom.

The abbot allowed Theos to photograph anything he wanted, and Theos did not miss a chance, regardless of how dim the lighting. "I was always in hopes that something would make its impression on the film as well as on my mind," Theos wrote that night, "so between the two, I would be able to store away unforgetable memories."

It was already late afternoon before a monk, swinging his leather thong to clear a path, led Theos out through the holiday crowd in the temple courtyard to his well-tended horse. Theos topped off the day by joining Captain Cable at his quarters for supper and gave him a circumspect account of his visit to the monastery. Later, back at their bungalow, Tharchin returned from dinner at a friend's house to tell Theos that the entire village was already talking about him. There was a groundswell of enthusiasm, Tharchin said, to help him in his "pursuit of understanding." They calculated that the news would reach Lhasa shortly, meaning it should arrive not long after his letters and gifts to the regent and the Kashag.

"Now let us see where it will lead to," Theos wrote. "To be invited to the world center of these teachings would be the first time the barrier has been broken. People have stolen their way in, fought their way in, and got in under various pretenses, but no one yet has been invited to make a pilgrimage to Lhasa and had the heart of their teachings open to him; so I carefully lay a diplomatic foundation."

The abbot invited Theos to return to the monastery the next morning to take pictures of their biggest dance performance of the year. At dinner Theos had made plans with Captain Cable to ride over to the monastery together, and the captain arrived at sunrise leading a fine regimental horse for him. The abbot was engaged in a service when they arrived, so Theos strolled with Cable about the nave of the main temple. Theos was happy to have a closer look at some of the images he had only glimpsed the day before—especially the intricately carved and richly painted butter sculptures, which would be destroyed when the festival ended—but with Captain Cable at his side, Theos didn't wander beyond the nave. "I had to see to it that he had the feeling that all was open to him," Theos wrote, "but after my tour of yesterday it was obvious how much they permit the outsider to see."

It wasn't long before the abbot arrived and they retired to his balcony room. After tea and a Tibetan sweet cake, they were served a delicious lunch of about fifteen courses and endless refillings of their cups with *chang*, the Tibetan barley beer. Now well fortified, they went down to the courtyard and pushed their way through a crowd of spectators packed twenty deep to a good vantage within the circle, where they remained for the rest of the afternoon photographing every aspect of the dances.

The orchestra was composed of cymbals, large drums, and a pair of *dung-chen*, the ten-feet-long telescoping brass horns used in Tibetan rituals. When the troupe of about two dozen dancers was ready, the accompaniment began and the ushers pulled out their long leather thongs to beat back the crowd and form an aisle through which the performers entered. The dancers wore large carved wooden masks—the faces of ghouls and fiends—and were draped with strings of human bone ornaments over their brocade gowns. In one hand each held a skull and in the other a long sword, and for the next hour they heaved from one leg to the other in time with the clashing cymbals and bellowing horns.

A brief intermission allowed the dancers to change costumes, and then, after another hour-long act, the performance suddenly stopped and the orchestra stepped out of its box and slowly filed off the stage, followed by the dancers in a measured procession. With the sun close to the western horizon and a heavy storm brewing, Theos and the captain gulped a last cup of *chang* and rode off through the parting mob.

Theos learned that the mail was going out early the next morning, and when he arrived back at the bungalow he hurriedly set to work with Tharchin packaging the film he had shot since leaving Gangtok to send off for processing in Calcutta. While they were working, Tharchin reported the gossip that the celebrated young couple Rinchen Dolma and Jigme Taring had just arrived from Lhasa at their estate near Gyantse. Jigme, a prince of Sikkim and only twenty-five years old, was second in command of the thousand-man Trongdra Regiment, Tibet's best-trained and best-equipped military unit. Educated at St. Paul's School in Darjeeling, Jigme spoke fluent English and was one of a small group of progressive nobles who believed Tibet should take some modest steps toward modernizing. His wife, Rinchen Dolma—Mary, as she was known to her English friends— had been born into one of the oldest noble families of Tibet, the Tsarongs. She also had been educated in Darjeeling and was the first Tibetan girl to read and write English. Tsarong Lhacham, the ally Theos had met in Kalimpong, was one of Mary's older sisters.

Mary and Jigme were close friends of the David Macdonald family, and Theos had been hearing about them in Kalimpong for months. He immediately sent off a letter to them, and the runner returned at ten that night with a note saying they would stop by to visit Theos in the morning.

The next morning, the boys got up early to clean the bungalow, and it wasn't long before the honored guests stood on the patio dressed in the most beautiful silk gowns Theos had ever seen. Jigme wore a funnel-shaped hat—richly studded with turquoise and pearls—that had a peak of gold and red silk tassels hanging down over the brim. Mary was arrayed as splendidly in brocade and jewels, and both had turquoise and jewels braided into their long raven hair.

They all had a leisurely visit for several hours in effortless English, and Theos judged that they were "about as fine a couple as one would ever want to meet in any race, for they have all the polish of our own culture with the grace of their own." On leaving, Jigme asked if Theos would offer his preliminary view on the potential he saw for the development of

Tibetan resources. There was boundless waterpower, Theos told him, and it seemed an ideal place for growing wheat. The Chumbi Valley alone could produce enough fruit and vegetables for all of India, and at little cost the trails across the plains could be improved to handle bullock carts rather than the current donkey trains, allowing a big increase of exports. And if they could just put the beggars to work, they would be able to compete with Japan for low-cost labor. Jigme concurred—there was much that could be done. At parting, Jigme and Mary invited Theos to the estate of Jigme's father for a luncheon the following day.

The next morning Theos was up at four again to catch up on his journal and gather his photo gear before heading back to the monastery for another of the Saka Dawa festival highlights, the hanging of the Kigu Banner. The hundred-foot-long *thangka* of Lord Buddha, done in silk appliqué, was considered so precious that during the entire year it was displayed for only one hour. By six Theos and Tharchin arrived at their seats next to the abbot, and then, with the aid of a monk, Theos climbed in the predawn light across the roofs of adjacent houses, taking black-and-white stills and color movie film of the event. Precisely at the moment the sun lifted above the horizon, the famous *thangka* was rolled up again and stored for another year.

The day was still young, but Theos and Tharchin were scheduled at noon for their luncheon with Jigme and Mary at the Taring estate outside of town, and immediately after breakfast they set off on the seven-mile ride. The estate was owned by Jigme's father, Taring Raja, who was the eldest son of the previous maharaja of Sikkim. Taring Raja could have succeeded to the throne when his father died in 1914 but, believing that he would be little more than a puppet of the British resident in Gangtok, he chose exile in Tibet instead.

The Taring household was known all over central Tibet for its informal hospitality, but Theos was eager to demonstrate on his visit that he was well schooled in the nuances of Tibetan etiquette, much of which centered on the fine art of hosting and visiting. Since entering Tibet, Theos had been continually tutored on the subject by Tharchin, who seemed to have friends in almost every village they passed through. When Tharchin arrived at one of those villages it was up to the friends who lived there to make the first move by sending a welcoming gift of meat—or grain for the pony—after which Tharchin was obligated to pay them a visit. The friends were then free to call on Tharchin as they wished. Along with *katas,* the friends always exchanged gifts when they met. "The Tibetan usually has a couple of dozen eggs which he passes around on this occasion," Theos wrote in his journal. "And by the time they have changed hands a couple of hundred times during the several years which they hold together, you can imagine what state they are in." Tharchin usually traveled with books to offer as gifts, and more than once had one ready at an impromptu moment to pull out of his pocket for Theos to present.

As Tibetan protocol demanded, when Theos and Tharchin arrived for lunch at the Taring estate—even though they were expected—they sent Norphel around to the back of the house to confer with Taring Raja's servants about whether the host was available. The head of the household staff informed Norphel that the Tarings were in and ready to welcome them, and he led Theos and Tharchin to the parlor, where the Tarings were waiting. Theos presented his *katas* and gifts, and then Mary and Jigme served biscuits and tea. It wasn't long before lunch was served, and, sitting cross-legged on cushions at a low table, they nibbled with chopsticks from fifteen dishes of appetizers. Then came the never-ending course of *tukpa,* a bowl of well-seasoned broth with long, flat noodles. The instant Theos finished his first bowl, another was forced on him, until he had eaten six or seven refills. For the rest of the afternoon Theos nursed as well a bottomless cup of *chang,* the Tibetan barley beer. Tibetan hospitality insisted that when Theos fell behind the pace of the others, the servant pick up his still-full cup and hand it to him, "a sort of delicate hint," Theos wrote, "that he cannot refill it as long as it is full . . . They will not take no for an answer."

Jigme was an avid photographer and did his own developing and printing in the well-stocked darkroom he maintained at his house in Lhasa. He showed Theos an album of photographs he had shot at different monasteries he had visited with the regent, and Theos was greatly impressed with their quality. They decided they should dress up and take pictures of each other, and Jigme outfitted Theos for his pose as a high official with the silk brocade robes, lampshade-like hat, and six-inch pencil-shaped turquoise pendant hanging from the left ear that denoted his rank.

Theos thought he might use the photos to illustrate an article on Tibetan fashion for *Esquire*, the point of which would be to explain that wardrobe standards for a well-dressed American man were rather meager when compared with the higher ranks of Tibetans. A high Tibetan official might require in his closet more than a hundred different ensembles of formal robes, hats, and boots, worn but once a year for some official function. A magazine devoted to Tibetan fashion would be a thick one, although it would have a small audience.

The next morning, over breakfast at their bungalow, Theos and Tharchin discussed their next move for getting a permit to visit Lhasa. Tharchin had talked with his good friend Choktey, the *jongpen*, or governor, of the Gyantse district, who had told him how impressed he was with the news of Theos' devotional prostrations a few days earlier at the Palkhor Chode monastery. To have a foreigner, especially an American, believe in their faith must be a gift from heaven, he told Tharchin.

As governor of a large district around Gyantse, the *jongpen* was one of the area's wealthiest and most influential men. He and the *jongpens* in all of Tibet's seventy districts collected taxes from the district's estates, settled disputes, and were responsible for maintaining law and order in their jurisdictions. Choktey was also a devoted Buddhist. Theos had met him, in fact, in Calcutta when he was on a pilgrimage to Bodh Gaya, the site of Lord Buddha's enlightenment. They met again on the *jongpen*'s return through Kalimpong, and so, by the intricate calculus of Tibetan etiquette, Theos and Tharchin concluded that courtesy required them to pay a call on him immediately.

They found the *jongpen* at home and eager to receive them. They told him of their hopes for making a pilgrimage to Lhasa, and the jongpen laid out for them a detailed plan of how to proceed. He predicted that if it was carried out, permission would be granted and even volunteered a personal letter to the regent.

Theos regretted that he had to rush back to town for lunch with Captain Cable, but at parting, the *jongpen* invited them to return the next day for an all-day party he was hosting. The road on the way back to town was congested for over a mile by a large Saka Dawa festival crowd trying to get through the narrow streets to the day's big event—archers shooting at a swinging target. Theos would have enjoyed seeing that, but Captain Cable had overwhelmed him with invitations to tea, lunch, dinner, and games, and so far Theos had been unable to make any of them. Now with the *jongpen's* encouragement that going to Lhasa might be possible, Theos realized that getting permission from the British might be the greatest remaining obstacle, and he was eager to cultivate the friendship.

Theos had written requesting an extension of time on his trade route permit to Hugh Richardson, the British trade agent for Gyantse, who was now stationed in Lhasa. Richardson had been sent to Lhasa the previous winter with Gould's mission, and after Gould left, he had stayed behind to establish a "temporary" British legation at the capital. Theos knew that on receipt of his letter Richardson would contact Captain Cable for an appraisal of him, and he wanted to make sure the report would be favorable.

During their discussion at lunch, Captain Cable showed "a very friendly interest" in Theos' plans and invited him that afternoon to play a practice game of polo. The captain had to keep in form, he said, as they had a match scheduled against the Political Department during Richardson's planned return to Gyantse. Cable was an experienced competitor, and Theos, being new to the game, tried "to catch on to the various tricks of advantage which are usually taught to you through some losing experience," as he put it. Nevertheless, he deemed it "a game that is impossible not to have a good time at, for just the mere fact of riding is a thrill. Outside of working cattle I know of nothing that requires one to be more on his toes for it is hard and rough riding from the moment of the take off until the bell."

At an altitude of nearly thirteen thousand feet, the unrelenting action of a hard match was a strain even for the rider, and Theos was amused to think that his cardiologist in New York would be the one to have the heart attack if he knew what Theos was up to. As part of a pre-trip evaluation of the damaged valves of his heart, Dr. Milton Raisbeck had recommended that Theos should get ten hours of sleep every night and limit his exercise to fishing at the wharf. But it was worth the risk, Theos decided, in order to develop a relationship with Captain Cable, who, along with being an avid horseman, was also a photography enthusiast.

Theos was at his typewriter by four the next morning, trying to keep up with the six to ten pages he added to his journal every day and the four legal-size, single-spaced pages he mailed to Viola twice a week. Mailing anything out of Gyantse required a large dose of faith to believe it would actually arrive in the right mailbox halfway around the world. From the Gyantse post office Theos' letters to Viola were carried by a relay of runners for several days before crossing the Indian border to Kalimpong. From there they went to Darjeeling by car and then by a series of trains to Calcutta, from where they were carried by air the rest of the way to New York. One week Theos addressed 125 cards as gifts to his stamp-collecting friends in America, but the post office had only seventy-five Tibetan stamps on hand and had to send an order to Lhasa to have more printed at the mint.

AN EARLY START was required for the *jongpen's* party—just one of a series the local nobility threw for one another during the fortnight of the Saka Dawa festival—because, like most of the all-day events, it started at eleven.

On arrival at the *jongpen's* estate, they were escorted through the stable courtyard into another small courtyard, at the end of which was pitched the *jongpen's* grand party tent. About fifteen Tibetan ladies and an equal number of men sat at opposite ends of the tent, with the men in their silk brocades congregated for conversation on carpets around two low Tibetan tables and the women seated in their finery on chairs at a European table.

Sweets and tea were served followed by their choice of drinks from a bar "as plentiful as any to be found on Park Avenue," as Theos noted. Fortunately, Captain Cable had arrived before Theos and Tharchin, and the waiter asked him first what he would like to drink. The captain ordered a whiskey and soda, thinking that would be the easiest for them, and Theos coyly delayed his order to see if what arrived bore any resemblance to that. Theos spied on the bartender—who apparently had his own recipe—as he added just a splash of soda to the tumbler of whiskey he had poured, and when the waiter returned Theos asked him to just bring his own favorite drink. The waiter came back with a full glass of crème de menthe, which Theos was happy to keep in front of him for the next three hours without a refill, while poor Cable had to "concede when the 'Tashi Delek' was ringing in the air demanding a topping off of all glasses."

The food arrived, and Theos was shown to a low table with a group of Tibetan ladies, Jigme, Taring Raja, Captain Cable, and an official from Nepal, all of whom spoke English except for two of the ladies and Taring Raja. The three-hour banquet began with about fifteen small dishes arrayed on the table between them. They all helped themselves with ivory chopsticks from the common bowls of stewed mutton in gravy, herring, green peach halves, stewed peaches, tinned pineapple slices, dried dates, Chinese sweets, peanuts, Mongolian ham, yak tongue, and pressed beef, all washed down by a continuous refilling of their *chang* cups.

These were just the appetizers and were cleared to make room for the main meal, another fifty courses of small dishes served five at a time. Theos noted down thirty of them before he lost track. Those included minced mutton rolled in butter with vermicelli, sea slugs in soup with boiled pork, meat dumplings, bamboo roots and boiled pork, eels in soup with pork and onions, shark's stomach, and minced yak. The only course served individually to them was a choice between a bowl of dumplings and a noodle soup, either of which offered the guest an opportunity to express his appreciation by eating as loudly as possible. Theos asked about the preparation of some of the unfamiliar dishes, but, to his amazement, no one at his table had the slightest idea, for, as he wrote, "never does a woman of this class have anything to do with cooking."

After dinner, they all stepped outside the tent into the courtyard to take photographs of one another, and Tharchin, who was learning to operate the movie camera, did his best to capture them all. After seven hours in their company, Theos averred that he had never "been in such a group where all the personalities present were so overwhelmingly charming." However, hearing that another meal would be served in the evening, Theos and Captain Cable offered their apologies for having scheduled dinner at another party, and rode back to Gyantse. The dodge, though, didn't mean the night was over. They hadn't gone far before the captain insisted that to avoid any possible affront if their deception was found out, Theos must join him for dinner at his place.

All this jolly diplomacy began to demand more of Theos' time than he had intended. To keep up with the work he needed to do, he started every morning at four and put in three hours at the typewriter before going off at eight to meet Captain Cable for polo. One day they varied the routine with an eight-hour game of cricket. While Theos regarded polo to be as exciting a thing as he had ever done, he dismissed cricket as being "the greatest excuse that I have yet seen to enable one to do nothing while he is supposed to be doing something. Outside of the fellows who bowl every-one else stands around and waits for the game to be finished." Theos re-gretted that he was taking so much time away from his work, but judged it was the "only avenue for the possibility of getting an extension of time."

By their second week in Gyantse, Theos and Tharchin again turned their diplomacy toward the Tibetans and began a series of obligatory afternoon calls at the estates of the district's nobles. In Tibet all land belonged in principle to the government, but it was held and worked ac-cording to the feudal arrangement laid down fourteen hundred years ear-lier by the first king of a unified Tibet, Songtsan Gampo. It is estimated that almost two-thirds of the arable land in Tibet was awarded by the government as estates, with about 60 percent of that amount held by monasteries. The rest was held by the nobility in estates whose size varied by a family's rank within the nobility. A family might keep its estates for centuries, and their holdings could be enlarged as a reward for service to the government or through marriage. However, estates could be confis-cated by the government because of treachery or malfeasance. Estate hold-ers were also required to supply one lay family member in each generation to fill an unsalaried administrative position in the central government, and failure to do so could result in confiscation of family property.

Along with the land, each estate came with a bound labor force of serfs to farm it. The lord generally contributed seed and plow animals for planting crops and received between a half and three-fourths of the es-tate's harvest. The rest of the harvest supplied the subsistence of the serfs. Instead of the farm labor, some of the estate's serfs might be diverted in childhood to lifetime obligations as soldiers, monks, nuns, or house ser-vants.

Remarkably, all of the lay estates in Tibet were held by about 160 families, who were ranked in four divisions of nobility: *yapshi, depon, midrak,* and *gerpa.* The *yapshi* were families into which incarnations of the Dalai Lamas were born. There were only six of these families, and although they held the highest rank, they all came from peasant stock and held smaller estates than the others. There were only four families composing the *depon* rank, all with enormous landholdings awarded at some time in the past by a ruler of Tibet for extraordinary government service. The third group was that of the sixteen *midrak* families. They had smaller estates but the same position in government as the *depon.* The families of all three of these top ranks of nobility kept large houses in Lhasa and generally preferred to live there while leaving the management of their country estates to stewards.

The fourth and by far the largest group of Tibetan nobility, the *gerpa,* were generally based in the provinces, and if they lived in Lhasa, they rented houses or apartments while there. In the Gyantse district, there were fifteen *gerpa* families, and it was on these Theos and Tharchin now called.

The entrance to the typical manor house lay through the courtyard stable, "so when you go calling you take your horse all the way into the house with you and finally leave him at the foot of the stairs which lead up into a dark, dingy, smoky, gloomy" living quarters, Theos wrote. Guests were hosted in the family chapel, which contained an altar and perhaps some *thangkas* and statues, and, as the one polished room in the house, served as the parlor as well. They sat on small carpets arranged on the floor around a low table, and Theos was invariably offered, as a sign of superior rank, the tallest cushion, which demanded his ritual demurring and their insistence.

An elaborate code of Tibetan etiquette governed social relations between people of different ranks. "One of an inferior rank will always speak to those above him in a whisper," Theos wrote in his journal, "and at no time will he ever permit his vile breath to be cast upon him. They hold their heads down and look at the floor or put their hand over the mouth and speak in a . . . silent undertone."

When someone of lower ranks accepted a piece of cake, for instance, "he will bend forward off his seat, or rise, and then with his head hung low, rake off a small crumb with his hands in the customary praying asana, sucking in his words of thanks in the usual undertone."

However, politeness demanded of both the high and low that they slurp their tea "so that it could be heard by the servants at the other end of the house." And no matter how elegant the gown of the host, it seemed that, in the provinces at least, "you are sure to be served by some greasy filthy servant or a half dozen of them if the person is of the higher rank."

Theos was by this time able to chat in simple Tibetan, and Tharchin was always available to translate what he missed, since none of the local nobility spoke English. It was typical on his visits, Theos noted, that "after a lot of sucking of breath and slobber whispering you finally get down to a friendly conversation," which always began with the host saying he hoped no misfortune had overtaken Theos on his journey and that he was now comfortably housed and his animals well cared for. Most of his hosts had heard stories about America, and they were spellbound by the slightest details of everyday life. And believing America must have a language of its own, they were amazed that Theos had learned to speak English.

The most fruitful of these visits was made one afternoon to a good friend of the *jongpen*, a noble reputed to be one of the intellectuals of the area. A fifteen-foot-high earthen wall surrounded his three-story house, and, as at most Tibetan houses, snarling mastiffs were chained at the gate. Theos wrote of his host, "There was never a more homely face attached to the shoulders of an individual, but never did a face pour forth greater radiance.... Behind that repugnant exterior was one of the finest minds that I have ever met." The man was fascinated that Theos had somehow in America learned Yoga and Tantra, and they had an exhilarating conversation of several hours that concluded with the host's offer to discuss with the *jongpen* how they could help Theos get an invitation to Lhasa.

That was the constant theme as well of Theos and Tharchin's conversations with the *jongpen* himself, as they seemed almost daily to be riding to his estate to consult with him on every move. It was during their visit on June 2, their ninth day in Gyantse, that the *jongpen* told them the time had come to send Tharchin to Lhasa in order to personally present to the Kashag Theos' request for a permit to visit Lhasa.

Tharchin was the ideal envoy. Not only was he highly respected as the editor of the *Tibet Mirror*, the only Tibetan language newspaper in print, but he also had personal connections with several important noble families. In 1926, a number of young aristocrats from Lhasa were sent to Gyantse for military training with the British. When the three-year-old English school they attended in Gyantse was closed in a government backlash against modernizing factions, the young artistocrats wished to continue their English studies and hired Tharchin to move from Kalimpong to tutor them. At the completion of their military training in Gyantse, the progressive young nobles invited Tharchin to return to Lhasa with them so they could continue their studies. Tharchin taught English in Gyantse and Lhasa for a total of three years and made many influential friends among the Tibetan nobility before he moved back to Kalimpong.

Tharchin was by this time familiar with all the cameras, and Theos decided to send them all—even the movie camera—with him to Lhasa. Even if Theos was himself denied a permit for Lhasa, he would at least return home with a complete photographic record of Tibet. Tharchin might also be able to find in Lhasa some of the Buddhist texts they were hunting for.

The only problem was the matter of gifts to send with him. It would be an egregious breach of Tibetan etiquette to go empty-handed, so, with the *jongpen*'s advice on what each official would like most, Theos sent wires to Calcutta with instructions to ship his orders as fast as possible. Just at that time, Theos got a reply from Tsarong Lhacham in Lhasa to his inquiries about the reception the letters and gifts he sent from Kalimpong six weeks earlier were receiving. She informed him that neither the letters nor the gifts had yet arrived in Lhasa. When Theos asked the Gyantse postmaster to check the date they had come through his office, he discovered that the letters and the packages were still sitting there awaiting transfer to an official who had been long out of town. It was a backhanded stroke of fortune, because they now had the gifts necessary to dispatch Tharchin immediately. The *jongpen* agreed that Tharchin should leave as soon as possible, and he sent out the order to prepare the first relay of transport animals.

However, when the *jongpen* examined the letters Theos had written to the Lhasa officials from Kalimpong, he felt that they could be improved and offered to write new letters to each of the four Kashag members in which he employed Theos' ideas but stated them, as Theos put it, with "the King's English and . . . proper Tibetan proverbs." Professional letter writers would copy the lettters the following day, and Tharchin could be off at daybreak the day after.

At five o'clock on the scheduled morning of departure, they heard shouting in the courtyard and went out to be informed that the house furnishing the transport would not have the animals until the following day. Theos and Tharchin had been up packing until two the night before, so Tharchin, at least, was not overly disappointed to delay the first day's thirty-two mile stage.

In the late afternoon, Tharchin went again to see the *jongpen* for some finishing touches on the letters and returned with a message from the *jongpen* saying that he was leaving town on the following day as well and he would like to come over that evening to say good-bye. It was already dark when the *jongpen*'s servants arrived to announce he was near, and Theos and Tharchin took a lamp out to meet him. With the *jongpen* were his charming and beautiful wife, their family lama, and the ugly but radiant noble Theos had visited earlier in the week. The noble, whom Theos never in his writings named, now greeted him with the news that he was a good friend of a young man who lived with the regent, and he was certain that whatever this friend requested, the regent would give. He asked if Theos had any objections to him writing two letters: the first to his friend, and the second—because his friend lived insulated within the household of the regent—to the young man's personal servant with instructions to deliver the first letter to his master. "From the looks of things it is going to be the winning card," Theos wrote in his journal.

It was still another backhanded stroke of fortune. If Tharchin had left in the morning on schedule, he would not have been able to take the noble's letters. But then they realized that Tharchin could not possibly arrive with these new letters without yet another substantial gift to accompany them. The *jongpen* insisted that the gift be a fine new wristwatch that he had bought in Calcutta, and he sent a servant back to his house to get it.

Even that, though, was only the beginning of the *jongpen*'s munificence. During their visits, Theos had talked with the *jongpen* of their mutual interest in Padmasambhava, and how Theos was eager to find the seven-volume set of his collected works. The *jongpen* had told him there were only a few sets in existence, and most of those were in far-off Kham. He, however, after years of searching, had found a set and bought it. And now the *jongpen* told him, if Theos could not find a set before he left Tibet, the *jongpen* would give him his own. "He offers to give them to me in order that I may be able to spread their teachings in America," Theos wrote to Viola. "Only with such a purpose in view was he willing, and even eager, to part with the books."

The *jongpen* admitted that he and others had been suspicious initially that Theos' interest in Buddhism "came from the head as a matter of curiosity," but after thorough questioning they decided it came from the heart. Theos was the first Westerner to come through during his lifetime, the *jongpen* said, who possessed genuine faith, and to him they were eager to pass the teachings of Padmasambhava.

But there was still one more gift the *jongpen* had for Theos. On one of their visits the *jongpen* had mentioned a Padmasambhava *thangka* on whose back the white palm prints of the high Kagyu lama who had commissioned it were impressed as a blessing. The *thangka* had been in the *jongpen*'s family for generations, but now that he was certain about Theos' sincerity, he wanted to give it to him. Earlier in the day the *jongpen*'s lama had conducted a ceremony to bless the transfer to Theos, and on the way to the bungalow the group encountered what they described obliquely as the most auspicious possible sign, and they stopped on the spot to give thanks with another ceremony.

They now hung the *thangka,* a large image of Padmasambhava seated on a lotus surrounded by other deities and lineage lamas, on the bungalow wall above Theos' altar. The *jongpen*'s lama had carried a lamp with the flame that had burned perpetually beneath the *thangka* at the *jongpen*'s home, and he used it now in another ceremony to light a small butter lamp beneath the *thangka* on Theos' altar. They sat in front of the *thangka* meditating on the spiritual qualities of Padmasambhava while the lama chanted a ritual passing the blessings of the sacred painting to Theos. Before they parted, the *jongpen* prayed that Theos would never sell the *thangka,* and that it would be a "foundation for the spreading of these teachings in the new world."

"Well, you now have a real Tibetan Lama," Theos wrote Viola. "This marks one of the deepest personal experiences, for I have had passed on to me the authority, so to speak, to convey the teachings of the Kargyupa sect."

The thing that touches me deepest of all is the fact that they have accepted me and are willing to impart these things to me, for it . . . tells me that I am entering the channels of my desire. To hear them talk it would sound as tho[ugh] the rest of my life in America is going to be the laying of the foundation for the spreading of these teachings and of course it is exactly what I hope that I will eventually be able to do once I have learned to live a better life because of them, for I never want to preach. Only by example will I ever endeavor to uphold these teachings. If they will not sound deeper depths of consciousness for me and make life a continuous inspiration by letting me live always in the flowing stream of creative energy, I do not want to call others to waste their lives.

AFTER THE *JONGPEN* AND THE OTHERS LEFT, Theos found it impossible to sleep, and he sat for hours in front of the *thangka* contemplating the past and the future.

Tharchin and Norphel had the mules loaded by five o'clock the next morning, and they set out with little fanfare on the five-day journey to Lhasa. Now with just twelve days remaining on his British travel permit before having to begin the trip back to Gangtok, every moment counted, and Theos made a list of his research priorities for the days that remained. He wanted first to understand every aspect of how monasteries operate, from construction and design details to the hierarchy of power, how one rose through the ranks, and how monasteries related to politics. His research goals for Tibetan texts centered on the ambitious project of creating an index to the 333 volumes of the Kangyur and Tengyur. "Imagine having to go through all of them in order to find the one book that you would like to devote your time to," he wrote in his journal. "By this time your life will be spent." Of all those volumes, the area that interested Theos most was an eighty-seven-volume section of the Kangyur containing the Tantric scriptures. He was driven to learn "the living principles of Tantra," he wrote, "the system and then the techniques with which to apply it."

While the possibility remained that the British could send him packing for India while Tharchin was still pleading with the Kashag in Lhasa, Theos could not slacken the intensity of his polo diplomacy. It was the vapid pastimes after the match, though, that wore on him the most. "We again accepted the hospitality of our host and enjoyed a pleasant lunch together," he wrote in his journal, "after which came the deadening experience of playing games." "Here we are a group from all the corners of the earth, with nothing to talk about, except regret that there is not a pack of cards around so that we will not have to play checkers."

And now Captain Cable recruited Theos to help entertain a colonel and his wife who had just arrived for a five-day visit. "I more or less have to do my bit since I am the only European around that Cable can call on to come and make up a party; and after all that he has done, I feel that it is a duty," he wrote in his journal for June 11. They played polo in the mornings for the colonel and tennis in the afternoon for the wife, but again, it was the wearisome conventions that gentlemen and ladies kept up in these remote imperial postings that bothered Theos the most.

> I would much rather talk about something else than the champagne consumed in her bedroom during a cocktail party given at her house [for] the elite of Calcutta. . . . She has all the latest on Simpson and the former King [Edward]. We now know how much money he has spent on her, what jewelry he has bought and has not yet been able to pay for; what furs he has bought, and where he buys them.

The climax of the entertainment staged for the colonel was a day at the races. Overnight, the regimental parade ground was fenced off, corrals built, a grandstand erected, and a grand tent raised with carpets, easy chairs, and blossoming potted flowers for the dignitaries.

All the Tibetans in the district turned out for the holiday, betting with gusto on every race in classes that featured—once the regimental horses had run—Tibetan ponies, mules, yaks, and even mongrel dogs. It was an extraordinary day of photography for Theos. The owners of the entrants in the mongrel heat were the "raggedest bunch of urchins" ever seen, who, with everything on the line, screeched every herder's expletive they knew at the yelping cloud of dust that raced to the finish line.

In the pony stakes, a winner emerged from the shrouding dust to claim the prize but was then discovered to be still on his first lap. In another race, the mule Theos bet on was out in front but then decided to go straight off the last curve. And halfway through the yak race, the leader, who was ahead by half a lap, decided to walk the rest of the way.

Between the races, the Tibetans mobbed dice games played on blankets spread on the ground and continued the revelry long after the dignitaries went off to the officers' mess for a concluding banquet. Taring Raja attended the banquet, as did Mary and Jigme. All assured Theos they had written letters to their powerful friends and were doing everything they could to intercede for him in Lhasa. Mary said that her sister, Tsarong Lhacham, was also doing everything she could, and they all believed his chances of getting a permit were exceedingly good.

While Theos was being saturated with the hospitality of both the British and Tibetans in Gyantse, Cable let him know that three other Westerners had been caught trying to sneak across the border. A German had made it over the pass but was rounded up and returned to India; an American who set out to visit some 1,700-year-old yogi was hauled back; and a Swedish girl who had arrived in India in a canoe made it across the pass disguised as a Tibetan woman carrying a heavy load, but she was now locked in the guardhouse at Yatung. Her apprehension was causing an international incident, requiring a flurry of telegrams to Europe. "The military officials are worked up as to what is the wisest thing to do," Theos wrote in his journal, "for after all, she is a woman, and it has never been known to have Indian troops arrest a white woman."

Five days after Tharchin left, Theos received a wire saying he had arrived in Lhasa. When after several more days there was nothing more from him, Theos sent a wire to him inquiring how things were going and received a reply that "was full of hope, but with not an iota of precise evidence on which to build up my faith." Theos sent several more wires to

Tharchin and each time got a reply with the confident line "You're going to be invited," but there was nothing included beyond that to substantiate the optimism, and Theos started to believe that was actually a sign he should expect the opposite.

Then a telegram came. "I shall never forget it as long as I live," Theos wrote in *Penthouse of the Gods*, the book he published in 1939 about his journey to Tibet. This one came not from Tharchin but from Reting Rinpoche, the regent of Tibet himself:

> BERNARD OF AMERICA, GYANTSE. RECEIVED YOUR LETTER. HOPE YOU RE-
> CEIVED WIRE FROM KASHAG THAT YOUR MUCH RELIGIONSHIP MAY VISIT LHASA
> AS YOUR DESIRE. WIRE IF YOU NEED DWELLING HERE. (SIGNED) REGENT.

It seemed too good to be true. The suspense that had for weeks sustained the ardor of his dream in an instant gave way to the realization this was not the climax but the beginning of his Tibetan experiences. He asked himself why, of all the people who so desperately wanted to make a pilgrimage to Lhasa, he should be the one to get an invitation.

"Now, as I was being swept up toward the crest of my adventure," Theos wrote, "it dawned upon me perhaps for the first time with astonishing clairvoyance that this was what I had been preparing for my entire life, and that some inner urge had been driving me and directing me toward some mysterious yet definite goal, from which I could not deviate without violating my best inner self.... To be sure, for fifteen years I had been building up the consciousness for the absorption of all that was about to be offered me."

A few days later, the telegram from the Kashag arrived with his official invitation:

> BERNARD OF AMERICA, GYANTSE. RECEIVED YOUR LETTER WHICH WE SENT UP
> TO THE REGENT AND PRIME MINISTER. AS YOU PROBABLY KNOW TIBET BEING A
> PURELY RELIGIOUS COUNTRY THERE IS A GREAT RESTRICTION ON FOREIGNERS
> ENTERING THE COUNTRY BUT UNDERSTANDING THAT YOU HAVE A GREAT RE-
> SPECT FOR OUR RELIGION AND HAVE HOPES OF SPREADING THE RELIGION IN

AMERICA ON YOUR RETURN WE HAVE DECIDED AS A SPECIAL CASE TO ALLOW
YOU TO COME TO LHASA BY THE MAIN ROAD FOR A THREE WEEKS VISIT.
(SIGNED) KASHAG

Along with that message, the delivery boy had with him as well a telegram
from Richardson, the Gyantse trade agent, allowing Theos a six-week extension on his travel permit.

The remaining days were filled with sorting out everything he wouldn't
need in Lhasa to store in Gyantse for his return and writing telegrams to
Lhasa to arrange all the details that suddenly had to be settled. Tsarong
Lhacham was soon able to get permission from the Kashag to host him
and sent an invitation requesting that Theos stay at Tsarong House with
her and her husband, one of the most influential and wealthiest men in
Tibet.

Theos was by now nearly out of 35 mm film for the Leica, and his
desperate wires to the Kodak offices in Calcutta and Bombay brought only
promises they would be getting more and would ship some in a couple of
weeks. But as for color movie film, there was only one more reel available in
all of India.

Mary and Jigme stopped in one morning to say good-bye. They were
moving to their estate near Shigatse for a few weeks but would be going to
India in July to pick up a consignment of arms for the Tibetan government, and over tea they made plans for a reunion in either Kalimpong or
Calcutta. They told him this was the most beautiful time of year for a
journey to Lhasa and gave him a list of sights he had to see along the way.

It didn't take Theos long to pack his boxes for the trip, but bureaucratic red tape delayed his departure. Even with the telegrams from the
regent and the Kashag, the district *jongpens* between Gyantse and Lhasa
needed to sign the *lamyik*, which was the actual passport for travel through
their territory. Official messages confirming permission had to be written
by scribes and sent through the proper channels and reviewed in each district. Without the *lamyik* to present to each village headman along the way,
there was no travel allowed through Tibet.

It was not an easy trail between Gyantse and Lhasa. Theos and Lhare
would have to average thirty-two miles a day and cross two high passes,

and Theos saw the delay in getting out of Gyantse as days nicked off the six-week extension he had just received from Richardson.

"Restless and impatient as I am by nature," he wrote, "matters always move too slowly for me, and there is a decided disadvantage in the Tibetan slowness when not able to cuss in the language which I must henceforth use. If I had to live this adventure over again, I should certainly learn this aspect of things before I undertook to study the legitimate literature of the country."

Chapter 6

GATES OF THE FORBIDDEN CITY

AT LAST, the final paperwork arrived with its official red seal, and on the morning of June 18, Theos rose at three-thirty to get the transport loaded. By seven the mules and their singing owners were on the trail to Lhasa, and Theos paused before setting off after them for an oatmeal breakfast and a last stop at the Gyantse telegraph office. He and Lhare then rode out through fields of green wheat and up narrowing gulches until they were forced to admit—after much discussion—they had missed a turn on the main trail to Lhasa. They backtracked until they found the telegraph line, and realized with a laugh at themselves that they could follow the poles all the way to Lhasa.

All morning, as Lhare—who spoke not a word of English—prattled on in Tibetan, Theos considered the historical importance of the *lamyik* he carried in his pocket. Beyond Gyantse, for the first time ever in his life, he felt that he had entered a world untouched by Europeans. "Indeed, even the character of the people seems to be different," he wrote. "They do not show that sense of inferiority, of submission, which the English knock into every race with which they come into contact."

Apart from the 144-mile extension of the telegraph line from Gyantse to Lhasa (installed by British engineers at the request of the 13th Dalai

Lama in 1923), little had changed in the sparse, dusty villages Theos passed through since the first Europeans got acquainted with Lhasa two hundred years earlier. But what had changed—diametrically, in fact—was what Westerners imagined Tibet to be. The Tibet Theos rode to was no longer a stubborn backwater of heathens needing salvation, as it had been for the first missionaries. It was even outgrowing the persistent image, spread by Victorian Buddhologists, that Tibet was a sort of spiritual Galapagos where a decadent branch of Buddhism introduced from India had mated with native shamanism, producing a unique species called Lamaism, which flourished in its isolation. By the 1930s a new conception of Tibet as the last surviving repository of the highest practices of Indian Buddhism was evolving in the West, and it was this image of Tibet that was drawing Theos to its iconic heart in Lhasa.

This shift in the West's conception of Tibet is illustrated by the history of foreigners' presence in Lhasa and their reasons for going there. The first Europeans to live in Lhasa were Capuchin and Jesuit missionaries, who, for most of the period between 1708 and 1745, freely evangelized among what they considered the godless and devil-ridden Tibetans. The friars even built a church in Lhasa, and the Italian Jesuit Ippolito Desideri lived and studied earnestly for a time at Sera monastery near Lhasa, where he translated Je Tsongkapa's massive *Lam Rim Chenmo*. He concluded from his studies that the source of all the Tibetan's false dogmas "is the absolute denial of the existence of any God." In Buddhist doctrine, he inveighed, there was no supreme judge; good and bad actions were believed to have a power of their own to reward and punish. The abbots at Lhasa's three enormous, city-like monasteries eventually grew tired of the missionaries' theological harangues and drove them out of Lhasa in 1745. They were enjoined to cease preaching in Tibet, leaving one Capuchin to lament after his departure that during all his years in Lhasa he had won only thirteen souls for Christ.

In 1792, the army of the Gurkha kingdom that had overrun Nepal crossed the Himalayas and invaded the frontiers of Tibet. The Tibetan army required Chinese reinforcements to repel them, and then—believing that the British had abetted the Gurkha invasion—the Tibetan government adopted the xenophobia of the Chinese emperor and closed the Himalayan border. Blockhouses were built at the passes to guard them, and the government announced a policy that Tibet was closed to all foreigners except the Chinese.

With the gates now barred to Europeans, the era of the trespassing adventurer began. Although many made the attempt, during the entire nineteenth century only three actually made it to Lhasa. The first was the Englishman Thomas Manning, an eccentric Cambridge scholar with an obsessive interest in Chinese culture and language who slipped across the border disguised as a Bengali pilgrim in 1811. At Phari, he impressed a Chinese general with his long, tapered beard and gift of two bottles of cherry brandy, and the general convinced the *amban*—the imperial Chinese resident installed in Lhasa—to permit Manning to continue to the capital. The high point of his four-month stay in Lhasa was an audience with the seven-year-old 9th Dalai Lama, whom Manning described as possessing the "simple unaffected manners of a well-educated, princely child."

Manning and his servant were under constant surveillance by the suspicious Chinese during their stay in Lhasa, and when a bright comet appeared over Lhasa, it was interpreted as a harbinger of evil linked to Manning's arrival. He began to hear rumors that he might be examined by torture, but no matter how fearful the timorous scholar grew, he would not compromise with the heathens in matters of religion, and he refused to spin Tibetan prayer wheels or show any sign of obeisance in their temples. He was allowed to leave without harm, however, and he eagerly returned to Calcutta by June of 1812.

The only other Europeans to reach Lhasa during the entire century were two French Lazarist priests who walked through the gates of Lhasa one day in January 1846. During the two months they were allowed to stay, they enjoyed frequent doctrinal debates with the regent, and although they were unable to convert him, the only obstacles they saw were their differences on the origin of the world and reincarnation. The *amban*, whose role had increased in Lhasa after 1792, was suspicious of the priests, and over the protest of the regent he expelled them. "If they remain long at Lhasa, they will spellbind you," the *amban* lectured. "You will not be able to keep from adopting their belief and then the [Dalai] Lama is undone."

There were a half dozen more attempts to reach Lhasa by Europeans in disguise during the late 1800s, but, beset by bandits, fierce storms, and intercepting troops, they were all turned back, some within days of reaching their goal.

The Tibetan government enforced its proscription of foreigners with a harsh policy of prosecuting any Tibetan who aided an interloping *philing*. In the 1880s the government decided to make an emphatic example of a high-ranking noble family that, perhaps unwittingly, helped the Indian spy Sarat Chandra Das get to Lhasa during his covert mapping mission for the British. After Das returned to India, accounts of his clandestine mission were published, and the Tibetan government concluded it must exact a terrible vengeance against those implicated in helping him. The estates of the Palha family, whom Das had stayed with while in Tibet, were confiscated, and then the noble and his wife were imprisoned for interrogation before having their arms and legs chopped off and being dragged to their deaths through the town streets. Even a venerated incarnate lama whom Das had studied with for three months was not spared. With bound hands and legs, he was thrown into the river to drown.

After that, it is no surprise that the first Europeans to reach Lhasa since the Lazarist priests in 1846, even though sent on a diplomatic mission, had to shoot their way in with a large military force. In the early 1900s the British saw signs they interpreted as plans of czarist Russia to expand its sphere of influence into Tibet, and Lord Curzon, viceroy of India, sent letters to the 13th Dalai Lama proposing that their countries should open the border to trade. When his letters were returned unopened, Curzon got permission from London to send Colonel Francis Younghusband into Tibet to insist on a trade treaty. A military escort to ensure the diplomat's safety grew into a large expedition of some two thousand fighting men and included a Royal Artillery battery with a pair of ten-pounder Maxim screw guns. Impatient to start, the expedition set out to cross the Himalayas in January supported by 4,500 yaks, 5,000 bullocks, 7,000 mules, 1,300 pack ponies, 6 camels, and some 10,000 porters, all of which stretched out more than four miles along the trail. But most important in that contingent to the Western imagination of Tibet were five London newspaper correspondents who unveiled the forbidden land with on-the-spot reports wired to their Fleet Street editors on a telegraph line that rolled out behind each day's march.

The Tibetans refused to send anyone to negotiate a treaty, and any delegates who did meet with Younghusband told him only that he must turn back. "The lamas believe that . . . their religion will decay before foreign influence," explained Edmund Candler to his readers in the *Daily Mail*. "The Dalai Lama, they say, will die, not by violence or sickness, but by some spiritual visitation. His spirit will seek some other incarnation, when he can no longer . . . secure his country . . . from the contamination of foreign intrusion."

After months of delay in freezing camps, the force received permission from London to advance as far as Gyantse. Near the village of Guru, they found the road blocked by several thousand Tibetans behind a long rock wall armed only with swords, matchlock rifles, and bits of paper bearing the Dalai Lama's personal seal, which they believed would make them bulletproof. Both sides held their fire until they were literally an arm's length apart, and then when the Indian sepoys in the Younghusband force were ordered to dismantle the wall, the Tibetan general in command shot the sepoy holding his horse's bridle, and Tibetans poured over the wall flailing with their swords. The Maxim guns opened up on the Tibetans still massed behind the wall, and after four minutes of withering fire, 628 of them lay dead and another 222 were wounded. The British suffered twelve wounded, none mortally.

For both sides, the carnage seemed to violate Tibet's mystical essence. Reporter Edmund Candler, who had just had a hand hacked off by a Tibetan sword, described the evident agony of the Tibetan forces remaining after the initial slaughter. They didn't cower or run for cover—even though still being fired upon—but rather slumped off the battlefield in "the most extraordinary procession I have ever seen . . . They were bewildered. . . . Prayers and charms and mantras, and the holiest of their holy men had failed them. . . . They walked with bowed heads, as if they had been disillusioned with their gods."

In Gyantse, the Tibetans still did not send anyone to negotiate a treaty, and Younghusband pushed on to Lhasa, planning to parley directly with the Dalai Lama. On the eve of walking the streets that only a handful of

Europeans had ever seen, Candler expressed the ambivalence that his readers in London undoubtedly shared. "Tomorrow when we enter Lhasa, we will have unveiled the last mystery of the East. There are no more forbidden cities which men have not mapped and photographed." For Victorians, filling in the last blank spots on the map meant the imagination had nowhere left to roam, for now, as Candler wrote, "there are no real mysteries, no unknown land of dreams, where there may still be genii and mahatmas and bottle-imps, that kind of literature will be tolerated no longer."

The 13th Dalai Lama had fled Lhasa for Mongolia days before the arrival of the British and left the government in the hands of the designated regent, the elderly Ganden Tripa. It took seven weeks in Lhasa for Younghusband to conclude the Anglo-Tibetan Convention, long enough for the mysterious to become commonplace, tawdry, and disgusting in the correspondents' reports. As Candler again reported, "If one approached within a league of Lhasa, saw the glittering domes of the Potala, and turned back without entering the precincts, one might still imagine it an enchanted city, shining with turquoise and gold. But having entered the illusion is lost ... We found the city squalid and filthy beyond description, undrained and unpaved. Not a single house looked clean or cared for. The streets after rain are nothing but pools of stagnant water frequented by pigs and dogs searching for refuse."

The Victorian disappointment in having Lhasa laid open for them was felt not only for the squalid city but also for the spiritual practices at its soul. Even Younghusband, who would have life-changing mystical experiences before he returned from Lhasa, wondered where was the "inner power for which Tibetan Buddhism was famous, especially here, in Lhasa, its holiest place?" The Ganden Tripa, one of the greatest of Tibetan scholars, was for Younghusband similarly disappointing: "His spiritual attainments, I gathered from a long conversation I had with him after the Treaty was signed, consisted mainly of a knowledge by rote of vast quantities of his holy books. The capacity of these Tibetan monks for learning their sacred books by rote is, indeed, something prodigious; though about the actual meaning they trouble themselves but little."

L. Austine Waddell, who accompanied the expedition as surgeon and its putative expert on Lamaism, was perhaps less disenchanted because what he found in Tibet was exactly what he expected to find. The son of a Presbyterian minister, his 1895 book *Tibetan Buddhism: With Its Mystic Cults, Symbolism and Mythology* propounded the accepted Victorian theory that since the death of the Buddha, the faith had steadily deteriorated from its original rational and agnostic philosophy to become a degenerate religion rife with ritual and superstition. The introduction of this corrupted form of Indian Buddhism to Tibet, a land of "rapacious savages and reputed cannibals, without a written language," produced, as Waddell wrote, "much deep-rooted devil-worship. . . . For Lamaism is only thinly and imperfectly varnished over with Buddhist symbolism, beneath which the sinister growth of poly-demonish superstition darkly appears."

Waddell concluded his 1905 book, *Lhasa and Its Mysteries*, saying: "The earthly paradise of 'The Living Buddha' is no longer the centre of fabulous conjecture. Its ring fence of mysticism has been penetrated, and the full glare of Reality has dispelled the mirage of spurious marvels that gathered over this Far Eastern Mecca during its long centuries of seclusion. . . . If in the new facilities for communication with the outside world the light of civilization should dissipate the dense mists of ignorance and unhealthy superstitions that cruelly harass the people, it would indeed be a blessing to The Hermit Land."

The view of the Victorian Buddhologists reigned unchallenged until the groundbreaking publication in 1927 of *The Tibetan Book of the Dead*, a Tantric text edited by W. Y. Evans-Wentz. Evans-Wentz, an American who studied with William James and William Butler Yeats at Stanford before going to study Celtic folklore at Oxford, was the editor of *The Tibetan Book of the Dead*, but the actual translator of the text that was its basis was Kazi Dawa-Samdup, a teacher at the maharaja's Boys' School in Gangtok. In 1919 Evans-Wentz acquired a Tibetan text, *The Profound Doctrine Self Liberation of the Mind [Through Encountering] the Peaceful and Wrathful Deities*, from a British army officer who had just returned from Tibet, and he asked Dawa-Samdup to translate it for him. Evans-Wentz edited the translation and gave it the title *The Tibetan Book of the Dead* to draw a comparison to the well-known *Egyptian Book of the Dead*.

The concept of reincarnation was well known to Western occultists, spiritualists, and Theosophists, but in the 1920s the subject began to draw scientific interest. *The Tibetan Book of the Dead*, published by Oxford University Press, attracted a wide and influential following ranging from Anaïs Nin to Carl Jung. Jung, the founder of analytical psychology, wrote in 1935 that since its publication, *The Tibetan Book of the Dead* had been his constant companion, and to it he owed "not only many stimulating ideas and discoveries, but also many fundamental insights." Jung was impressed with the incisive wisdom of the book's psychology and the way it instructed the dead, as well as the living, to recognize all appearances, whether beautiful or terrifying, as the projections of consciousness, and he compared its insights on prenatal experiences to what he saw as the more limited views of his colleague Sigmund Freud.

Almost overnight, Tibet, a land many believed to be filled with degenerate demon worshipers, became in the Western imagination the land of ultimate wisdom. Most amazing in this transformation was the fact that it was wrought by the first Tantric Buddhist text to be presented without apologies to the West—a *terma*, or time-capsule treasure, buried by Padmasambhava in the eighth century with the intention it would be discovered when its spiritual message would have the most beneficial impact. A fifteen-year-old Tibetan, Karma Lingpa, is said to have discovered the original *terma* on a mountaintop in southeast Tibet in the fourteenth century, but for the rest of the world, it remained concealed until 1927, when it was published as *The Tibetan Book of the Dead*. Tibetan Buddhism, the argument now went, was not a degeneration of the Buddhist path but its culmination. As Evans-Wentz wrote, Tibetan Buddhism was not "in disagreement with canonical, or exoteric, Buddhism, but related to it as higher mathematics to lower mathematics, . . . the apex of the pyramid of the whole of Buddhism."

After Younghusband withdrew his military force from Lhasa in 1904, the British took charge of ensuring that, from the southern frontier at least, Tibet would remain a forbidden land. The mirage of marvels, which Waddell said cloaked Lhasa only because of its seclusion, again asserted its allure, but now—with the growing psychological and philosophical sophistication in the West's conceptions of Tibet—those determined to peek behind the cloak thought they would find there something profound.

The British granted a few permits to travelers to go as far as Gyantse, the newly established trade mart, but aside from two British diplomatic missions (Charles Bell's yearlong consultation on modernizing the Tibetan army in 1920 and Basil Gould's attempt to reconcile Lhasa and the Panchen Lama in 1936), only one party of foreigners received permission to travel all the way to Lhasa. In 1935, the American gentleman explorer Suydam Cutting (who the Tibetans believed had opened the American market to Tibetan wool) and his English companion, Arthur Vernay, were invited to Lhasa for a ten-day visit. Aside from Cutting and Vernay's social call and the two British diplomatic missions, only two other Westerners had made it to Lhasa since 1904. Both, however, were unable to get permits to travel in Tibet and stole across the border disguised as peasant travelers. And both, as a consequence, suffered horrible privations along the way.

The first of those trespassers, the Oxford Orientalist William Montgomery McGovern, crossed the Tibetan border from India in the winter of 1923 disguised as the servant of a Sikkimese teacher. McGovern's disguise included attempts to tint his blue eyes with lemon juice and to darken his skin with walnut juice and iodine. It also required that he carry a load and sleep in cowsheds. During the six weeks of his adventure, Montgomery became infested with lice, subsisted on a scant ration of dried meat, and nearly froze to death wading through chest-deep snowdrifts. When, with his heroic endurance, he finally did get to Lhasa, dysentery and pneumonia forced him to drop the disguise and present himself to the authorities. When the rumor circulated that a foreigner was in Lhasa, a mob began stoning the house where he was staying, and troops stood by to protect him if the angry citizens broke through the door. He was allowed to remain in the holy city under virtual house arrest for a month while he recovered, and after an audience with the 13th Dalai Lama, he was deported with an armed escort guaranteeing he crossed the border into India. His story was serialized in the *Daily Telegraph* on his return to

London, and his book, *To Lhasa in Disguise*, came out the next year, but added little, aside from the tale of his suffering, to the corpus of 1904 accounts.

The French mystic explorer Alexandra David-Neel arrived in Lhasa a year later after a circuitous eight-thousand-mile, six-year odyssey from Peking. Disguised as lowly pilgrims, she and her adopted Sikkimese son, Lama Yongden, carried little, often slept outside, and ate what scraps the poor villagers along the way offered as alms. They were menaced by bandits and tigers, but in February 1924 they arrived in Lhasa for the start of Monlam Chenmo, the great annual three-week prayer festival. They were able to stay undetected for two months among the throng of a hundred thousand Tibetan pilgrims, but were forced to leave suddenly when they were called to appear before a magistrate as witnesses to a domestic dispute.

In May, when Alexandra David-Neel and Yongden—weakened by influenza, wasted to skin and bones, and now very willing to be deported—finally left Tibet through the Indian border, they presented themselves in Gyantse to the British trade agent, David Macdonald, and asked for help. Macdonald, who had been to Lhasa already twice himself, saluted her achievement but qualified it by telling her: "Madam, you have undergone incredible hardships. Your courage and vitality have succeeded where others failed. Unfortunately, by reason of the disguise you adopted, you saw Tibet only from the viewpoint of a poor pilgrim."

Theos Bernard, riding his first day out of Gyantse with a *lamyik* in his pocket and an invitation to stay at the home of one of Lhasa's wealthiest nobles, would not suffer that limitation on his spiritual research. The project for preserving Tantra that Theos had outlined for himself in his master's thesis at Columbia required him first to "gather together those manuscripts which are left so that the future may have them," and then to "devote several years . . . to the practice of its method . . . to gain by experience an estimate of the truth of the teachings." And now Lhasa, he hoped, was being opened to him, not just to map and photograph and demystify, as the Fleet Street reporters had done, but to plumb the spiritual potential of the Tantras.

Tibetans seemed to recognize Theos' high intentions. The regent had termed him in his telegram "Your Much Religionship," and the Kashag had stated plainly in its telegram: "Understanding that you have a great respect for our religion and have hopes of spreading the religion in America on your return we have decided as a special case to allow you to come to Lhasa." That recognition guaranteed that Theos Bernard would receive a much different welcome in Lhasa than any other Westerner ever had.

THEOS AND LHARE COVERED seventeen miles out of Gyantse before they stopped for lunch at a flat-roofed stone house. After climbing the ladder from the stable to the second floor, Theos was welcomed to the place of honor by a grinning man who spat on the table, then wiped it with his grimy sleeve. They covered the remaining fifteen miles to their destination for the night by four-thirty, and were welcomed by the village headman bearing a *kata* and a small tray of eggs. Theos had already eaten his dinner of yak meat and potatoes before the transport arrived at nine with his bedding, and he unrolled it on a bench so filthy that he wished he had brought his own tent.

There was no charge for sleeping quarters or basic meals, but at departure the next morning, Theos followed the custom of a reciprocal offering in the form of cash to, as he wrote, "express your deep appreciation in accordance with the position they have assigned to you."

They were off by five, and as the trail climbed along the snout of the glacier falling off the south flank of 23,600-foot Nojin Gangsang Ri, the shaded valley they climbed through was filled with a luminous twilight from the sunrise reflection off the blue ice. Shortly after reaching the pass at the head of the valley, the 16,400-foot Karo La, Theos spotted a party coming up the trail and recognized Norphel's hat. Tharchin had sent him back to lead the way to Lhasa, and when they met, Norphel erupted with a jubilant account of all that had happened in the holy city.

At the end of the second day, they reached Nagartse on the shore of the brilliant turquoise water of Yamdrok Tso, Tibet's largest freshwater lake, and even though they had started the day at four, Theos felt "as fresh as a kitten, filled with love to the brim and too wide awake to sleep." He planted himself on a mat near the open fire of the hovel they stayed in, and when he was finally ready for sleep, he simply rolled over on his side and closed his eyes, oblivious to the frigid draft from the open door and the dense smoke that refused to rise to the hole made for it in the roof. As he wrote in his journal, "My falling in with Tibetan ways did more than astonish the native, it convinced him that I was one of them."

The next day they rode along the broad bays of the scorpion-shaped Yamdrok Tso and left it at its northern end as the trail climbed to Kamba La and a view across the broad valley of the Tsangpo, the upper end of one of Asia's greatest rivers. Flowing east through Tibet for a thousand miles before abruptly bending south, the Tsangpo breaches the Himalayas through the world's deepest canyon. In India, where it is renamed Brahmaputra, the river flows six miles wide in some places before joining with the Ganges to form vast deltas on the Bay of Bengal. From the tall cairn and streaming prayer flags at Kamba La, the trail dropped precipitously four thousand feet to the Tsangpo Valley bottom, where grew the first trees Theos had seen since leaving Gyantse.

Lhasa was still a day and a half away up the Kyichu Valley on the other side of the Tsangpo, and Tibetan ferrymen waited at the well-used crossing. Each ferryman had an oval-shaped craft made of a willow lattice covered with yak skin well coated with pitch. Called kowas, the boats were light enough in weight to be carried back upstream by one man after crossing but were capable of floating large payloads. Crossing the river with Theos and his party were also the boatman, four Tibetan muleteers, a goat, a dog, and a large load of lumber. They left the ferry station on the south bank and floated diagonally across the swift current to the river's north bank at the confluence with the Kyichu.

Having made thirty miles already by midday, they had a cup of Tibetan tea, arranged fresh transport animals, and set off up the long valley leading to Lhasa, now only fifty miles away. The trail the entire way was bordered on both sides by large willow trees and fields of blooming yellow mustard divided by walls of stacked stone. The headdresses and earrings of the men were distinctly different now, and Theos could even detect a difference in the dialect. Everyone they met, Theos noted, was "wrapped in a mood of the pilgrim on his eternal quest." Advancing the beads of their rosaries as they murmured *Om mani padme hum*, "they seemed hardly aware of us as we passed them."

Theos and his party covered nearly sixty miles that day, only to arrive at the filthiest hovel of the journey. They had already eaten the little that remained in the saddlebags at lunch, and the old woman at the house where they stayed had nothing to offer but some Tibetan butter tea and a few old eggs. Theos had been eating so lightly during the three days since leaving Gyantse that for the first time he was feeling fatigued, and he realized that the reserves that had fueled him were now exhausted.

The long day had left one of their ponies with a limp, and the next morning, with no other ponies available, Norphel volunteered to walk the next stage. The valley bottom was filled with cultivated fields, and all along the way women were out directing water through the irrigation ditches or banking up a broken spot where the water flooded out. They soon reached the main Lhasa Valley, and they galloped around the last bend to a high pile of stones that marked the first view of the blessed Potala, faintly visible through the scrim of a rising morning mist. Theos added a stone to the tall cairn marking the spot just as the sun rose above the high ridges hemming in the valley and the golden pagoda roofs of the massive Potala burst forth in all their glory like a "mirror of the gods."

They were only eight miles away from the city gates now, and the trail was bordered with four-foot-high *mani* walls, built of stacks of slate on which the mantra *Om mani padme hum* had been laboriously carved. They soon reached Tibet's first steel bridge, the parts of which had been fabricated in India and hauled over the passes to be bolted together piece by piece. Still under construction, the bridge was another modernizing project promoted and managed by one of the wealthiest men in Tibet, Dasang Damdul Tsarong, Theos' host in Lhasa.

At last they crossed a final rock ridge and entered a broad thoroughfare crowded with yaks, donkeys, and horses heading to Lhasa. It was not far to the spot along the road designated as the official reception area for arriving guests, and there waiting for them was a plump official with an ever-smiling face and a long braid of black hair that fell below the yellow hat that signified his high rank. Immediately after the official's cordial welcome, Theos spotted Tharchin, only a moment late, racing through a cloud of dust. Theos mounted a fresh, prancing Chinese thoroughbred sent by Tsarong, and Tharchin insisted on recording the historic moment with the movie camera.

As they rode together, Tharchin recounted every carefully planned move that had led to the invitation. He mentioned that Richardson, the chief of the British mission in Lhasa, had offered to put Theos up in a tent at the British compound, but since Tsarong had received permission from the Kashag to host him, Theos preferred not to lodge with Europeans outside the city gates, and they rode on.

They came at last to the huge Pargo Kaling *chorten*, the thousand-year-old, bell-shaped monument that contained holy relics of the Buddha Mindukpa and served as Lhasa's western gate. Theos rode through the portal built into the massive structure and presented his *lamyik* to the policemen stationed there. The government official who was sent to escort him added a few words, and the guards stood aside. Theos kicked his horse into a trot but a few paces inside the gate abruptly reined him to a stop, for there, seeming to penetrate the clouds themselves, loomed the Potala. Set atop the solitary prominence of Red Hill, Marpo Ri, the majestic sweep and massive flowing rhythm of the palace complex left Theos breathless. This was a view that could only be seen from within the fabled forbidden city. So many Westerners for so many varied reasons had dreamed of standing here, but Theos Bernard was the first in all of history to arrive at the invitation of the Tibetan government as a spiritual pilgrim from the New World. As Theos described the moment, "I had to pause for a few moments, to take it in, to feel it, to let it sink into my soul."

Chapter 7

THE PILGRIM'S WELCOME

MOST HIGH-RANKING NOBLES lived in two- or three-story mansions in the middle of Lhasa. Tsarong, however, decided in 1923 to build his new house on the eastern outskirts of town near the Kyichu River. Tsarong drew the plans for the two-story rectangular house himself, and his design created a sensation among the nobility for its incorporation of nontraditional elements discovered on his travels through India, China, Russia, and Outer Mongolia. Among those foreign elements were the city's first glass windows, which replaced the traditional shutters and admitted, even during the cold months, the site's beautiful views of the near peaks and the gleaming golden roofs of the distant Potala.

Theos and Tharchin dismounted at the mansion's gate and walked through a large courtyard to a garden of blooming flowers at the main entrance of the house. There, waiting on the steps to greet them, was their friend Tsarong Lhacham and her fifty-seven-year-old husband, Dasang Damdul Tsarong, whom Theos described as being "as jolly as though he had been my life long friend; just a little chubby ball of enthusiastic fire with his face split from ear to ear with hospitality." Tharchin had two silk *katas* ready for Theos to present and translated their cordial and respectful welcome, for neither of the Tsarongs could speak a word of English, and the colloquial Tibetan that Theos had become practiced at with servants and muleteers demanded a whole new honorific vocabulary for addressing anyone of their rank.

Theos was shown to his home for the summer, the expansive eastern suite on the ground floor. Along with a bedroom, the suite included a spacious living room, a storeroom for Theos' boxes, an office, and a bathroom that featured a modern toilet and portable bathtub. There were carved beams and columns throughout the suite—all painted in brilliant red, green, yellow, and blue—and beautiful carpets and cushions covered the floor. The suite even had its own shrine room, which the lama of the house maintained daily by changing the water in the offering bowls and by filling with melted butter the silver lamp that burned perpetually on the altar.

Lunch awaited them all upstairs and along the way their hosts led Theos and Tharchin on a quick tour of the upper floor's banquet hall and the library, where they paused to browse the titles of a large selection of foreign books. They arrived at the dining room and settled on cushions around a low table crowded with lunch's multiple courses, and Tharchin translated the introductory volleys of questions and answers while they nibbled leisurely with chopsticks from the communal plates. Tsarong, who accompanied his lunch with a whiskey and soda, had been a leading spokesman in the 1920s for a faction in the Tibetan government that advocated the adoption of some modest modernizing reforms. The modernizers received encouragement from the 13th Dalai Lama, and an emboldened Tsarong proposed that Tibet should join the International Postal Union, produce a typewriter with Tibetan characters, and develop a road system for motorcars. A conservative backlash ended the first tentative steps taken in that direction, however, and over lunch they discussed the question of whether modernization would be beneficial for Tibet. Tsarong now believed, he told Theos, that Tibetans were on the whole a happy people, and change would mainly bring problems. The Tsarongs insisted that Theos have all his meals with them and suggested that, to speed up his progress in learning the honorific vocabulary, Tharchin should have his meals in the kitchen.

They had only finished lunch, but it was already nearing the time for afternoon tea, and Theos had promised Hugh Richardson he would pay a call to present himself at the British mission as soon as he arrived in Lhasa. Theos also had a few telegrams he wanted to send on his way out to the British compound, but while preparing to leave, he got a message on the true local telegraph, the network of always-gossiping household servants. The Tsarong staff had current information that the telegraph operator was out of the office and that Richardson was away that afternoon as well, and they insisted it was pointless for Theos to set off on his errands. Theos was skeptical and decided he would take his chances, but discovered that in both cases the servants were right. Gossip traveled as efficiently at the other end, however, and as soon as the telegrapher heard that Theos was on his way, he returned to the office, as did Richardson, who was happy to have an excuse to leave an all-day Tibetan party he was attending.

Richardson was just dismounting at the stable of the British compound when Theos rode up, and they introduced themselves with a hearty handshake. Richardson was only three years older than Theos and, as Theos put it, "in the typical Oxford manner, was droll and overflowing with brilliance, not knowing much about anything, but one should never be able to detect this because of all they do know."

They went inside, and Richardson introduced Theos to Reginald Fox, the British wireless operator who had been dispatched to Lhasa the year before to balance the capacity of the Chinese wireless set installed in Lhasa three years earlier. Fox, like Richardson, was a photography buff, and when they heard that Theos had been invited to study Buddhism in Lhasa and that he was also a photographer, they brought out their Tibet photo albums and made use of each picture to illustrate a discourse that, as Theos put it, was meant to correct any errors he might hold on the subject of Lamaism. They invited him to continue listening through dinner, and when he finally left, Theos rode home at a full gallop under the moonlit Potala and entered the Tsarong courtyard to find, to his great surprise, that the house was illuminated with a dim yellow wash of electric lights.

THEOS WAS UP EARLY the next morning and typed six single-spaced pages in his journal before joining the Tsarongs upstairs for a breakfast that included a variety of fine cuts of yak meat, eggs, toast, Tibetan tea, and jam, all concluded with a cup of fine English tea. Theos had been hearing bits of the Tsarong story ever since meeting Tsarong Lacham in Kalimpong, and he was eager now to hear from him how the son of a bow and arrow maker had been able to enter Tibet's system of hereditary nobility and become one of the country's richest and most powerful men.

Dasang Damdul Tsarong, as he was now known, had acquired the name Tsarong (the name of one of the oldest and highest-ranking families in Tibet) only in 1913 when he was given the family and its wealth as a reward for service to the 13th Dalai Lama. He had been born with the name Chensal Namgang on a small peasant farm plot north of Lhasa, and at age twelve he was taken to Lhasa as a student of the monk who managed Norbulingka, the Dalai Lama's summer palace. One day the 13th Dalai Lama noticed an uncommon air of confidence and intelligence in the boy and decided to bring him on to his personal staff. Chensal Namgang served well in the palace, and when the troops of the Younghusband expedition invaded Lhasa in 1904, he was one of about a hundred officials and staff who fled to Mongolia with the Dalai Lama.

The Chinese reacted to the Dalai Lama's flight by officially deposing him, and after two years in Mongolia, the Dalai Lama and his entourage began a slow, circuitous return to Lhasa while they negotiated with the Chinese over his status. The Tibetans eventually ended up in Peking where they spent several humiliating months attempting to convince the dowager empress, Cixi, and her tottering Qing court that his rule should be reinstated. The Chinese responded by disdainfully appending "Our Loyal and Submissive Vice-Regent" to the Dalai Lama's official title, and Western diplomats at the capital assumed they had witnessed the end of the Dalai Lama's temporal power in Tibet.

In late December 1909, after more than five years of exile, the Dalai Lama—and Chensal Namgang—returned to Lhasa. The Qing government had decided, in the meantime, to reinforce the authority of their *amban* in Lhasa with two thousand troops, and an advance force arrived in Lhasa on February 12, 1910. The Dalai Lama concluded that the troops had been sent to enforce his government's subservience, and after being back in Lhasa for only six weeks he chose to flee Tibet again, this time racing toward the Indian border with two hundred Chinese cavalrymen in close pursuit.

Chensal Namgang, with sixty-seven men and only thirty-four rifles, decided to make a stand on the broad Tsangpo River at Chaksam ferry. They took all the *kowas* across to the far bank, and as the Chinese waded and swam across, the Tibetans opened fire, killing 170 of them. Having given the Dalai Lama the time he needed to escape, and having run out of ammunition, Chensal Namgang dispersed his troops and in various disguises was able to elude the Chinese garrisons on the way to the border and make it across the Himalayas to join the Dalai Lama in Darjeeling, where he was received as a hero.

While the Chinese troops occupied Tibet, the Dalai Lama stayed in Darjeeling and contemplated the circumstances that had forced him to spend all but six weeks of the previous six years out of his own country. He developed a close friendship with Sir Charles Bell, the government of India's political officer in Sikkim, and learned a great deal about modern politics. During the three years of his exile in India, the 13th Dalai Lama saw firsthand how an efficient and dedicated bureaucracy and army could rule a vast country, and he conceived a new vision of Tibet. To implement his vision, however, Tibet would need a new breed of civil servant, and, seeing Chensal Namgang as his prototype, the Dalai Lama arranged for him to train with the British army.

It was during this time that the rebellion in China against the Qing government spread across the country, and exactly two years after the Dalai Lama fled Lhasa, the six-year-old emperor, Puyi, abdicated, putting an end to more than two thousand years of imperial rule. The revolution had begun, and Chinese troops throughout the empire—including those occupying Lhasa—mutinied and killed their commanders. The Dalai Lama recognized the opportunity the chaos presented and appointed Chensal Namgang as commander in chief of the Tibetan army. He was dispatched immediately to Lhasa to root out the marauding Chinese forces, and by April 1912 Chensal Namgang had accepted the surrender of three thousand Chinese troops and permitted them to leave Tibet through India.

Once the Chinese were evicted, the Tibetans settled scores among themselves with a wave of bloody reprisals. Shape Tsarong Wangchuk Gyalpo had served as a trusted minister of the four-person Kashag since 1903 but was now suspected of collaborating with the Chinese because (due to the success of his diplomacy, his children would later write) the minister did not receive the same harsh treatment as some of the other nobles. While attending a high-level meeting at the Potala after the Chinese eviction, Shape Tsarong was arrested and dragged down the long stone stairways and beheaded. His son Sampdup Tsering was also arrested and brought to see his father's head before being executed on the same spot at the foot of the Potala.

On his return to Lhasa in January 1913, the Dalai Lama rewarded those who had served him during his absence with titles and estates. Chensal Namgang was given the title of Dzasa (a government official ranked directly under that of cabinet minister) to accompany his title of Chida (commander general). The Dalai Lama saw as well that the executions of Shape Tsarong and his son had left the Tsarong family with no males to serve as officials in the government, and under the thousand-year-old rules governing land distribution, the family's long-held estates were in danger of confiscation. To prevent that, the Dalai Lama eagerly approved the suggestion that Chensal Namgang marry the widow of the murdered son and take the name Dasang Damdul Tsarong.

After the wedding, however, some of the family began to worry that the new wife, Rigzin Chodon, had only become a Tsarong by marriage, and so they requested that the newly created Dasang Damdul Tsarong take the family's eldest daughter, Pema Dolkar, as his second wife to preserve the blood lineage. The two wives lived happily together in the same house, but after several years the first wife decided to become a nun, which left Pema Dolkar, the woman who now hosted Theos in her Lhasa mansion, as Tsarong Lhacham, the senior wife.

A servant interrupted Tsarong's account of his life to announce that a representative of the Kashag had just arrived with the customary welcoming load of gifts. They went down to see stacked in the middle of the reception hall fifteen dozen eggs, eighty pounds of yak butter, a large tray of vegetables, and six large sacks of *tsampa*, the Tibetan staple of roasted barley flour. The envoy was over six feet tall, had a shaved head, and wore the red robes of a monk. He had a handsome, intelligent face, and his eyes sparkled as he presented Theos with a *kata* and delivered a heartfelt oration in Tibetan. As Theos looked in Tharchin's direction for help translating, the monk switched to perfect English "without the hint of an accent, and with a diction that would have pleased the most exacting headmaster," as Theos described it. Khenrab Kunsang Mondo was one of the four "Rugby boys" sent to England by the 13th Dalai Lama in 1913 to study at the famous Rugby boarding school. Mondo stayed in England for another two years of training in mining and mineralogy, and on his return to Tibet he entered a monastery and became a government official. Mondo joined them upstairs and regaled them with tales of his years in England while they enjoyed a proper tea poured from a silver service along with cookies and cake baked by the household chef, whom the Tsarongs had sent to India for four years of training in haute cuisine.

Tsarong had to leave to spend a few days out of town at his bridge project, and so the party broke up to allow him to get under way before dark. The Lhacham then showed Theos their private shrine, a thirty-foot-square room in the center of the upper floor with three life-size, gilded copper images of Tibet's legendary dharma kings. The shrine had been under construction for years and only a few details remained before it would be finished and ready to be consecrated. Dinner soon followed, and Tsarong Lhacham and Theos talked until a midnight cup of tea without using a word of English.

THEOS WAS UP EARLY again the next morning and got in four solid hours of writing, language studies, and organizing photographs before being called upstairs for another full English breakfast. Shortly after his arrival in Lhasa, Theos had sent the prescribed messages to the regent, prime minister, and members of the Kashag announcing his desire to visit them, and he promptly received responses from them all with a coordinated schedule of calls. The regent, Reting Rinpoche, would be leaving Lhasa in a few days for a long visit to his home monastery at Reting, three days north of Lhasa, and Theos was eager to visit him first.

After the sudden death of the powerful and dynamic 13th Dalai Lama in December 1933, Reting Rinpoche was appointed to govern as regent during the expected twenty-year interregnum before the 14th Dalai Lama—whose infant incarnation had yet to be discovered—would reach the age of majority and take the throne. The fifty-eight-year-old 13th Dalai Lama had been sick for about twelve days with what was thought to have been only another of his frequent colds or a case of flu, but after the state's Nechung oracle forced a dose of medicine known as the "the seventeen heroes for subduing colds" down his throat, His Holiness soon lost consciousness and never spoke another word.

The mourning period proved to be a dangerous and volatile time, with leaders of reform, monastic, and military factions vying to claim the regency. While continual prayer ceremonies were held at Lhasa's monasteries and temples for the quick return of the Dalai Lama, behind the doors of the National Assembly a five-month power struggle resulted in purges, exile, the confiscation of estates, and, for one principal contender for the regency, mutilation and imprisonment. Two of the three longtime favorites of the Dalai Lama were pitted against each other, with each accusing the other of complicity in the Dalai Lama's death. The third favorite, Tsarong, escaped being drawn into the dispute only because he had taken a year's sabbatical from the government and was living at his estate away from Lhasa.

After months of wrangling, the National Assembly—dominated by monks representing the three great monasteries near Lhasa—was unable to agree on a choice between the rival candidates and resorted to divine lottery at the Potala. Reting Rinpoche, a revered incarnate lama, was only twenty-three, frail, and had no political experience when his name was chosen. Tragically, during this decisive period of Tibet's modern history, his interregnum would focus obsessively on the shifting alliances of internal politics and deadly palace intrigues.

Since his installation, Reting Rinpoche had built a small but exquisitely appointed palace in Lhasa, and Theos and Tharchin rode to their meeting there on two of Tsarong's finest stallions with a suitable retinue of servants behind them. They were met at the gates and led across green lawns and through a garden of blooming flowers to an antechamber where they were served tea and instructed on protocol. When the tall door opened, Theos crossed the threshold into the regent's room and then prostrated himself three times, bringing his folded hands to the top of his head and then his forehead, throat, and heart before kneeling and touching his forehead to the carpet. He then approached the regent, who laid his long, delicate hands on his head in blessing and then returned the silk *kata* Theos offered, placing it around his neck. Theos sat on a low cushion in front of the regent's elegant "living box," which Theos describe as a small gilded davenport enclosed by a frame of carved panels in which the slight lama sat cross-legged all day. A modern wall of large glass windows with a view onto the garden patio brightened the room, and an electric fan hung incongruously from the frescoed ceiling.

"There was no doubt about him being a truly spiritual individual," Theos wrote that night in his journal, "but at the same time very keen, for his mind was sharp and grasping as well as filled with ideas."

The regent skipped the usual pleasantries Theos had come to expect at the beginning of his conversations with members of the higher ranks and went straight to the reason he had invited Theos to Lhasa. He attributed Theos' interest in their religion to a past life in Tibet as a spiritual teacher, and he wanted to know all about Theos' plans for spreading Tibetan Buddhism in America. Reting Rinpoche even offered to travel to America to add his blessings to the effort. They spent several hours together, and before parting, Reting Rinpoche told Theos to make a list of all the scriptures he hoped to collect; before he left town he would give orders to find them. He then tied a small red silk scarf with a distinctive triple knot around Theos' neck as a final blessing.

As Theos rode through the city on the way back to Tsarong House, people came out of their doors to gawk at the white-skinned and bearded young man riding through the streets in a Tibetan gown with this red, triple-knotted scarf around his neck, a blessing they themselves prayed their entire lives to receive.

"Gossip traveled fast and far," Theos wrote in *Penthouse of the Gods.* "Who was this fortunate individual who had come from a strange world to be so generously welcomed by their great Divine Soul? From that instant, every one in Lhasa, from the highest to the lowest, was eager to do everything to help me."

AFTER LUNCH AT TSARONG HOUSE, Theos had an appointment to call on the *lonchen,* or prime minister, who lived in a large three-story house on several acres around the corner from the Tsarongs. Unlike the straightforward conversation with the regent in the morning, the prime minister preferred pleasant formalities, and it was difficult for Theos to gauge what kind of impression he had made, "as everything done in Tibet is so indirect." "It is the custom always to be amiable and smiling and jovial," Theos wrote, "to talk about everything except what is uppermost in your mind, and for which indeed you have made the visit; yet when you leave you know the answer by implication."

More loads of *tsampa* and eggs arrived during the day at Tsarong House from individual members of the Kashag, and the following morning at eight Theos and Tharchin paid their call at the home of Langcunga Shape, who Tharchin warned could be "loquacious and argumentative." Weeks earlier, Tharchin had to make two visits to him with Theos' petition, and each time he had to listen to a long lecture on the evils of allowing strangers into Lhasa. Again, during this visit, no matter what Tharchin or Theos said, Langcunga forcefully corrected them. "I realized that behind this extraordinary manner he was testing me, trying perhaps to confirm the suspicions he had about me," Theos wrote.

After lunch at the Tsarongs', they hurried off to visit Kalon Lama Shape, who filled the one slot designated for a monk-official on the Kashag. He had been instrumental in getting approval for Theos to come to Lhasa, and Theos was glad for the opportunity to express his appreciation. Kalon Lama's house sat within the outer walls of the sacred Potala, and the sixty-seven-year-old lama met them with open arms at the top of the steep stairway leading from his stable to the second-floor living area. He humbly insisted that Theos enter his parlor shrine room ahead of him, and Theos anticipated, with this flood of amity, "a conversation that it would take years to forget." But after settling himself in his painted living box, Kalon Lama said little, beaming all the while with joyful affection. A servant brought English tea, and then, finally, Kalon Lama asked what kind of shrines Americans kept in their homes. When Theos described the "matter-of-fact Western ways" at home, Kalon Lama was "profoundly shocked. He thought religion was the most important thing in life, and the sole justification for existence was spiritual development," Theos wrote.

On parting, Kalon Lama offered a guide to show them a few of the important shrines of the Potala, the Dalai Lamas' thirteen-story, fortress-like palace complex that rises on Marpo Ri more than a thousand feet above the valley floor. The Potala's White Palace, whose construction was begun by the 5th Dalai Lama in 1645, served as the residence of the Dalai Lamas and housed government administrative offices, a monastery, and printing house. The Red Palace contained a many-leveled complex of shrines, chapels, and galleries, as well as the great stupas housing the re-mains of the Dalai Lamas. Altogether, the Potala's thousand rooms housed ten thousand shrines and two hundred thousand statues, all within stone and wood exterior walls that averaged ten feet in thickness and rested on foundations reinforced with poured copper.

Theos and Tharchin followed their guide up a massive stone stairway that zigzagged up the Potala's inward-sloping walls to its main entrance. Stepping across the high threshold at the top of the stairway, they passed through endless corridors that were art treasures in themselves. Every square inch of their columns, beams, and rafters was ornately carved and brightly painted in red, yellow, blue, and green. Life-size murals narrating the miraculous feats of Lord Buddha, the great yogis of India and Tibet, and Buddhist deities were painted in equally bright polychrome and cov-ered every wall.

Inside, they climbed up dimly lit, ladder-like staircases and emerged at the very top of the Potala at the shrine of Chenrezig, the embodiment of all the Buddha's compassion and the patron bodhisattva of Tibet, who emanates as the Dalai Lamas. Their guide's narration was interrupted by a messenger who said that the doors to the chapel containing the stupa of the late 13th Dalai Lama were about to close for the day, and they hurried on to see it before it did. They arrived just in time at the Red Palace's Great West Hall, where stand the enormous jeweled stupas that hold the mummified and perfumed bodies of five Dalai Lamas. The grandest of these five is the forty-nine-foot-high stupa of the great 5th Dalai Lama, which was built of sandalwood and then covered with more than four tons of solid gold and studded with eighteen thousand pearls and semi-precious jewels.

The stupa of the 13th Dalai Lama is located in a separate chapel outside of the Great West Hall, and Theos and Tharchin followed their guide up another ladder-like stairway lit by butter lamps to reach it. The splendorous reliquary of the 13th Dalai Lama, which had recently been completed after three years of work, was fifty feet square at its base, rose to a height of forty-six feet, and was covered with one ton of solid gold—"not gold leaf, but slabs thicker than a good piece of cardboard," as Theos described it. The entire structure was inlaid with "the finest gems to be had on earth—jade, turquoise, ruby, coral," and "the top of it was covered with large necklaces of jade and coral—a fortune in and of itself," Theos wrote that night in his journal.

In front of the stupa stood several four-foot-high solid silver butter lamps with a multitude of burning wicks in a melted pond of yak butter two feet in diameter. The stupa's altar was filled with precious offerings from the noble families of Tibet and from wealthy monasteries of Mongolia and China; among which were small trees of solid coral, large jade carvings, and a mandala pagoda made from more than two hundred thousand pearls. The walls on both sides of the room were filled with pigeonhole cabinets holding the bundled pages of a Kangyur and Tengyur written by hand with letters of gold.

From there, the tour continued to the printing rooms, where the copy of the Kangyur that Theos purchased in Calcutta from Ngagchen Rinpoche had been produced. The walls were filled with cataloged shelves organizing the wood printing blocks, and dozens of small boys scurried with stacks of blocks on their shoulders to the printers, who sat on the floor, spread ink, and made the impressions.

They concluded the tour with a visit to Shol prison, a cluster of buildings at the foot of the Potala, where prisoners sat on the stone floors in groups of three or four with their outstretched legs locked in timber stocks. As Theos and his companions were about to leave they heard an eerie voice rising through the grate of a trap door in the corner. They "listened to the faint echo that came up from this dark dungeon below where this crying soul was going thru his ritual that he might gain happiness in the next life," as Theos wrote, and learned from their guide that held below was a friend of Tharchin, the famous Lungshar. Lungshar had been one of the most powerful men in Tibet, but he found himself, as a contender for the regency, on the losing side. Lungshar had for decades advocated governmental reforms that would have shifted power from the large landholders to the National Assembly, a group dominated by the three huge Gelugpa monasteries near Lhasa. In the power struggle after the 13th Dalai Lama died, Lungshar was accused of leading a plot to overthrow the government and replace it with a Bolshevik system. His arrest and conviction were based on the testimony of a sole informant, and the investigating committee concluded that although a death sentence was appropriate, Lungshar might become a vengeful ghost and interfere with the discovery of the new Dalai Lama. They therefore recommended a lesser punishment: confiscation of the family's property, life imprisonment, and the gruesome torture of squeezing his skull between two yak knucklebones that were tightened by twisting leather thongs with a stick on top of his head until his eyeballs popped out. During the actual mutilation procedure, only one eye popped out, and the other had to be cut out. Boiling oil was then poured into the sockets to cauterize the wounds.

Lungshar had spent the three years since his fall purifying his karma in the Potala dungeon. He told his wife that the reason he lost his eyes was because he had carelessly put out the eye of a sheep with a slingshot when he was young, and he warned his children not to even think of revenge. The sound Theos and Tharchin heard echoing off the stones on their tour to Shol prison was the incessant repetition of the *Om mani padme hum* mantra, which before his parole a year later, Lungshar said, passed his lips one hundred million times.

THE NEXT DAY Theos and Tharchin continued their round of calls to members of the Kashag with an appointment at the home of Tsarong's good friend Tethong Shape. The lean and tall forty-seven-year-old Tethong had once commanded the Dalai Lama's bodyguard and been governor of the eastern Tibetan province of Kham. Now a minister of the four-person Kashag, Tethong was one of the most influential men in the country. The recent death of his wife left a lingering sadness, but his native enthusiasm and vitality remained unsubdued, and Theos judged Tethong to be one of the government's most charming personalities.

Theos was beginning to formulate a request to the Kashag for permission to head east through China when he left Tibet rather than return by the Gyantse route on which he had arrived. He figured it would take three months to travel overland through eastern Tibet to the Chinese border and then another month to reach Peking. Along with the allure of being the first to leave a record of traveling from India to Peking via Lhasa, Theos was beginning to think that the only way he would ever get a high-quality set of the Tengyur was to go to eastern Tibet himself and have it printed in Derge. A Tengyur printed from the more commonly available Narthang blocks would not serve foreign scholars, Theos thought, because the Narthang blocks had become so worn that their prints were nearly illegible. The Narthang editions were used mostly by that time to place inside stupas or in a noble's private temple, where once installed they were never opened. The Derge printing house preserved the quality of its carved wood blocks by producing only limited editions for important families and selected monasteries and temples of Tibet and Mongolia, and consequently, its printings were the finest and rarest. Theos realized that in order to fulfill the lofty plan he had outlined with the regent for introducing Tibetan Buddhism in America, he would require a legible and authoritative copy of the Tengyur for his translations, for without the 3,600 texts of commentary contained in the encyclopedic Tengyur, the straight discourses of Lord Buddha contained in the fine edition of the Kangyur that he had bought from Ngagchen Rinpoche would be nearly impossible for Western scholars to understand.

Theos talked openly with Tethong Shape about his hope to travel through Kham to China, and Tethong let him know that friends who had just arrived from Kham reported that not only were fierce battles flaring between Tibetan and Chinese forces in the region, but also gangs of desperate bandits roamed the country, making travel anywhere in the area extremely dangerous. Tethong explained that Chinese Communist forces driven out of Hunan by Nationalist forces the previous summer had been forced across the Tibetan border and had captured, for a time, most of Kham, including Derge. But even more menacing than the Communists that summer were the threats of the 9th Panchen Lama, Chokyi Nyima, now in the fourteenth year of his self-exile, who was camped across the border in China and continued to organize for a march back to his monastery in Shigatse at the head of a large force of Nationalist Chinese troops.

The Tibetan government had hopes that after the death of the 13th Dalai Lama the feud could be ended, and toward that end it offered to restore many of the Tashilhunpo estates confiscated in 1923 and also to reduce the heavy taxes imposed to support the military. However, the Tibetan government would not allow the Panchen Lama to raise an independent army, nor would it recognize his Tashilhunpo monastery as autonomous. And the government would not permit an escort of Chinese troops and officials to accompany the Panchen Lama to Shigatse.

The previous summer, in anticipation of an imminent return, the Panchen Lama had sent a large advance shipment of baggage to Tibet in which border guards discovered a cache of rifles, hand grenades, and ammunition. Civil war seemed at hand when, only three months before Theos arrived in Lhasa, the Kashag intercepted a copy of a *lamyik* written by the Panchen Lama instructing all district officials on the way to Lhasa and Shigatse to prepare to receive him and his entourage, which would include twenty Chinese officials and five hundred well-armed Chinese soldiers. Consequently, in mid-May 1937, just a month before Theos was inquiring about going to the area, the Tibetan government ordered 2,700 of its troops in Kham to take up defensive positions and prepare to block the entry of the Chinese escort.

Despite the evident danger, however, Theos insisted to Tethong that he should have the choice of going to Derge if that proved to be the only way to get a high-quality Tengyur to take back to America. Tethong agreed and said he would do everything in his power to secure permission.

Theos had still one last call to finish up his initial visits to the members of the Kashag. The visit to Bhondong Shape later that afternoon was less cordial and more of the formal *kata* offering and humble expressions of gratitude and piety that Theos had expected of the first visits. Both host and guest were happy to keep this visit brief.

Now that the protocol for the first visits to the highest government officials had been observed, it was time to make plans for the round of ceremonies that the important monasteries near Lhasa wished to perform for Theos. The abbots at each monastery wished to perform special ceremonies to welcome the West's first Buddhist pilgrim to Lhasa and to bless his mission to bring their religion to America, and after consulting their astrologers they selected auspicious days for the events. When the schedule came back with the first ceremony set for the last of the three weeks on his permit to stay in Lhasa, Theos realized he had been handed the perfect justification to request a two-month extension.

Tsarong gave Theos detailed advice on how to maneuver for the extra time and promised also that if Theos still insisted at the end of his stay on requesting a permit to leave Tibet through China, Tsarong would outfit him with the horses, tents, and guns required for the much larger group of attendants Theos would need as an escort. Theos sent off the requests to the Kashag and then filled the next days with first visits to some more of Lhasa's landmarks—the thirteen-hundred-year-old Jokhang and Ramoche temples, and the Dalai Lamas' summer palace, Norbulingka. He also began a series of long introductory meetings trying to ferret out book collections he wanted to purchase.

Theos' tenth day in Lhasa, July 4, was scheduled full with social events. Not only did he have lunch planned with the regent, but immediately afterward Theos himself was hosting a tea party at Tsarong House to break the ice between the British and Chinese delegations in Lhasa. At seven-thirty a stream of servants entered his room and removed everything before bringing in a great stack of mats and carpets, which they arranged on the floor around low Tibetan tables. Theos thought that he was beginning to look like a "jungle man" and decided he needed a haircut for the occasion. The barber arrived but had forgotten his scissors and left immediately, Theos supposed, to go get them. The barber returned again in a few minutes, sat Theos on the floor, and began cutting. Theos was curious about the tugging on his scalp and the loud grinding and was more amused than outraged to find that the barber had returned with Tsarong's garden shears.

Tsarong accompanied Theos and Tharchin on this second visit to the regent, and they set out from the house in a regal procession with the appropriate number of servants to denote his rank. Tsarong wore a golden gown and sat erect on a very large horse that was itself adorned with a jeweled crown. All these trappings signaled even from afar that the common people on the bazaar streets must bow their heads in mandatory obeisance as the entourage passed.

When he entered the audience hall of the regent, Tsarong humbly prostrated himself three times, but from that moment on he was, as Theos described, his usual self: direct and outspoken, "like lashing tongues of fire, occasionally cooling down to an effervescent glow of radiant heat." The regent had a small table to himself, while the guests sat at a larger but lower table. Two young boys—who appeared to be relatives of the regent—and their lama chaperone joined Theos, Tharchin, and Tsarong at lunch. The regent wore a robe of spotless yellow silk, a great contrast to the younger of the boys, who Theos guessed had just come in from playing in an alley; he was certain "that water has not touched him for months on end."

It was called a light lunch, with only about fifteen courses, and at the first opportunity Theos brought up his hope to travel through eastern Tibet to China. The regent replied that he had already discussed the idea with the Kashag, and they all agreed that because of the danger it would be unwise to go. But considering that it would give him an opportunity to secure a Tengyur from the Derge blocks, they would not stop him if he insisted. Endless refills of Tibetan tea were brought, and, expecting that he would be able to get only a fraction of his requests, Theos gave the regent a long list of Buddhist texts he hoped to take home to America. To his surprise, the regent said he would leave orders to help Theos get everything, which left Theos wondering how he could possibly pay for them all.

The regent said he would be leaving in a few days to spend about a month at Reting, his home monastery three days north of Lhasa, and that on his return he would have a party for Theos. This implied, of course, that the regent expected him to be in Lhasa for some time after his initial three-week permit expired. Theos restrained an exclamation of joy, said merely that it was very considerate of him, and carried on with the meal. At their departure, the regent presented Theos with a white silk *kata*, the red piece of silk with the triple knot, and two gifts to inaugurate his American collection. The first was a small, fine image of Lord Buddha, and the second a large bundle wrapped in beautiful yellow silk. Inside was an exceedingly rare copy of *The Sublime Mahayana Sutra on the Golden Eon*, a 1,176-page volume illustrated with brilliant images of all one thousand Buddhas and captioned with the Buddha's names, making it possible to identify them all. Reting Rinpoche told Theos that the reason he had selected this particular text for him was that in it were gathered all the blessings of Buddhism. It had been presented to him on the day he was installed as regent, and he thought it would be a great aid to support Theos in bringing Buddhism to America.

Theos had to hurry back to Tsarong House for the tea party he was hosting that afternoon for the two most important foreign delegations in Lhasa—the temporary and informal missions representing the Chinese and the British. The two Chinese officers had been in Lhasa almost three years and there had been a British delegation in Lhasa for two years, but so far they had refused to meet each other. As the situation was explained to Theos, it is the custom of the incoming guest to make the first call, but since the British refused to recognize the Chinese officers as official representatives of the Chinese government in Lhasa, they refused to put them on their diplomatic visiting list.

To have any Chinese officials in Lhasa at all was a touchy issue fraught with great diplomatic significance. After the death of the strong-willed and fiercely independent 13th Dalai Lama in 1933, Chiang Kai-shek saw an opportunity for restoring what he considered China's traditional hegemony over Tibet and deputed General Huang Mu Sung to deliver the Republic's condolences to Lhasa. It was the first high-profile official visit to Lhasa since the Chinese Republic was created in 1911 and was allowed by the Kashag—only after much debate—because some rapprochement with China was considered necessary to end the costly border clashes and prevent another of the marches on Lhasa that had forced the Dalai Lama to flee in 1910.

The Huang mission arrived in Lhasa in August 1934 with about eighty people, and General Huang made a show of piety by touching his forehead to the throne of the Dalai Lama and distributing to the combined twenty thousand monks of the Lhasa monasteries about two Chinese silver dollars each. It wasn't long thereafter that Huang got permission to use the wireless set he had brought to communicate with Nanking. When, after several weeks, Huang got around to discussing political issues, he pressed the Chinese demand that Tibet accept inclusion into the Chinese Republic. He was clear that meant the Chinese authority to approve all appointments to high government positions in Tibet as well as taking over the training and equipping of the Tibetan army.

The National Assembly diplomatically rejected every point and stated that because Tibet was a self-governing, independent country, there was no reason for China to station civil or military officials in Lhasa. Huang and his delegation felt rushed to leave Lhasa before snow closed the passes between Szechuan and Tibet, but he asked to leave the wireless unit and two officials behind to facilitate a continuation of their new dialogue. As Hugh Richardson noted in his account of that period, "From that time too the Chinese Government began to make regular payments to a number of Tibetan officials, from the Regent downwards."

The British sent a delegation to Lhasa the following year intending to monitor and balance whatever influence the Chinese presence might have on the Tibetans, and they hoped in particular to broker a settlement between the Panchen Lama and the Lhasa government that would keep Chinese troops and officers from moving into his monastery at Shigatse, Tibet's second-largest city. The delegation, led by the Sikkim political officer F. W. Williamson, arrived in the summer of 1935, but soon after his arrival in Lhasa, Williamson developed kidney problems, and by November he was in critical condition with uremia. Williamson died in mid-November, and in February 1936 Basil Gould, Williamson's replacement as political officer in Sikkim, arrived to take command of the effort to reach a settlement. Gould's staff included Hugh Richardson, the newly appointed Gyantse trade agent. When Gould returned to Sikkim with most of his staff in February 1937 (just a few weeks before Theos met him in Kalimpong) he left Richardson in charge of the Lhasa mission, which included a wireless transmitter of its own. The Tibetans, considering both wireless installations to be temporary, assured the indignant Chinese that the British wireless would be removed as soon as they removed their own.

Theos had paid an earlier visit to the Chinese officer, S. H. William Tsiang, to discuss a visa for his proposed return through China, and Tsiang wished to reciprocate by hosting a dinner for Theos to which he would invite some other officials—perhaps even Richardson, if the protocol could be worked out. Theos knew as well that Richardson would be leaving soon to spend some time at headquarters in Gangtok and was eager to meet the Chinese unofficially before he left Lhasa. The two could be brought together, Theos realized, over tea at Tsarong's house on his "neutral soil of friendship." Theos had forgotten it was the Fourth of July until Tsiang arrived at the party with a *kata* in honor of America's Independence Day and congratulated him for "belonging to a free people which had the sense to throw off the shackles of the outworn forms of the Middle Ages."

So as not to appear too overt in his diplomacy, Theos invited the other foreign delegations in Lhasa, and looking over the group, he thought there was no finer way of celebrating the Fourth of July than by sitting at a table at which six nationalities—Chinese, Nepalese, Sikkimese, English, Tibetan, and American—were all amicably talking. The Chinese group included, along with Tsiang and the wireless operator, a young Chinese man who spoke fluent English, knew Greek philosophy, and was undertaking the twenty-year course of monastic study for the *geshe* degree. Richardson's group included his wireless operator Reginald Fox, two clerks, and Rai Bahadur Norbu Dhondup, the British trade agent at Yatung. Norbu, whom Theos had first met in Kalimpong, had just arrived to take over temporary command of the British mission when Richardson left for Gangtok. They spoke eighteen languages between them all, but confined the conversation to English and Tibetan. Richardson and Tsiang, Theos observed, had a good talk "about little nothings, which might break down the ice of national pride and make way for new maneuverings."

The tea Theos hosted didn't have the geopolitical consequences he had hoped for, but this one event, at which almost all the foreigners in Lhasa were gathered, illustrated powerfully the difference between the reason Theos Bernard was in Lhasa and the reasons for all those who came before. What the Tibetans wished for most from both the Chinese and British delegations was that they just pack up their wireless units and go home. The temporary British mission was tolerated as a counteragent to the unwanted temporary Chinese mission, but the thrust of Tibetan policy was to resist the influence of both. Theos Bernard, on the other hand, had been specifically invited to Lhasa as a way for Tibetans, through him, to influence the rest of the world. The historic series of blessings and initiations intended to groom this Western pilgrim as a fit emissary of Tibetan Buddhism to the New World were about to begin.

THE ABBOTS OF LHASA'S three great monasteries chose the last day of the Tibetan lunar month, July 8, as the auspicious day for the first ceremony to honor Theos, which was to be held at Tibet's most sacred temple, the Jokhang. The four-story Jokhang was built in 642 CE by the dharma king Songtsan Gampo to house a statue depicting Lord Buddha at the age of twelve, the Jowo Sakyamuni, and it was the dream of all Tibetans to make a pilgrimage to see it before they died. As Theos approached the temple entrance on the morning of his ceremony, he joined the other pilgrims in prostrating themselves full length on the plaza stones worn smooth by generations of their ancestors. Some had walked—or even prostrated—the entire distance from districts months away, but they all recognized that this white-skinned one had come from an even more remote home. As Theos noted, "They could not quite figure out . . . my nationality; so the main question was, 'Who is he?'"

Theos was first escorted on a tour of the temple's holy shrines. Scattered butter lamps marked a path through the dark hallway that circled the main shrine room and the five-foot-high, heavily gilded, and jewel-studded Jowo Sakyamuni. The shrine that displayed statues of King Songtsan Gampo and his two queens reposed upstairs in gloomy dignity, and around it ran a hall off which opened small cells housing more gilded statues. At all the shrines, countless mice darted between the shadows of the butter lamps and feasted on the bowls of rice offered to the deities.

Down in the temple's main courtyard, eight hundred monks had been reciting since daybreak a Buddhist refuge prayer Theos had requested, but there was no need for him to take his place among them until the officiating lama, His Eminence the Ganden Tri Rinpoche, arrived. The Ganden Tri Rinpoche is the spiritual head of the Gelugpa lineage—of which the

Dalai Lama is the temporal head—and is appointed after competitive examinations to a seven-year term by the Dalai Lama. He is considered, as Theos wrote, "to be the most learned lama of all Tibet, having acquired his position...without the aid of a fortunate reincarnation." With little hope it would be accepted, Theos had sent an invitation requesting Tri Rinpoche to preside at the Jokhang ceremony, and all were surprised when His Eminence agreed.

Still awaiting the arrival of Tri Rinpoche, the monks took a break from their recitation, and the courtyard was suddenly empty and silent. The high altar in the courtyard was arrayed with a thousand bowls of blessed water and rows of foot-high *tormas* arrayed three deep. On a visit to see the preparations for the ceremony the day before, Theos had photographed about twenty monks kneading two tons of barley flour into the dough for the thousand cone-shaped *torma* offerings on the altar. He also photographed a full ton of yak butter being melted in great copper vats to fuel the thousand butter lamps that now burned in front of the altar. The butter was brought in eighty-pound yak-skin bags from the great herds of the Chang Tang a thousand miles to the north. This one temple alone, Theos was told, required more than ten thousand pounds of yak butter a month just to fuel its lamps.

The deep vibration of a gong signaled that Tri Rinpoche had arrived and was installed on his throne. The monks shuffled back to their cushions, rearranged the wraps of their robes, and, almost in unison, the entire group sat down. In an instant the soft rustling was stilled and the low mumbling chant of their prayers filled the hall. Immediately after the completion of the first prayer, the tea prayer, the novice monks sprang up and ran to the rear of the room, where women with large earthen jars of Tibetan butter tea filled urns for the novices to pour from as they moved, humbly bent low, down the rows of monks.

After all were served, a lama sitting on a raised platform in the back strode up the center aisle, made three prostrations, and read a petition that Theos had written requesting the consent of the assembly to conduct the ceremony and recite the secret mantras specified by Tri Rinpoche. There was a low rumbling response of assent, and then the monk read the prayer Theos had written using the prescribed formula that mentioned his name and nationality and his fervent wishes for the health, wealth, and happiness of the whole world.

This was the cue for Theos to enter. They had permission to photograph the event, and as Theos was escorted up the center aisle, Tharchin snapped away. At the front he made his three devotional prostrations and then approached Tri Rinpoche and presented offerings to him symbolizing the body, speech, and mind of a Buddha, and then a *kata*. Tri Rinpoche placed the offered *kata* around Theos' neck as well as a red silk triple-knotted scarf and then gave him a benediction with the touch of his sacred hands. Backing away in humble respect, Theos offered *katas* to each of the other high lamas, who likewise gave him their blessing.

A long period then followed during which the monks continued reciting prayers while the high lamas at the front followed a choreography of graceful mudras punctuated by ringing bells and rapping *damaru* hand drums. At a certain point Theos was cued to walk through the ranks of monks and make symbolic offerings to them with a bundle of burning incense sticks, and then tea was served again. This time it was lunch, and the monks mixed pinches of *tsampa* from pouches they carried in the folds of their robes with the butter tea poured for them. This they kneaded into a ball of dough from which they silently nibbled their main meal of the day. After the brief break, the chanting continued for another three hours, and then Theos was advised he could leave. The monks would continue their rumbling recitation from the *puja* scripture until it was finished at about seven that evening.

Outside the Jokhang, a line of beggars waited to give Theos a chance to act on his wish for the health, wealth, and happiness of the whole world. He offered copper coins to all those in line and made arrangements for offerings to reach the city's other beggars, as well as Lhasa's dogs and prisoners.

WHILE THEOS WAS IN TIBET, his experience continually alternated between the ritual austerity of the monasteries' celibate monks and the sumptuous hospitality of the highest ranks of nobility and foreign delegations. And so it was that two days after his ceremony at the Jokhang, Theos was invited to a party at the home of Tethong Shape. Each year a different *shape* hosted the official twelve-day festival of the Kashag, and this year it was Tethong's turn. The festival gave Tethong a chance to show off his new three-story house, which everyone agreed had surpassed even Tsarong's as the finest in Lhasa. The day Theos was invited as the honored guest was already the eighth day of the festival, and many of the guests had been camped for days in their own tents at the house, "making it one continuous meal," as Theos put it.

Tethong greeted Theos when he arrived and led him on a tour of the house. Every room they passed through had a small party of its own in swing, and their progress was slowed by endless introductions. They finally reached the exquisite shrine room, which featured nine large hand-embroidered *thangkas* depicting the life of Lord Buddha, and then they returned to the dining room, where they drank cup after cup of butter tea and discussed the problems Theos was having finding the scriptures on his list.

Soon lunch was served. It was the usual myriad of dishes, but all were of the finest quality. Theos had by this time learned to nibble his way through the courses, but by the end, five large bowls of noodle soup had been forced on him. And then the *chang* girls arrived to boisterous cheers of *"Tashi delek!"* Theos drank with decreasing reluctance cup after cup of the low-alcohol sweet-and-sour barley beer, and it seemed to him that one of the *chang* girls had special instructions to make sure he was keeping up the pace. He tried to avoid her by circulating around the house, but every few minutes she showed up and, with sparkling eyes, insisted on refilling his glass from her keg. "They go so far as to . . . stick you with needles if you refuse," he wrote, "and by this time the eyes of everyone in the room are on you, all begging you to have more. One would not mind a few glasses, but when it gets up to around thirty you begin to realize that it is not water."

With no interruption in the flow of *chang*, the tables were cleared and set up with the ivory tiles of the popular Chinese game mahjong. Tsiang, the Chinese officer, "showed the boys how it is possible to lose their money in a hurry," while the women, as was typical, left for the other side of the house, where they had a party of their own.

Throughout the entire day and night a group of Tibetan musicians accompanied the traditional dances of three women who tapped their feet from time to time and occasionally swung in an arc the long sleeves that hung far below their hands. Theos talked with a few of the lamas and some of the minor officials there whom he had heard of but not yet met; all of them knew about the ceremony at the Jokhang and were keenly interested in the progress of his studies and his plans for collecting a library to bring to America.

A grand thirty-course dinner was served, washed down again with a continuous flow of *chang*. Theos tried to resist, but Tsiang insisted he join the old Chinese drinking game of predicting the number of fingers he flashed. The loser had to down another glass, and, as at mahjong, Tsiang never lost. Theos realized that the only way he would escape eating and drinking late into the night was to go home, and he sent for the servants who had come with him.

It was only a short way back to Tsarong House, but Theos had learned that no one of any rank ever went anywhere without at least a syce to stable his horse and one personal servant. It was more than just a matter of parading status, especially at night. Theos had been warned that many of daylight's beggars became bandits after dark, and just recently two men had been robbed and killed in Lhasa. The danger was so serious, in fact, that city authorities enforced a nine o'clock curfew. Rather than attempt to police the dark and winding streets of the city, the government instead ordered everyone indoors after dark, and as soon as the curfew hour was signaled with the explosion of a giant firecracker at each of the four corners of the central city, the streets were deserted. It was common, Theos noted, for lower-ranking Tibetans to pick up their hats around eight forty-five and hurriedly say good-bye. However, as with many of the rules needed to control the Tibetan rabble, the nobility seemed to be exempt from this one; they left when they wanted, but with an entourage.

AS IN GYANTSE, Theos found it prudent also to accept some of the frequent invitations he received from the British mission. The day after Tethong's party, Richardson invited Theos out to their compound (which was set outside the city gates in a dense grove of willows) for an early dinner and a screening of the Lhasa movie that Theos helped Chapman edit in Calcutta. After a leisurely dinner, Richardson set up the projector. For Theos, the large crowd of Tibetans who filled the room were the most entertaining part of the show.

> They were teeming at the door when we first came down, and when the door was opened they swarmed in like an army of migrating bees. The guests arranged themselves in the chairs in the large dining room, while their servants flocked in on the floor, crawling forward until they were sitting directly beneath the screen itself. Against the wall in the rear they clambered over and upon one another's shoulders and stood up on chairs or on any other piece of furniture within reach.

Chapman had brought the projector to Lhasa on his visit with the mission a year earlier, and now Richardson got requests for showings of movies at children's parties and even from the regent himself. The Rin Tin Tin adventure *The Night Cry* was the favorite, and no matter how many times they saw it, the film never failed to move the Tibetans to gasp, cry, and shout warnings and encouragement at the characters on the screen. Charlie Chaplin was also popular, and they had their choice between *Easy Street* and *Shanghaied*. Screenings typically ran over four hours and included newsreels of the jubilee procession of King George V and of the Grand National, whose horses and riders always thrilled the Tibetans with their jumps at the hedges and fences of the Aintree course.

Chapter 8

LIVING RITUAL

THEOS HAD BEEN IN LHASA nearly three weeks already—the time limit stipulated in his original invitation—but no one had the least concern that he would be suddenly expelled. Ceremonies for him were scheduled still in the weeks ahead at the Ramoche temple and at the Drepung, Sera, and Ganden monasteries. As expected, just as the expiration day arrived, the Kashag sent a message that he had been granted a two-month extension.

For the ceremony at the thirteen-hundred-year-old Ramoche temple, another of Tibet's most sacred pilgrimage sites, Theos requested a service to "propitiate" Dorje Jikje, or Yamantaka, the Slayer of the Lord of Death. Yamantaka practices are strictly secret rites reserved only for initiates of the Unsurpassed Class of Tantra. Images of Yamantaka, his mantras, mandala, and practices are closely guarded, and the description Theos gives of the ceremony suggests that the "propiation" was actually his initiation into the secret world of Buddhist Tantra.

The Ganden Tri Rinpoche again presided over the ceremony, and since most of the monks who had participated in the rites the week before at the Jokhang were actually headquartered at Ramoche, "it was a matter of greeting one another again," Theos wrote. Hanging from the high beams of the assembly hall was a large *thangka* of Yamantaka's mandala, a graphic representation of his paradisiacal home. The ceremony, as Theos described it, revolved around entering through a gate in the outer circle of the mandala and progressing through the intricate passageways to his "abode of bliss" in the center. The main shrine in the temple featured an enormous image of Yamantaka, whose midnight blue body had a bull's head and eight other faces, thirty-four arms holding fearsome weapons, and sixteen legs, all surrounded by an aura of flames.

The service began with a high lama reading Theos' request for the ceremony and then his prayer that all beings find ultimate happiness. There was a murmur of consent from the monks, and then Theos walked to the front of the center aisle, made his three prostrations, and presented four sacred offerings to Tri Rinpoche, one symbolizing the universe and the others the body, speech, and mind of a Buddha. The lamas on this day were dressed in silk brocade capes and elaborate two-foot-high crowns representing the dress of the deity. The chant master began with the first syllables of the scriptural text and was quickly joined by the eight hundred seated monks, whose rumbling recitation was punctuated at points by the mass tinkling of their ritual bells.

At one point the monks symbolically offered everything good in the universe to their guru as they heaped up rice in silver rings over beautiful silken scarves in their laps. Later the monks tied red scarves on their foreheads and then picked up their *dorje* scepters with their left hands and their ritual bells with their right hands and performed a series of mudras as they chanted secret mantras.

In this ceremony and in all his later experiences in the temples of Tibet, Theos was always watchful for signs of how the practice of ritual in Tibetan Buddhism either generated or repressed true spiritual experience. In his account of the Ramoche ceremony Theos wrote,

It was a feast for the imagination.... The endless formality is only for the purpose of awakening the imagination.... All this ritual was devised by the learned ones who compiled the Tantras countless centuries ago, aware of the incapacity of the human animal for seeking strength and solace within. Before the individual can receive the blessing of his devotion he must first be awakened, and they are fully aware that nothing is bestowed upon him from the outside, that everything must come from within through this emotional awakening.

After several hours of ceremony, rice and tea were served and the monks brought out their *tsampa* bags. After lunch, Theos offered devotional *pujas* before the main deities of the temple as well as the wrathful forms hidden in the temple's secret sanctuaries. He returned to Tsarong House with a mob of Tibetans running ahead of him trying to figure out who was this bearded foreigner who was dressed as a Tibetan and being treated this way at their holy temples.

DAYS NOW BEGAN at five for Theos with three hours of Tibetan grammar studies before breakfast followed by sessions with a well-known Nyingma lama whom Tsarong had introduced him to. The first day the lama made a gift to Theos of a small image of Padmasambhava, the greatest teacher of the Nyingmas, and then Theos listened for six solid hours to the lama's teaching while sitting cross-legged without moving. Unlike the Gelugpa monks Theos had met, who shaved their heads and took vows of celibacy, this lama, as was common with Nyingmas, had long hair, owned his own house, and had a wife and family. He was filled with laughter, and, with his comprehensive knowledge of Tibetan scriptures, was quick to point out the apparent contradiction between certain Tibetan beliefs and their philosophical foundations. But what Theos hoped for out of these sessions was to receive secret oral instruction on Tantric practice. After a few days of teachings Theos concluded:

> This wheedling information out of esoteric priests is certainly a delicate job of silent tugging, for you more or less have to keep them talking and . . . then whenever they find that their wind is about to give out, they say that the rest is esoteric and that it will be necessary for you to take the [Tantric] vows before the next step can be revealed to you.

As the lama explained, the Tantric vows were not easy to get. The vows were received during Tantric initiation, and among Nyingma lamas a long preparation, or *ngondro,* that typically included one hundred thousand full-length prostrations and another hundred thousand mantra recitations was required before a student would be considered ripe for initiation. Theos was envious of anyone who could devote his entire life to spiritual practice, and he wrote in his journal, "This life is so transitory and short that it is a pity that we must waste so much of its precious energy on misdirected externals when the source of eternal life is within." He felt a longing to create a life of contemplation and reflection, but cherished the hope that it could be "adapted to the everyday life of the individual in the world of affairs who can not give up all of his time."

Theos recognized that the world of affairs required that he stay on good terms with the British, and he reluctantly gave up part of his study time to accept an invitation from Norbu Dhondup (who was left in charge when Richardson returned to Gangtok for a visit) to come out to the mission for a game of badminton. Theos stayed to dinner, and during the meal Norbu mentioned that he had received a letter from Giuseppe Tucci, one of the leading Sanskrit and Tibetan scholars of the era, asking Norbu to recommend him to the Tibetans for permission to visit Lhasa. Tucci, a supporter of Mussolini and a member of the Italian Academy, had already conducted two expeditions, in 1933 and 1935, to Dungkar in western Tibet, and he wrote in the Calcutta newspapers before he left that he was headed to Shigatse. Theos had inside information that the Tibetan government had refused Tucci's request to go to Shigatse, but Tucci had decided to go as far as Gyantse on a limited British permit anyway in hopes that after he got that far he could inveigle the authorities for a permit to go on to Shigatse or even Lhasa. Tucci also asked in his letter that Norbu find copies for him of several Tibetan scriptures that even Theos—who had the full assistance of Lhasa's most powerful officials—was still unable to locate. As in Gyantse, where his British friends regaled Theos at dinner with stories about the arrest of foreigners trying to sneak across the Tibetan border, the gossip about the problems that the renowned Tucci was having getting beyond Gyantse made Theos appreciate all the more the remarkable and unprecedented access he was being given to Lhasa's sacred landmarks.

The British stationed at this most far-flung of imperial outposts, however, seemed to Theos to be thoroughly unappreciative of the unique potential their residency in Lhasa offered. After dinner, the group went upstairs and the two head clerks put bells around their ankles and performed parodies of Indian dancing girls, a "first class entertainment," Theos wrote,

> but what leaves me speechless is the reason for the necessity of such things. I find that they are doing this every night and now they are building a tennis court, having just erected the badminton court so that they can have one game in the morning and the other in the evening with dancing in the night, all because they want to find something to pass the time.

Theos was invited out to the mission for another party the next afternoon and went hoping to meet some Tibetans whom he knew still only by reputation. When he arrived, he found the British on the lawn decked out in white ducks excitedly volleying the shuttlecock over the badminton net. Theos took a racket and joined the competition, and it wasn't long before one of the Tibetan guests arrived with his family. Theos noted with surprise that Norbu greeted him in English, and deduced that this must be R. D. Ringang, another of the Rugby boys. Ringang had been only eleven years old when, in 1913, he went off to spend a year at the Rugby school in England. He returned to England two years later to study electrical engineering at what is now the Imperial College of the University of London and stayed for another eleven years. He went home to Tibet in 1927 to build a small hydroelectric plant on a rushing stream three miles from Lhasa. The plant's generator was shipped from London and carried across the Himalayas in pieces by twenty men. Ringang directed all the work of reassembling the generator, building wood flumes to carry water to the turbines, stringing power lines, installing transformers, and building a substation. Eventually all of Lhasa was connected. The Tsarongs and Tethongs and some other aristocratic families had electric lights installed in every room of their houses, while the humbler houses might have a single light in the main room. Ringang was still in charge, and even though it was impossible to predict on which nights there would be power, and when there was power, it was "hardly bright enough to attract the bugs," as Theos put it, the plant was nonetheless a source of great pride in the city. Ringang took off his Tibetan gown, under which he too sported English white ducks, and joined the game with the remark that he had not handled a racket in fifteen years. The Tibetan women, decked out in their rainbow aprons and arrays of pearls, turquoise, and rubies, joined in as well and laughed uproariously as they batted the feathered shuttlecock in all directions.

While waiting for dinner to be served, Fox tuned in some music on the shortwave radio, and throughout the meal they listened to broadcasts from Java, China, and Hong Kong. Afterward they retired to the large room downstairs and watched yet again the movie Chapman had shot in Lhasa, the room even more crowded than before with Tibetans who wanted to see themselves on the screen.

Theos concluded his description of the night in his journal with this observation: "It is amazing the roles one must play in order to keep up. . . . [I]n Gyantse I had to play polo and carry on with military gossip, . . . when [Richardson] was here, it was necessary to indulge in the ostentatious sophistications of Oxford, . . . and now it is necessary to indulge in a few of the juvenile pleasures of the simple minded." Younghusband's life had been transformed by his mystical revelation on the road back from Lhasa in 1904, but this British delegation appeared oblivious to the spiritual essence Theos had come to Lhasa to taste.

Theos rode home from the British compound on one of Tsarong's finest prancing horses, and, as he described it, every pore of his body was stimulated by the diffuse moonlight and the vitality of life bounding beneath him. In this heightened mood every architectural detail in the deserted lanes below the Potala palace seemed imbued with spiritual meaning, and he sensed some guiding genius in this solitary, antique culture that had died or was yet to be born in his own.

It is my contention that . . . people can learn how to live in our modern hubs of civilization, . . . where all has become so mechanical and matter of fact, . . . and still cling to that other side of life thru the principles and techniques of Yoga. . . . In any event we are going to try, for it is not reasonable that there can be one hundred fifty million people striving for happiness and no possible salvation ahead. . . . The first test of all this will be to find just how much of this side of life I will be able to hold on to after my return to the world.

IT WAS MIDNIGHT before Theos got to sleep, but he had to be up again at three the next morning to leave for Drepung, the first of Tibet's three great Gelugpa monasteries to hold a ceremony for him. The ceremony was scheduled to start at daybreak, and it was still dark when Theos and Tharchin passed through the *chorten* gate at the city's edge. Drepung was located in the mountains six miles west of Lhasa, and from a distance Theos could see the dim outlines of the entire monastery complex, which sprawled in warrens of three- and four-story whitewashed buildings half-way up a broad natural amphitheater. Drepung, like the others of "The Three Seats," Sera and Ganden, was a bustling town in itself. Of the three, Drepung (founded in 1419) was the largest and had a population of about 10,000 monks, while Sera housed about 7,000 monks and Ganden about 5,000. Almost a fifth of all males in Tibet were monks—estimates range up to a 120,000 total—and the infrastructure required to support them all was financed mostly by the income from the vast property holdings deeded to the monasteries by the government. Drepung, for example, was said to control 185 estates, 20,000 serfs, 300 pastures, and 16,000 no-mads.

A delegation of senior monks met Theos and Tharchin at the monastery gate and led them up a steep stone staircase lane to the main temple, whose golden roof could be seen for miles in the valley below. The stone-paved courtyard of this, the world's largest monastery, was filled with a mass of shaved heads mumbling mantras and hunched into the mounds of their robes as they waited to catch the first glimpse of the sun just now beginning to gild the distant peaks. Theos hurried past them into the great temple, which was likewise filled with monks chanting in the dusty gloom of the dawn, and as the first radiant crescent of the sun broke above the horizon, a chorus of trumpets, horns, conch shells, and cymbals welcomed it and continued their bray until it had fully risen.

Unlike his visits earlier to the Jokhang and Ramoche temples, there was no great ceremony staged at Drepung specifically for Theos. He was there as an honored guest simply to tour the vast monastery, and after about an hour of the morning chant, his guide led Theos upstairs to the monks' everyday breakfast of *tsampa* and butter tea. The head Lamas of the monastery joined them and offered welcoming *katas*, and after breakfast they began a four-hour tour of the temples of each of Drepung's four colleges. One of the colleges was a Tantric college, and in a dark cell of one of its secret shrines was the large figure of a demon who generations earlier had been securely chained to prevent him from returning to his depredations.

Theos described his reaction to the day's visit in a letter to Viola:

> And so your Theos enters . . . these sanctified dungeons of deified ignorance. . . . You do not mind a few stories, but by the time these images commence to sweat and grow finger nails and then have to resort to anchoring the fiendish demons in heavy chains, your emotional tolerance breaks. . . . There is no doubt it embodies a certain amount of truth as given by their ancient teachings, but the maya of ignorance that has cast its veil is too thickly covered with religious soot for there to be much hope for those who aspire today.

Theos maintained hope that with a few of the better-educated monks to guide them and the essential Buddhist scriptures as a foundation, modern scholars could unearth the essence of Lord Buddha's Yogic path, which the monasteries, as Theos saw it, had encrusted with centuries of now meaningless ritual. However, after a month already in Lhasa, and despite the efforts of the regent and Tsarong, Theos had made little progress in finding those essential scriptures.

His first task had been to develop a list of texts to acquire as the foundation for his American library, which in itself required considerable research and discussion with scholars at the monasteries. He also got help, inadvertently, from Tibet scholars all over the world. Tharchin and other Tibetans showed him letters from Japan, Germany, Russia, France, Italy, England, Austria, Hungary, Czechoslovakia, Sweden, and Finland—almost everywhere except America—whose lists of requested texts revealed clearly what other scholars thought important to collect.

From all these sources, Theos assembled a list of a hundred titles to acquire, but, as he wrote, "it looks like a hopeless search for such a short period." Much of the problem resulted from the fact that all the printers in Lhasa were currently employed working on the massive biography of the late 13th Dalai Lama. In Tibet there were no bookstores with shelves of inventory for sale. When someone wanted a particular text, he placed an order directly with the printer who owned the set of hundreds or thousands of hand-carved printing blocks for that manuscript. In the summer of 1937, all the printers in Lhasa were assigned by the government to the project of completing the hagiography of the 13th Dalai Lama, making it impossible to find even books that otherwise would be common.

Beyond that, the routine complications of Tibet's isolation made every individual process in book printing a slow and laborious one. Before the books could be printed, the paper had to be made. The best paper at the time came from Bhutan, about 350 miles away, and the cost of transportation alone made it expensive. The paper arrived in oblong sheets about two and half feet wide and four or five feet long that first had to be hand-cut to the necessary size for the manuscript. Then several sheets were pasted together and ironed to stiffen it sufficiently. After several rounds of paste and ironing, the paper was ready for the printer.

Tharchin had been searching for weeks before he was able to report his first bit of encouraging news. He had located the blocks for a complete set of medical texts and a rare biography of the 5th Dalai Lama, which contained a valuable history of the country as well as the development of the Gelugpa lineage. They were stored, however, under lock and key in a government warehouse, meaning printers had no access to them. Theos was confident that he could convince the government to release the blocks if only he could find an available printer. He already had an order in for about forty other volumes with a printer, but he had no idea when the printer might get started on them.

Tsarong, as always, was ready to help however he could. Theos had sent two cables to Viola asking her to double the amount of her monthly wire transfer to Theos' Darjeeling bank account to a thousand dollars, but no cables of any kind had made it through from her, and Theos was low on cash. Tsarong offered to extend a line of credit to Theos for the myriad bills he was running up, which would allow Theos to cover his routine expenses with a wire to Viola for a lump sum after he got back to India. He could thus use all of his remaining cash to buy books.

Of all the Tibetan scriptures that were proving impossible to find—in this, the one place in the world where they should be the easiest to get—what most threatened Theos' aspirations for acquiring a comprehensive library was the fact that, even with the aid of the government, he was still unable to find a copy of the Tengyur for sale. Tsarong had recently received for his new shrine room a complete set of the Kangyur and Tengyur printed in Derge, which had taken four years to produce, and he was just then having the cover boards carved for them. Tsarong had earlier promised Theos that he would find a Tengyur as a companion to the Kangyur Theos had bought in Calcutta, but after a few weeks of fruitless searching, he went further to guarantee that if he couldn't find a set, he would sell Theos his complete new Kangyur and Tengyur and wait four more years to have another set printed for himself. Theos was hugely relieved by that assurance and swore in appreciation that if after all this he managed successfully to get the Kangyur and Tengyur to America, he would make them available to every student who wanted them by translating them into English and publishing them as paperbacks.

ONE AFTERNOON a few of the lamas who were writing the biography of the late Dalai Lama stopped in to visit Tsarong. Like the biography of the 5th Dalai Lama that Theos hoped to have printed, this one would chronicle virtually every event of the great 13th's life as well as be a complete history of everything that happened in the country during those years. Tsarong was one of the few still alive who had accompanied the Dalai Lama on his exile march to Mongolia when the British invaded Lhasa in 1904, and the lamas wanted to consult with him about some of the events along the way. They had already written accounts for the biography of how the Dalai Lama had miraculously parted the waters of several deep rivers they came to, and they wanted corroboration from Tsarong. Tsarong, understanding the ramifications, replied cagily that it might have happened sometime when he was not around, but at the moment he couldn't recall having ever been away. Satisfied, the monks left with the request that, should the opportunity ever arise, he do them the favor of substantiating what had been written. That night during dinner, Tsarong entertained Theos and Tsarong Lhacham with American jazz on his phonograph and was eager to hear all about the size of New York City. The thing that concerned Tsarong most was how it could ever be possible to grow enough food for that many people living in such a small area. That indeed was a miracle of modern society to which Theos could testify.

EXACTLY A MONTH after his arrival in Lhasa, Theos was invited to the Potala for a Tantric *puja* for Yamantaka, the deity whose practice he had been initiated into at the Ramoche temple. The ceremony was scheduled for eight-thirty at the glorious stupa of the 13th Dalai Lama in the Potala's Red Palace. They climbed the solid rock flights of stairs up the Potala's lower walls and then, inside the massive gates, were drawn through a maze of halls and up steep and dimly lighted wooden staircases by a growing clamor of braying horns and clashing cymbals. The orchestra's din brought them to the temple of the Nechung oracle, who was about to invoke the temple's spirit to possess him. With plenty of time still before the Yamantaka ceremony, Theos and Tharchin slipped into the temple hoping to witness the event and perhaps even to receive a blessing from the oracle. This was a new state oracle, the last having been replaced after concocting the potion that failed to cure the cold that killed the 13th Dalai Lama.

He was costumed in a seventy-pound outfit of several layers topped by an ornate robe of golden silk brocade. A polished steel circular mirror was mounted on his chest and surrounded by clusters of turquoise and amethyst. When not in a trance, the regalia were so cumbersome he could hardly walk. About thirty seated monks chanted prayers, and the slow beat of the horns, cymbals, and drums continued to work up the atmosphere for coaxing the spirit to enter the oracle. At last he began to quiver, and the drummers and the trumpeters drew closer and closer to him, increasing their volume and finally drumming and blowing directly into his ears.

The oracle began to vibrate, and four strong attendants, barely able to control the volcanic energy of the possessing deity, tried to hold him

down. Suddenly, still seated with legs crossed, the oracle seemed to rico-
chet off the floor to a height at least an arm's length above the heads of his
attendants, and he continued this yogic feat several times before he
stood and paced back and forth, gesturing as if his body were made of
rubber and driven by a coiled spring of enormous power. He was escorted
to his throne, where he knocked back several cups of some drink offered
to him and then broke into an entranced mumbling punctuated at short
intervals with a kind of hiccupping while a scribe wrote down his every
word on a slate for later interpretation.

The oracle then began abruptly to sway from side to side, and that
seemed the cue for an attendant to hand a stack of short red silk scarves to
him, which he tied into sacred knots and cast in all directions. One fell in
Theos' lap, and this was interpreted, he wrote, "as a sign of favor conferring the blessing of the oracle's controlling spirit."

A crowd had gathered at the doors to watch the spectacle, and when
the oracle noticed the onlookers, he threw a silver cup at them and then
hurled whatever was within reach in that direction with a hysterical fury.
By this point it was time for Theos to get on to his *puja*, and he took advantage of the pandemonium to make his way to the chapel containing the
golden *chorten* of the 13th Dalai Lama. He arrived to find an assembly of
about a hundred monks crowded into every corner and awaiting his arrival.
Theos had requested to see a slightly different form of the Yamantaka
ceremony than was performed for him at the Ramoche temple, and today
the officiant was the abbot of the Gyuto Tantric college, Yongdzin Ling
Dorjechang. Ling Rinpoche, as he was known, would become famous as
the senior tutor of the 14th Dalai Lama, and Theos had been fortunate to
have had some informal studies on the "inner teachings" of the Yamantaka
practice with him since his initiation. Theos again had been given permission to photograph the event, and he took the approach that "all we can do
is never stop clicking and hope for the best, for the conditions are most
unfavorable and we must see to it that it is done very quietly, for they are
very touchy on the subject and prefer that it is not done at all."

Theos got his cue and stumbled through the congestion of brocade
capes and crowns to the narrow center aisle, at the head of which he
prostrated himself three times, made his offerings to Ling Rinpoche,

and received his blessing. The monks in unison waved their *dorjes* and rang their bells, and the chamber vibrated with blaring horns, beating drums, clashing cymbals, and the monks' mumbled bass chant. Each precious gem studding the golden *chorten* flickered under the dim rays of light that found their way through the small cupola window, and the myriad yellow flames of the butter lamps created a mood designed to awaken "the most agonizing pangs of yearning for an intenser devotion," Theos wrote. The ritual had its intended effect, "for with flowing emotions, one could not help but feel the meaning."

The difference between his spiritual rapture at that moment and his experience during his first visit to the great stupa three weeks earlier as a tourist illustrates the gulf between Theos Bernard's pilgrimage to the holy shrines of Lhasa and that of all other Westerners before or since. "On our last visit," he wrote, "all was cold and calculated, the same lights were burning on the altar of this priceless treasure, but one did not look thru the same eyes as when taking part in a ceremony under the influence of its mystical rhythm." The massive golden stupa of the 13th Dalai Lama and all the baroque spiritual monuments of Lhasa inspire awe in anyone who sees them—even as snapshots and postcards—but Theos Bernard was very likely the only Westerner in all of history to have experienced them come alive as part of the divine regalia of Tantric ritual.

IN THE MIDDLE of his fifth week in Lhasa, the schedule of ceremonies called for Theos to visit the second of the Three Seats, Sera monastery. Theos and Tharchin were again expected to arrive before daybreak, and as they rode through the twilight fields of mustard, a drenching shower overtook them. They were already rushing to reach the monastery on time, and Theos decided to ride through the squall rather than wait it out under a roof. The soaking left his silk gown looking like a "wrung-out dishrag," but Theos rode on in a buoyant mood, recognizing, as his Tibetan teachers explained to him, that the value of his ride to Sera—and the rituals that awaited him there—depended entirely on what he put into them. If he could hold the right thought, no matter what came, good results would ripen in many lives to come, just as actions in his past lives were responsible for him wanting to come to Lhasa in the first place to take part in these ceremonies.

"Who is to deny that they are right," Theos wrote. "For the scientists cannot disprove it, and the Yogi has his own answer for all actions of man. He does not believe that things just happen to him. Everything is governed by a law of which he can gain understanding, and thereby learn the meaning behind all unfathomable answers."

A group of monks greeted them outside the monastery gates and led them to the main assembly hall, the entire way laid out with the eight auspicious symbols chalked on the paving stones. They were escorted to a protected corner and, as the chanting of the long tea prayer began, were offered the standard *tsampa* breakfast. Theos by this time had developed a taste for the cookie-like dough, and admired the simplicity of being able to carry every meal of the day in a pouch of flour. Even as the monks kneaded the tsampa into the butter tea in their bowls, they didn't sacrifice a syllable of the chant to the preparation of their breakfast.

With the preliminaries finished, Theos went to the center aisle in his drenched gown and, after prostrating himself, made his offerings to the abbot of the monastery and received his blessings. He walked through the files of monks with a bundle of smoldering incense sticks as a symbolic offering to them and then set out on his tour of the monastery, which again offered open access to all its secret Tantric shrines.

After the tour, Theos had lunch with the abbots of Sera's three colleges. Their conception of the cosmos was so different from his scientific view that Theos could not get them to understand why it was possible for it to be night in America when it was day in Tibet. It was fascinating anthropology, but Theos felt the dread of certainty that "change is inevitably coming, and I fear within my own lifetime, which means that my next visit to Tibet may be entirely different, unless I can make it very soon."

EVEN ON DAYS Theos didn't have a predawn appointment, the songs of the household's workmen guaranteed he would be up long before the sun came over the high ridges shading the valley. As he discovered, the moment a Tibetan began to work—man, woman, or child—he immediately broke into song and didn't stop singing until the job was finished. The chorus began at five outside Theos' windows when the servants watered the flowerpots and continued through the day with the men and women laying stone in the courtyard. The constant voices could make it difficult to concentrate on his studies; "however if you but give into it and go to the windows and watch them," Theos wrote, "you are more thrilled than disgruntled to feel that creatures can get such a joy out of their burden and that nothing ever seems to be too much trouble."

Theos was told that every occupation had its own songbook. Whether it was plowing, sowing, harvesting, or loading for market, rock breaking, road building, sewing, weaving, or grinding barley, every job was a specialty distinguished by the tunes that accompanied the labor. When Theos asked what would happen if a whole new category of work such as stringing electrical wires was introduced, he was told that the words mattered less than the rhythm, and some tune in the occupational repertoire with the proper beat could always be found for the job. All agreed that crews could stay at the job longer with less fatigue when they were singing, and as Theos noted, "When twenty or thirty of them are working together at the same task they produce something that is worthy of being recorded."

Often the songs drifting on the breeze through his open window were accompanied by the metal clack of Theos' typewriter keys. Along with the four single-spaced pages Theos typed in his journal every day without fail, he continued to type long letters to Viola, which he sent out with each of the twice-weekly postal runners leaving Lhasa. The typewriter mesmerized the Tibetans. Theos wrote in one letter that there were three Tibetans on the mat with him watching with the fascination of a child as each key struck the page and left a letter behind. Over and over again they giggled as each demonstrated the finger movements in the air to the others, and Theos had to be cautious about returning the carriage so that it didn't poke one of them in the eye. Although they were mystified by the action of the levers and gears, they did understand that it would take a scribe hours to draw the Tibetan letters saying what Theos tapped out in minutes. Seeing a similar inscrutable mechanics at work, they gave the Underwood the same name they used for the harmonium that one of the Nepalese had with him in Lhasa.

Although Theos was sending out letters to Viola twice a week, after a month he still hadn't received one from her, and he worried that his might not be getting through either. His two cables brought no reply as well, and in a letter he warned her: "If I continue to go like this without a word from you, I am going to fly straight home to see what is wrong, for I cannot carry on in this part of the world, if there is the slightest feeling that things are not absolutely perfect with you." At last, during his fifth week in Lhasa, a long letter arrived that Viola had written two and a half months earlier.

She had been writing at least once a week but, not trusting the instructions from Theos to address his mail simply to "Bernard, Gyantse, Tibet," she continued to use the Kalimpong address and the delays had come in forwarding from India. As for the cables, they discovered that Lhasa wouldn't accept foreign telegrams and the cables had been routed to Gyantse and put in the mail to Lhasa from there.

Viola, as the first letters to come in explained, had finished her internship in the Jersey City Medical Center's obstetrics ward at the end of April and was transferred then to work in the men's and women's psychopathic wards. Not long after she started there, the intern in charge of the ward isolating contagious diseases quit, and she was assigned to cover that ward as well. On top of that, there was only one intern rather than the usual two in the men's and women's pneumonia wards, and every other night Viola had to handle those as well. Her shifts for the two and a half jobs she was doing required her to be on duty for thirty-six hours straight (a day, a night, and the next day) before she got the next twelve hours off. Not surprisingly, the fatigue left her vulnerable to her own illnesses, and she developed a succession of infections on four fingers and a toe and then got the worst cold she'd ever had, which infected her left sinus.

She realized that her summer's experience could hardly be more different from her husband's, and wrote: "Your letters sound as though you were on the trail of your rainbow and from down here I salute you." In another letter she wrote, "I am happy for you that you are having a chance to soar inside . . . and damn it you're making history. In fact it . . . scares me a little . . . in the sense that you are existing on such a peak of experience right now that it will be difficult not to let everything afterwards seem rather anticlimax-ish."

She felt strongly, especially after reading his letters from Gyantse, that he should shelve for the time his ideas for a book of photographs and an academic tract for his Ph.D. and write instead a popular book about Tibet while the experience was "all hot and fresh." They decided that Viola would take a six-month break between the completion of her internship at the end of December and the start of her psychiatric residency, and they both agreed that what they needed first was, as she put it, "just some plain being together ... before rejoining the beehive." That time, Viola urged, should be used for Theos to organize his movies and photographs and to write his book, and she would be his secretary and manager. Viola proposed that they rent a rustic chalet in the Alps for the winter and then get a country house in England for the spring "and just play house and be together and exist and let the experiences you've had digest into me." They would return to the United States in May and by that time be ready for the inevitable round of New York parties. For his part, Theos was ready to "rub off a little of this Lamaistic Sainthood and feel like a human being once again ... I am anxious to ... see how refreshing it feels to cuss and raise hell again."

But beyond that point, they still didn't know how they would meld their diverging lives into a single future. The regent offered to arrange for Theos to spend a few years studying in one of the monasteries, but, he reassured Viola, he preferred building his own and working close to her. What the world needs today is not one to reveal the truth, for that can be found, but a leader who can show us how to adapt those teachings to our new set of facts."

Viola concluded one of her letters—written at the end of a thirty-six-hour shift—saying she felt discouraged. "Why? Because what's the use of all this effort at the grubby side of this medical business—I just don't see the end of it fulfilling for me unless I pay too big a price because of its lack of place ... in the future you are envisioning."

Theos replied: "Come and join hands with me and give your medical training to the world thru a new channel." His goal was to reveal the truth of the Yoga teachings thru modern means and methods, which would require the kind of experimentation that Lindbergh was urging. "It will not be possible without you," Theos pleaded, ". . . for all of the physical and psychological researches on the work of Yoga are to be directed by you."

As their wedding anniversary neared, Viola wrote, "In a couple of days I'll be . . . remembering a certain August first when a young feller and me waved a marriage certificate in the face of a cab as they hurried hell bent for their own wedding! Well we haven't behaved like other people then or since—have we—but as long as we know why and we like it that way what the hell—so say I three years later."

Chapter 9

THE HERMIT'S BLESSING

ON JULY 29, near the end of his fifth week in Lhasa, Theos set off on a trip to visit the last of the Three Seats, Ganden monastery. The great complex of five thousand monks was set at the top of a high ridge thirty miles east of Lhasa, but the six days they planned for the excursion would allow a leisurely pace. Even though it had already been a wet summer, the government continued with ceremonies to bring rain, and Tsarong and the whole household came out on the porch steps to see them off with the hope they wouldn't get too wet from the lowering black clouds.

The entourage Theos set off with had grown to a party of seven. Along with Tharchin and the two attendants from Kalimpong, Norphel and Lhare, there was the official guide appointed by the Kashag and his servant, and the two servants from Tsarong's household staff who had been assigned to Theos on his arrival.

They were off by ten and within a half hour arrived at a sandy spot on the Kyichu River where three yak-skin *kowas* were propped on sticks waiting to ferry them across. A change of transport greeted them on the far bank, but after traveling only about five miles with them, they had to switch again to another owner's stock. While waiting for the headman to bring the ponies in from the fields for the next stage, they talked with a few of the traders and sheepherders hanging around and with one man who shuffled about with heavy iron shackles on his ankles. Since the *jong-pens* who tried local cases didn't have prison systems in their districts, many of Tibet's convicts were sentenced to roam about in leg irons or in a cangue, a collar-like pillory about three feet square that locked around the convict's neck. This heavy board collar was large enough so that the convict couldn't feed himself with his own hands, and he was left to depend on the kindness of his family or passersby to put food and water in his mouth. The man Theos talked with was sentenced to wander in shackles for life because a device he had made to kill foxes had found a human victim instead.

They rode up the valley all day through fields of ripening wheat and fragrant yellow mustard against a steady traffic of lamas, pilgrims, traders, sheepherders, and women towing clutches of snot-nosed children, all walking to sacred Lhasa. By dark they reached the base of the Ganden ridge and settled for the night in a large rock house abandoned by some absentee noble. The government guide broke the seal on the long-unoccupied private room of the owner and offered the dusty quarters to Theos for the night. By six the next morning they started the climb up the rocky trail to the monastery, and just before the top they encountered a lama posted there to warn visitors to take the bells off their animals; Tri Rinpoche was in residence and nothing should disturb his meditations. As they crested the ridge they got their first sight of Ganden, a large complex of three-story buildings arrayed up the slope among the gathering clouds, a sight to "awaken all the religious awe any soul might possess," Theos wrote.

They were guided to the main temple and escorted to their quarters in a long room above the main entrance, an entire wall of which was filled with the pigeonhole cabinets holding the six-hundred-year-old sets of the Kangyur and Tengyur used by the incomparable Je Tsongkapa, the founder of the Gelugpa lineage of the Dalai Lamas, and the founder in 1409 of Ganden monastery. Every five minutes a different boy—curious to see this bearded American who wore Tibetan robes and spoke to his servants in their own language—would arrive with an earthen pot of tea. Each boy removed the silver lid from Theos' cup, topped it off with butter tea, and then handed it to him for an obligatory sip before topping it off again.

Theos and his entourage had arrived early and had most of the day to tour the monastery. Almost every bump and crevice of the hillside had some story connecting it with a miraculous feat of Je Tsongkapa. Their guide explained that the great saint had once thrown the cuttings from his hair to the winds, and they had been growing ever since as the patches of moss before them. At another spot, he pointed out the high-water mark of the next flood that would destroy the world and then a rock marking the height of the flames when the world was destroyed by fire. Both indicated that Ganden was safely above them and would survive the destruction.

The next morning, Theos was awakened long before sunrise by the chorus of a few thousand monks gathered for morning prayers. He was filled with an inexpressible joy, and as he wrote in his journal that night: "I tried to feel all that was happening to me at the moment so that I could relive it someday when I am a thousand or so miles away from here and have almost forgotten that such things exist any longer."

Even though it was the middle of summer, snow had fallen during the night on the higher peaks, and at Ganden's fourteen-thousand-foot elevation, the crisp air had Theos getting hastily from the warm bed into his clothes. His attendants fussed over every fold in his robes and ironed the sash that tied around his waist, and when the monks downstairs in the temple reached the end of their tea chant, Theos went down to join them. The hall vibrated with the prayers Theos had requested supplicating the protection of Drolma, or Tara, who is often referred to as the "Mother of all the Buddhas" and is connected with longevity and overcoming obstacles to spiritual practice. He was conducted down the center aisle between what appeared to be all five thousand Ganden monks sitting in twelve long rows. When he reached the altar at the front, a monk poured saffron water from a silver vase into Theos' cupped hands. He sipped the purifying nectar and then put the rest of it on his head.

Tri Rinpoche was seated on a ten-foot-high throne with a small enclosure atop it that concealed him from the monks below but allowed him a view of everyone in the hall. Theos slowly ascended the stairway of the throne, and at the top he found Tri Rinpoche wrapped in golden robes with a smiling face that seemed to flicker like a candle flame under the single beam of sunlight that shined on him from a high, small window. Theos promptly made three prostrations and then sat on a cushion in front of him and meditated while Tri Rinpoche recited mantras. Theos next presented the customary offerings of a small image of Lord Buddha, a scripture, and a sacred knotted scarf, representing enlightened body, speech, and mind, and then bowed his head to receive the warm, blessing touch of Tri Rinpoche's fingers and then his forehead.

Theos wrote that, "overflowing with the energy which he had caused to be released from my subconscious," he descended the stairs "to the world of name and form, symbolized by the endless rituals performed in the temple room below, where the Lamas were still repeating their chants." He then slowly felt his way up and down the twelve aisles, making symbolic offerings to the vast assembly of monks with sticks of smoking incense. In their ranks Theos saw that "just about every specimen of humanity living is to be found amongst them, cock-eyed, deformed, crippled, and maimed . . . Really it is almost as bad as visiting one of our institutions for the mentally deficient." There were some (presumably belonging to the clubs of fighting monks that made up between 10 and 15 percent of the population at each of the big monasteries) who had ghastly scars on their heads. These, Theos was told, resulted from fights with the big iron keys they carried, "beating one another until both are a gory mess and one confesses defeat. Then they patch one another up and continue on the friendship in full light of who is the most powerful."

After tea was served, Theos followed a committee of guides and their small butter lamps down the long, narrow passages leading to the monastery's innermost sanctuaries and the tomb of the illustrious Je Tsongkapa. An antechamber with large protector deities guarded the tomb, and a number of stuffed yaks, said to be heroes of the monastery construction, hung from the ceiling. The room also looked to be some sort of celestial armory, with a great variety of spears, shields, armor, bows and arrows, swords, and crude muskets lining the walls.

They entered the shrine, and Theos offered a *kata* at the altar and then walked clockwise around the large *chorten* in which reposed the body of one of Tibet's greatest scholars, authors, and yogis. His guide told Theos that the tomb was opened periodically and that they always found the body of Je Tsongkapa, who died in 1419, still perfectly preserved. In fact, Theos was told, the fingernails and hair continued to grow, and when the tomb was opened they received a trimming.

After the tour, Theos visited Tri Rinpoche alone in his sanctuary for a couple of hours. About those hours, Theos wrote in his journal only that there was "the performance of a private ritual," and "the results of these discussions will appear at odd intervals in the diary." But with the rush of events that followed, Theos never returned in his journal or letters to a description of his private hours with Tri Rinpoche. It was still early in the day, and Theos and his entourage hoped that by getting a head start for home, they might arrive back in Lhasa a day earlier than planned. And so, having spent a total of about twenty-four hours at Ganden, they departed immediately after the interview.

They rode back down the steep trail to the braided river and arrived at their campsite at sunset. There, under a large tent, a group of lamas chanted the third day of a ceremony to bring rain and a good harvest, and on this night, without even a hovel nearby to sleep in, they put up their own tent. After a greasy meal prepared over an improvised pot of burning dung, Theos was typing the day's journal pages by candlelight in the tent when a fierce storm blew in and rained torrents on them.

The tent shook and flapped in the deafening roar of the wind, and within minutes everything in the tent was wet. Theos threw the typewriter and his papers into one of the pack boxes and covered them with yak-hair rugs while the boys rigged a tarp under the leaking tent ceiling, which provided just enough space for them all to huddle between the dripping edges.

With the sudden intimacy, Theos and Tharchin shared their thoughts about their experiences at the great monasteries around Lhasa. Drepung, Sera, and Ganden, they agreed, operated more like towns than universities, and in their combined population of twenty-two thousand monks, the range of intelligence, activities, and spiritual acumen was great. Less than a third of all monks there were "readers," studying in the monasteries' colleges. The rest could typically read and recite only their prayer books. In contrast to the surge of devotional rapture Theos had felt during his Yamantaka *puja* at the stupa of the 13th Dalai Lama, his visits to Lhasa's big monasteries left Theos with a growing impatience for what he called the "superstitions of the ignorant believers," who treat as literal what the great teachers regarded merely as "an essential beginning, in much the same way that among us the belief in Santa Claus is supposed to help small children in doing the right thing."

Theos concluded that the ritual-bound practices he saw dominating spiritual life at the monasteries were worse "than our own conduit of dissatisfaction." "Never did Buddha try to formulate a religion," he wrote when he got back to his typewriter.

It was philosophy first and foremost—and what we need today is philosophy first and last.... Today we are unable to see how anything that was taught to the people of mythological times has anything to do with us who seem to know so much, but...are battling with the same problems of love, hate, graft, greed, jealousy, envy, ambition for power. However, a leader will come and give expression to the universal truths of life in light of modern understanding.

As Theos Bernard sat typing his reflections by candlelight in a wet and flapping tent in remote Tibet, he was fully aware that history was offering him a unique opportunity and demanding a unique responsibility. Would he be that leader to recast the universal truths around which the monastic rituals had become encrusted? Would he be the one to deliver to the modern world the essence of these 2,500-year-old antidotes to hate, greed, and jealousy? "What," he wondered, "is the best means to serve as a vehicle of universal happiness?"

He had been in the Lhasa area five weeks and completed his pilgrimages to Lhasa's monumental temples and monasteries, but what now? He had made little progress in finding copies of the essential scriptures to bring home with him, and he had received only scant instructions on the esoteric practices that he believed could turn arid ritual into life-changing realizations. For all the pomp of his welcome in Lhasa and the historic open access he had been given to secret shrines and ceremonies, he had found little so far that might serve as a foundation for happiness in the modern world.

THEY WERE UP EARLY the next morning and had to pack their gear before it dried out in order to visit a hermitage high on a ridge across the river. The river had risen several feet during the night, flooding sections of the trail and forcing them to take high-water detours to get above obstructing cliff bands. Along the way they stopped at the small village of Dechen—not much more than a mud alley between a dozen rock houses—and heard that the nearby monastery was having a dance festival. Theos was delighted to hear that the climax would be a performance of the famous Black Hat Dance, a commemoration of the assassination of King Langdharma, the usurper king who, two generations after King Songtsan Gampo built the Jokhang, tried to revive the Bon religion and wipe out Buddhism in Tibet. They joined the small crowd at the monastery, and Theos was amazed that the quality of the costumes and the dancers in such a backwater was better even than what he had seen at Gyantse. That was explained when he was told that the 13th Dalai Lama had been a patron of the festival and, as well as attending performances, had paid for both the dancers' training and their costumes.

They spent the night at the village, and it was three o'clock the next afternoon before the Black Hat dance concluded and they resumed their journey to Drag Yerpa, a small, remote monastery that was famous for its meditation caves. To get there, Theos and his group first had to cross the swollen river in a *kowa* and then wait on the other side for an hour while horses were brought in from the fields for them. It was already late afternoon, and with five miles still to climb up the high valley to Drag Yerpa, Theos was happy to be given an excitable stallion "who was ready to mount anything and everything." Ahead of him they put a mare, which, in trying to escape, led them in a gallop up the rocky trail, blowing past two stations where they were supposed to change animals with a wave.

It was already dark when, about a quarter mile from the top, they found a guide waiting with a lantern to lead them through clusters of *chor-*

tens and a dense thicket of wild roses to Drag Yerpa. They left the horses at the main gate of the temple and followed the lamp of another monk up several flights of rock stairs to a small room with a view overlooking the whole moonlit valley. Rumors of the reception Theos was receiving from Tibet's highest officials and lamas had spread even to this remote hermitage, and the abbots here as well insisted on arranging a ceremony to honor him on the following day.

The next morning Theos was escorted by a group of monks through a dense cloud that shrouded the ridge for a brief look at the twenty or so temples built into walled-off caves in the limestone cliffs. The meditation caves at Drag Yerpa were considered to be among the most sacred sites in all Tibet. The caves had been consecrated by the retreats of the dharma king Songtsan Gampo in the seventh century, the frequent stays of Padmasambhava and his consort Yeshe Tsogyal in the eighth century, and the meditations of the illustrious Indian sage Atisha in the tenth century. In view of that history, Theos asked if, along with the hundred monks that lived at Drag Yerpa's small gompas, there might also be a hermit living in one of the caves. His guides led Theos to a small wooden door in the stone wall blocking off a cave entrance, and a monk reverentially whispered to Theos that behind that door lived a hermit who had been in solitary retreat for ten years. Before coming here, the hermit had spent twelve years in a cave in a different valley, and when he finished twelve years at Drag Yerpa, he planned to move to the area where the great yogi Milarepa had had his cave and start another twelve-year retreat there.

The silence of all those years was shattered by a gasp from the monks when, against all protocol, Theos brazenly knocked on the rough planks of the door. After a few dread-filled moments, all were equally shocked to hear a voice inviting him to enter. Inside the small cell, Theos found a lean but strong-looking man sitting placidly in his square meditation box. The monks had said the hermit was sixty-five, but he looked to Theos to be closer to forty. There was not a gray hair on his head or in his beard, his skin was supple, and his voice—although unused in conversation for years—was vigorous.

The small rock cell held a large image of the thousand-armed Chenrezig and several *thangkas* depicting the Kagyu masters Tilopa, Naropa,

Marpa, and Milarepa, the Tantric lineage into which the hermit had been initiated. Most of the hermit's life in retreat was spent in his small meditation box, a cockpit where he meditated and slept upright in the same cross-legged position. One small window in the cell admitted just enough light to read by, and on a small shelf, within reach of his box, were four large folio volumes of scripture and several smaller ones wrapped in silk. On his left, also within reach, were his ritual articles. In fact, he could reach almost everything in the room without moving from his box. His caretakers brought one helping of tsampa and a little milk each day, which they left at the door without seeing him.

Theos could hardly contain his enthusiasm. This was exactly the kind of yogi he had hoped to meet in Tibet, and he had endless questions for him. The hermit refused to answer any of them with the crowd of monks around his door, but, sensing in the direction of Theos' questions "a little different approach than had ever come his way," he told Theos to come back with only his interpreter a little later, and he would tell him what he wanted to know.

Theos left and continued with his stunned guides on the tour of the dark cave shrines in the fog. They came at last to the shrine of Padmasambhava, the place that Theos had requested be the location for the ceremony they wanted to do for him. The ceremony was intended to be the highlight of the day, but Theos could hardly keep his mind on the ritual proceedings, and the minute it was over, he returned with Tharchin to the cave of the hermit.

The hermit was waiting and told Theos to lock the door. Theos prostrated himself, requested three times "the desires of my heart," "crawled to him as is customary when making a request from a learned master of divine wisdom," and then offered him a *kata*. Before beginning, the hermit placed over his left shoulder and under his right arm a cloth sash in which three lines were sewn in reddish thread, representing the three main channels through which the winds of the subtle body travel—Sushumna, Ida, and Pingala—and, at a position representing the location of the chakras, the secret syllable of each was woven.

The hermit had open on a small table in front of him several folio scriptures, from which he "mumbled with a ringing voice in the typical

Tibetan rhythm which one can never forget nor can he ever repeat." At prescribed points he placed a variety of sacred objects on Theos' head and at other points tossed wheat seeds and passed to Theos holy water, holy butter, and precious peas of blessed *tsampa* to put in his mouth. And with this, Theos wrote in his journal, the unnamed hermit passed on the direct lineage of Milarepa and the authority to carry on his teaching and spread them to those who were worthy.

The hermit then gave Theos oral instructions for a collection of completion-stage Tantric practices called the Six Yogas of Naropa: "practices of meditation, concentration, breathing, and the union of the two spiritual poles within," as Theos wrote. The practices, known as Naro Choe Druk in Tibetan, were first taught by the Indian master Tilopa about a thousand years ago and are usually described as including *tummo*, the yoga of inner fire; *gyulu*, the yoga of the illusory body; *osel*, the yoga of the clear light; *milam*, the yoga of the dream state; *bardo*, the yoga of the intermediate state between death and rebirth; and *phowa*, the yoga of the transference of consciousness to a Buddha paradise.

The hermit told Theos that during a retreat, he should spend two hours on each of the Six Yogas and take a two-hour break between them, which created of the set a twenty-four hour practice. During the practices, Theos was instructed to regulate his breath so that each round of inhalation and exhalation was marked by the time it took a six-inch stick of incense to burn down. Perfection of the practices, the hermit assured, would lead to full enlightenment in this lifetime.

The hermit produced a chart and referred to two small handwritten books in which the Six Yogas were outlined to describe how the practices related to the three main channels of the subtle body. He then offered to let Theos take these secret handwritten scriptures with him so that he could have a copy made of them in Lhasa and be able to refer to them himself when instructing others. Theos remained sitting cross-legged almost the entire afternoon before his "holy master of this divine line of saints on earth." It was only because he had offered himself as a true disciple, Theos realized, that a portion of the secret scriptures he had so ardently sought had found him. The hours sped by, and as Theos made his prostrations at the door before leaving the hermit, the words of the Kagyu

Lama in the Chumbi Valley on his first day in Tibet returned to him. When Theos had asked how to find a teacher to prepare him for Tantric initiation, the lama replied, "When you are ready, the answer will come." As Theos closed the rough plank door on the hermit's cave, he realized with gratitude and wonder that by that calculus, the arrival of the answer was proof that the disciple had been ready to hear it.

When Theos and Tharchin arrived back at their quarters, "the monks were more than amazed," Theos wrote in his journal, "for even they who take care of this holy one had not been able to ever be given such an audience. Who was I that I could walk right in, they didn't know but they thought it must be something divine."

It was already late afternoon, but rather than face a night of stupefied inquiries from the monks, Theos decided to attempt the fifteen miles back to Lhasa before dark. The monks brought more gifts of eggs, butter, and a lump of *tsampa* bread, and then paid him the great honor of presenting a *thangka* to link their hermitage with America. Theos and his entourage were on the trail by six, and even though they had to change horses five times, they pushed their mounts as fast as they would go in between, and made it to Lhasa in just two and a half hours.

They rounded the bend revealing the first view of the Potala—still faintly visible in a fading purple glow—but they were at last forced by darkness to a walking pace, and Theos could at last reflect on what happened to him that afternoon. His initiation from the hermit was not only the culmination of his pilgrimage to Tibet but something he had dreamed of finding for years: "the direct teaching of the meditative principles passed down from Mila, the great Yogi of Tibet ... So I am more or less ready to return home," he typed in his journal that night.

Tsarong was astounded to hear that the hermit had granted Theos the Lung, Wang, and Tri—that is, the recitation of the sacred scripture, the empowerment to practice and pass it on, and the oral instruction—but he was even more amazed that the hermit had allowed Theos to take those treasured secret books to have them copied. "This was all a miracle of the first order," Theos wrote. "He just cannot make it out."

FEELING NOW that he had already reached the climax of his pilgrimage, Theos abandoned his plan to leave Tibet through China and the war zone on the eastern border. The Kashag, delighted to hear that, eagerly granted his request for permission to detour into western Tibet on his way back to India. He would turn off the main trade route back to Gyantse to visit Shigatse, Tibet's second-largest city and the home of the Panchen Lama's monastery, Tashilhunpo. From there, he would continue another three days west and south to the rarely visited home of the fourth and once domi-nant lineage of Tibetan Buddhism, the Sakyas.

It was already the first week of August, and Theos realized that it would take a month to reach Kalimpong by this route. He would have to leave Lhasa by September 15 or risk crossing the Himalayan passes in deep snow. With a long list of details to take care of during his last five weeks, his focus shifted from "the depths of inner consciousness to skip-ping along with the external actions of daily living." The heavy rains con-tinued, encouraging him to stay inside and continue his studies, which along with Tibetan grammar now included the Tibetan handwriting script called U-me, a system of entirely different letter shapes than the U-chen printed script. He had also received another batch of his devel-oped film and contact prints from Kodak in Calcutta, and when he real-ized that he couldn't remember the names of the bungalows on the way to Gyantse, he decided he had to dedicate some time to the laborious task of identifying and indexing the several thousand photographs he now had.

By this point as well, Tsarong had realized that he wasn't going to find a suitable set of the Tengyur for Theos, and as promised, he agreed to sell him his for a very reasonable price of 2,500 rupees. Tsarong had spent much more than that when the books first arrived after their 1,300-mile trip from Kham just for a group of high lamas to bless the volumes with a lavish ceremony attended by all his friends. He'd then spent 5,000 rupees (almost $1,900 at the time) for the fine silk to wrap them in. "I am more or less compelled," Theos wrote, "to demonstrate my intentions of taking care of them as I would if I adopted one of his children."

The first thing to be done with the 333 volumes was to have the neces-sary markers made, which, hanging over the edge on the outside, allowed a particular book to be found without unwrapping the bundle. The markers were made from three different colors of silk—red, yellow, and blue—with each layer being slightly larger so that the color below created a border for the one above. Below these, on a piece of plain yellow silk, the volume was identified with a sequence of Tibetan letters, and then finally, below that, was written on a piece of white silk a descriptive title of the book. Theos brought in two lamas to help with the job, one a *geshe* from Sera and the other a monk from Drepung. They both moved right into the Tsarong household and spent long days and nights checking every one of the pages of all the volumes and creating a separate index.

The *durzi*, or tailor, required thirteen assistants just to cut out the markers. The yards and yards of red, blue, and yellow silk they strewed across the floor of his rooms reminded Theos nostalgically of autumn in New England. Across the hall in the other wing of the house, ten carpenters sat on the floor with rough boards clamped between their toes and buried themselves in shavings as they planed their way down to a suitable board to make the wood boxes for the books. Once the boxes were made and the books indexed, each volume would be wrapped in handmade Tibetan paper, and then the boxes would be sewn up in waterproofed yak skins for safe transport by mule, train, and ship, halfway around the world.

Aside from the Kangyur and Tengyur, some of the other scriptures they had ordered started coming in from the printers. The printer commissioned to find the sixty-four-volume set and the very rare seven-volume set that together were reputed to contain virtually the complete corpus of Tibetan Tantra had to travel several days from Lhasa to find them and was now making daily visits to Theos to settle on a price. "One never buys on the first two or three tries," Theos wrote, "for by the time the seller has dragged them back and forth a few times, he is more or less willing to come down to something which you consider reasonable.... Then too, we find that the psychology of making them bring the books here and inspecting them amongst all the rest which we have already purchased has a strong effect."

They were still unable, however, to get copies of the twenty-five volumes on Tibetan medicine Theos wanted, and now, complicating the picture, they got word that all the printers in Lhasa were being called back to work by the government in a few days. Again the regent came to their aid.

When Theos explained the situation to him, he sent orders to unlock the government warehouse that secured the printing blocks Theos needed and to assign sufficient printers to ensure that Theos got not only the medical texts but also anything else he wanted from their inventory before he left Lhasa.

While Theos attended to all those details, Tharchin searched the bazaar for some of the other things on their list. Theos found it ironic that while a powerful taboo kept monasteries and individual owners from selling sacred art or texts in their collection, the markets were full of articles that the government had confiscated in lieu of back taxes from the exiled Panchen Lama and his officials in Shigatse. "In all there were thousands upon thousands of thangkas that were sold," Theos wrote, "and they have gathered a reputation with every mile that they have traveled from Shigatse on the way to Indian markets."

Theos noted as well that an item's value increased greatly if it had been blessed by a high lama. His standard reply was to keep the blessing and sell him the object. One day a trader brought over a *dorje* priced at several hundred rupees because of the blessing that could stop bullets and protect a person from all harm if he kept it with him. Theos proposed to buy the *dorje* at a much higher figure if the seller would demonstrate its power by tying it around the neck of a dog and shooting it. There was no deal on that item.

HIS FRONTIER PASS from the Government of India was set to expire on August 15, and on the day before it did, Theos went out to the British mission's compound to get a renewal. Norbu nonchalantly gave him a two-month extension, and then, after a quick drink, they went to the lawn for a few sets of badminton accompanied by the songs of the workers building Lhasa's first tennis court.

Over dinner, Norbu filled Theos in on the latest about Tucci, who was still stalled in Gyantse with his troupe, which included—along with a head secretary, clerks, cooks, and bearers—a crew of photographers shooting four hundred frames a day at the monastery in anticipation of his publishing a book about it. Tucci's trade route pass was expiring soon and he had given up hopes of getting to Shigatse, but in a last-ditch effort he had sent four letters to the Tibetan government and several letters to the British trade agent arguing that since this fellow Bernard was virtually living in Lhasa, he, as one of the world's greatest Tibet scholars, should be given at least equal consideration. One letter to Norbu offered, crazily, to recommend him to Mussolini for an Italian title if he could help him get a permit to Lhasa.

Even the telegraphers seemed to be conspiring against the Italian. Theos had sent a wire to Captain Cable, his polo partner in Gyantse, that gave him a good-natured ribbing about being stuck at that outpost and not getting up to enjoy the luxuries of the British mission in Lhasa. The message, however, was mistakenly delivered to Tucci, who, outraged at the perceived insult, found Cable and spat out a string of passionate invectives against this Bernard he was hearing so much about. Captain Cable, as the story was told to Theos, was obliged to defend his friend and coolly "took him down a notch."

Theos could appreciate Tucci's frustration. He knew the scholar had been trying for over ten years to get a full set of the Kangyur and Tengyur and that he had undoubtedly been hearing reports about all the assistance the government had been giving Theos with his collecting in Lhasa. He must have known that the long list of books he was looking for would be going to America rather than Italy. "I am just a few months ahead of him and there are only a few copies to be found," Theos wrote, "and he does not have the prize I do with Tharchin."

Theos was acutely aware that much of his success in Lhasa was due to the goodwill Tharchin had built up over the years with Lhasa's elites. At home, however, Tharchin's dedication to the mission was causing trouble. His wife, who had been born in Lhasa and hadn't seen her family in ten years, was complaining about his long absence and that he hadn't brought her with him. There was also a threat that because he had been away so long, his family might be thrown out of their house in Kalimpong. One of Tharchin's several jobs in Kalimpong was with a Scottish missionary society, which, along with a small salary, provided a tiny three-room house. They had given Tharchin a leave of absence, but it had expired six weeks earlier, and when he applied for an extension, the director replied that he should consider the work of the Almighty before his own.

Complicating things even further was the fact that, because of the problems Viola was having with the bank transfers, Theos had been unable to pay Tharchin since they left. Tharchin, however, wasn't about to abandon the project at this point. He knew the historic significance of this American pilgrim's visit and was thinking about writing a book of his own. They were also discussing plans for Tharchin to join Theos the following year at Oxford, where they would begin translating some of the texts they were collecting for Theos' doctoral degree.

THE REGENT RETURNED to Lhasa in the middle of August from his five-week trip to Reting monastery and invited Theos to a three-day performance he was sponsoring of the Ache Lhamo, or Tibetan opera. For only one week of the year, from the first to the eighth of the Tibetan seventh month, the traveling companies of the Ache Lhamo were permitted to perform within the walls of the city. The rest of the year these professional troupes traveled across Tibet dramatizing religious history and the lives of the Buddha and important saints.

Theos planned to leave at nine for the first day of the performance sponsored by the regent, and on his way out of the house, he found Tsarong at the weekly task of leveling his sundial, the first step in synchronizing the clocks of the house, all of which seemed to run at a different pace. Theos was never sure which standard to set his watch to. In Lhasa, Sun Time, Daylight Saving Time, Indian Standard Time, Calcutta Standard Time, and Potala Time were all used, and with over an hour's difference between them, it was necessary, if he wanted to be on time, to start early for an appointment.

The opera must have followed one of the earlier time standards, because the pavilion of the monastery behind Reting's living quarters was already packed with a crowd of about five thousand and the performance was well under way when Theos arrived. All eyes, however turned to follow this tall, white-skinned foreigner dressed as a Tibetan noble as he made his way to a special tent set up for him and the British on a top-tier balcony.

All Lhasa seemed to be invited, and the crowd ranged from those wearing their only set of rags and sitting on the paving stones in the court-yard to bejeweled noblewomen in outfits saved only for this appearance. The more honored guests sat at different levels of the enclosed pavilion according to their rank. Theos and the British legation were honored with a tent on the top tier directly opposite the regent and prime minister, and next to them was the tent of the Chinese mission.

The opera told the story of the Tibetan king Songtsan Gampo win-ning the hand of the Chinese princess. The Chinese emperor staged a competition between her suitors—the most powerful sovereigns of the East—with the winner taking his daughter home. The tests culminated with the arrival of a batch of alluring girls, one of whom was the princess. The contestants were forced to drink huge amounts of *chang* and were then told they could keep the girl of their choice. Songtsan Gampo had wisely offered the *chang* to his deities before drinking it, and they sent him an astrologer who told him the real princess would have a turquoise fly buzz-ing about her face. Of course, he chose wisely, and the emperor sent the princess off to Tibet with the sacred statue of the twelve-year-old Buddha now in the Jokhang as part of her dowry.

All of this was performed during the course of nine hours to the ac-companiment of incessant drumbeats and cymbal clashes while the per-formers, in an array of costumes, tossed one foot back and forth and every now and then raised their arms like soaring wings and occasionally added a whirl. There were two intermissions, during which meals were brought to the tent, and the usual constant servings of tea throughout the day.

At one point during the performance, Tsiang, the Chinese official, came next door to say hello, and Norbu felt obligated to tell him the latest news heard on the wireless about the fighting between Chinese and Japa-nese forces in downtown Shanghai, the first full-scale battle in China of World War II, a horror that would last eight years there and claim an es-timated thirty-six million casualties.

Tsiang flew into a rage at the mention of the fighting "and commenced to drool and froth at the mouth and his armed escort drew their guns," Theos wrote in his journal. "It was a tense moment and we all thought that there was going to be a killing, and the crowd was gathering rapidly— you could hear him holler above the drone of the beating drum and all eyes were focused in our direction." Norbu diplomatically left the tent without another word. Theos went to the Chinese tent later and was able to calm Tsiang, but he dared not mention the Japanese again.

They rode to the second day of the opera festival in a drizzle, and the mud in the streets was worse than ever. As they rode splashing down the lanes, the elegantly dressed Tibetan women holding up their skirts and wading through the filthy ooze—"none of them with less than 25,000 rupees worth of ornamentation"—provided an incongruous scene to be found nowhere but in Tibet.

The story of the second day's performance involved a king who, disappointed that none of his five hundred queens had given him a son, married the beautiful daughter of a forest hermit. Naturally, the displaced queens' jealousy inspired intrigues, and, believing their lies, the king banished the new queen, who returned to the forest to become a nun. After twelve years, one of the jealous queens confessed her treachery to the nun, beginning a chain of scenes reconciling old enemies, and after nine hours everyone lived happily in the kingdom.

Near the middle of the performance, a servant came into the British tent and asked if they needed to use the restroom. Theos and Fox gladly followed the servant down to the street and past an alley in which men, women, children, and lamas were squatting together; the dogs, as Theos described it, almost knocked the small children over before they could finish their task. As dignitaries, Theos and Fox were led past that alley to a specially constructed shack, where twenty of the loveliest Tibetan ladies Theos had seen yet waited in a line. "So there we all stood together," Theos wrote, "watching the other ladies lifting their beautiful silk skirts in a room with three slits in the filthy floor. . . . I must confess it was a queer feeling to be attending to the wants of nature with the elite of Lhasa."

A FEW DAYS LATER, Theos was back at work organizing the growing thousands of contact prints and negatives of his photographic record of Lhasa when he became concerned about the unknown quality of the movie film he was shooting. Some of the still photos that were coming in weekly now from the Kodak lab in Calcutta were underexposed, and because he was having the lab send all the processed movie footage directly to Viola in New York, he still hadn't seen any of the results. He decided to send a telegram to the Kodak lab manager asking his candid professional opinion about the quality of the exposures he was getting in the dim interior lighting of the shrines so he could reshoot if necessary before he left town. It wasn't long before Theos got the reply he had hoped for. "I'm sure you'll feel good," the lab manager wrote, "when I say without exception that your movies on the road to the great city are the best I've seen and if your Kodachrome are comparatively as good, I am sure that you have the finest pictorial record in existence." Coming as it was from the office that had seen every film ever made in that part of the world, Theos was greatly encouraged by the opinion. What still worried him, however, was the fact that he had been waiting for over a month for good weather to take some important pictures—such as the Potala exteriors—and with less than three weeks remaining before he left, he was growing impatient for the daily clouds and rain to give way again to the blue skies that had greeted his arrival in Tibet.

Regardless of the weather, however, unique opportunities for photography continued to be offered to Theos. Theos and Tharchin had heard about a large set of rare medical *thangkas* owned by the 13th Dalai Lama that were missing. With a little investigation, they found that the set had been taken years earlier to Norbulingka, the Dalai Lamas' summer palace, to be copied, but after His Holiness died, everyone forgot where they had gone. Theos told the regent that since he already had the complete twenty-five volumes of the medical texts, he should photograph these medical diagrams as well to illustrate them. The regent readily agreed, and the prime minister himself took charge of finding the *thangkas* and then called Theos out to Norbulingka when they were ready for display.

Norbulingka, the Jewel Park, was a hundred-acre complex of palaces and formal gardens set a mile outside the city behind twelve-foot-high walls on the banks of the Kyichu River. After the death of the 13th Dalai Lama, the Norbulingka gates were locked and special permission from the Kashag was required for Theos' visit. The prime minister met Theos and Tharchin at the gate and led the way to a large hall where the medical *thangkas* had been specially hung for them.

The series of eighty-nine *thangkas* began with the azure body of the Medicine Buddha holding a bowl of long-life elixir and the potent myrobalam fruit, the only remedy in Tibetan medicine for all three basic types of illness that have their causes in the conflicting emotions of lust, aversion, and ignorance. The series illustrated the entire process from conception through the developmental stages of the egg on up to birth, and then the anatomy of the organs and the diagnosis of illness, all the way through the preparation of herbs for treatment. This was the only complete set of medical *thangkas* in all of Tibet, the prime minister told them, and never before had a European seen them. What intrigued the prime minister, though, was how Theos had even guessed at their existence. The best explanation, he said, was one Theos had been hearing frequently since he arrived in Lhasa: it was all a memory of his previous life in Tibet.

They set up the camera and tripod and had progressed through the series to *thangka* number thirty when the prime minister suggested they should break for a light fifteen-course lunch. He said it was a big job and they shouldn't worry if they couldn't finish before the light failed. He was happy to come back to unlock Norbulingka for them another day. It was on another of these later occasions at Norbulingka that the prime minister offered Theos another unique acquisition and personally supervised for them the printing of a secret collection of *thangkas* picturing the thirteen Dalai Lamas. "Never before has anyone ever taken a print of these out of India. . . . There are very few who know that they even exist," Theos wrote in his journal.

DURING HIS LAST WEEKS in Lhasa, two more unique collector's prizes were offered to Theos as blessings to help spread Buddhism in America. The regent sent an order to Sera monastery to make several prints for Theos of a rare and precious sacred charm block that was locked in a vault there. No one was able to tell Theos much about the history of the block, but it had the reputation of being one of the most highly prized of all charms, and rare prints were going for several thousand rupees in Mongolia and China. Theos heard there was an edict that no prints were to be made this year, even for the highest official, but an exception was now being made for the American.

From Sera also came what Theos described as "the prize of our trip . . . and Oh! What a triumph." Through the influence and effort of the Sera *geshe* who was indexing his Kangyur and Tengyur, the monastery offered to sell Theos a complete set of a ritual Tantric dress carved from human bone. Theos knew there was not as complete a set anywhere outside of Tibet and very few even within the country. Worn only by the highest lamas for Tantric ceremonies, the outfit consisted of a shirt, a vest, four amulets, two anklets, a set of earrings, a cap with a double *dorje* crown, a forehead band of carved human skulls, and several other items. Theos was told that the 13th Dalai Lama had had a set carved exactly like this one and it had taken over six years to complete.

All of the treasures Theos acquired now had to be carefully wrapped and placed in the wooden pack boxes. And then came the final gratifying step of sewing the pack boxes into waxed yak skins, which sealed the precious loads against dust storms, downpours, river crossings, Himalayan snowfields, and the cargo holds of ships on their journey to New York. "My only hope," Theos wrote, "is that the books do not take on the smell of those hides, for it has been a long time since I have smelt anything much worse." The biggest problem at the moment, however, was getting enough wooden boxes made. The price of wood was extremely high, and the carpenters had all started other jobs.

Another milestone was reached when they finally agreed with the printer on a price for the sixty-four volumes of the collected Tantras, meaning they had succeeded in getting everything that was on their original list and quite a bit more. Their Sera *geshe* was kept busy making the index for the new arrivals before they could be packed, and with the chance for the first time to see the deep stacks of folios covering the floor, they all agreed this was a prize collection.

Their Sera *geshe* was also a chief assistant to Rahula Sankrityana, a pandit from the Bihar Research Society who came to Tibet regularly to collect palm leaf manuscripts for the library at Patna, which was then reported to have the finest collection of Tibetan books outside of Tibet. Rahula had been trying, their *geshe* said, to get a Derge Kangyur and Tengyur for more than three years without success, and in general, he believed, Theos' collection was more complete than that of the famed Patna library. "As it stands," Theos modestly appraised his success, "the collection is perhaps one of the best to ever be brought out all at one time."

TSARONG TRIED TO CONVINCE Theos to delay his departure from Lhasa until after the official weeklong party he would host beginning September 17, but Theos was firm in his plan to be off by the fifteenth, and, anyway, as he pointed out to his host, Tsarong would need the lower floor of the house that he had occupied all summer for the three hundred guests he expected. Since Theos was going to miss "the biggest show in Lhasa," Tsarong insisted on throwing a three-day party for him at the end of August. With Theos' cargo still occupying much of the lower suites, and the lamas and tailors still at work with the indexing, they decorated as best they could and erected in the garden Tsarong's huge holiday tent, the most beautiful Theos had yet seen.

The guests began to arrive before noon, and until the last day, when the members of the British mission came, Tsarong insisted proudly that no English be spoken, allowing Theos to show off his skill with Tibetan. Among the fifty guests on the first day were the three remaining Rugby boys, both of the Chinese officials, a number of monks and nuns, and several minor officials. The guest of honor was Tethong Shape, who for Theos was "the finest personality among the lot which probably speaks for why he is considered about the most powerful."

Theos sat all day next to Tethong explaining the pictures in a tall pile of back issues from Tsarong's long-running *National Geographic* subscription. Tethong remarked that as an official, he found it next to impossible to introduce new approaches in Tibet, but he hoped that as he gradually and judiciously modernized his own household, others would take note. For example, Tibet was famous in explorers' accounts for being a society without wheeled vehicles (forgetting, of course, the Dalai Lama's two Baby Austins and a Dodge, which had been carried to Lhasa from Gangtok on the backs of porters). Tethong had recently introduced the first wheeled cart—which Theos was shocked to see one morning on his way out to Sera—and, after two years of use, three other families were trying them. Everyone was amazed, he said, that one cart could carry the loads of fifteen donkeys. He advertised their use by pointing out to his compassionate friends that the chief advantage of the cart was that it eliminated the ghastly sores so common on the backs of Tibetan donkeys.

They topped off the day with the servants scattered over the floor to watch Tsarong's home movies, and after everyone had left for home in a heavy downpour, Theos and the Tsarongs went upstairs for more tea "and a big family talk."

On the party's second day, after a sumptuous twenty-five-course lunch, Tethong went inside to take a look at the collection of Buddhist scriptures Theos was taking to America. He was greatly impressed with the care Theos was taking in indexing the volumes and preparing them for shipment, and suggested that he should make a list of anything he was unable to find and he would try to get it for him in Kham. They had a long conversation about how each of them sought to encourage the evolution of their vastly different countries by offering something of what the other had. And Tethong was certain, he said, that the reason Theos had any interest in bringing all this to America lay in his past lives as a teacher in Tibet.

EVER SINCE ARRIVING in Kalimpong nine months before, Theos had been hearing reports that Suydam Cutting, who became in 1935 the first American to visit Lhasa, was applying for permission for a return visit that fall. Suydam Cutting was a gentleman explorer and big-game hunter who had spent years in remote parts of Asia bagging specimens for the displays at the American Museum of Natural History. Hoping to add Lhasa to his trophy case, Cutting began in 1928 cultivating a friendship with the 13th Dalai Lama, and over the next years sent His Holiness a pair of dachshunds and then a pair of dalmatians. The Dalai Lama reciprocated by sending to Cutting three pairs of Lhasa apsos, the first of their breed in America, and asked Cutting to pass on his letter inquiring about the market in America for Tibetan wool to the State Department. As it turned out, Tibetan wool made excellent automobile carpets, and it wasn't long before that industry provided the major part of Tibet's hard currency. In gratitude, the Kashag invited Cutting and his English companion Arthur Vernay to visit Lhasa for ten days in October 1935.

Cutting had hardly returned from his first visit before he began proposing a second trip to Lhasa, this time with his wife, Helen. Perhaps recalling what they believed to be Cutting's influence in opening the American market to Tibetan wool, the Kashag responded with an invitation for them to come to Lhasa in early September 1937, just as Theos was preparing to leave.

Theos decided that, as a fellow American, he should be the first to welcome Cutting back to Lhasa, and he sent a message down the telegraph line to find out where they had last been seen. When he heard they were getting close, he rode with Lhare twelve miles down the road to meet them and found that much of the main route was flooded. Frequent detours were required through fields of ripe grain that were filled with peasants bent over and swinging small sickles or hauling huge bundles of the harvest on their backs. Theos and Lhare stopped at a small village to wait for the Cuttings, and it wasn't long before they spotted a foreign entourage coming up the trail. The Cuttings were the first Americans Theos had seen since Glen left Kalimpong seven months earlier, and he went out to greet them with what he considered the Tibetan courtesy of escorting visitors on their arrival.

The Cuttings' only reaction at seeing him, however, was to inquire coolly what he was doing so far out of town—was he on his way home? "It was indeed interesting to listen to him during the three hour ride back into town and the various questions which he asked," Theos wrote in his journal. "So far I can't figure out if he is as dumb as he appears or as smart as it could indicate."

The road into Lhasa was crowded with monks returning to Drepung, and although Cutting had told the newspapers that he was going to Lhasa to study Tibetan religious and social customs, his comments wondering how anyone could exist in the monastery's barren cells with nothing but *tsampa* to eat made Theos doubt his sincerity. Cutting might have wondered as well if Theos himself had some inclination toward being a monk. He had heard that Theos had spent the winter in Kalimpong, and remarked that there was nothing to do there and the winter months would have driven him insane. The conversation led Theos to observe: "With such feelings . . . about the only reason that I can attribute to his coming is that of trying to do something commercially with a film that he will probably make. . . . There is certainly something besides the love of the country."

The Cuttings' arrival in Lhasa made Theos keenly aware that although his experiences in Tibet were unique, he was an unknown, and if he was to bring to the West more than museum artifacts and fables of Shangri-La, he would have to compete for the public's attention. Theos noted that although Cutting had been coming to that part of the world for almost ten years as a big-game hunter and museum collector, he had "never taken a manuscript out of the country—I doubt if he even knows that they have a body of knowledge worth investigating." However, Cutting was an excellent photographer, "capable of that professional touch," and although he would never have the pictures of the monasteries that Theos had, "he does everything else so perfectly and already has a well built up piece of machinery for its exploitation which will indirectly make it that much more difficult for myself."

Theos wrote to Viola suggesting that she hire a movie editor to immediately begin cutting up the film that was being sent directly to her from the Kodak lab in Calcutta, so that "if anything comes up along the commercial line, everything will be set to go. With Cutting coming to this section, I more or less have to keep such in mind, for we are investing too much in this trip to let someone else take all the bows."

In another letter, he wrote to her on the same theme: "As others have been saying, they are amazed that I have not advertised my coming and remaining here in all the papers of India, England, and America. Maybe they are right, and we will take up a line of action in that direction on my return. And it is for this reason that I am so anxious to return to America before he does, because I know that he will advertise himself sky high."

THEOS HAD ARRIVED in Gyantse with fields just sprouting at the beginning of Tibet's brief summer, but now the signs of fall were unmistakable.

The leaves on the trees were turning yellow, the harvested fields were crowded with migrating cranes, and in the chilly mornings, "the transition between jumping out of bed and wrapping up is made more quickly each day."

Beginning his last week in Lhasa, Theos looked back over the last two and a half months with the dejected feeling he had accomplished little, but the undeniable proof of his achievement was packed in the twenty finished boxes on the patio and thirty more in the stable. And more was still coming in. The medical books had finally arrived and were being indexed, and the regent sent word that he had ordered his men to cross the dangerously flooded Kyichu to bring Theos a thirty-volume biography of the Dalai Lamas that Theos had given up on. Also, a printer had brought over another, lesser-quality set of the Kangyur, and after weeks of showing no interest, Theos finally couldn't resist a price set so low it angered the rest of the printers, who threatened to throw the man out of the guild. Along with the priceless Derge Kangyur Theos had gotten as part of the set from Tsarong and the Kangyur he had bought from Ngagchen Rinpoche in Calcutta, this new set made a total of three Kangyurs he shipped to America. If they proved to be unnecessary duplicates, Theos was confident he could easily sell the extras at a nice profit in America or Europe.

In the final days, there were countless details to settle with Tsarong. He offered to arrange for the carving of a shrine to display the statuary the regent had just sent over for Theos, and he promised he would ship them all together in the next three or four years when the shrine was completed. He then offered, as still another gift, a beautiful Tibetan carpet that Theos had openly admired since his arrival.

But now, along with everything he had done for Theos during his eleven weeks in Lhasa, Tsarong refused to accept even a token amount from Theos to cover the expenses of hosting him. Tsarong had housed and fed not only Theos in grand style, but Tharchin, Norphel, and Lhare as well. And along with them Tsarong had for the last month housed and fed the lama from Drepung and the *geshe* from Sera who had been working on the book indexing. He would accept no reimbursement even for the expenses of the tea party Theos hosted for the British and Chinese. And then, as a final gesture of his magnanimity, he insisted on reducing the agreed price for the Derge Kangyur and Tengyur that he was sacrificing by another 250 rupees. "And such is the Tibetan custom of friendship," Theos wrote in his journal. "It more than amazed me when I realize how royally he has treated me, and that he never knew me until I arrived in Lhasa. I have a life-long friend in him and one that I am very glad to claim."

Another group of friends, all penniless monks at Drepung, delivered as a farewell gift the full carcass of a sheep and a couple of hindquarters, a supply of meat they hoped that would last through the entire five-hundred-mile trip back to India. "I regret that it is impossible for me to box up a few of these Lamas and store them away with the books," Theos wrote, "for their counsel is going to be missed next year. . . . I have driven a few of them crazy with questions."

THEOS HAD ONLY SIX ROLLS of film left for the Leica and a few reels of movie film to get him to Shigatse. Hoping for the best, he sent a wire a few days before he left to Kodak in Calcutta with instructions to ship all their available movie film and sixty more rolls of 35 mm still film to Gyantse. The plan was that Theos and Tharchin would split up on the way back, with Theos taking Lhare and Norphel with him to Shigatse and Tharchin leading the long caravan down the main trade route to Gyantse. Tharchin would then pick up the mail in Gyantse—with its fresh supply of film—and make the two-day trip to meet Theos in Shigatse. Theos then would have the film he needed to document his unprecedented trip back through Shigatse, Sakya, and the Himalayan passes.

On the way to the telegraph office, Theos ran into the Cuttings, out for a stroll through the city. He was dressed in jodhpurs, she in an immaculate gray country suit, and they gave Theos a thorough razzing for riding about town in his silk Tibetan *namsa*.

The network of Lhasa's gossiping servants had kept Theos fully informed of the Cuttings' every move since their arrival, and he knew they planned to leave just three days after he did, which made two weeks total for them in Lhasa. Theos offered his assistance as interpreter in the bazaar, but Cutting replied there was no need to buy any more curios in Tibet because he had gotten everything on the last trip. Theos smiled at the thought that, even aside from the books, Cutting had never even seen any of the two hundred articles that he was shipping home in yak skin, but he politely agreed that it was all a lot of trouble to pack the stuff. Wishing them good day in Tibetan, he rode off on his errands.

WITH ONLY TWO DAYS left before his departure, Theos began the round of farewell visits to the *shapes*. All were "more than pleased," Theos wrote, "for they feel that I have a noble purpose . . . All asked that I return to Tibet soon." He then stopped at the Chinese mission to say good-bye to Tsiang, who, as it turned out, was bidding farewell to Lhasa as well. Because of the war with Japan, he was being recalled to China and would depart through India in two weeks. They made plans to meet in Calcutta, where Tsiang promised a huge party at his favorite Chinese restaurant.

When Theos returned to Tsarong House and entered his room, he was hit immediately with the overpowering stink of uncured yak skins. Each of their wooden pack boxes required a full skin, and, having exhausted the available supply of cured hides, animals were now being slaughtered and skinned just for this purpose; three men were busy sewing them on "hot." Tsarong had looked into the unexpected supply problem and found that the army had requisitioned every available hide to accompany troops headed for eastern Tibet. They were mobilizing to oppose the heavily armed Chinese escort of the Panchen Lama, who, according to one report among the conflicting intelligence, was preparing at any time to leave his Chinese base for Tibet.

Ironically, the day after Theos entered that information in his journal, September 13, 1937, Tsiang received in Lhasa a copy of a secret wireless message sent by the Chinese government to the Panchen Lama advising His Serenity to postpone his departure for Tibet. Because of battles raging with the Japanese in Shanghai and the growing threat to Nanking itself, there were no troops to spare for his escort. The Panchen Lama consequently sent a message to Lhasa saying that because the Tibetan government had not been sincere in its welcome, he had decided to spend another winter in China. Within weeks of that, he became sick, and on December 1, 1937, the 9th Panchen Lama died. His death ended his fourteen-year exile before he saw his home monastery, Tashilhunpo, again, and strangely, the death of Tibet's second-highest incarnate lama postponed for a time the threat of Chinese troops marching across the eastern border.

THE DAY OF THEOS' DEPARTURE from Lhasa, September 15, 1937, began at four-thirty in the morning with the hope that they would be able to seal up the last of the pack boxes and get the transport under way by nine. Getting ready, however, required almost the full day, and it would be four in the afternoon before the transport finally set off and even later before Theos got on the road. More than sixty pack boxes had been sewn up, but four boxes still awaited the arrival of additional skins.

The transport of more than fifty mules arrived on time, filling the small courtyard and forming a long line outside the compound. At seven o'clock Theos heard that the prime minister was leaving town, and having yet to say good-bye to him, they hurried over to his house. Lonchen Langdun had heard about Theos' research and practice of Yoga, and out of the blue he burst out with a long line of questions about Pranayama. There was more he needed to learn from their final meeting as well, such as the clothing style of the American king and high-ranking military officers, and what rank Theos' dress represented. "He was a bit taken," Theos noted, "when he found out that we all dress alike."

Still on the morning's schedule was a final visit with the regent. Theos arrived to find stacks of heavy camera equipment in the waiting room, which indicated that the Cuttings had the appointment ahead of him. It was only a matter of minutes, however, before they took their shots and were on their way. The Cuttings again seemed startled to see Theos dressed in his golden *namsa* and conversing with the attendants in Tibetan, but when they passed in the garden, Mrs. Cutting remarked only that never in her life had she seen flowers in such abundance.

Theos was soon shown in to see the waiting regent, and after Theos' humble prostrations, all formality vanished and they behaved with each other as if they were best friends. They began with some final pictures and the regent remarking that Theos' cameras seemed "small and innocent" compared to Cutting's professional machinery.

Theos took a few shots of Reting in his chambers, and then they walked out together into the garden. Tharchin captured them with the movie camera coming down the stairs hand in hand, but as Theos described, "What is going to bring down the house is when the public sees the King Regent of Tibet, playing with my beard—it simply fascinated him." They finished off the photo session with Theos getting some equally unique footage, a close-up of Reting taking his snuff.

They were talking about how Buddhism would spread in the United States when Reting suddenly suggested that he should write a letter to President Roosevelt. Suydam Cutting, a family friend of Roosevelt, had just moments earlier walked out his door, but it was Theos whom the regent asked to personally deliver his letter to the White House.

The letter was written on special paper reserved for correspondence of the regent or Dalai Lama and for currency printed by the Tibetan mint. The outsize page—measuring almost four and a half feet by two and a half feet—was filled by the official scribe; impressed with the large, square, red official chop of the regent; and then folded accordion-wise across its length forty-three times and then once in half.

The letter, as it was translated—most likely by Tharchin—read as follows:

To His Excellency the great Mr. Roosevelt, President of America, White House, Washington . . .

The bearer of this letter, a citizen of your country (kingdom), Mr. Theos Bernard, has great faith in the Buddhist Religion, and is possessed of great wisdom, mild, and a good discipline.

Especially has he the greatest desire to cement the friendship between Tibet and America. It is of importance that all of you who are concerned, should have a high regard for this matter, and render such assistance as lies in your power, in order that Buddha's doctrine may prosper exceedingly in all directions.

This letter is sent by the Regent of Tibet, the Hu-thuk-thu of Ra-dreng Monastery, from the Happy Grove of the All-Good Beautiful Palace of the Shi-de Gan-Den Sam-Ten-Ling, on the Auspicious Date, the tenth day of the eighth month of the Fire-Bull year.

Theos spent two and a half hours with the regent, and at parting Reting gave Theos two images, one of Padmasambhava and the other of Amitayus, the deity of long life. As a final farewell blessing, the regent took off his own monk's shirt, which he wore under his robes, and gave it to Theos. Reting requested that Theos return to Lhasa as soon as possible, and again offered to go to America to help Theos sow the seeds of dharma in the New World.

It was already midafternoon before Theos got back to Tsarong House to find everyone still waiting for the last yak skins to come in. Giving up at last, they wrapped the last boxes in heavy Tibetan wool and got the mules loaded. Norbu had been waiting patiently for Theos' return to wish him well on behalf of the British mission, and at four o'clock, with the sun already nearing the ridge, the long line of transport animals finally got under way. Theos rode out ahead through the middle of the city to a strategic point to take some photographs of the procession and then hurried back for a last cup of tea and farewell with the Tsarongs, who "really cracked the old heart with their expression of regret that I was to leave them." As Theos wrote that night in his journal, "There is no way to tell the silent inner strain at the moment of turning my back on them and riding away, perhaps never to see them again in my life."

Theos had promised still one final stop on his way out of town, that at the humble home of Tharchin's mother-in-law. They had a cup of tea, and she placed *katas* around their necks to bless their journey, which for Theos was "very touching—for here I stepped from the high to the low and find the same feelings of love."

The sun had dropped behind the ridge and they were already at the four-mile post out of town when Theo spotted his Sera *geshe* ahead waiting for him at a crossroads. They had already said good-bye at Tsarong's, but the *geshe* had walked all that distance out to offer a final *kata*. They had developed a close friendship during the month the *geshe* had lived at Tsarong House and supervised the book indexing, and they had "had a lot of fun teasing one another in the wee hours of the morning after the task of the day was finished."

Theos realized the *geshe* would have an eight-mile walk back in the dark before he reached his bed at Sera monastery, and that although he didn't have a cent, he offered the finest *kata*.

> I damn near cracked right there, but fortunately, I was able to hold myself together long enough to accept his token and offer him mine and have a short farewell, but I must admit that I had to whip my horse around in a hurry and face the other direction.... It is so seldom that you find people expressing such a high regard of friendship for one another that I could hardly take it, for only a couple of months ago we were total strangers to one another and here we part perhaps never to see one another again.

Theos never would see any of them again: Tsarong, the Sera *geshe*, the regent, Tri Rinpoche, or even Lhasa itself. This one time in history they had welcomed a pilgrim from the West who they believed had an earlier life among them. Now they were shipping home with him the finest collection of scriptures ever to leave the country, the seeds of wisdom and compassion to plant in a world they had never seen but knew would be colliding with them soon.

Chapter 10

THE TREASURE OF
PADMASAMBHAVA

THE CARAVAN REQUIRED TWENTY-FIVE MEN and a steady diatribe of whistles, shouts, and rocks to keep the fifty mules ambling between their stubborn halts to graze on whatever grew within reach. Nevertheless, by the afternoon of their first full day out of Lhasa, they reached the flooding Tsangpo, which after a month of rain was flowing, as Theos described, as broad as the Hudson and as swift as the Colorado. They ferried the cargo in the waiting *kowas*, but all fifty mules had to swim across and, miraculously, all made it to the far shore without mishap. They followed the same trail they had come to Lhasa on, until on the fourth day, at a junction beside the turquoise-colored lake Yamdrok Tso, Theos split from the rest of the caravan.

Tharchin would lead the long line of pack mules down the main trade route to Gyantse, and eventually from there retrace the route they had come in on back to Kalimpong. Theos, with just the attendants Lhare and Norphel, would spend the next three weeks exploring seldom-visited Shigatse, the home of the exiled Panchen Lama's monastery, and the even more rarely visited town of Sakya, the home and source of the name for the fourth major branch of Tibetan Buddhism. He would then cross the Himalayas over an 18,000-foot pass into Sikkim—ahead, he hoped, of the deep snow that could close it for the winter at any time.

With just their riding ponies and two mules, Theos, Lhare, and Norphel turned west up the barren Rong Valley for Shigatse, traveling a route Theos was told repeatedly that had never been seen by a white man. The people of the area even spoke a different dialect, which they dashed off in a high-pitched voice that sounded to Theos more like a crying baby than mental deliberation.

They traveled at least twelve hours every day through terrain that varied from crumbling trails hundreds of feet above raging torrents to desolate plains covered with huge golden sand dunes. On the fourth day after leaving the caravan they crossed a low ridge and got the first distant view of the fertile farms surrounding Shigatse. They rode through fields of wheat stubble and scattered stacks of harvested grain and went directly to the manor house of Tsarong's Shigatse estate, just one of seven he owned in the provinces.

The headman was expecting them and showed Theos to his quarters, a room displaying an extraordinary collection of *thangka* paintings depicting Lord Buddha and various Tantric deities. During the five days that Theos waited for Tharchin to bring the mail up from Gyantse, he rarely left his room and reveled in the chance to catch up on his grammar studies, write long letters, bring his journal up to date, and continue the laborious task of organizing the thousands of photographs he had taken since leaving Kalimpong. The days of rest provided a chance for Theos to pause finally and absorb all that had happened during his months in Lhasa. Every day had required his full attention, and without taking some time to contemplate what he was learning, he feared, "it would be wiped away as a child cleans a slate in order to write its next lesson."

In Shigatse he fell into the slow rhythm of a country manor. The entire household, it seemed, started snoring before the sky was completely dark and woke fully rested well before first light. But aside from the hours when everyone was asleep, Theos found his contemplations continually interrupted by a stream of visitors who had come to witness the rare occasion of a fair-skinned visitor, and some waited hours with the hope of catching sight of him at work on the strange typing machine. Theos finally gave up trying to discourage the most curious from putting their faces right next to the keys, where they could see every action that led to a letter being printed on the page.

At last, on the fifth afternoon after his arrival in Shigatse, Theos was happy to see Tharchin walk through the door. He had been delayed in leaving Gyantse by the typical problem of finding transport, but while he was getting things organized there, Tharchin made use of the time for the obligatory visits to the nobles who had helped them get to Lhasa. They were all remarkably well informed about the details of Theos' reception in the capital and were proud of his historic achievements.

In the bundle of accumulated mail Tharchin delivered were yellowing copies from Theos' subscription to the Sunday *New York Times* and packages of film he had ordered from Kodak before leaving Lhasa. Most important, however, there was also a letter from Viola. It had been weeks since the last one from her, and he wouldn't get mail again for almost another three weeks when he reached Kalimpong. His joy at opening the letter, however, was soon tempered with the worrying news inside of her continued long hours on the ward floors and her persistent illness.

The next day, an official from Tashilhunpo monastery brought a load of welcoming gifts, which included two sacks of *tsampa*, four sacks of yak butter, eight bricks of Tibetan tea, a small amount of Tibetan cash, and eight sacks of grain for the ponies. Theos sent word back with the official that he would like to return the visit, and the following day rode out to the great walled monastery for an appointment with the abbot. During his visit, Theos spotted an extraordinary set of *thangkas* depicting the previous lives of the present Panchen Lama, the ninth of the line, and hinted about buying them. The abbot said this was the only set in existence and he couldn't possibly part with them; however, the monastery did have a master set of blocks with the outline of the images used to create the *thangkas*, and he could have a set printed for Theos before he left. The abbot also offered to obtain a biography of all the past lives of the Panchen Lamas, which would be another first outside of Shigatse.

Theos went back to Tashilhunpo the next day (dressed as always in his golden silk *namsa*) for a ceremony with thousands of monks chanting a prayer he requested entreating the deity Drolma to remove obstacles to the happiness of all beings. That was followed by a full tour of the monastery's treasures. The huge doors guarding the inner temple were thrown open and the pomp of his entrance, Theos wrote, could be compared only with that of the Pope in Rome. They passed from one shrine to another whose artistry and grandeur surpassed anything Theos had seen even in Lhasa, and all of it, he was told, had been made in Shigatse. He was conducted to a vast hall with giant gilded stupas containing the remains of five of the Panchen Lamas that were similar in size and in the wealth of jewels adorning them to the stupas of the Dalai Lamas in the Potala. Beaming down on these from high above, however, was the massive golden face of Maitreya, the Buddha who will appear next in this world. Theos climbed steps in the room for a view from the top of the seven-story-tall seated Buddha and counted thirty steps to get just from the nose to the crown on Maitreya's head. The entire image was covered with gold—several inches thick on the face—and its huge eyes were said to have shed tears shortly before the late Panchen Lama fled to exile in Mongolia.

The last day of his stay in Shigatse brought Theos a final unique experience that had eluded him in Lhasa, one that he would call "the prize of this Tibetan trip." He had been trying for months to witness and photograph the grisly Tibetan practice for disposing of the dead, called "sky burial." One morning a few days before he had left Lhasa, he went out before sunrise to the sandstone outcrop near Sera where one was scheduled, but as it turned out the corpse had to be buried rather than fed to the vultures because the woman had died of a contagious disease. But now Theos got word that he would have another chance to witness the most common way in Tibet to recycle the bodies of the dead, and he left the Tsarong manor at four to make certain that he would have his cameras set up at the site by sunrise when the butchering of the corpse began.

As Theos told a magazine interviewer after his return, Tibetans recognized four means of burial—by air, water, fire, and earth, the elements to which the body must return after the mind leaves it. In Tibet, the ground was generally too hard and rocky for digging graves—especially when frozen during the long months of winter—and, except for the cremation of high lamas, wood was considered too scarce and valuable to be burned in a pyre. And while the bodies of criminals and paupers were sometimes dismembered and thrown into a river, sky burial was by far the most common, and perhaps tidiest, method for disposing of the dead.

The job of dismembering the corpses was generally performed by members from a specialized and fairly prosperous group of beggars called the Ragyapas, who had their own powerful guild. Along with disposing of corpses, the Ragyapas' responsibilities also included providing monks with human skulls and thighbones for special rites, chopping off the limbs of the few criminals who received that terrible sentence, and keeping other beggars away from parties if the hosts didn't want to be bothered. These particular Ragyapas in Shigatse were not, like those in Lhasa, full-time professionals, but had their own fields and performed sky burials only as a sideline.

The charnel ground remained in the cold shadows of the eastern ridge when Theos arrived, but far above he could see a broad gyre of vultures soaring on ten-foot-wide wings in the first rays of the morning sun. The corpse of a Tibetan woman who had died in childbirth waited on a pile of rocks, and after finishing their tea, the Ragyapas rolled the corpse onto the large stone-slab work area.

The Ragyapas had no objection to Theos filming their gruesome chore, which progressed, of course, to the rhythm of its own specialized work song, and they began by pulling all the hair from the head of the corpse. Then, with knives just sharpened on the adjacent rocks, they made two long perpendicular slashes through the chest and stripped off large pieces of skin. At this point, the sharp-eyed vultures began to drop from the sky like hailstones, and one of the men was forced to whirl a rope in a wide circle around him to keep them back until everything was ready. Four men worked with the knives, and after the flesh had been flayed from the face and skull, a rope was tied around the neck and anchored to a large rock to prevent the vultures from dragging the corpse away.

Theos counted two hundred of the huge, powerful birds on the ground, but more kept arriving and he gave up trying to number them. "Getting away from the carcass," he wrote, "was like running after igniting a fuse." In an instant the vultures swarmed the corpse and ate greedily.

The feast required only a few minutes, and when they were driven back again with the whirling rope the skeleton they left was picked clean.

Six Ragyapas gaily disjointed the elbows, shoulders, knees, and hips, and then all sat down in a circle to pulverize the bones with round rocks. When the mash of bone and marrow was gathered and presented at the serving area, the vultures again dove in and fed in a frenzy. Finally the skull and brains were pounded into a pudding, which the leader of the crew put into a folded cloth and carried to the top of the hill to attract the vultures away from the site of the butchering so that the smaller crows could clean up the last signs of the morning's work. The brains were kept from the vultures until the very end, Theos was told, because once they had tasted that delicacy, they would refuse to eat the pulverized bones.

A nearby fire reduced the hair and the crown of the skull to an ash that the deceased's relatives would mix with *tsampa* or clay and use to mold images of deities, which they would place in some auspicious spot. For their morning's work, the Ragyapas were rewarded with a small parcel of food and the blanket the corpse arrived in. Theos joined them at the fire on which a pot was now set to boil tea, and the disposers of the dead sang a final frolicking chorus of the song that concluded their work.

When the crows had finished pecking the crumbs of the pulverized bones on the rock slab there was no trace left of the peasant mother who had died while giving birth. "I must admit that I have never visited a graveyard which showed less sign of death," Theos wrote in his journal. There was as well an absence of any sign of tragedy or grief. Since childhood these illiterate farmers had heard the Tashilhunpo lamas teach that the path to enlightenment begins with three realizations: *my death is certain; the time of my death is uncertain; and at the moment of my death the only thing of any value from this life is the wisdom I have cultivated in my heart.*

Theos had gone about the business of getting his historic movie footage of the sky burial as dispassionately as the Ragyapas had gone about their work, but the morning had nonetheless provided him another initiation of sorts. He now knew, whenever it happened, the song the Ragyapas would sing when it was his turn to feed the vultures. There would be no dirges.

———————

THEOS WAS PACKING to leave on the morning of his tenth and last day in Shigatse when he decided he would make an offer on a beautiful *thangka* he had seen of Yamantaka, the deity whose practice he had been initiated into at the Ramoche temple in Lhasa. The owner of the house in whose shrine it was hanging told him that it actually belonged to Tashilhunpo, and because it was on their inventory list, it was impossible to sell it. He was more than willing, however, to let Theos borrow it. He could take it to America, reproduce it in the book Theos told him he wanted to publish, and return it when he was finished with it. Theos told the man that he could not promise that he would return it even in this lifetime, but the man was happy to lend it to him, and as Theos noted, "I don't even know his name or he mine."

When Theos returned to Tsarong's manor house and asked the headman about buying some of the exquisite Shigatse-made *thangkas* on the wall of the room he had been living in, the same thing happened. The headman asked which ones he liked and then gave him his top six choices as a gift to help spread Buddhism in America. He insisted it was a sacrilege to sell sanctified Buddhist images and would accept nothing for them. Nor would he accept anything for the food, fuel, or feed for the animals he supplied during Theos' stay. The headman had been in Lhasa during the summer and seen the friendship between Tsarong and Theos, and he said nothing more was necessary.

Theos set off with Norphel and Lhare in a cold drizzle and after two days reached another of Tsarong's estates. They were heading into an even more remote area between Shigatse and Sakya, and the next day met just one solitary person on the isolated trail they traveled. When they reached the pass overlooking the Sakya valley, they saw ahead of them the source of the icy headwind that howled through the gap where they stood: rank after rank of snowy ridges that ran all the way to the cloud-filled horizon, beyond which still was the haven they needed to reach before winter— India.

They dropped quickly from the pass and followed a stream in the valley bottom to the village of Sakya, whose clusters of flat-roofed houses were dominated by the massive, square, fortress-like Sakya monastery. As planned, the transport arrived before Theos did, and the peasant wrangler made arrangements for him to stay in a tiny house at the edge of the village. Norphel was outraged that they would put an honored guest in such a dump. He asked Theos for the letter of introduction he carried from Tsarong to the king of the Sakyas and stormed off immediately to deliver it. A messenger soon arrived to say that a room awaited Theos at the palace, and the moment he reached its gates, gracious servants came running to greet him and escort him to an immaculate suite decorated with a royal collection of carpets and *thangkas.*

Arrangements were made immediately for Theos to make a formal call on His Holiness, and he unpacked his one remaining gift, a clock. Promptly at two, an attendant showed him into a large audience hall. Theos made his devotional prostrations at the entrance and then approached the high throne for a blessing, sensing immediately that before him was the sort of burning personality he had met so far in Tibet only in Tsarong. Before a word was spoken, Theos felt as though he were visiting a lifelong friend. The Sakya Trizin, or king, as he was still regarded in this area, was filled with questions, and even though the Sakya dialect differed from Lhasa's, they conversed without an interpreter for two and a half hours. Theos was only the second foreigner to ever visit the area, the Sakya Trizin told him, the first being F. W. Williamson, the former Sikkim political officer. He wanted to know all about religion in America, why Theos was attracted to Buddhism, what he planned to do with it when he got home, and why he had come to Tibet. He then shared his insights about the political situation between Tibet and China and the standoff with the Panchen Lama, and he was eager to hear the latest on the war between China and Japan.

His Holiness invited Theos to attend the next morning's sunrise prayer assembly in the main temple, which was reputed to be the largest single building in all Tibet. When Theos arrived at the hall the next morning the entire room was vibrating with prayer chants, clapping hands, and trumpet blasts. An old monk was appointed to help Theos through his small part in the morning's ceremony, and all eyes were fixed on him as he made his prostrations and offerings at the altars before the main deities.

After tea was served, the old monk guided Theos through the temple and explained the illustrious history of the Sakya lineage. Beginning in the mid-thirteenth century, under the patronage of the Mongol emperor Kublai Khan, the Sakyas ruled all of Tibet from this capital. Sakya rule lasted about a hundred years before Tibet fragmented again into regional kingdoms, which were reunited in 1642 under the Gelugpa rule of the Dalai Lamas.

Huge timber columns measuring four feet in diameter and fifty feet high supported the carved and painted roof beams of the nave, and when the tour reached the vast hall's far end, the guide led Theos through a concealed door between a statue and an altar and then down a dark passage to the famous Sakya library. One very long wall was filled from its floor to its high ceiling with rare handwritten texts, and there was even a section of original Sanskrit manuscripts inscribed on palm leaves. Theos didn't want to be accused of exaggerating the room's dimensions, so he stepped it off and counted 103 paces down its length. "In all of Tibet I have never seen anything that even compared with it," he wrote.

The Sakya Trizin had two sons and three daughters. The fifteen-year-old daughter spied on Theos and reported that she saw him doing something very strange, and now the king wanted Theos to perform on the typewriter. The Sakya Trizin, his three daughters, and his wife—dressed in a gown more splendid than anything Theos had seen in Lhasa—huddled with Theos atop the royal throne and shrieked with laughter as he tapped the keys and the ink letters on the paper spelled out a transliteration of their names.

Theos thought that with this king's keen curiosity, Tibet would make great strides if the Sakya Trizin were once again to be the sole ruler of the country. The king had picked up some progressive ideas during his pilgrimages to India and said that, if given the chance, he would build a road and introduce cars, trucks, and buses. He was just as eager to help Theos spread the flowers of Tibetan culture in the modern world and suggested that Theos make a list of all the *thangkas*, images, and texts he needed, and the king would send them to him in a few months. He also suggested that, as the regent had done, he should write a letter to the American king, and he asked that Theos personally deliver it. The Sakya Trizin called in a scribe and dictated in Tibetan what translated as:

> To the Most Illustrious King of America who is interested in all the Virtues.
>
> This letter is sent by the President of the Phun-Tshog Pho-Drang (The Perfect Palace) of Sakya with greetings.
>
> An American gentleman named Bernard, who has great faith in the religion, arrived here. Rest assured that I have rendered him all the assistance that lay in my power. If a Buddhist Monastery is estab-lished in your Precious Majesty's Kingdom, there will be no pesti-lence, nor will there be war or famine in your country. Perfect happiness and prosperity will prevail.
>
> Pray remember that in whatever state you may chance to be re-born, you will have long life, and fortune, power, and glory beyond description will be yours.
>
> It is good to hear that that the King of America sympathizes with the spread of the Buddhist Religion to other countries.
>
> As I have requested earlier in this letter, please be graciously in-clined to render all the assistance that lies in your power, to help this gentleman, Bernard, who has a pure mind.
>
> This letter is sent with a Silk Scarf of Greeting from the Phun-Tshog Pho-Drang of the Noble Sakya Monastery, on the Auspicious Date, the fifth day of the ninth month of the Fire-Bull Year.

The king's scribe executed the letter with elegantly drawn Tibetan script on large fine paper and affixed the red seal of the Sakya Perfect Pal-ace. Theos again was being asked to be the courier between kings. Both the letter from the regent and the letter from the Sakya Trizin to the President of the United States attested to Theos' character. The regent wrote: "Mr. Theos Bernard, has great faith in the Buddhist Religion, and is possessed of great wisdom, mild, and a good discipline." The Sakya Trizin wrote to Roosevelt that Theos had "great faith in the religion" and "a pure mind." Both letters asked Roosevelt to do everything in his power to help this worthy one establish a monastery and spread Buddhism in America. There could be no clearer announcement from the highest ranks of Tibetans about why they had invested so much in this pilgrim and what they saw his mission to be on his return to the New World. In his self-effacing, homespun style, Theos wrote to Viola: "Poor old Franklin is sitting in the path of an avalanche of Buddhism and doesn't know it."

THE NEXT MORNING, Theos saw the transport off and then went to the large audience hall to bid farewell to the Sakya Trizin. From his high throne the king expressed regret that Theos had to leave so soon, and insisted that when he returned to Tibet he must enter through northern Sikkim and come to Sakya first. He would show him all the monasteries in his small kingdom, and Theos could spend some time studying in their library. The king draped a white *kata* and a small knotted red silk scarf with his blessing around Theos' neck and gave him a final gift of some Tibetan medicine. Theos packed these with the rare and valuable texts he was given and the first movies ever taken of Sakya and set out at a fast pace to make up for the late start.

Theos asked the Sakya Trizin about the fastest way to Khampa Jong—the last village before the trail headed over the Himalayas—and was told there was a shortcut out the east end of the valley. It went straight up and over a 20,000-foot pass, but by that route they could make the trip in two days rather than the four required down the normal trail. The pass was so high that it was covered with snow and ice most of the year and, because it was so rarely used, there was virtually no trail. The Sakya Trizin sent a man along to guide them, but he immediately got lost, and they went a couple of hours in the wrong direction before Theos insisted that they retrace their steps. A lonely yak herder pointed them in the general direction, and they wound their way the rest of the morning through a box canyon so narrow they could have, as Theos put it, "spit across [it], had we been from Texas and well trained."

The only company was that of the wind that howled at them from the snowcapped pass whose small rock monument, when they reached it, marked the highest elevation at which Theos had ever stood. Theos, however, still had energy in reserve and could have, he wrote, easily hiked up the side of the hill to gain another three or four thousand feet just for the view. His resting pulse increased only from its normal forty-two to about fifty-seven at the pass, which considering his damaged heart valves and the warning from his cardiologist to take up fishing from a pier, seemed a testament to the restorative effects of his yoga practice.

The steep pitch and icy, gusting wind on the other side made the descent almost as arduous as the climb, and the sun was setting behind the western ridge before they reached a tiny village beside a creek on which ice was already growing. The transport, however, was far behind them, and until it arrived with his bedding in the middle of the night, Theos had only two thin, short blankets under which to attempt sleep. He noted in his journal that the frigid night inspired him to perform some practical experiments in the art of *tummo*, or inner fire, a practice the Lachen Gomchen had outlined for him during his visit with Glen the previous winter. "If you drape a blanket of any pretense around yourself and do a little breathing, it matters little how cold it may be, you will find that in a short while, you are ready to perspire," he wrote.

It was long before sunrise that Theos called the boys to start packing, and they soon had a fire going and poured hot tea. They were under way for Khampa Jong by six, and by midmorning they arrived at a low pass that led them onto the open Tibetan Plateau. They spent the rest of the day trotting across a desolate plain of scattered bunch grasses with the glaciers of Mt. Everest as their landmark. Their haste was rewarded by their arrival at Khampa Jong at sunset, and Theos dashed out to get some pictures of the pointed top of the world's highest peak, still incandescent in the last rays of the departed sun, while all around it the blue black night enveloped fathomless space.

Theos had been planning to cross the Himalayas into Sikkim by the 18,400-foot Donkia La, "just for the fun of it," but heard in Khampa Jong that the pass was already deep under snow and that only the day before, two Tibetans and their animals were killed attempting to cross it. They decided instead they would take a fork of the trail that led over the somewhat tamer Kongra La.

They set out on fresh ponies in the morning up a barren hillside filled with grazing dèer driven to their winter range by the lowering snow line, and headed directly for the towering Himalayan ridges, "straight up and up and up, into the land of perpetual ice, behind which lies sweating India," Theos wrote. A frigid wind howled down on them from the ridges, demanding that Theos pull down the earflaps on his Tibetan fur hat and wrap a scarf over his face to avoid sudden frostbite. Scattered bare spots had melted since the last heavy dump of snow, but in lees where the scouring wind left fresh deposits, they had to break trail through deep drifts.

Just as the chilling shadows lengthened and the sun was about to disappear behind a western rampart, they rounded a bend in the trail and saw not far ahead the stacked-rock walls of the hut that would shelter them for the night. It was by far the coldest night of the trip, but now at least, traveling together with the transport, Theos had the luxury of sleeping in his own bedding. He created a cocoon of his Yeager camel hair sleeping bag laid in the fold of a wool Tibetan blanket, and he stayed snugly warm until a little after three, when he roused everyone to begin packing the transport loads. While Lhare and Norphel supervised that job and got a smoky fire started, Theos hammered with stiff, ungloved fingers on the typewriter's frozen keys, and with heroic diligence was able to catch up on the previous day's journal pages.

They left camp long before the warming sun arrived to melt the firm crust that had frozen over the snow on the trail, but after it rose high above the eastern ridge and thawed the solid footing, weak spots gave way, and the animals broke through. Suddenly, rather than walking on top of the snow, they were floundering through it, and everyone had to heave and push and tug while the animals struggled to regain their footing. As the drifts grew deeper, they had to walk ahead and pack down a trail for the animals and then lead them one by one through the rough parts while bracing them when they slipped off the trail. When the ponies fell on their sides, Theos and the boys had to remove the boxes and haul the thrashing animals back to their feet, though they would often go down again as soon as they were reloaded and took their first steps. At one point, the horse carrying the bedding fell and slid on its side, legs flailing, down a frozen slope. Miraculously it came to rest at the very edge of a rushing stream.

They kept up the wallowing progress for several miles, but as Theos wrote, "I must confess that when you took your mind from the difficulties at hand, the old heart commenced to pound with all the raptures of human kind for there is little in this world that holds more beauty than the frozen north of Sikkim." Finally, at about ten-thirty, they reached the top of Kongra La and crossed the border into Sikkim. The south-facing slopes had melted and the fatigue of the riders and their ponies vanished as they went down the easy descent, splashing mud. Theos quickly left the transport behind and hurried down to Thangu, only a short distance from the retreat cave of the Lachen Gomchen. Theos expected that the Gomchen would not have moved down to Lachen yet for the winter, and after a quick cup of tea at the Thangu bungalow, he dashed up to say hello.

Only nine months earlier, when Theos and Glen had visited him in Lachen, Theos could not speak a word of Tibetan, and now the Gomchen was surprised and delighted to hear the story of Theos' remarkable travels in his own language. Theos had to be brief in his account for the Gomchen, however; it was still twelve miles to their destination for the night at Lachen. Just below Thangu, he came to the first real sign of the world he was returning to, a milepost indicating that Gangtok was a mere sixty-two miles down the trail. Their final destination, Kalimpong, was only three days away.

Theos would have been happy, however, to spend an eternity at any point along the trail if, as he wrote, he had only been able to cling to the feeling stimulated by the grandeur of the environment. They crossed great piles of avalanche debris and then the first small liquid stream of aggregating snowmelt. From that point, the trail constantly crossed streams of increasing size, and the colors and smells changed with each hundred feet of elevation they dropped. First came stunted cedars, then dwarf spruce and firs, and then, as the atmosphere grew noticeably thicker with oxygen, the trees grew taller and wider, until they rode through a dense forest whose canopy towered hundreds of feet above them and lower branches suspended flowing veils of moss.

Autumn was rapidly making its way to the lowlands, and entire hillsides were painted a solid mass of red with splashes of yellow. The last few miles to Lachen followed a narrow, unstable trail—only a foot wide in places—that was eaten away by landslides and dropped from its crumbling edge a thousand feet or more to snarling rapids.

They reached Lachen just before dark and found beds in the dak bungalow, but they had left the transport far behind in their race down from the pass and it was three o'clock in morning before the rest of the party came in. When the muleteers arrived, they woke Theos to say that one of their animals had stepped off the trail in the area of the landslides five miles back and had tumbled out of sight with its load into the darkness.

On that disappeared load was Theos' bedroll, inside of which was all the film he shot since leaving Shigatse, along with his journal. Now that he had crossed the border and his odyssey to Tibet was already memory, the alarming thought that he had lost his documentation of the journey sent Theos into instant action. They returned with ladders, flashlights, and ropes the miles back on the dark trail to where a hole on the narrow edge marked the spot where the mule had tumbled into the night. They belayed each other from tree to tree with the rope, and as they descended through the blackness to the increasing roar of the stream, Theos wondered if they would find a way to get everyone back up.

The bedroll had worked free of the load at some point during the tumble, and Theos found it resting providentially at the edge of the frothing water. The mule as well seemed to be all right, but now how were they going to get it back up the cliff to the trail? Lachen was to be the end of the stage for this set of animals anyway, so Theos and his boys scurried out of the canyon and left the logistics of the mule to its owner. "They are a bit ingenious in getting things done," Theos wrote, "so I feel confident that the animal is now on his return journey to Khampa Jong."

It was noon before they got back to Lachen, and despite advice from all sides to relax and spend the short afternoon there, Theos was determined to travel all night with a candle if needed to stay on schedule for his return to Kalimpong. They got as far as Chungtang before the light completely faded, and dismounting at the dak bungalow, Theos saw thick smoke coming out of the stone chimney. He strode in through the back porch and wandered through the well-set dining room to the front porch, where several Englishmen with their ladies were sitting in chairs having a whiskey and soda. They had seen an article about him in Calcutta's *Statesman* and, guessing this must be the American returning from Tibet, they asked him to join them for dinner and ordered their servants to prepare a bath for him. It was the first occasion for Theos to speak English since leaving Cutting and the British in Lhasa, and that excitement, coupled with the memories that flooded back with the sight of each detail of imported society, made it difficult for Theos to sleep that night.

He enjoyed a leisurely breakfast with his hosts the next morning, and it was ten o'clock before they got under way to Dikchu, smiling at the Englishmen's insistence that it would take a full two days to travel the twenty-seven miles. They set off again at a gallop and reached Dikchu an hour before dark.

The next morning, Theos roused Lhare at four and sent him ahead to Gangtok to wire for a car to meet him there at the dak bungalow and take him the remaining way down the road to Kalimpong. Theos and Norphel followed later, and on the nine-mile climb straight up the ridge to Gangtok, they talked about their reluctance to end an experience that would be hard to match the rest of their lives. However, at the top of the hill, neither of them considered turning back or even putting off their return another day. "It is needless to say how good it felt," Theos wrote in his journal, "when I rounded the last bend and knew that over the hill lay the end of my long, long journey." They arrived at Gangtok's dak bungalow around noon and found Lhare waiting with tea ready. The car would be there soon, he assured Theos.

Sitting alone on the porch of the dak bungalow, Theos realized that the tranquil autumn afternoon was a brief intermezzo between two of his life's most dramatic acts. What the next act would bring, he didn't know, but judging from the crescendo with which the last one had ended, it would be exciting and he was eager to get on with it. But for a few more hours, anyway, Theos had to be patient. He sent some telegrams, drank more cups of tea, strolled the streets, and repacked the kit he wanted to carry with him that night to Kalimpong, but still the car he had called for did not arrive. Finally at five-thirty, his Tibetan pony spooked at the sound of the first car engine it had ever heard laboring up the steep jungle grade, and eventually a Baby Austin pulled up to the corral. It wasn't, however, the car dispatched to pick up Theos. Instead, the man who stepped out of the car, by sheer coincidence, was a friend of Theos from Kalimpong, a tea planter named George Hall who had driven up to show the sights to his visiting brother-in-law. Hall had seen the long dispatch in Calcutta's leading British newspaper, the *Statesman*, that Tharchin had sent out shortly before leaving Lhasa. The feature was illustrated with dramatic photos of monks and monasteries and detailed the entire trip, including the history-making passport, Tsarong's hospitality, ceremonies at the temples, and a description of the huge library of Buddhist scriptures now on its way to America. Theos had become instantly famous and had better prepare for a clamor to broadcast his story on the radio, Hall warned. "It more or less took my breath away," Theos wrote in his journal, "for I did not have the slightest idea that anyone but a couple of friends knew anything about my weird wanderings, but I was completely wrong."

It was after seven o'clock before the car sent to pick up Theos pulled up to the bungalow. They all agreed that since it would be midnight before he got to Kalimpong, they should stop off at Hall's bungalow on the way down for something to eat. Theos left his pony and the baggage with Lhare and Norphel and finished his descent from the Himalayan passes coasting on rubber tires. They had hardly started down the long grade when the first evidence of India—a bullock cart—slowed their progress, and Theos knew he was back. They were forced to pull off the single lane for up to a half hour at a time, yielding the road to the night's procession of carts hauling supplies up from the railhead on the Indian plains at Siliguri. They cautiously followed Hall's taillights down the steep, narrow road, but at last they arrived at his bungalow, and as they drove into the yard Theos leaned out the open window and snatched a ripe orange from the heavy boughs along the driveway. They improvised a banquet of cold chicken, orange juice, California peaches, and meat patties; then, impatient for the waiting reunion in Kalimpong, Theos and his driver resumed the evening's crawl down the valley of the Tista River.

All along the road, as they wove their way down the dusty canyon in the moonlight, Theos looked for landmarks and tried to recall his emotions on every one of his passages past them, especially the last journey in the opposite direction to begin the greatest adventure of his life.

Theos Bernard in Kalimpong with a Tibetan noblewoman modeling her jeweled Tsang province headdress. *Phoebe A. Hearst Museum of Anthropology, University of California at Berkeley.*

Abbot of the Kagyu Monastery in the Chumbi Valley reputed to be a master of the Six Yogas of Naropa. *Phoebe A. Hearst Museum of Anthropology, University of California at Berkeley.*

Jigme Taring in Kalimpong. *Phoebe A. Hearst Museum of Anthropology, University of California at Berkeley.*

Theos Bernard at Palkhor monastery with 1,000 butter lamps lit to honor his arrival in Gyantse on the great Buddhist festival day, Saka Dawa. *Phoebe A. Hearst Museum of Anthropology, University of California at Berkeley.*

The silk Kigu Banner, displayed for only one hour each year during the Saka Dawa festival in Gyantse. *Phoebe A. Hearst Museum of Anthropology, University of California at Berkeley.*

ABOVE: Drepung
Monastery, Lhasa.
With 10,000 enrolled
monks, it was the largest
monastery in the world.
*Phoebe A. Hearst Museum of
Anthropology, University of
California at Berkeley.*

RIGHT: Theos Bernard
during his visit to
Drepung. *Phoebe A. Hearst
Museum of Anthropology,
University of California at
Berkeley.*

LEFT: The Potala, the former winter residence of the Dalai Lamas and seat of government administration. Its thousand rooms housed 10,000 shrines including the great tombs of eight Dalai Lamas. *Phoebe A. Hearst Museum of Anthropology, University of California at Berkeley.*

BOTTOM: A Tantric ceremony Theos was invited to attend at the tomb of the 13th Dalai Lama in the Potala. *Phoebe A. Hearst Museum of Anthropology, University of California at Berkeley.*

ABOVE: Theos Bernard with a senior lama at Ganden monastery. *Phoebe A. Hearst Museum of Anthropology, University of California at Berkeley.*

RIGHT: Theos Bernard with Reting Rinpoche, the Regent of Tibet, on the day Theos departed Lhasa. *Phoebe A. Hearst Museum of Anthropology, University of California at Berkeley.*

BOTTOM: A village in the Rong Valley. Theos Bernard was probably the first white person ever to travel through this remote section of Tibet on his way to Shigatse. *Phoebe A. Hearst Museum of Anthropology, University of California at Berkeley.*

ABOVE: Ragyapas flay the flesh from a corpse to feed to vultures during a sky burial near Shigatse. These were probably the first photos ever taken by a westerner of this common Tibetan practice for disposing of the dead. *Phoebe A. Hearst Museum of Anthropology, University of California at Berkeley.*

Uttanakurmakasana (stretched like a tortoise posture).
Courtesy of The Bancroft Library, University of California, Berkeley.

Theos demonstrates Pasini Mudra (noose posture) in a studio photograph published with his doctoral dissertation, *Hatha Yoga. Courtesy of The Bancroft Library, University of California, Berkeley.*

When the car finally pulled into the courtyard of the Himalayan Hotel, waiting with a lantern on the porch—as if he had been keeping watch ever since his exuberant send-off more than five months earlier—was his dear friend Frank Perry. "I think that he was happier over all that had happened than I had been," Theos wrote in his journal, "for he has been watching them come and go for many years and never has there been anyone who ever approximated the way I went to Tibet."

They had reserved for him the corner room he had occupied the previous winter, but the party began the moment he walked through the door without giving him a chance to clean up or unpack. Everyone, including the hotel guests, rolled out of bed, and for the next four hours Theos told one remarkable story after another. They had been following his adventures in the news dispatches Tharchin sent back and were eager to hear more. Even the servants said before they went to sleep that regardless of how late the sahib arrived, they were to be roused so they could fix him something to eat.

It was near daybreak when the last of the well-wishers returned to bed and Theos was alone. In the stack of accumulated cables and mail in his room waited the recent letters from Viola, whom he had not seen now for almost a full year.

She had written the most recent of her waiting letters five weeks earlier, and it was a matter-of-fact four pages whose tone was all business. She was of necessity, she said, "omitting much that I would like to be writing and that I know you are eager to hear" because a brush with poison ivy had swollen both eyes shut and the message was being dictated to a secretary. She appreciated his desire to make it home for Thanksgiving but she admonished him to make sure his work was finished before leaving India.

> Now please do not fail to take the necessary time in Calcutta to collect your photographs, ship your books, and pull yourself together according to what is necessary for you. I would strongly regret it if your work and the completion of a big job should fall short of its mark because of undue impatience over a mere matter of days, in view of the months put in. And as for myself and the situation here, a few weeks on either side of the balance makes relatively little difference.

Theos had only just learned of the "situation" she referred to in another letter from the same stack of mail. Viola's mother had two lumps on one of her breasts and, even when resting in bed, she was short of breath. Viola had rented an X-ray machine and installed it in the Persian Room at Sky Island in Nyack, which allowed her mother to have treatments without having to drive back and forth to Manhattan, but by the time of the most recent letter, her condition had deteriorated to the point that Viola was forced to take a month's leave from her internship to care for her. The crux of the matter was that the month Viola was taking off would unavoidably have to be made up in January in order to complete her twelve-month internship. She had planned to finish the internship before Theos returned to New York, but now that she would be forced to spend the entire month of January back at her all-demanding schedule in the hospital wards, she saw no reason for Theos to hurry back for the holidays. "We both have a great many years ahead of us," Viola wrote, "and a few years from now thirty days more or less will appear very irrelevant." For Theos, however, the prospect of another thirty or even sixty days away from Viola was agonizing, and he replied to her: "Get mad if you want to—I want to be home. . . . I am badly in need of you. . . . [I]t is simply hell being alone in this world—I just have to get home."

But now another situation complicating his departure arose: everdependable Tharchin was still in Gyantse, sick in bed with a 104-degree fever. The most recent wire from him said he might not be ready to travel for two more weeks and, until then, stacked in a stable across the Himalayas in Gyantse lay Theos' fifty-muleload cargo of precious Buddhist scriptures along with the bulk of the ten thousand photographs he had shot in Tibet. And all knew that the deep snows of winter might close the passes at any time. Theos considered making the ten-day trip back to Gyantse and bringing the transport out himself but then decided he would have Tharchin open some of the boxes and send him the essentials by express post.

BEFORE THEY LEFT Lhasa (spurred perhaps by the perceived competition with Cutting) Tharchin insisted that he employ his newspaper connections, and he mounted a publicity campaign about their historic reception in Lhasa. He sent dispatches back to the Kalimpong headquarters of his *Tibet Mirror*, to the *Statesman* in Calcutta, and even to a reporter he knew in America, who ended up writing a feature on Theos for the Sunday *Detroit News*. Now one of the first jobs for Theos after arriving back in Kalimpong was negotiating with media outlets that wanted to make him famous.

The *Statesman* wanted another story, there was an offer from a radio show in Calcutta, and there was a stack of cables from others, but the most compelling offer came from London. Frank Perry worked as a stringer for the *Daily Mail*, and it was undoubtedly his enthusiasm for his friend's accomplishment that spurred the newspaper to offer Theos £50 to write a three-thousand-word story, a rate that at today's values would be about a dollar per word and put it among the top-paying serial markets. Published in London with a circulation of more than two million, the *Daily Mail* aimed at the lower-middle-class market and set out to entertain its readers with human-interest stories, serials, and competitions. The editor insisted on first rights to Theos' dramatic story, and as soon as he signed a contract, Theos sent out a thousand-word press release that announced his return and stated that he would not give any interviews until after the *Daily Mail* published the story. To keep the story under wraps, the editors went so far as to assign Frank to be Theos' constant companion. In one of his daily letters to Viola, Theos told her:

> From the communications that I have received, you would think that perhaps I had something—it all makes me smile and wonder where I am going, for the current is mighty swift at the moment. . . . If I listened to everything that they say, I would tend to believe what you wrote in one of your letters—"you are making history." It is impossible to anticipate the reaction that I will find in America, but I must confess that England is certainly willing to receive me; so I am letting come what will.

Aside from dodging reporters, the biggest job for Theos during his twelve days in Kalimpong was organizing the fifteen hundred photographs he had with him. Knowing he would finish those soon, he wired Calcutta to urge the lab to expedite processing the last twenty-five hundred frames he had sent them, and he also wired Tharchin to send by postal runner all the photographs in the pack boxes. There was also the matter, now that he was back in India, of transferring funds to his Lloyd's account in Darjeeling to cover his still-outstanding Lhasa expenditures. Theos sent two wires to Viola over four days without a reply, but was certain, as with the problems they had in Lhasa, "your answers are dancing in space around the end of a broken line or something."

But then on October 24, a telegram got through from Viola that eclipsed all his mundane arrangements. Her mother had died. Most of that message, however, was used to again urge Theos not to change his plans and to be sure that all his work in India was wrapped up before heading home to New York. Theos had felt a close bond with the socially progressive and spiritually questing Mrs. Wertheim, and after cabling a reply, he elaborated in a letter to Viola the same day.

> Truly dear, I do not see how on earth you can think that it will be possible for me to continue on here. My own feeling is that I am much more upset than yourself about it. . . . Work is out of the question, my feelings are running the show at the moment and I feel a great need for you. . . . One of the regrets of my life is that I have not been able to be with you during this period. At no other time does one need the companionship of the one he or she loves so much, and on the other side of the world, I am forced to sit back while you share those longings of the heart with some one else.

Four days later, having received from Viola the funds to pay off the remaining bills from Lhasa, he left Kalimpong and completed his descent "from the frozen passes . . . to the sweating, sticky, stinking, slippery slime of the plains of Bengal," checking in, as usual, at the Great Eastern Hotel.

The first of the movie film that he shot after leaving Lhasa was ready at the Kodak lab, and the gasps of the private group that saw the first-ever footage of the sky burial in Shigatse made Theos realize just how unique had been his access to the little-known practices of the Tibetan lamas. As he wrote to Viola: "You should see my movie and hear the reports I am getting on it. . . . It will be enough for anybody—even I say it is wonderful—they say stupendous—just that alone justifies the entire trip." The reaction to the preview screening encouraged Theos to think of larger audiences. "If [the] Tibet color [film] is anything near what I have—it is a world-beater. Do not let it . . . out of your possession until I arrive—I have ideas."

As intended, the dramatic film footage was testimony for the incredible stories Theos brought back from Tibet and whetted the appetite of the *Daily Mail* for its three thousand words. Frank sent daily cables to London apprising the editors of everything Theos did to be sure there was no opportunity of letting their exclusive slip out. The expense account to sequester him the few days he was in Calcutta ran to more than 500 rupees, almost $2,400 in today's currency. "Hell they are spending many times over the little pocket money they are donating to me for an evening's entertainment," Theos wrote to Viola. The British consul general in Calcutta insisted on a visit, and then the American consul general invited him to dinner. More offers for radio interviews came in, but all had to be deflected because of his exclusive contract with the *Daily Mail*. The flood of attention left Theos to conclude, "This public is a fun lot."

The point of being in Calcutta, however, was to make arrangements for getting home, and it was probably the *Daily Mail's* connections that secured a seat to London for Theos on the next Empire Flying Boat, the new aircraft put into service only a few months earlier to open airmail delivery to all the capitals of the British Empire. The flying boats cruised at 164 miles per hour but had to land for refueling every 800 miles, which meant a week was required to reach London from Calcutta. But for Theos, who still hoped to be home by Thanksgiving, that was certainly an improvement on the three weeks required by sea. The entire trip was flown at less than a thousand feet above the ground, and although the turbulence could be upsetting, the close-up aerial view of the parade of cultures between the two great capitals of the empire was alone worth the hefty fare, which at today's values would cost almost $7,000.

Theos spent two weeks in London and reacquainted himself with Western luxury by headquartering at the five-star Ritz Hotel on Piccadilly. On November 12, 1937, the day after his arrival in the city, Londoners were greeted with this banner headline in the *Daily Mail:* "Young Explorer

Writes the Greatest Adventure Story of the Year Exclusively for 'The Daily Mail.'" The subheads cascaded down half the page—"Secret Rites I Saw in Darkest Tibet," "I Was a Lama," "Oracle in Jewelled Cloak"—and under the misspelled byline "Theo Bernard" and in a breathless tone undoubtedly more the editor's than his own, Theos rolled out a new persona.

"I am the first white *lama*," the piece opened, "the first Westerner ever to live as priest in a Tibetan monastery, the first man from the outside world to be initiated into Buddhists' mysteries hidden even from many native *lamas* themselves."

To a public tantalized by the dispatches from the reporters who had accompanied Younghusband thirty-three years earlier, the occasional glimpses captured by British diplomatic missions to Lhasa, and the accounts of a handful of trespassers, the promise of an inside view was truly sensational news. The article was illustrated by three photographs from Lhasa that represented a collection the editor said was "being described by competent authorities as the greatest photographic record of Tibet ever made." One of the photos showed high lamas conducting a service in a dimly lit Lhasa temple; another showed Theos in a Tibetan robe and boots turning prayer wheels in a temple courtyard; and the third showed Theos, again in silk robes, standing among rows of seated monks. The last was captioned, "Mr. Theo Bernard being initiated as a lama." One edition of the paper even included a facsimile of the telegram from the Kashag inviting Theos to Lhasa.

A bulleted list at the head of the second page of the *Daily Mail* article offered the highlights of Theos' five months in Tibet. "I have," it read:

- seen a service to evoke the spirit believed to occupy the body of an oracle during trance.
- attended and photographed the ceremony of "air burial," in which the body is fed to vultures and ravens.
- studied thumo, the art of raising the heat of the body to fever pitch and of lowering it to icy cold by concentration of thought.
- lived with a hermit who had not lain down for 22 years, and seen him cease to breathe whenever he wished, sometimes for several hours.

- photographed secret temples which natives themselves have never entered.
- brought back with me complete copies of the Kan-Gyur (Buddhist Scriptures), Ten-Gyur (commentaries), and other works, comprising 333 volumes printed from engraved wood blocks.

The body of the article skipped along with a few sentences of detail for each of these dazzling plot points, but the most dramatic lines of the entire piece were those explaining why Theos was the first to be honored with such open access to Tibet's secrets: "The Tibetans told me they believe that I am the reincarnation of a great and saintly lama and that I was sent by fate to their country to gather knowledge to take back to the West. That was why they granted me special privileges."

Overnight the scope of Theos Bernard's celebrity grew beyond the small club of Tibetologists. A few days after the *Daily Mail* article, Theos wrote to Viola: "As strange as it may seem everyone seems to be tremendously interested, including Douglas Fairbanks, who I met the other day. This morning I had an early engagement with the head of one of America's largest newspaper syndicates—yesterday I discussed the matter with their keenest competitors, so one in all, it seems that others besides myself (and you) think my experience is of public interest."

Some of the reasons for the others' interest were quite surprising. Five days after the appearance of the first article, the *Daily Mail* ran a second piece headlined "Church Leaders Praise White Lama's Story." The leader of a Scottish missionary society (perhaps the one that employed Tharchin in Kalimpong) wrote: "The article deserves the widest publicity. Already it has been read by millions of people, but I am so enthusiastic about it that I think it should be published in leaflet form and given an even greater circulation.... Last Sunday when I was preaching I referred to its importance, and told my congregation that it proved beyond all doubt an assertion I have made for many years—that there is sufficient gold in Tibet to relieve any world shortage."

Theos found an eager reception among scholars as well. During his first weekend in London, Theos was able to schedule his long-anticipated trip to Oxford, the university at which he hoped to complete his doctoral studies.

Of the Oxford visit he wrote to Viola:

I sat around a glowing fire and enthralled the tottering gray heads while I balanced an unfamiliar teacup on my knee. You should see them—one would almost think that they were biologists and I was a new species. I have had to go to the library and museum to go over special finds which they thought they had. It all gives me a funny feeling when I find myself going over manuscripts etc. with the would-be scholars of the world—one of us is crazy I am sure. One in all, I did everything but pay my entrance fee . . . in fact, they are even planning on the literature which I am going to be able to bring out on my next trip . . . I am sold 100% . . . I have to look no farther.

While still in Tibet, Theos had broached the idea in a letter to Viola of bringing Tharchin to England with him and staying on at Oxford to start translating the texts he had collected rather than returning immediately to New York. That idea, however, depended on Viola joining him there during the six months after her medical residency ended in New Jersey, and when she balked, he gave up the proposal. It was not the tottering gray heads or their collections that attracted Theos to Oxford, but rather the possibility of collaborating with W. Y. Evans-Wentz, the pre-eminent English-speaking Tibetologist of the time and the scholar most interested in Tibetan Tantra. Two years earlier, in 1935, Oxford had published his *Tibetan Yoga and Secret Doctrines,* another exposition of Tantric practices that, like the earlier *Tibetan Book of the Dead,* was based on Tibetan texts translated by Lama Kazi Dawa-Samdup. Evans-Wentz was still in San Diego, but according to Glen, who had frequent conversations with him about Theos' research in Tibet, he would be arriving at Oxford in a few months, and although he was not actually a member of the faculty, he offered to help Theos design a program there. Theos wrote to Viola that he had heard through Glen that the scholar hoped to retire after his next book and open an ashram in India where he could devote the rest of his life to the actual practice of Yoga. Evans-Wentz was looking forward to meeting him, Theos told Viola, "more than I am waiting for him, for he feels that I am the only person living who is capable of carrying on his work."

A few days after his trip to Oxford, Theos made another excursion out of the city, this time to spend the night with Charles and Anne Lindbergh at their home an hour to the southeast in the Weald of Kent. Charles had grown tired of the adulation of the massive crowds that greeted him everywhere he went in America and had fled the spotlight in search of a dignified privacy, if not anonymity, in Europe. Charles found that he could walk the streets of London without being accosted, and in the spring of 1936, he and Anne signed a lease on a six-hundred-year-old house in the nearby country named Long Barn. From here Lindbergh spent long days keeping up a massive correspondence with a coterie he considered to be advancing civilization and pursued his research in the collection of the British Library on sleep, hypnosis, and esoteric Yoga practices.

Charles wanted to know whether Theos saw a possibility for developing airfields in Tibet, but he was even more eager to talk about deep states of meditation. He wondered if Theos had encountered any yogis in Tibet who could enter a state of nonawareness that lasted for days at a time and from which they could not be roused. He was curious also about the position of the body and the respiration and pulse rates associated with deep meditation, perhaps for his speculations about the possibility of suspended animation during space flight. One of his correspondents was Dr. Robert Goddard, a pioneer of rocket technology.

Anne had been pregnant when Theos met them in Calcutta and had given birth to another son since they had seen each other. With the joyful commotion of five-year-old Jon and six-month old Land and their dogs—a German shepherd and Scottish terrier the Lindberghs shipped over on the *Queen Mary*—the night at Long Barn offered Theos a cherished idyll that he hoped to duplicate upon his reunion with Viola in New York.

But before that, there was another reunion to attend in London. His friend Basil Gould, the British political officer in Sikkim, was still in London and invited Theos to a meeting of the Royal Geographic Society for yet another viewing of the color film Chapman had shot during their stay in Lhasa—the very film that Theos had helped edit. While still in Lhasa, Theos had heard the news at the British mission that the film was a sensation in London and Gould had received a special order to show the film to King George and the queen.

Also in attendance at the Geographical Society that night were Sir Francis Younghusband, returned from the spring's travel to Calcutta, and Sir Charles Bell, the legendary career diplomat and friend of the 13th Dalai Lama. After the film, the group quizzed Theos on his return route from Lhasa through Shigatse and Sakya. The illustrious group apparently had no challenges to Theos' belief that he was the only living Westerner to have visited Sakya, and they requested an article describing his journey and Sakya's great library for the Geographical Society's noted journal.

WITH MOST OF HIS BUSINESS now concluded in London, Theos spent the last few days there working out the complications of his reunion with Viola. She wired her approval of his arrival date, November 29—four days after Thanksgiving—and he finalized his booking for a stateroom on the *Queen Mary*. Even though Theos had become an overnight celebrity in London, and it had been by this point more than a year since he had seen his wife, he realized that when he got back to New York, he would still, for a time, get little of Viola's attention. She had returned since her mother's death to the long shifts at the Jersey City hospital, and Theos prepared himself for the possibility that she might not be able to get the day off to meet him when he docked. "You are not to give my return the least bit of attention so far as the work is concerned," he instructed her. "Your work has had far too many distractions and I do not approve of any more and do not want any on my account. . . . I am perfectly willing to stay in a hotel until the weekend when you probably can be off."

In another note to her just days before his departure, Theos wrote: "As you can well guess, I want you near for the homecoming—but it doesn't make a tinker's damn so far as the feelings within are concerned. . . . In this instance, work is first and then me—I can be first some other time, but not just yet. You have that job and must look at it in that light and let me come in where it is possible. . . . Them's orders."

Theos insisted also that she keep his arrival day a secret. He was adamant that Viola be the first person he saw in New York, and if it took days before she could get the time away from the hospital to see him, he preferred to stay anonymously in a hotel until then. He did not want to be greeted at the gangplank by the press or even his friends. "There is to be no one until after you," he wrote to her, "or I am raising hell!"

AT LAST, ON WEDNESDAY, November 25, Theos boarded the *Queen Mary* for the trip across the North Atlantic from Southampton to New York. Since her maiden voyage seventeen months earlier, not only had the *Queen Mary* set a new speed record by becoming the first vessel to make the crossing in less than four days, but her interiors redefined luxury afloat. The brochures advertised that no two staterooms were alike, and the ship's tailors could even redecorate if the existing colors did not satisfy one's taste. More than thirty artists contributed to the diverse collection of paintings and sculptures of this "city gone to sea," and the frequent appearances of the very rich and famous made the *Queen Mary* the height of the transatlantic social scene.

In Tibet Theos had tried to fit in by speaking the language and wearing his golden silk *namsa*. Now with a new suit from a London tailor and fresh haircut and shave, he looked right at home in the ship's first-class salons, and his screen idol good looks and self-assured manner must have set many debutantes to gossiping about who he was. But none aboard would have guessed they were sailing to America with, as Theos told millions of readers in the *Daily Mail*, the incarnation of a great Tibetan saint. He didn't name the saint in this article, but he soon would announce that Tibetan lamas recognized him as an incarnation of Padmasambhava, the great eighth-century Tantric master revered as the Second Buddha.

Theos felt a powerful personal connection to Padmasambhava that had begun soon after he started his Tibetan studies with Tharchin in Kalimpong. He obtained a copy of Padmasambhava's biography, titled *The Lotus Born*, while still in Kalimpong and made that his first translation project. He finished the rough draft before he left Lhasa, producing the first translation into English of *The Lotus Born* (although it was never published) more than fifty years before another English translation appeared in print.

The life story of Padmasambhava was written down in mystical verse by his consort, Yeshe Tsogyal, who hid the manuscript under a statue at Samye, Tibet's first monastery, where it remained for three centuries before it was found. The name *Padmasambhava* means "Lotus-Born" in Sanskrit, an epithet describing the miraculous appearance of Padmasambhava as an eight-year-old child in a giant lotus blossom and his discovery by a servant of the childless king of Uddiyana. The boy was taken to the royal palace, where he was raised as a prince and heir to the kingdom, and one day while doing a sacred dance on the edge of the palace roof, he dropped his ritual trident and *vajra* scepter into the crowd below, killing the wife and son of the king's most powerful minister. As punishment, Padmasambhava was exiled, and he took up residence in the charnel ground of another kingdom. This remained Padmasambhava's home while a famine in the land left more bodies lying in the charnel ground than walking the village streets, and the young prince competed with jackals and vultures to rip the meat off the decaying corpses that were dumped there. Witches haunted the charnel ground and terrorized the village, and Padmasambhava realized that to subdue them he must conquer all revulsion and attain the wisdom that everything he saw was a dream-like illusion projected by his own mind. As Theos put it delicately in his translation, Padmasambhava "effectuated coition with all the corpses that happened to be of the female sex," and attained from that practice the magical power to subdue the witches. The grateful villagers named him Sin Po Shanta, or "Demon Butcher," and having now achieved what he needed to at the charnel ground, Padmasambhava moved on and entered a monastery, where he became a master of Buddhist scriptures.

Padmasambhava's fame spread after another miraculous display in India. The king of Zahor was deceived into believing that Padmasambhava's teaching at his daughter's convent had defiled them both, and he ordered them burned alive. The pyre continued to burn for a week, and when the king arrived to investigate, he found that the pyre had become a lake and in it was a lotus blossom upon which was seated the Princess Mandarava and Padmasambhava as Tantric consorts.

Across the Himalayas, Tibet's great dharma king, Trisong Detsen, was attempting to promote the spread of Buddhism in the kingdom by building Samye monastery. The great Indian Buddhist scholar Shanta-rakshita was brought in to bless the foundation and supervise the project, but the local spirits, opposed to the new religion, united to prevent any progress. They sent a series of earthquakes and floods, and whenever the king's workers raised a wall during the day, the local spirits tore it down at night.

Master Shantarakshita tried to pacify the hostile spirits with *bodhichitta*, great compassion, but they were too savage to respond to the subtlety of that approach. Finally Master Shantarakshita admitted that the malicious gods and demons of Tibet must be tamed by wrathful means, and he advised the king to call in Padmasambhava, who at the time lived meditating in a cave in Nepal. When the king's envoys found Padmasambhava, they offered him bags of gold dust to entice him to return with them, but Padmasambhava strewed the offering across the ground, saying: "I have no need for your gold. . . . For me, all appearances are gold."

He consented nonetheless to help the king, but as soon as he got under way, the war goddess tried to crush him between two moving mountains. The white fiendess Nammen Karo hurled lightning, another demon tried to swallow him, and still another gathered all the icy winds from the three northern plains into one gale and blew them onto Padmasambhava and his terrified retinue. Padmasambhava responded by spinning, on the tip of his finger, a wheel of fire that melted the snowy mountains where these demons lived as if they were butter touched by a red-hot iron.

Padmasambhava then proceeded to the Samye building site, where he found the king waiting at the head of a large reception party. As Theos translated the account of their meeting, the king proudly thought when he saw Padmasambhava, "I am the king of all the black-headed men of Tibet and so the teacher will first salute me." Padmasambhava, however, thought, "I am a devotee who has attained to perfection and have been invited as a teacher, so the king should first salute me." Divining the king's proud thoughts, Padmasambhava sang a song about the poison of arrogance, and with his right hand raised in a salute, emitted a beam of light from the palm that set the king's robes aflame.

With similar miraculous displays Padmasambhava easily bested all the local spirits who opposed him. "Then all the nojin of Tibet, both male and female, offered to him their life-essence and so were exorcised," as Theos translated it. The same spirits that had been working at night to tear down the day's progress on the Samye walls now became allies of Buddhism and helped complete the project.

Working with Shantarakshita, Padmasambhava then helped shape Samye into a preeminent center of scholarship, and it was there at the new monastery that many texts of the Kangyur and Tengyur were first translated from Sanskrit into Tibetan. But Padmasambhava knew that this first flourishing of dharma would not last, and, anticipating the great persecution of Buddhism in Tibet by another king a generation later, Padmasambhava and his disciples hid numerous scriptures throughout Tibet and sealed them with magical time locks that prevented their discovery. These *termas,* as they are called, began to be found shortly after the second flourishing of Buddhism in Tibet was under way near the end of the tenth century. The treasure finders, or Tertons, are considered to be emanations of Padmasambhava himself or of his direct disciples, and they use their powers—which may include clairvoyance and X-ray vision—to find the texts or icons concealed in caves, on high cliffs, underground, in rocks, or even in trees.

Among the treasures discovered in this way was the text that provided the basis for *The Tibetan Book of the Dead.* As Buddhist scholar Robert Thurman put it in the introduction to a recent translation of that text, sometimes the Tertons even "found treasures in their minds, hidden there by the master during their former lives, sealed in the memory codes of their spiritual genes, and discovered at the right moment when people had need of them in some later life and century."

For Theos Bernard, there was no more satisfying explanation than that it was his spiritual genes that were the source of all the miraculous events of his five-month pilgrimage in Tibet. Lamas and high officials told him repeatedly that the karma of his previous life as a teacher there had brought him back to collect everything he needed to spread Buddhism in his new home. And in this way, at least, the seminal role his friends foresaw for Theos was similar to the one Padmasambhava played in the introduction of Buddhism from India to Tibet—clearing the way for others to follow. During the remaining decade of his life, Theos continued to translate not just the words of the biography into English, but also the broad archetypes of Padmasambhava's life into a modern American sequel.

If the memory codes of Padmasambhava were now steaming in a tailored suit at thirty knots to an America filled with demons of different faces but powers similar to those he overcame at Samye, he seemed aware, at least, of the hazards awaiting on the shore. When he began his trip home Theos wrote in a letter to Viola a sentence whose incongruous clauses must have sounded even as he wrote them to be an augury: "The best-informed people say that I have done something that has never before been accomplished and that my dangers lie in the future." The White Lama was about to land in the New World, and the demons were waiting.

Chapter 11

AMBASSADOR
OF SHANGRI-LA

WHETHER ANY FRIENDS, reporters, or even Viola herself was at the dock to meet Theos when the *Queen Mary* tied up in New York is unknown, but his return from a year and three months abroad did not go unnoticed. The day before his arrival, the *New York Times* ran a seven-hundred-word article on page one of the inside section, headlined, "Buddhist Worship in Tibet Pictured; Young Explorer Is Returning Tomorrow with Results of Five-Month Study." The piece included a two-column portrait of Theos dressed in a suit and posed as if he were the handsome leading man in the fantastic movie the article described.

Viola, however, seemed to take less notice of her celebrity husband than the newspapers in London and New York did, and if she did manage to get the day off from the hospital to meet Theos at the dock, she nevertheless saw little of him over the next months. She continued to live at the Jersey City Medical Center, pulling long shifts in the maternity ward, until she completed the full year of her internship at the end of February. "I have put in too much vitality and effort to waste the investment already made for a matter of thirty days," she had written to Theos while he was still in Kalimpong, and that continued to be her appraisal after he returned.

Theos stayed in a New York hotel for the first two weeks of December sorting his films and writing supportive and endearing letters to Viola just as he had from Tibet. That routine, however, led them to conclude that Theos might as well use the time while Viola was still fully occupied at the hospital to spend Christmas in Arizona with his family and then go on to Los Angeles to see Glen. Viola was able at least to see Theos the night before he departed, and he left her a note saying: "Last night was a night that I won't forget for many a day—not until it is blotted out by many more just like it." Theos, it seems, was willing to be patient and to endure the continued separation as an investment of his own. He wrote to her again on the airplane to Tucson: "Don't think that I will ever try leaving you to get away, for the farther I go the closer I get . . . rest assured that we are spending all of our time together."

His flight over the timeless expanse of the American West reminded Theos of the broad vistas on the trail to Gyantse, and he realized just how well his youth in the Southwest deserts had prepared him for the hundreds of miles he traveled on horseback across the bareness of the Tibetan Plateau. He was thrilled by the aerial view of the "endless canyons of solitude and joy" in the sky-island ranges of the Guadalupes, the Chiricahuas, then the Santa Ritas, and delighted in the memories that arose of his adventures on each peak they flew over.

Aura and the family were overjoyed to have him home, and even his stepfather, Gordon—who remained living in Tombstone after the rest of the family moved to Tucson for the boys' university education—came up for the entire visit. "God the affection they have for me dam[n] near smothers me," he wrote to Viola at the end of December.

Aura had provided the Tucson newspaper with updates from Theos' letters to her, and at the reunions he scheduled, his friends and former university professors all knew the outline of his adventures and were keenly interested in his research. One day Theos drove twenty miles into the desert to visit a friend at home, and when he arrived, he was overcome with rapture for the beauty of the barren landscape. "I wanted to jump out of that car and run, holler, as well as get down and roll in the dirt. . . . God I am carried away when I stand on a knoll and gaze across these expanses— every nadi of the system opens," Theos wrote to Viola.

The day after Christmas, a copyrighted story released through the North American Newspaper Alliance appeared in Sunday newspapers across the country. The headline as it appeared in the *New York Times* declared: "American Details Tibetan Mysteries; Young Lawyer Says He Saw Hermit Who Stood Erect in Cell for 20 Years; Attained Height of Several Feet Without Jumping—Saw Temperature Trick." The article was a straightforward description of some of the more sensational things Theos witnessed in Tibet and was similar in its astonished tone to the *Daily Mail* article.

The publicity preceded Theos to Los Angeles, where he arrived on New Year's Eve for a three-week visit with Glen. During his stay, Theos met some of Glen's colleagues who all had been following the news accounts and were eager to discuss his research. Of the group Theos met, two would a few months later be asked to write comments on his doctoral dissertation for Columbia. The first was Hans Nordewin von Koerber, professor of Asiatic studies at the University of Southern California, and the second was the well-known author of *The Tibetan Book of the Dead,* W. Y. Evans-Wentz, who drove up from San Diego for the occasion. Evans-Wentz had been advising Theos on his research through Glen for nearly two years, but this was the first time they actually met. The four of them viewed Theos' uncut Tibet movie footage and spent hours discussing what he should do with it and his plans for the future. But the best moments of the stay in Los Angeles for Theos were in the long, undisturbed hours he spent with his father. "Yesterday was a perfect day," he wrote to Viola. "We saw no one—and never stopped talking."

Before Theos left New York for the West, he talked with a literary agent named Carol Hill about the possibility of writing a popular book about his travels in Tibet. Theos liked to believe that she was one of the biggest agents in the business, but her most important credential was her good relationship with the legendary editor at Charles Scribner's Sons, Maxwell Perkins. Perkins had become famous through the literary success of his discoveries F. Scott Fitzgerald, Ernest Hemingway, and Thomas Wolfe as the model editor who championed, developed, befriended, and lent money to new writers. Although he was modest and polite, Perkins' close editing and insistent advice on revisions amounted in some famous cases almost to coauthorship. He had what one of his novelists, Vance Bourjaily, called an "infallible sense of structure," and his advice on rewriting a rejected manuscript was, at the very time Theos met him, guiding Marjorie Kinnan Rawlings to produce her runaway bestseller and Pulitzer Prize winner, *The Yearling*.

Theos gave Carol Hill an outline for the book and an excerpt from his journal, and she forwarded those to Perkins, who read them and immediately wanted to discuss the project. He called two numbers he had for Theos in Los Angeles without reaching anyone, and the third the person who answered informed him that Theos was very busy and probably didn't want to be disturbed. Perkins persisted with a letter that he sent to the hotel where Theos was staying: "I have gone through all your outline very carefully . . . and I am very anxious now to have a talk with you about the whole matter of the book. It is extremely interesting to me, and has great possibilities. At any time that you are in New York I could suit myself to your convenience."

Theos hurriedly put together a first chapter and sent it to Perkins, but when his agent inquired if Scribner's was ready to make an offer on it, Perkins replied:

> I wish you could wait until I get Mr. Bernard's second chapter. The reason is not that I have any idea, of course, of changing from what I said, but that I want to be able to tell people here better things about the book than I could simply on the basis of the first chapter.
>
> I think he got off on a wrong start, and I want to talk to him again and try to clarify the situation. I had a very nice talk with him and I am sure he has the book in him, but if you would be willing to wait until I get the second chapter, which he said he would bring me, and we can talk again, it would be better for me anyhow.

Theos worked on the second chapter while in Los Angeles and wrote to Perkins that he would have it for him when he returned to New York at the end of the month.

ANTICIPATING THAT THEOS WOULD NEED a quiet place to write when he returned from Los Angeles, Viola rented a hidden cottage called Stepping Stones just a few miles from Princeton University in New Jersey. When Viola described it to him, Theos replied: "Nothing could sound better and you will never know how much the old heart craves it—for once, I am home sick—and home to me means solitude with you. We will store more memories away in that little kitchen corner than it will be possible to forget in two lifetimes by a race of people."

That fantasy and the realization that their marriage would not withstand another long separation led Theos to decide that he would finish his doctorate at Columbia rather than leave again in the fall to study at Oxford. Immediately after settling in at Stepping Stones Theos enrolled for the spring term at Columbia, and Dr. Herbert W. Schneider of the philosophy department agreed to be his dissertation advisor. By this point Theos' interest in academics had devolved to a desire to finish his Ph.D. as fast as possible—perhaps even by the end of the spring term in June. He made infrequent trips to New York to consult with Schneider but spent most of the next months settled in at Stepping Stones to work on both the dissertation for Columbia and the Tibet book, titled *Penthouse of the Gods*, for Perkins.

Viola, still in the last month of her internship, rarely got away from the hospital to be with him, and when magazine reporter Stewart Robertson visited Stepping Stones to interview Theos for a long article he was writing on him, he reported that his visit was the first contact Theos had had with outsiders in fourteen days. "Mr. Bernard was letting his beard grow again, his manner was utterly restful, and he sat quietly in the Buddhistic posture on high cushions," Robertson wrote in his article for *Family Circle*.

During the rare times Theos and Viola did see each other, however, the hours were tense with irritation. The stresses of having cared for her mother and dealing with her death were compounded by the impossible hours and conditions for interns at the hospital, leaving Viola vulnerable to months of infections and chronic sinusitis. Her fatigue led to emotional outbursts that left them, as Viola described it, "alternating between explosive heights and depths those last weeks at the hospital." Theos pressed her to tell him what she wanted for the future, but she resisted, believing that her physical weakness left her emotional state unreliable and that careless phrases "may make permanent a false attitude."

The anxiety and Viola's apparent ambivalence about their future together were intolerable to both of them, and at the beginning of March, with her internship finally completed, Viola agreed with Theos that she needed a rest cure and fresh air. She decided she would go alone to Hot Springs, Virginia, to try to recover her health and determine whether it was really sickness and fatigue causing the problems she was having with her husband or some intractable difference.

Theos hid an encouraging and supportive note in her suitcase and put her on the train. Viola wired on her arrival in Hot Springs: "PRETTY DONE IN BUT WILL LET PINE TREES DO THEIR STUFF IN TIME." She signed the wire with a glaringly neutral "GOOD LUCK. VIOLA."

Theos sent an immediate reply: "STARTING TO WORK WITH STEAD-FAST HOPE GET LOTS OF REST BIG FUTURE AHEAD MUCH LOVE. ME." They talked on the phone and exchanged telegrams, and after about a week Viola moved farther south to the Carolina Inn, in Summerville, South Carolina. She then moved again, this time to Charleston, and by April 2, a month after she left Theos at Stepping Stones, she reached a watershed decision and wrote Theos a three-page letter with her conclusions. "I have fairly conscientiously exposed myself to some sleep and air while turning off the tides of our difficulties as much as possible," she began. "As a result, much of the emotional fatigue is rested, and I know now that my feelings are more reliable and more truly the digest of our years together." She could now write "neither from emotional outburst . . . nor intellectual calculation, but out of all honesty and sadness."

It's all up—you and me making a go of it together. We have both guessed it and feared it. . . .

The practical result of the attempt to fuse our lives, has been un-happiness and a sense of insecurity for us both . . . a rootlessness, in spite of the desire for some sort of permanence and assurance—a house—children—the desires you have often expressed and which I share—but I am afraid to build these things with you—there would be so much more to uproot—and so much more life time of each of us used up. There is an undermining divergence in our activities, our beliefs & standards, our friendships, our work, till now there is so little we share. . . .

I am far from unaware or insensitive to the many ways you have made efforts to compromise and bridge the gap—including these recent weeks. But I do not want to cause you to be untrue to yourself even if you would (which you couldn't for long).

Is our love sufficient bond to hold us in spite of these divergences? Apparently not for me. I have a great affection for you that will doubtless go on, . . . [but] as a wife my feelings have ceased to function completely enough to make either of us happy. . . .

The one thing I hope out of all this may be impossible to achieve—there may be too much intensity, . . . but if we could come out the other end of this thing with a real friendship, we would be able to salvage something that can mean much.

Wanting to close this chapter of her life before she started her assistant residency in psychiatry at Grasslands Hospital in Valhalla, New York—scheduled to begin only ten weeks later—Viola didn't delay in figuring out the mechanics of moving from separation to divorce. In New York at that time, the only ground for divorce was adultery, and so about a third of all New York divorces were executed out of state, with Havana, Mexico, and Reno being the most popular destinations. Viola chose Reno, the self-styled "divorce capital of the world," which had—since the state liberalized its laws in 1931 to require only a six-week residency—created a multimillion-dollar industry out of what Walter Winchell termed "Reno-vation." A plaintiff simply had to prove that he or she had been a continuous resident for six weeks, and if the divorce was uncontested, it was granted immediately on any number of grounds.

Viola arrived in Reno to begin her residency period around the beginning of May, but the atmosphere she found there was hardly conducive to continuing her recuperation. About two-thirds of the plaintiffs seeking a Reno divorce were women, and although there were always a number of celebrities in town, the large majority supported hundreds of motels, hotels with kitchenettes, tawdry boardinghouses, and the phenomena of the divorce ranch, which featured well-appointed gambling parlors, dancing, wide-open drinking, and the opportunity to rediscover the joy of life in the strong arms of a handsome cowboy. At one of the most exclusive ranches, the TH, about thirty miles outside of Reno, owner Cornelius Vanderbilt Jr. offered a $795-a-week divorce package that included room and board, a horse, two trips to Reno, a bottle of liquor, and a daily pack of cigarettes. It may have been the TH that Viola checked in to for the first days of her stay in Reno. She wrote to her attorney and supportive friend in New York, Louis Weiss: "There is much that goes on at the best of Reno ranches that a sense of humor can feed on."

Usually an aggrieved wife's personal attorney at home referred her to a "correspondent" in Reno who guided her through the paperwork, which culminated in a hearing that, if the divorce was uncontested, averaged no more than fifteen minutes and resulted in a decree recognized in all states except South Carolina, New Jersey, and Massachusetts. Legend has it that when the proceedings were concluded, grateful divorcees left red lipstick prints on the columns of the Washoe County Courthouse and flung their wedding bands from the Virginia Street Bridge into the rapids of the Truckee River.

After about a week of the Reno carnival, Viola needed a change of scene and decided to finish waiting out her six-week residency requirement at the elegant Glenbrook Inn on the shores of Lake Tahoe. Since 1907, the Glenbrook Inn had been an exclusive summer getaway for the likes of Mark Twain, Thomas Edison, Henry Ford, Rita Hayworth, and Clark Gable. A coat and tie was required of gentlemen at dinner, to which the butler would call guests from their cocktail hour across the meadow.

Still, despite the serenity and grandeur of Lake Tahoe and the confidence with which she insisted on a divorce so soon after Theos' return from a thirteen-month absence, Viola suffered through periods of black uncertainty about what she was doing. One letter from Louis Weiss alludes to those, saying, "I am so sorry at what goes on in your gizzard. You say it with humor and with sorrow and with warmth and understanding, but that extraordinary epistle of yours makes it abundantly clear that the suffering did not end when you took flight for Reno."

She did not share her doubts with Theos, however. Viola asked him not to write to her until the divorce was finalized, but he found it necessary to inquire about the lease at Stepping Stones, and while he was writing, he took the opportunity to tell her in his irrepressibly lyrical style how he felt about the sudden turn that was ending their marriage.

If I did what I wanted to do most of all, I would fill up the rest of this page and perhaps another sheet or so with all those things in the heart that come under the category of Love, for I am finding it no easy matter to reconcile myself to the new world [in] my heart with one who I admittedly love. But wanting to be as helpful as I can in the situation, I will do no more than mention it except to suggest that you go into the middle of the vastness of a Nevada desert and take one great big deep breath for me—and hold it for a few seconds—do it until you have forgotten that you yourself exist, but for a fleeting moment are completely absorbed in the breath of the universe—and then you will be with me completely for that space of time which we designate a moment, but which will be an eternity for you if you never try to replace it with the mind.

Although he regretted it would be without Viola, Theos was as eager as she was to get on with the next chapter of his life. While Viola was still in South Carolina sorting things out, Theos signed a contract with Charles Scribner's Sons to publish *Penthouse of the Gods* for a $500 advance, payable on delivery of the completed manuscript. With the contract, Max Perkins enclosed a note to Carol Hill: "I wish Mr. Bernard would get on faster, but it is better not to push him. He is far from lazy, I know, and will do the best he can. I think there will be a good deal of work to be done on the manuscript, but that is as we foresaw."

Back at Stepping Stones, Theos was not only working on his book, finishing his Ph.D., and getting a divorce, but also managing the growing media attention focused on his twentieth-century fairy tale. He began organizing a national lecture tour to present the film from Tibet that he was editing, and hired the renowned speakers' agency, W. Colston Leigh, to manage it. Offers came in for radio appearances on Robert Ripley's *Believe*

It or Not! and bandleader Rudy Vallée's top-rated variety show, *Royal Gelatin Hour.* At the same time, radio's most famous broadcaster, Lowell Thomas, sent scouts to preview Theos' film-illustrated lecture—also called "Penthouse of the Gods"—and booked him as the headliner for an upcoming event. Theos and Lowell Thomas soon became friends, and Theos quickly realized that the broadcaster's own career provided the most alluring model for how to market his Tibetan odyssey.

During that time, Lowell Thomas was best known as the man who made Lawrence of Arabia famous. He met T. E. Lawrence, a captain in the British army, in Jerusalem in 1918 while on a film expedition dispatched by President Woodrow Wilson to drum up support in isolationist America for the unpopular world war. Lawrence worked as a liaison between the British and the Arabs, who were in revolt against their common enemy, the Ottoman Turks, and Thomas and his cameraman spent several weeks with Lawrence in the desert.

After the war, Thomas toured the world narrating his film *With Allenby in Palestine and Lawrence in Arabia* in dramatic performances that featured backdrops of the pyramids and exotic dancers accompanied by the band of the Welsh Guards. The extravaganza was seen by four million people around the world and ran for six months in London alone, making Lawrence—and Lowell Thomas—household names. Thomas made $1.5 million on the tour, and then in 1924 published *With Lawrence in Arabia*, the first of what would be fifty-six books in his career. Over the next years Theos would consult frequently with Thomas for advice on how to create an audience for his adventures and how to package his presentations.

One day that spring Theos got a call from the famous polar explorer Admiral Richard Byrd. He was canceling a trip to Chicago, he said, and needed to meet with Theos immediately. On his second expedition to Antarctica, between 1933 and 1935, Byrd spent four and a half months alone at a meteorological base in the perpetual night of Antarctic winter, sheltered from the -85°F temperatures in a nine-by-thirteen-foot prefabricated hut. Drifting snow completely buried the hut, and Byrd developed carbon monoxide poisoning when a pipe venting the generator that powered the radio became occluded with ice. Two months into his stay, he collapsed during one of his thrice-weekly radio conversations with base camp at Little America, but it was another two and a half months before a rescue party reached him and two months more after that before a plane arrived to evacuate him.

"He has made a deep contact with his subconscious self as the result of that period of isolation," Theos wrote about their meeting. "As he puts it, something popped on the inside and . . . from all that he had read and heard about me, he felt that I should understand him."

DESPITE ALL the interruptions and the fact that it was hardly the focus of his life at this point, Theos finished writing his dissertation on schedule and in the third week of May defended it at his oral exams. In the dissertation—titled "Tantrik Yoga"—Theos attempted to document the techniques used in the spiritual training transmitted by the Tantric Yogis with whom, he said, he had studied in India. There was already abundant literature on the theories of Hatha Yoga, Theos wrote in his preface to the dissertation, but when it came to the actual practice of Hatha Yoga, those texts were more confusing than informative. "I have not attempted to contribute to the theory of Yoga, nor to its history," he wrote. "My aim has been to become acquainted with the practical application of the theory." To achieve that, he said, he became the sincere disciple of a highly esteemed teacher and settled down at his retreat in the hills near Ranchi to practice the rigid discipline of Hatha Yoga under his supervision and guidance. With one sentence in his acknowledgments at the end of the preface, Theos tried to deflect the question of why he didn't anywhere in the dissertation name the teachers he studied with. "To my teachers in India and Tibet, who, shunning public acclaim, must perforce remain anonymous, I am deeply indebted."

The six-person review committee from the philosophy department asked several outside authorities to read "Tantrik Yoga" and offer criticism to pursue during the oral exams. Chief among those readers were Glen's friends Hans Nordewin von Koerber and W. Y. Evans-Wentz. Koerber wrote that it "shows a highly subjective viewpoint in so far as he obviously accepted verbally the teachings given to him by Gurus or Lamas and simply incorporated them in his dissertation without first carefully weighing them." And even though Theos was not attempting a survey of Yoga scholarship, the bibliography was incomplete, Koerber wrote, without listing the leading publications in Latin, German, French, Russian, Hungarian, Chinese, and Japanese from as long ago as the fourteenth century.

The comments from Evans-Wentz that were included in the official report of the examining committee were minor criticisms about the glossary and suggestions to distinguish Buddhist from Hindu Tantra. He also stated there should be an emphatic warning in the text that because of the "physical, mental and psychic dangers inseparable from certain Yogic practices" they should be attempted only under the supervision of a competent guru. He further advised that, when published, "Tantrik Yoga" should be circulated only to qualified associates to protect the secrecy of the practices.

It is interesting, however, that the examining committee chose to omit in its report the glowing praise that Evans-Wentz (undoubtedly the most competent authority on the subject in the Western academic world) wrote in his letter to Schneider:

I am of the opinion that the Dissertation constitutes a genuine contribution to the advancement of philosophical and anthropological learning; I should, therefore, recommend that the Dissertation be accepted by the Examination Committee. . . .

Mr. Bernard deserves unstinted praise for his remarkably successful penetration of the Sacred Places of Tibet, especially Lhasa; and I wish to append here my own appreciation for his arduous research.

I have no doubt that the Examiners will recognize the pioneer character of Mr. Bernard's research and, accordingly, make due allowance for its shortcomings. I take it that Mr. Bernard is merely at the thresh-hold of a scholarly career which promises much for the future. And it is the duty of those who are his academic seniors to extend to him Right Encouragement along with Right Guidance.

The examining committee, however, offered little encouragement and concluded in its report: "As it stands ["Tantrik Yoga"] attempts more that it adequately achieves." They suggested that, because the candidate chose to approach the subject as "a field trip exploring contemporary cults and mythologies," he needed to cite clearly both his oral and written sources and distinguish the Yoga schools represented by the gurus who instructed him in both Tibet and India. He also needed, the committee stated, "to distinguish his personal experiences from the theories about them." All in all, the committee's report concluded, the submission would require so many additions and excisions to address the criticisms that they suggested he start over and send the committee an outline of his new approach before beginning.

The examining committee rejected Theos' dissertation submission largely because he did not answer a question that still beguiles researchers and avid readers today: Who taught Theos Bernard the practices of Hatha Yoga that he had so evidently mastered?

AFTER THE ACCEPTANCE of a dissertation, the Department of Philosophy required that it be published and a hundred copies filed at its office. Publishing entailed a large expense, and months before he submitted the dissertation Theos proposed a plan to pay for it by packaging the dissertation with a popular book on Yoga that would, as he wrote to Perkins, "deal with the subjective results of the training." Perkins read the dissertation about the same time the examining committee did and replied to Carol Hill that it didn't have enough commercial potential for Scribner's to publish it, but "we do think that Mr. Bernard could write a popular book on Yoga, and this shows that he could. . . . It seems to us though that *Penthouse of the Gods* is much the most important project and should precede a book on Yoga and prepare the way for it."

The following year Theos signed a contract with Scribner's for the popular book on Yoga, but it would be five years before he got around to rewriting his dissertation and finally completing his Ph.D. at Columbia. The calculation for Theos since he started his studies at Columbia four years earlier was that it was necessary to endure the bothersome investment in a doctoral degree before he could establish the Yoga institute he was dreaming of. Now he believed the publicity being showered on him would take him there faster.

In the last week of April, just as he was finishing his dissertation and Viola was on her way to Reno, Theos was thrust irrevocably into the national spotlight with a two-part series and cover photographs in one of the largest-circulation magazines of the day. *Family Circle* was one of the first and most successful of a new concept for magazines that, like radio programs, was distributed free and supported by advertising. The twenty-four-page tabloid weekly was available only at the checkout counters of chain grocery stores, such as Piggly Wiggly and Safeway, and quickly reached a circulation of three million. The covers featured large photographs of celebrities and newsmakers ranging from Bing Crosby to Mussolini to attract readers to the romantic fiction, feature articles, and, of course, advertising inside.

On April 22, 1938, Theos joined the celebrity ranks with a cover photograph shot in Lhasa that showed him in the official hat and silk gown of a *shape*. The photo was captioned, "Theos Bernard . . . is a Buddhist lama—the only white man ever to be made one." His picture the next week dominated the cover and showed him "in his lama's cap and robe at Lhasa" while from the other side of the page a scantily wrapped Dorothy Lamour was posed with her gaze directed admiringly at him.

Theos made the cover of *Family Circle* four times in eighteen months, sharing the space in the following issues with Errol Flynn, Bette Davis, and Norma Shearer, but each time he upstaged them with photos twice the size of theirs. The first two of the four articles, "White Lama," parts one and two, were given five full pages in each issue and were illustrated by twenty-three of Theos' photographs, including "the first photos of a Tibetan air burial ever published in a magazine."

The articles, written from his multiple interviews with Stewart Robertson, provided the same kind of publicity in America that the *Daily Mail* provided in London, and Theos used the opportunity to tell the same story. "Mr. Bernard . . . became the only white man in the world's history to be made a lama . . . of Tibetan Buddhism," Robertson wrote. "They saw in him the reincarnation of the sainted Padmasambhava, of whom the legend runs that he will someday return in the guise of a white man to carry Buddhism into the western world. And that is why the Tibetans gave Bernard a welcome such as no soldier or statesman could ever receive.

They escorted him into Lhasa as one who was in touch with them spiritually—as one who was coming home."

IMMEDIATELY AFTER HIS RETURN from Los Angeles at the end of January, Theos began his attempts to deliver the letters he carried home from the regent and the Sakya Trizin to the president of the United States. In his own introductory letter to the White House Theos wrote:

> Dear Mr. President,
>
> I have recently returned from an extended visit in Tibet where as a student of Tibetan religious and social life, I was permitted to live for several months in the Lhasa home of Kashag member Tsarong-Shape, and was honored by audiences with the King-Regent of Tibet who has commissioned me personally to deliver to you a letter of friendly greeting.
>
> I should appreciate the opportunity of discharging this honored obligation.
>
> Should you be interested in seeing at the White House unique motion pictures in color of the land from which I bring you greetings, I should further be happy to have you the first to see these pictures. . . .
>
> Most respectfully yours, Theos C. Bernard

Theos received a quick reply from the chief of protocol at the State Department.

> The President desires me to thank you for your . . . suggestion that he might be interested in seeing the motion pictures you brought back from Tibet. Your thoughtfulness is appreciated and the President regrets that he is unable to take advantage of your kind offer. As for the letter of greeting for the President which you have brought from Tibet, if you will send it to me I shall be glad to forward it to its destination.

Theos replied to that message saying he would very much like to personally present the letters to the president as he had promised, and then enlisted another contact in the bureaucracy, a friend of Viola's family,

Frederic A. Delano. Delano wrote to Mrs. Roosevelt and received a telegram from the Roosevelts' summer home saying the president would be interested in seeing Theos when he returned to Washington. But when the president found out that Theos lived in New York and would have to make a special trip to see him, he wrote to Delano, "Never mind, I will see him some other time, whenever he is in the city."

Delano concluded from all that, "I do not know that it would be worth your while to make a special trip to Washington for ten minutes, but I am inclined to think that if you did have ten minutes with him you could perhaps interest him enough so that he would say 'Stay over and let me see the thing in the evening.'" In June Theos got a call saying that the president might be able to meet with him after Congress adjourned for the summer, but nothing came of that either.

A letter through whatever channel with overtures of friendship from the head of the long-isolated Tibetan government should have been a noteworthy event for the American State Department, and Roosevelt's apparent indifference to receiving the letters Theos carried from Tibet most probably reflects diplomatic calculations rather than simple disinterest. There was a great sensitivity in Washington in 1938 to avoiding any offense to the Nationalist Chinese government of Chiang Kai-shek, which not only was fighting the Japanese but also offered the only hope of defeating the Communists in China. With the Nationalist Chinese reviving the imperial claim that they were the legitimate rulers of Tibet, diplomats in Washington chose repeatedly in the 1930s not to risk offending their ally by opening direct communications with Lhasa.

At the death of the 13th Dalai Lama in 1933, Roosevelt accepted the advice of the State Department and decided against sending a message of condolence to the Tibetan government, reasoning that the message might be construed as recognition of a fellow chief of state. Four years later, Roosevelt showed a similar deference to the Nationalist Chinese when he listened to Undersecretary Sumner Welles' advice against sending an official letter of greeting to the Kashag with Suydam Cutting on his visit. Welles warned that Tibet is "still technically under the suzerainty of China" and the letter would be "liable to misconstruction" by the Chinese Nationalist Government.

Roosevelt might also have been concerned that a meeting with Theos would have offended his old friend Suydam Cutting. The attendant publicity and implicit endorsement of Theos' trip to Lhasa could be perceived as a slight and require some compensating public acknowledgment of Cutting's brief trip to Lhasa as well. At any rate, with all the diplomacy, Theos didn't have the opportunity in 1938 or 1939 to deliver the letters from the regent of Tibet and the king of the Sakyas to Roosevelt. In February 1940, Lowell Thomas offered to help arrange a meeting and mention it in a radio broadcast, but nothing came of that either, and the whole issue was forgotten. The president of the United States never saw the large pages of regal paper meticulously lettered by the court scribes with their forty-four folds, red seals, and hopes that he would help Theos Bernard promote Buddhism in America, and they became just another artifact of the White Lama's trip to Tibet.

WITH HIS FANTASY of tranquil months making memories with Viola in the kitchen corner at Stepping Stones now shattered, Theos decided to move back to Manhattan and rented a room from Blanche DeVries in the apartment on 57th Street that served as one of New York's first Yoga studios, the Living Arts Center. Despite their separation, Theos continued to be financially dependent on Viola, and he sent a letter to her at Lake Tahoe to let her know that there was no money in the joint account. He was beginning to organize his national lecture tour and needed a deposit to cover—in addition to his living expenses and $300 to pay off Tharchin—$500 for the lecture brochures, and the cost of a Bell and Howell thousand-watt projector and screen. As she had throughout their marriage, Viola continued during their separation to underwrite without complaint Theos' ambitious projects.

It was mid-July when Viola had her hearing in Reno's Washoe County District Court and walked out after fifteen minutes with a routine, uncontested divorce decree. She was generous in the terms she had her New York lawyers draw up, and established an $80,000 trust for Theos from which he received the interest and the investment profits in quarterly payments. He could also withdraw up to $2,500 a year of the principal until, at age fifty, he would receive the remaining balance. Her sense of fairness extended even to a $100,000 wedding gift from her mother that had been deferred because of worries over the course of the Great Depression at the time of their marriage. Her mother's will stipulated that Viola would receive the gift after the death of an invalid niece for whom she had established a $200,000 trust, and Viola had the lawyers include a clause that Theos would get half when she received it.

Viola wrote in the breakup letter from South Carolina that she wanted to avoid bitterness and salvage a friendship from their marriage, and it appears they did succeed in that. Theos wrote blithely in his last letter to her before she left Nevada with the divorce decree: "I am looking forward to being with you this coming Saturday—arriving around two o'clock or shortly thereafter as I possibly can—and then for a swim."

THEOS HAD BY THIS TIME FINISHED editing his ten thousand feet of movie film into a forty-five-minute presentation, and to prepare for his national lecture tour he staged on the evening of July 26 a preview at Manhattan's exclusive Lotos Club. The presidents of both the Fox and Paramount studios were there along with Robert Ripley from *Believe It or Not!* and a producer from NBC. "It is perhaps one of the best advertising things that I could have done," he wrote to Viola as soon as he got home that night. "I wish that you could have seen and heard the people at the Lotos club rise in their seats and bring down the house when I finished the lecture.... Every one of them says that I have a fortune wrapped up in the story."

Theos had asked Lowell Thomas for some advice on preparing for his lecture career, and Thomas suggested that he start by hiring a voice coach. Theos invited his voice coach to the Lotos Club preview to criticize the lecture, and received another boost of confidence when his instructor told him it was the finest lecture presentation he had ever seen. It wasn't long after that when Theos received still more encouragement. He had sent a description of his program to the American Anthropological Association, and they wished to give him an entire evening at their annual conference.

Theos continued to work on his book, *Penthouse of the Gods*, and by the third week of July had written eight hundred pages of a first draft but said he was still not half finished. Nevertheless, he thought he could finish the first draft by the end of the following week, but it might require hiring another typist—the first was already working ten-hour days and falling behind.

After a week with a second typist, however, Theos realized that he needed more help than just a pair of stenographers to keep up with his dictation, and he hired the writer John Cournos to help him turn his sixteen-hundred-page draft into a finished manuscript. Cournos wrote poetry, short stories, essays, criticism, translated Russian literature, and by the time he went to work with Theos, he had already published ten novels of his own. Perkins wrote to Theos, "I am delighted by the conversations with John Cournos. . . . I have found him really enthusiastic about the book, and particularly after he talked with you. I believe no one could have a better understanding of it, or a greater ability to handle it in complete sympathy with your conceptions. It seems to be certain to turn out to be a very fine book indeed."

While the ghostwriter worked at the book manuscript, Theos shifted his focus to polishing the narrative script and final film edits for his "Penthouse of the Gods" national lecture tour. He debuted with a presentation to the Woman's Club of Fall River, Massachusetts, on October 24, 1938, and continued over the course of two separate tours between 1938 and 1940 to more than ninety venues in almost every major city in the United States. On the first tour alone, he crossed the country four times in six months with a total of forty-five engagements at colleges and universities, women's clubs, geographical societies, and service clubs. In New York City he lectured at Town Hall, the venerable auditorium that had lectures scheduled also that season by Winston Churchill, Will Durant, and Carl Sandburg.

The tour's brochure cover featured a large photo of Theos—alluringly handsome, bearded, and in his yellow silk Tibetan *namsa*—sitting at a low table covered with stacks of loose rectangular Tibetan manuscript pages and counting beads on a *mala* in his left hand. A large headline exclaimed, "The Most Exciting Illustrated Lecture Attraction of the Season," and the text inside explained why.

Theos Bernard went to Tibet, not as an explorer, photographer, or collector of Asiatic curios, but as a student of Buddhism and Tantric Ritual. He was received and treated by the Tibetans as has no other American or European who has ever penetrated the fastnesses of that little-understood Himalayan upland.

In its fifteen hundred feet of color motion pictures, the advertising promised "a living page from what the school-texts call 'Ancient History.'"

The film and scripted narrative took the audience along on the entire trip—from entering Tibet over Natu La to leaving it five months later over Kongra La. Theos paced dramatically across the stage costumed in his gold Tibetan *namsa* and high crescent-shaped *geshe*'s cap declaiming to audiences mesmerized by film images of the monastery and Tantric shrines at Gyantse:

> The head lama took hours to examine me, making certain who I was and why I had come, for it was an auspicious event that one of the Western world should arrive on this holy day. They heralded me as a reincarnation of the famous Saint Guru Rimpoche, and ordered that the ceremony of burning a thousand butter lamps be offered in my honor.

From Lhasa there were stunning color images of Tsarong's house, Norbulingka, and the regent's dance festival. Even the sublime tombs of the Dalai Lamas in the Potala were captured in motion pictures.

> Climb these forbidden stairs and go through its sacred halls.... Within are literally hundreds of shrines and behind those walls the tombs of all the Dalai Lamas...covered from top to bottom with gold and studded with priceless gems. Placed at the altar are butter lamps several feet high made from pure gold, holding enough butter to burn for three months without being replenished.

The excursions to Drepung, Sera, and Ganden monasteries were depicted, and then came scenes showing the piles of priceless Tibetan manuscripts Theos had collected as they were being sewn into yak skins to be hauled on the backs of fifty mules over the Himalayas, from where they would "be shipped on to America that the teachings may be brought to the western world and peace may come to the soul of all."

After the film images showed him crossing the snowbound Kongra La safely into Sikkim, Theos concluded his narrative script with these enigmatic lines:

> Like a flash before death I realize that I have reached the end of my journey and review every detail of my Twentieth Century Fairytale: . . . my first glimpse of the Penthouse of the Gods, my initiations, and the last instruction of my guru: "The end of human existence is to learn to follow the eternal stream of life."

As unique as these first documentary movie images of Tibet were, the twentieth-century fairy tale Theos narrated had by the time of his "Penthouse of the Gods" tour become a leitmotif in America and England called "Shangri-La." The term, which came to mean an imaginary paradise on earth or exotic utopia, was introduced to the English lexicon by James Hilton in his bestselling novel *Lost Horizon*. First published in 1933 with a small print run, the book reached number eight on the bestseller list after being reissued in 1935. In 1939—just as Theos was beginning his national lecture tour—the book was reprinted again as one of the first-ever paperbacks, Ballantine's Pocket Book No. 1. This edition alone sold 1.3 million copies in less than a decade.

Hilton's story is set in a hidden valley on the frontier of northeast Tibet where the glaciated peaks of the Kunlun Mountains shelter below its high passes an idyllic society of surpassing beauty, wealth, artistry, and tranquility called Shangri-La. Here, in the Valley of the Blue Moon, people live three hundred years or more, and the masterpieces of the world's philosophy, art, and science are safely preserved from a holocaust that will destroy the rest of earth's warring civilization. The plot revolves around the arrival of a uniquely qualified Englishman in Shangri-La and his grooming as the successor to the valley's High Lama.

While Theos Bernard was in Lhasa during the summer of 1937, Hollywood was turning Shangri-La into a household word. Frank Capra's ambitious and high-budget adaptation of Hilton's book produced a block-buster film seen by more than 250,000 people at a single theater in Hollywood. Another three million people saw the film in a hundred cities around the country, and the film was nominated for seven Academy Awards, including Best Picture.

The record audiences were the American culture's heartfelt response to the question posed on the first of a series of title cards at the opening of the film:

In these days of wars and rumors of wars, haven't you ever dreamed of a place where there was peace and security, where living was not a struggle but a lasting delight?

The last card of the series states:

One man had such a dream and saw it come true. He was Robert Conway—England's "Man of the East"—soldier, diplomat, public hero.

In the film, Conway—played by Ronald Colman—has been dispatched to an outpost in war-ravaged China to aid with the evacuation of the remaining Westerners escaping the battles of the Chinese civil war and Japanese invasion. Three of the evacuees board the last DC-2 out of the flaming airport along with the suave adventurer and foreign secretary–designate, Robert Conway. When they are safely under way, the passengers discover the plane has been hijacked by their pistol-wielding Mongolian pilot, who is now flying them deeper into the glaciered mountains of Tibet in the west. The plane runs out of fuel and crashes into a snowfield in the Kunlun Mountains, killing the pilot and leaving the passengers marooned among the frigid peaks. When all appears lost, a party of fur-robed travelers appears, and the elderly Chinese leader, Chang, gives them warm clothes and takes them safely roped through the treacherous glaciers to a pass where they look down upon the warm and verdant Valley of the Blue Moon, the uncharted Himalayan paradise of Shangri-La. They descend to a mysterious civilization of beautiful gardens, fountains, marble palaces, and a happy and perpetually youthful population.

The book supplies a number of details not in the screenplay. The High

Lama and founder of the valley's unique society was a Capuchin monk, Father Parrault, who in 1719, at age thirty-three, left Peking with three other friars on a mission to search the mountains of northeastern Tibet for remnants of the Nestorian Christians who once settled in remote parts of Asia. Father Perrault was the only one of the group to survive a succession of mountain snowstorms and, near death, stumbled into a hidden valley inhabited by Buddhists who nursed him to health again. He spent years trying to convert the Tibetans, who listened tolerantly, and at the age of ninety-eight he began to study some Buddhist texts found in the old temples and undertook the mystical practices of Yoga and its Pranayama breathing practices.

At age 108 Father Perrault thought he was dying and gathered his friends and servants for a farewell. He lay for weeks without speaking and on his deathbed had an apocalyptic vision. He saw the nations of the modern world increasing not in wisdom but in violent passions and the will to destroy. He saw their machine power multiplying until a technician with a single weapon could match a whole army of the Grand Monarque. New tyrants would rage over the world, and every precious thing would be in danger, every book and picture and harmony, every treasure garnered through two millennia. The small, the delicate, the defenseless—all would be lost.

Lost Horizon tapped the gestating worldwide fear that the globe was on the brink of a cataclysm from which it might never recover. On November 12, 1937—the very day the *Daily Mail* published its exclusive story on Theos' pilgrimage in Tibet—people throughout the world observed a two-minute silence to commemorate the nineteenth anniversary of the armistice that ended the Great War. An article on the front page of the *New York Times* stated, "The keynote of the world-wide celebration was hope that statesmen somehow would be able to find a way to peace and save the peoples of the world from suffering the horrors of another great international war." That article had to share the front page, however, with stories of the surrender of Shanghai to the invading Japanese army and Japan's refusal to attend a nine-nation parley in Brussels. The infant industry of scientific opinion polling found that in the fall of 1939 two-thirds of Americans believed Hitler was driven by ambition to be emperor of the world and would attack the United States if he defeated England and France.

In *Lost Horizon,* the High Lama—having found the secret to longevity in Pranayama, but growing infirm now at the age of 350—tries to convince Robert Conway to succeed him as Shangri-La's High Lama. Conway was a man of the Lost Generation—one of the millions disillusioned with modernity by the mechanized carnage they saw in the trenches of the First World War, and alienated from the following decades' materialism, shallow pleasure seeking, and ideology of unrelenting technological progress. Conway had attracted the attention of the High Lama from afar with some essays he had written expressing his disillusionment with the modern world, and the High Lama had staged the evacuation and plane crash to maroon him in Shangri-La.

In recruiting Conway to succeed him, the High Lama was asking Conway to oversee Shangri-La's repository of the world's great philosophy, art, and science, the finest examples of which he had clandestinely purchased over the centuries with the plentiful gold found near the valley's streams. These would be the only seeds of human culture to survive the great and searing holocaust that approached. "The time must come, my friend, when this orgy will spend itself, when brutality and the lust for power must perish by its own sword. Against that time is why I avoided death and am here and why *you* were brought here. For when that day comes, the world must begin to look for a new life. And it is our hope that they may find it here."

The tone of apocalyptic dread suffusing American culture before World War II was poignantly expressed by James Hilton, conceiver of Shangri-La, in a full-page op-ed piece in the *Los Angeles Times* for Easter Sunday, 1938. Headlined "Humanity Can Be Saved! An Easter Challenge to a Groping World," the article began: "Rarely have the skies of the future been darker; never have we been so thoroughly warned of their darkness. The collapse of civilization, a fantasy to our grandfathers, is a schoolboy's cliché today. . . . We are alive at our own funeral."

Unless we want to begin our cultural evolution all over again, Hilton wrote, we must find a way to ensure that the wisdom produced by our millennia of civilization survives civilization's approaching collapse. And with the stakes so high, Hilton proposed here an approach to preserving the wisdom of the ages opposite from the one the High Lama took in *Lost Horizon*. Wisdom could not be preserved by filling vaults with cultural treasures in a remote land, but must be realized in each of us with the hope that those who survive will carry the seeds of wisdom in their hearts.

"It may be that for a lifetime wisdom must hibernate in catacombs.... While the tyrant conquers the earth, he who is eventually to dethrone him must first conquer himself.... There can be no new quality in our civilization till there are new qualities in our minds and hearts. We must be born again as individuals before we can save ourselves as humanity."

Hilton's inspirational piece offered no advice, however, on a path to achieve the individual transformations he saw as civilization's only hope to survive. "What shall we do to be saved?" Hilton asked. "In an earlier age men believed that they knew, and in the shelter of that belief the mind and conscience of humanity flowed in ever-deepening channels. Today, all over the world, that belief is weakened, dying, or dead.... Many of us cannot, even if we would, accept the simple faith of our fathers."

The hero must first conquer himself before conquering the tyrant, but as to how that could be achieved, all Hilton had to suggest in his piece was, "We must watch—perhaps we must even pray." Politics offered no reassurance against the pandemic fear that another generation was about to be shattered by some unstoppable inertia in world events, and if the tyrants could not be kept from destroying the world, the true hero must prepare himself with the wisdom to build a better world on its ashes.

For Theos, America's urgent interest in the refuge of Shangri-La provided a marketing bonanza. Everywhere Theos took his "Penthouse of the Gods" tours over the next two years, the press found the *Lost Horizon* connection irresistible. On his visit to San Francisco, just six weeks after his return from India, the *San Francisco Chronicle* captioned a front-page, two-column picture of him "From Shangri-la: Dr. Theos Bernard, He Saw Forbidden City in Tibet." The article began: "A slim, completely modern young man sat in a Pacific Avenue home yesterday and spoke of 'Lost Horizons,' of a Shangri-la that exists in fact as well as in the fancy of novelist James Hilton." The headline of the second of the four *Family Circle* cover articles about Theos read: "Seen 'Lost Horizon'? Read Lama Theos Bernard's Story of What Tibet Is Really Like." And typical of the advertising for his lecture tour was this ad in the *Reno Gazette* promoting 25¢ and 50¢ tickets at the Civic Auditorium with the line: "Explorer brings to Reno for the first time the inside story of Lost Horizon."

Theos' story provided an intriguing parallel to the fictional High Lama's choice of the debonair but disillusioned Englishman, Robert Conway, to be custodian of Shangri-La's library, the seeds for the renaissance of wisdom in a decayed West. Following his lecture in Pittsburgh, the *Telegraph* printed an article Theos wrote describing his reception in Tibet as the fulfillment of prophecy.

> The priests of fabulous Tibet have initiated me as the first white man, into the anxiously guarded ritual of their religion [for] a reason so strange that I myself did not know about it at first. Only gradually I learned about it from the highest Tibetan priests in their capital, Lhasa. They believe me to be the reincarnation of the god who founded that religion....
>
> Perhaps the strangest prophecy of the Tibetan Holy Books is this: that there will come a time when the world will seem in chaos. There will be floods and cold, wars will threaten the universe. Then a new, great teacher, like Buddha, will appear to spread law and order throughout the world. And this teacher, Tibetan tradition says, will be a Westerner.
>
> When I was about to leave Tibet, my friends gave me the holy books and admonished me to spread the word of man's brotherhood and peace in my country.
>
> I saw their meaning, and assured them I did not feel I was destined to be the great teacher. But they only smiled the inscrutable smile of mysterious Tibet and said:
>
> "Guru Rinpoche, whose incarnation you are, also might have said that once."

The Sakya Trizin wrote to President Roosevelt in his undelivered letter: "If a Buddhist Monastery is established in your Precious Majesty's kingdom, there will be no pestilence, nor will there be war or famine in your country. Perfect happiness and prosperity will prevail.... Please be graciously inclined to render all the assistance that lies in your power, to help this gentleman, Bernard, who has a pure mind." The myth of Shangri-La now had its first champion, returned from the quest with not only the essential ancient books but all the pictures to document his story and inspire faith in his individual transformation. The White Lama had arrived in America.

THEOS STARTED his first "Penthouse of the Gods" lecture tour in the last week of October 1938 and spent much of the next six months traveling between forty-five venues in almost every major American city and speaking before audiences as large as three thousand people. While Theos was traveling, his ghostwriter, John Cournos, and editor, Maxwell Perkins, were collaborating to turn the sixteen-hundred-page manuscript he left them into the book *Penthouse of the Gods.*

Months earlier Perkins had written to Theos' agent, Carol Hill, that the first chapter "got off to the wrong start," but by July 5, 1938, after several meetings with Theos, Perkins was able to write to her:

> Now I think . . . he has . . . devised a good method for going at the book. . . . He will need a lot of help, but I think now it ought only to be in detail. He begins the book in a monastery in Lhasa with his initiation into the priesthood. At the end of that initiation, the neophyte puts in a week of solitary confinement and then he is supposed to review his life. . . . When he gets into his cell he goes back to the beginning of the story of how he got interested in Buddhism, and how he determined to master it. Then he tells of his journey to Lhasa. I think now on this basis he will work out a very good book at least.

Penthouse of the Gods was released by Charles Scribner's Sons on March 30, 1939. As Theos and Perkins had worked out in their early meetings, the book opens with the plot device of the final initiation with Tri Rinpoche at Ganden and then Theos being installed in a tiny retreat cave. He spends three days and four nights in his meditation box without lying down to sleep, and as the book tells the story, between his four meditation sessions each day he recalled (in a three-hundred-page extended flashback) the dramatic events that brought him to that point: the arduous journey across the Himalayas, maneuvering for permission to visit Lhasa, living with Tsarong, collecting texts, his open access to the Potala and Norbulingka, his initiations at the great temples and other monasteries of Lhasa, and his recognition as an incarnation of a Tibetan saint.

The story in the book climaxes with Theos leaving the cave and having one last illuminating meeting with Tri Rinpoche, who had been meditating in his chamber and in psychic contact with Theos the entire time. The sun had not yet risen, Theos wrote, when he stepped into the private shrine of Tri Rinpoche and sat down on a cushion beside him for three hours of silent meditation. Tri Rinpoche finally broke the silence by reciting some mantras and then explained to Theos the meaning of his experiences in Tibet.

> He pointed out to me that now I had gained contact with an old soul that was within me, this was, he said, the reason for my pilgrimage, that I had by no means come as a disciple to acquire learning, that I had, indeed, previously possessed this knowledge, and that it had been only a question of making the contact. Now, having brought consciousness into it, he said, it would be possible for me to continue my development throughout life.

Now that Theos had awakened this latent wisdom from a past life, his work in Tibet was finished and he could go home. In the concluding paragraph of the book, Theos wrote:

> Secure in my knowledge that I had a way of communing with this mind from any corner of this earth, it had now become possible for me to return to the world of affairs. And my own land, America, suddenly beckoned to me, and my return to it, I was aware, would be fraught with meanings which I had not even suspected when I left it for my wanderings in India and, above all, Tibet.

With the nationwide mania for Shangri-La, Theos must have been confident when Scribner's released *Penthouse of the Gods* in the spring of 1939 that he had a sure bestseller. The book, which was dedicated to Viola, was illustrated with sixty dramatic but grainy black-and-white photographs of Tibet, but even with the publicity over those, Scribner's showed a notable lack of confidence in the book and released it with a modest initial print run of 3,270 copies. A year after its release, the total sales had reached only 4,758 copies, netting for Theos—after the agent's 10 percent and the $500 fee for the ghostwriter—a total of $565 in royalties.

The reviews weren't bad overall and should have aroused some interest among anyone who hadn't yet heard of Theos Bernard. The *Los Angeles Times* called *Penthouse of the Gods* "one of the most curious books to be found on the spring lists" and concluded that, "Mr. Bernard makes his adventure into a wholly readable book . . . and his photographs of these wonders of the world would convince the most skeptical that 'Lost Horizon' was no exaggeration."

Katherine Woods, writing in the *New York Times*, spent much of her review discussing the book's literary shortcomings. "Theos Bernard's story is unique, and so is his way of telling it," she wrote. "The book is not mystical, or sensational, or sophisticated. It might more nearly be described as naive. It is open and childlike. It is written with the colloquial English, the laboriousness in dealing with thought or emotion, the awkwardness and occasional confusion, of a traveler who is not naturally a writer." Nevertheless, she concluded, "on its thread of unprecedented opportunity—it makes very interesting reading. It is illustrated with many telling photographs, and the narrative's very imperfections strike a note of sincerity."

Although it sold fewer than five thousand copies in the United States, *Penthouse of the Gods* rose in July 1939 to number four on the most-read nonfiction book list at the Los Angeles Public Library, and despite Scribner's trepidation, the London publisher Rider and Co. picked up the book a couple of months after its release in America and published it under the title *Land of a Thousand Buddhas*.

Perkins was at least well enough satisfied with the project that shortly after the release of *Penthouse of the Gods* he offered Theos a contract—with a thousand-dollar advance this time—for the popular book on Yoga they had discussed the year before. Theos pitched the book to Perkins in the middle of his first lecture tour with an outline of the book, which was to be titled *Heaven Lies Within Us: The Attainment of Health and Happiness Through Yoga*. Theos described the concept for the book to Perkins as "the Timeless Spiritual Science as taught by the ancient sages of India and passed down to us thru a long line of discipleship."

"The book should be a tale rather than a handbook of information," Theos wrote, and the reader would glimpse his subjective experience as he recounted the training that promoted his own quick progress in the physical techniques of Hatha Yoga and the meditative practices that focus on the subtle body, which are classed as Raja Yoga. The tale would include "a short dramatization of my arrival in India and receiving word that my teacher had passed away," Theos told Perkins, "then my odyssey for happiness over the length and breadth of India, and finally my arrival at the jungle hermitage in Central India of the one who was to be my Spiritual Guide. I will describe the different initiations, the techniques given to me, my experiences and difficulties in my effort to perfect them and the philosophical background of all these practices as given to me by my Guru as I proceed along the path."

Perkins replied within days of receiving the outline, "A glance through it makes me think you have the best plan possible." Theos left New York to spend the summer of 1939 writing the rough draft of the Yoga book at a cottage in a wooded canyon of Beverly Hills and again hired ghostwriter John Cournos to smooth out the prose.

Theos told Perkins the book should be a tale rather than a handbook, and as with *Penthouse of the Gods,* some fictional invention was employed for the sake of the story's plot. The scenes at the beginning and the end of *Penthouse of the Gods*—the final initiation with Tri Rinpoche and the days of solitary meditation in the cave—are set in the book at Ganden monastery, the last of the Three Seats Theos visited. And although the scenes contributed a good narrative structure, the events are recorded nowhere in his journals or letters. Indeed, Theos' journal is very clear that he spent only about twenty-four hours at Ganden. Just before he left the monastery Theos had a private interview with Tri Rinpoche, about which in his journal he wrote only that there was "the performance of a private ritual," and "the results of these discussions will appear at odd intervals in the diary." But he never did return in his journal or letters to Viola to a description of those hours alone with Tri Rinpoche, and the first journal entries on the evening after he left Ganden were filled mostly with criticism of the ritual-bound practice he saw there.

It is impossible to know how much of the narrative invention is due to the advice of the genius of fictional structure, Maxwell Perkins; *Penthouse of the Gods* was, after all, one of the few nonfiction books Perkins edited in his career. The ghostwriter, John Cournos, who also worked in fiction, may have found the essence of the scenes in the long manuscript Theos dictated and, as well, found no harm in taking some fictional license for the sake of narrative structure. Evidently, neither the editor, the ghostwriter, nor the first-time author was overly concerned with the journalistic standards of veracity in contemporary nonfiction. But even though it may have been Perkins who suggested the confabulation and Cournos who actually wrote it, clearly Theos could have protested and not allowed the invented scenes in his book.

Aside from the fictional scenes at the beginning and end of *Penthouse of the Gods*, almost every detail in the intervening three hundred pages is well documented in Theos' journals and letters and often follows the journals verbatim. In *Heaven Lies Within Us*, however, it is not just the beginning and ending scenes that are fabricated, but almost the entire story line is pure fiction, an allegorical device for the extraordinary information Theos presents on Hatha and Raja Yoga techniques.

Much of *Heaven Lies Within Us* purports to be the description of Theos' practices during a three-month retreat with his guru at his jungle ashram near Ranchi in Bihar state. Theos didn't keep a journal of the time the book covers in India, but virtually every day of his travels there—from his arrival at the docks in Calcutta with Viola to the day he leaves Gangtok for Tibet—is accounted for either in Viola's diary of their travels or his long, frequent letters to her after they parted in Colombo. There are no weeks, let alone months, unaccounted for in the documented timeline during which Theos might have undertaken a Tantric retreat in the jungle.

In the book's preface, Theos stated (as he had in his rejected dissertation) that his teachers must remain anonymous to protect their privacy.

That explanation, though, is hardly convincing considering that in Yoga, Buddhism, and Tantra, the names of the individual gurus of the lineage are venerated in prayers and adduced as proof of the unbroken purity of the teachings delivered from the founder to the current student "thru a long line of discipleship," as Theos had put it to Perkins. It seems certain that the real guru whose identity Theos was concealing was his father, Glen, and that most of the plotline in *Heaven Lies Within Us* describing a three-month retreat with a Tantric guru at Ranchi was actually based on Glen's experiences at the jungle camp.

The story line, however, was intended only as a device to present the book's detailed descriptions and practical advice on the poses of Hatha Yoga, Kriya cleansing practices, and especially rich sections on Pranayama and Kundalini. Most of this "Timeless Spiritual Science" came directly from Theos' research for his rejected dissertation and the insights based on his own dedicated and highly advanced practice.

In the book, the climax of his "personal story" at the jungle ashram comes with his initiation into Hindu Tantra by the maharishi and a vividly described, all-night immersion in the bliss of Kundalini. "The ultimate success of all Yoga practices depends upon awakening Kundalini," Theos wrote. "On Kundalini is founded the whole of Hatha Yoga teachings and practices."

He describes preparing for the initiation by fasting for twenty-four hours, ritual bathing, drawing yantras in the dust, performing mudras, and reciting mantras. He was given a cannabis potion called bhang to offer to the deities at his head and heart and then to the Kundalini at the base of his spine before he drank of it himself. He then ringed himself with a visualized wall of fire and snapped his fingers in the four directions to create a pure habitat that no malevolent spirits could penetrate. He visualized in meditation the dissolving of the four elements of the body, simulating the process that occurs at death, and awakened the Kundalini energy by practicing Pranayama while his teacher recited mantras. Theos wrote that he completely lost awareness of his surroundings and with his eyes wide open could see nothing but a brilliant light. As he described the experience in his book:

I had the feeling of being under the influence of some mystic light. I was conscious of its unremitting, penetrating, warm rays. There was a restful dawn of a soft glow. I was held by the awe of it and, as with the sun, there was no cessation of its light. Indeed, its brilliance increased, and its intensity grew more penetrating....

The element of Time had vanished. In the midst of all, something snapped, and all was quiet. The light was still there, and I had become absorbed in it. I could no longer find its source. All was light. And I was light. All was peace....

The return to my conscious faculties was gradual. I was then to reflect for a short while upon the fact that I had fully realized the identity of the individual and Brahman, or the complete Union of the Individual Consciousness with the Universal Consciousness. There was no longer any doubt in my mind. I felt very much like one who has experienced his first love. Something had happened to my inner consciousness, which I was certain would be mine forever. My only future concern would be how to direct it. I now had everything. The question was how to use it.

The full account is one of the great descriptions of the subjective experience of Kundalini in Yoga literature. But considering that the maharishi and the three-month retreat of which this night was supposed to be the culmination were both fictional creations, one must ask whether the sublime Kundalini experience Theos describes actually happened to him at some other time and in some other setting or if it too was the dramatization of someone else's experience.

The outline of the Kundalini practice and its hoped-for results was introduced to the West in John Woodroffe's book *The Serpent Power*, which was published in 1918 and was an important source for Theos' master's thesis at Columbia. With that description and instructions from Glen, Theos practiced the Pranayama breathing practices that are preliminary to the rising of Kundalini in the central channel of the subtle nervous system and reported his results in a letter to Viola from Kalimpong. He told her that he could suspend breathing for a full six minutes of *kumbhaka* and that "my imagination cannot conceive of any joy that would surpass the experience of going into *kumbhaka* and remaining there time on end. The experience and after effect is incommunicable." In another letter he wrote that he had gained "somewhat of the consciousness which we are seeking, the inner essence of man, Kundalini to be exact." But as he explained to her, the full achievement of the goal was a gradual process. "You may ask why not just settle down to the job of gaining this end—well it is impossible—it is impossible to make such jumps in nature—when you plant seeds, you have to wait until they finally sprout and start to grow—once the process is commenced, then you can continually encourage it by proper cultivation."

Perhaps nothing illustrates how the invented narrative was nonetheless underpinned by rare and disappearing sources better than the line drawings of Yoga poses at the head of each chapter. The simple drawings depict yogis with topknots and halos in a series of asanas associated with the Six Yogas' of Naropa that are found in an extremely rare Tibetan text produced in the early 1800s in either China or Inner Mongolia. A note at the beginning of *Heaven Lies Within Us* states only that the illustrations come from a text given to the author by his teacher. The drawings were used not only at the chapter heads but also as illustrations for newspaper advertising for the book seen by millions of people. Until recently the copy of that book given to Theos was the only copy known in the West to exist. In 2002, a copy that had been lost in the dusty inventory at the Library of the Russian Academy of Sciences in St. Petersburg was discovered during the first-ever cataloging of the 128,000 titles in its Tibetan collection by the American group Asian Classics Input Project. Until the excited discoverers learned that the asana images had been published sixty years earlier in Theos Bernard's book, the copy in the Russian library was thought to be the only one extant. Since then, another solitary copy has surfaced in Mongolia.

HEAVEN LIES WITHIN US was released in October 1939—with a dedication this time "to my father"—but again Scribner's slight confidence in the softening prewar market for a Yoga book resulted in a first print run of only 2,455 copies. Scribner's never printed another edition, but again

Rider and Co. quickly published it in London under the same title and over the next fifteen years brought out five editions. Although Theos told Perkins he didn't intend to write a handbook, the book's practical advice on Hatha Yoga practices—rooted as they are in Theos' experiments with them—has made *Heaven Lies Within Us* an enduring classic in the field, and the book continues to this day to be reprinted in small-press paperback editions.

Theos may have invented the story line for his book and exaggerated his attainments at the time, but his obsession with Hatha Yoga and Tantra and his unique sources and experiences in Tibet undoubtedly made Theos in 1939 the best Western authority on the actual practices of Tantric Yoga. As he wrote at the end of his Kundalini description in the book, "The question was how to use it." For many Yogis who experienced the bliss of Kundalini throughout history, the answer to that question was that they now had a responsibility to teach others how to do it.

THEOS GOT THE CHANCE to teach directly the Hatha Yoga program that he describes in *Heaven Lies Within Us* with the opening of his own studio on October 1, 1939. Having learned from his uncle's success with the Clarkstown Country Club that his clientele would come first from among the city's Brahmins, Theos opened his studio across the street from Central Park in suite 403 of the Pierre, one of New York's most elegant hotels. He wrote on the cover of the studio's first brochure: "The purpose of physical re-education is more than a physical end; it is to culture, refine, and tone up the material of which we are composed, to make it a perfect instrument for registering a deeper consciousness."

The Pierre Health Studio, as it was called, taught the "Science of Breath and the corrective postures and exercises of Yoga" adapted to modern needs. The price of classes ranged from $25 for a twelve-class package with one of the studio's staff to $200 for twelve sessions in a course of Hatha Yoga personally supervised by Theos. The "full course in Yogic Physical Culture," as Theos called it, was intended for serious aspirants only and included a series of eleven classic asanas: headstand, shoulder stand, fish posture, plow, cobra, locust, bow, twist, western stretch, peacock, and corpse pose. Typical of the standard he expected his students to work toward was the goal of maintaining headstand, or Sirshasana, for twelve minutes, and rolling the abdominal rectus muscle with the Nauli Kriya practice for eight minutes.

The Yogic Physical Culture Theos taught at the Pierre Health Studio was only one element, however, of a larger organization he created, the American Institute of Yoga. Even with the upheaval of his divorce, the academic work trying to finish his Ph.D., touring the country for six months with his lectures, and writing two books and numerous magazine articles, less than two years after his return from Tibet Theos was able to found the institute he had been contemplating since his summer with the Indians in New Mexico. He gave himself the title of director and organized courses in the Applied Philosophy of Yoga as adjuncts to the classes of the Pierre Health Studio.

The curriculum of the American Institute of Yoga included courses in both Hindu and Buddhist philosophy. The underlying premise was: "There is no mystery. Everything can be explained. . . . We are not dealing with a religion. We are dealing with a science. The whole principle of Life."

There was a course on the basic philosophical systems of India that outlined each system's rites and ceremonies as well as their arguments of logic, which Theos believed was "necessary for keeping the mind on the right path during its investigations." There was a course on the chakras discussing the "subtle forces known as the Tattvas that control every manifestation," and a psychology course that analyzed the laws of the mind: "how it functions, how and why we think, where our thoughts come from and where they go, what is the effect left behind, and how they may be directed to certain lines of thought to increase our power." The catalog also included a course on the Bardo, and the science of death: "What is the essence of man, what laws bring about the phenomena of death and rebirth, where do we go, what happens there, how long are we away, how, when and why do we come back, and what will be the nature of our next existence?"

Theos' students ranged in age from nineteen to seventy and included college students, doctors, housewives, artists, socialites, lawyers, and men and women in business. Five nights a week when he was in New York, from seven-thirty until midnight, Theos instructed groups studying the higher forms of Yoga. "My dream is to build a Shangri-La in the heart of New York," Theos told a reporter, "to fill the needs of the driven people of this seething metropolis."

Theos inaugurated the course series teaching a subject that captivated him more than almost any other. Twenty years before the first Tibetan Lama began teaching in the United States, Theos offered a course at the American Institute of Yoga on Sipay Khorlo, the Tibetan Wheel of Life, which he described as "a study of the laws pertaining to the coming and going of human existence, why we are born, why the law of Karma is an absolute fact, and how it operates and what conditions make for its operation."

Already in Kalimpong and later in Tibet, Theos showed as much interest in collecting and translating texts on Sipay Khorlo as he had on Padmasambhava. When Glen left Kalimpong to head home, Theos gave him the commission of collating the various Sipay Khorlo texts they had collected to that point, and used that assignment as part of the rationale to Viola for keeping him on his $100-a-month stipend.

Theos published a short scholarly article in the May 1939 issue of *Review of Religion* in which he explained that Lord Buddha personally directed the painting of the Wheel of Life, a circular flow chart depicting the complex interrelationship of life and death's twelve causes. A painting or *thangka* of the Wheel of Life is found near the entrance of every Tibetan temple, Theos wrote, and frequently in Tibet a lama will hang up a large *thangka* at a crossroads or outside a bazaar and explain the twelve links of dependent origination to passersby desperate to find out how their actions bring either happiness or suffering.

Theos' lecture notes for the course state that "the beginning and the end of Buddhism is to wipe out the sin of ignorance. There is only one sin—ignorance." Ignorance is depicted on the Wheel of Life as a blind man probing the unseen world with a cane and is explained in the commentaries as being more than a mere mistaken perception of the world. Ignorance is the conviction that the world exists opposite of how it actually does. It is the belief, along with the mistaken perception, that the qualities we perceive in an object are part of the nature of the object rather than projections of our own minds.

The Wheel of Life illustrates how ignorance leads to the beginningless round of rebirths in this realm of suffering through the complicated web called the Twelve Links of Dependent Origination. Ignorance produces action, or karma. Karma produces consciousness. Consciousness produces name and form. Name and form produce the senses. Senses produce contact. Contact produces craving. Craving produces grasping. Grasping produces existence. Existence produces rebirth. Rebirth produces old age. And old age produces death. Ignorance is the root of all. If we can cut the chain at the link of ignorance, we end the world of suffering.

"The whole purpose of our destiny on this plane is to escape," Theos wrote in his lecture notes. "The only things holding us are ignorance and desire. Why are we ignorant? It is due to past lives; things we have done before; actions we have done. The seed of those actions is left in our being." The antidote to ignorance is wisdom, he said, which results from realizing directly that "the world that we are in right now is a dream."

Just weeks before Theos launched the American Institute of Yoga, he was thrust for the fourth time before three million housewives with another long illustrated article in the pages of *Family Circle*. The article, again written by Stewart Robertson, was titled "The White Lama on Yoga," and began:

> So many readers have written to the *Family Circle* to ask about the present whereabouts and activities of Theos Bernard, the famed White Lama of Tibet, that I called on him the other day to persuade him to tell me something of the classes in Yoga which he is conducting.... Mr. Bernard has just returned from one of his extended lecture tours, and as usual he is full of enthusiasm about life in general—making him an excellent advertisement for the things he advocates.

On the question of who is a yogi and what is a proper motivation for practice, the article quoted Theos:

> Although every Yogi is a practitioner of Yoga, not every practitioner of Yoga is a Yogi. That state comes only after the student has successfully advanced through and mastered the various steps.... A good

teacher makes a careful study of the mental and physical make-up of every applicant before he gives any lessons. I turned down a man the other day because he was interested only in studying Yoga to find out if he could learn to get along with scarcely any sleep. That man had too much vanity to make his mind properly receptive ... And likewise it has nothing for the spiritual tramp who flits from one cult to another, approaching them with the lackluster gaze of some oaf wandering into a great museum to give it the once-over.

Theos said that people who practice only the asanas, or physical postures, and don't go any further with Yoga never become real yogis. "The asanas are merely preparation—the sound body for the sound mind that we Westerners like to talk about as if we invented the idea."

When the body is strengthened and the mind quieted, Theos said, the student should progress to Pranayama, or control of the breath, the purpose of which is to move *prana,* a subtle but palpable energy sometimes thought of as the life force, to specific target points in the subtle nervous system. The article included a large illustration of the three main channels of the subtle body and the six chakras arrayed up the spine. In Tibet, the description of the subtle body and even Yoga asanas were kept secret as part of the practice of Tantra. Now in America, three million patrons of Piggly Wiggly and Safeway saw in the tabloid pages of *Family Circle* what, if they had been Tibetan monks, they would learn only after years of preparation studying karma and wisdom in the open scriptures (exemplified in the Wheel of Life) and initiation by their lama into the secret world of Tantra.

AFTER HIS RETURN FROM TIBET, Theos kept up a regular correspondence with Tsarong and Tharchin. Tsarong was happy to hear of Theos' plan to create a proper home for the library he brought from Tibet, writing, "I must say, there is nothing more beneficial for this and the next life of self and others than the work you have proposed to do. I ... shall pray regularly that your religious work will be done according to your wish without any misfortunes."

The regent was in good health, Tsarong wrote, but in the spring of 1938 the reincarnations of both the Dalai Lama and the Panchen Lama were yet to be discovered, and he prayed they would be found soon. Tsarong also mentioned that he "received a letter from the King of Sakya in which he praises you a lot and seemed to like you very much." Another letter requested that Theos research the technical details for a water mill, for grinding flour, that he hoped to install at one of his estates; he also mentioned that he would appreciate some California apple seeds for his orchards. In due time Tsarong sent three altar images Theos had commissioned while in Lhasa and a bill for the balance of 201 rupees for their jeweled ornaments and the gilding of their bodies and faces.

Every time Theos got a letter from Lhasa, he was gripped by the unsettling intuition that the Tibet he had visited would not survive much longer. He wrote in an article titled "The Peril of Tibet" for the September 1939 issue of *Asia* that his friends would witness wrenching upheavals in their lifetimes. "Far reaching changes, little short of cataclysmic, threaten the land of Tibet and Lhasa its capital," he wrote. "Lhasa the Forbidden, the Mysterious, is in danger at no distant date of losing its unique place on this planet. This would mean the throwing open of the vast territory of Tibet, hitherto sacred and untouched, as a new era of exploitation by modern militarist powers previously held in check by the might of the British Empire."

The inexorable logic of the market, Theos warned, would bring a military invasion from either of Tibet's behemoth neighbors in a race to grab its untapped natural wealth for their own malnourished populations. "Lhasa...will, and within our own lifetime, become transformed into the Chicago of Asia," he prophesied, "a great stockyard and industrial center radiating not spiritual light but iron roadways and commercial airways spanning the continent east and west, and south and north."

This vision of the imminent obliteration of the Tibet he had visited made Theos appreciate even more his unique experiences there, and he wanted to write one more book about it. During the first months after the Pierre Health Studio and American Institute of Yoga opened, Theos was also busy at work on a manuscript with the working title of *Tibetan Pilgrimage*, which recounted his return trip from Lhasa to Kalimpong and his historic stops at Shigatse and Sakya. At the beginning of February 1940, Theos wrote to his agent, Carol Hill, that the manuscript was nearly finished and he would be turning it in at the end of the week.

"This one had all the time the others should have had and it shows the results," he told her. Theos had apparently been so busy that he hadn't had a chance to discuss the project with Maxwell Perkins, who knew about it only in the most general terms. After reading the manuscript, Perkins wrote to Theos, "I must tell you that I do not think your 'Tibetan Pilgrimage' would be wisely published now. It is simply because of what seems to me to be the fact that it records a journey in Tibet which as recounted, is not as impressive or moving as was 'Penthouse of the Gods.' In a rough sense it is very like it, and yet it has not the novelty, of course, and I do not think for some reason that it is as striking in its events or its descriptions. And if this is so, it would come as a disappointment even though it is really as well done. It is simply that a second journey must have new features."

There was also the fact, as Perkins noted in a letter about the royalties of the first two books, that "we have not come out very well so far on *Heaven Lies Within Us.*" After getting this, his first rejection letter in two and a half years of telling the story of his summer in Lhasa, Theos wrote to his agent, "This winds up the Tibetan saga. I wonder what is next."

Chapter 12

TIBETLAND

ONE DAY, in the first months after the Pierre Health Studio opened, a woman walked through the door who offered to be for Theos what Mrs. Vanderbilt was for his Uncle Pierre and the Clarkstown Country Club—a wealthy patron. Madame Ganna Walska would have been instantly recognizable. For two decades the press in both Europe and America chronicled her succession of marriages to some of America's wealthiest men and mocked her disappointing attempts to prove to opera critics that she could sing the great soprano roles in performances from Havana to Carnegie Hall.

Madame Walska would become Theos' second wife, but this self-styled "enemy of the average" could not have been a more opposite type from his egalitarian first wife, Viola, who at that time in 1939 was turning Sky Island, the Nyack estate she inherited at her mother's death, into a hostel for refugees from Nazi Germany.

Ever wrapped in the operatic story of her own invention, Ganna Walska was born into a middle-class family in Poland as Hanna Puacz, in either 1887, 1892, or 1893, depending on which of ten passports and countless conflicting news reports one chooses as authoritative. Hanna grew into a tall, raven-haired, blue-eyed beauty, and she began what would become her career of marrying and divorcing wealthy men with her elopement two weeks before her twentieth birthday with the Baron Arcadie D'Einghorn in czarist St. Petersburg, Russia. A portrait of her showing a bejeweled dark-haired beauty was commissioned, she said, by Czar Nicholas II after he selected her as the most enchanting woman at one of his royal balls. When the Baron D'Einghorn contracted tuberculosis, he moved to a sanitarium near St. Moritz, Switzerland, and after a few years of his absence, Hanna decided to divorce him.

The divorce financed her move in 1914 to Paris, where she pursued a career on stage. She adopted the performance name Ganna Walska ("divine waltz" in Polish) and added the title 'Madame,' a conceit commonly employed by opera singers and actresses of the time. She enjoyed some success in Paris as a cabaret singer and continued to train her voice for opera but with France embroiled in the Great War, Madame Walska decided in 1915 to visit America. As the war in Europe dragged on, Madame Walska decided to stay in America and got a job singing at a French theater in New York. When she developed a throat problem, the theater owner recommended she see the famed endocrinologist Dr. Julius Fraenkel, and on her second visit to his office, Dr. Fraenkel, who was twenty-eight years older than she was, proposed marriage. They were wed in September 1916.

The newlyweds bought a four-story row house just off Park Avenue on Ninety-fourth Street, and Ganna filled her days with morning music lessons, luncheon musicales, opera matinees, and evening concerts. After two years of this immersion, Madame Walska felt ready for her grand opera debut, and in December 1918 she opened in *Fedora* with the Havana Opera. She was all but hissed from the stage on opening night, and sensing when she returned the following night that the singer was not sufficiently chastened, the antagonistic audience pelted the stage with rotten eggs and vegetables.

Madame Walska fled the blistering reviews in Havana and returned to the comfortable existence of a pampered but restless wife. During this period she began a long investigation of mysticism and spiritualism. She attended séances, consulted the Ouija board, and explored Yoga, astrology, meditation, telepathy, numerology, and Christian Science.

Her explorations in Yoga led her to the Clarkstown Country Club and Theos' uncle, Pierre Arnold Bernard, who, as she wrote in her memoir, *Always Room at the Top*, "advocated washing the stomach three times a day as well as standing on one's head for protracted lengths of time." She succeeded beautifully with headstand, she wrote, but didn't make it a regular practice, and concluded, "If Dr. Bernard knew how to apply Yogi wisdom I could not tell, for being just a plain doctor's wife I was never permitted to even approach the great man. I only looked with a little jealousy at the door behind which the Vanderbilt girls received enlightenment by the hours."

In the spring of 1919, Madame Walska read in the newspapers that Harold F. McCormick, the founder and principal sponsor of the Chicago Opera Company, was visiting New York and staying at the Plaza Hotel. With the sort of single-minded devotion that marked the next ten years of trying to make a career in opera, she got a call through to McCormick and insisted that he must meet her for just five minutes before he caught his train back to Chicago. McCormick, the president of the giant farm implement manufacturer International Harvester Company, reluctantly agreed to the five minutes, but after an hour with Madame Walska, he had to be reminded about his train. The regal bearing of the would-be diva seemed to magnetize men, and after hearing her sing, McCormick was convinced that Madame Walska had a voice the world had to hear.

McCormick invited her to join the Chicago Opera and signed her to sing the title role in Leoncavallo's *Zaza*, scheduled to open December 21, 1920. Eight months before the opening, Dr. Fraenkel, husband number two, died of a "stomach ailment" and left to Madame Walska the Ninety-fourth Street house and $500,000 in cash.

Her "black despair," as she described it, prevented her from singing, and three months after Fraenkel's death, "close friends"—hoping that the change of scene would excite her to prepare for her Chicago Opera debut—persuaded her to sail with them to Paris. Harold McCormick, as it happened, was also sailing to France aboard the *Aquitania* in June 1920 on his way to see his wife, Edith, the daughter of John D. Rockefeller, who had spent the previous seven years pursuing psychoanalysis under Carl Jung in Switzerland. McCormick had fallen in love with Madame Walska at their first five-minute meeting the year before in New York, and now that she was a widow, McCormick intended to ask Edith for a divorce so he could marry her.

Aboard the *Aquitania* on that voyage as well was Alexander Smith Cochran, who, with an estimated $80 million fortune, was called by the press "the richest bachelor in the world." The forty-six-year-old Cochran made his money as a carpet manufacturer and spent it on his yachts and thirty houses around the world. McCormick introduced them on the last day of the voyage, and after Madame Walska and Cochran spent the afternoon together, he proposed marriage to her over dinner. She refused, and the next day he disembarked for London while she went on to Paris. Accustomed to getting what he wanted, Cochran went to Paris the next day, but again Madame Walska refused his proposal. Twice more he made the trip, and on September 15, 1920, she at last relented; and they were married in Paris that very afternoon.

McCormick received the telegram from Ganna announcing her marriage to Cochran just as he was sending a wire to her informing her of his freedom from Edith. He flew immediately to Paris and showed up at the newlyweds' hotel the morning after the wedding. Cochran had spent his wedding night roaming the streets of Paris, and the next morning, while the bridegroom slept it off, the bride served McCormick coffee in the adjoining room and listened to his pleas to immediately divorce Cochran and marry him as soon as possible.

Her husband and her suitor began a lavish competition of gifts to woo her. About Cochran's offerings, she wrote: "A million francs worth of sable coat that I found in my room that afternoon, Alex's invitation to go with carte blanche to Cartier and choose anything I desired as a wedding present, and his announcement that my bank would receive a hundred thousand dollars yearly for my 'pin money,' all that went by me without actually touching my inner being." Not to be outdone, and perhaps to symbolize his enduring love and faith in the future, McCormick immediately set up a trust fund for Mrs. Cochran guaranteeing her $100,000 per year *for life*.

Madame Walska had to leave Paris a few days after the wedding to reach Chicago for the beginning of rehearsals for *Zaza*, and McCormick insisted on personally escorting her there. At the last minute, so did Cochran. The rehearsals were a disaster from the start. Director Gino Marinuzzi urged her to project her voice beyond the orchestra pit, and eventually gave up on the production and turned the show over to Pietro Cimini. At a dress rehearsal, three days before the opening, Cimini pleaded with Madame Walska to sing louder. Finally, exasperated, Cimini called a halt and said, "Madame, please sing in your natural voice."

Through the glare of the footlights, Madame Walska glowered down at Cimini and snarled, "Pig! You would ruin my performance!" and marched off the stage. The Chicago Opera Company announced with much embarrassment that the production of *Zaza* was "postponed indefinitely," and Madame Walska left immediately for New York. From there she caught the next ship for Paris, without, as was noticed in the New York headlines, Alexander Smith Cochran, her husband of three months.

Six months after their marriage, Cochran and Madame Walska formally separated, and the papers reported an "amicable financial arrangement" allowing their divorce in Paris in the spring of 1922. At one point she had demanded half his fortune and later $1 million a year, but she settled for $100,000 cash. She also got Cochran's Paris mansion in the Rue de Lubeck and, a few miles west of Versailles, the Château de Galluis. At his death seven years later, she received as part of the divorce settlement another $3 million.

In the meantime, Harold and Edith McCormick divorced, and a few months later Madame Walska and Harold were married in a private civil ceremony in Paris. From the day of their wedding, the *New York Times* and *Chicago Tribune* carried frequent installments of the tragicomedy of McCormick and "the prima donna," the story of a rich and beautiful woman with an obsession for singing grand opera who was repeatedly scorned by critics and heckled by audiences. The young Orson Welles grew up in the milieu of the Chicago Opera and said years later that one of the plotlines of his 1941 film *Citizen Kane* was inspired by McCormick's million-dollar attempts to make his wife into the diva she craved to be.

Her Paris debut came on June 26, 1923, at a special charity concert that McCormick entirely financed on the stage of the French National Opera House. She sang Gilda in Verdi's *Rigoletto*, and as the *New York Times* correspondent wrote, "When she reached the famous aria 'cara nome' she faltered, stammered, and produced a series of squeaks. The tension in the house was more than even the cultured people who filled it could stand. A ripple of laughter broke across the stalls and rose to the highest galleries."

It was a year and a half after her Paris debut—about which the city was still talking—before she attempted *Madame Butterfly* in Nice, and again the audience was provoked to laughter. Although she was under contract for two more performances, the mayor of Nice thought her first performance was so injurious to the musical reputation of the town that he issued a fiat that she must not appear again. He said she should consider herself lucky that she appeared in an orderly town such as Nice; at Marseilles there would have been a riot.

It was another four years of similar attempts and responses before she realized a dream by appearing in recital on February 12, 1929, at New York's Carnegie Hall. She had to rent the hall herself, but a distinguished audience listened in "courteous but unencouraging silence," as the reviewer put it the next day in the *New York Times*. Like most of the audience, the reviewer was drawn to the performance by the decade-long drama of "a famous and beautiful woman whose obsessing ambition is to sing." The central question in that drama, the reviewer wrote, was:

> Why, after all, should Mme. Walska, whose resources and opportunities for study are unlimited, and who is also known to labor unceasingly for advancement in the singing art, remain so far from the achievement which she so greatly desires?
>
> The explanation lies probably in the impression received of a singer who has never mastered the fundamentals of her task, and who has leaped for glory before it was sensible or prudent to do so. This, indeed, seems the only possible explanation of such bad singing.

It was the last major performance of the frustrated singing career that had begun eleven years earlier with being pelted by vegetables in Havana.

BEGINNING IN THE FALL OF 1927, there were press reports that McCormick would file for divorce from Madame Walska as early as the following week. The *New York Times* reported that the divorce petition charged Madame Walska with desertion, and stated that despite McCormick's pleas, she refused to leave Paris and take her place as his wife in Chicago. "I have been terribly disillusioned by this marriage, and I feel very bitterly the ridiculous position I have been forced to occupy. I can feel the pity in my friends' hearts for me," McCormick was quoted as stating in the divorce petition. It took four years, however, to finalize the divorce while their lawyers wrangled over the value of a large block of International Harvester stock that Madame Walska had received as a wedding gift and insisted was worth $4 million.

During the years between 1933 and 1940, Madame Walska split her time between France and America, and when asked in 1934 if she had found any new romance during her five-month stay in New York, she replied: "Romances are not made to order. I still believe in them, however. One may overtake me at any time." It was more than six years after her divorce from McCormick, though, before another marriage, if not romance, overtook her again.

In a most unlikely pairing, she wed in January 1938 her fifth husband, Henry Grindell-Matthews, a reclusive British electrical research scientist, known in the press as "Death Ray Matthews." Among his many inventions were an automated system to pilot aircraft and a wireless communication device for motorcars. In the year of his marriage to Madame Walska, he invented a laser-like ray that he said would bring down airplanes at a distance, and he was also reported to have designed a rocket-propelled aircraft capable of traveling twenty-eight times the speed of sound.

The fifty-seven-year-old "mystery man of science" worked and lived in carefully guarded secrecy at a laboratory and bungalow surrounded with electrically charged fences and burglar alarms on the top of a mountain near Swansea, Wales. The announcement of the London wedding of Madame Walska and Grindell-Matthews wasn't made until the week after the event, and by that time Madame Walska was back at the Château de Galluis and Mr. Grindell-Matthews had gone back to his Welsh mountaintop, from where he issued a statement saying he was so busy on his latest invention, an aerial torpedo, that he could not spare time for a wedding trip or say when he expected to join his bride.

In her histrionic *Always Room at the Top*, Madame Walska wrote that when Grindell-Matthews proposed to her, she replied she would never marry again. The inventor, she wrote, became so depressed as a result that mutual friends and even government officials pleaded with her to reconsider, "as it was feared that my indifference might kill him before his invention for detecting submarines and defending London against bombardment through rocket shooting could reach the hands of the War Ministry."

She did her duty for the war effort even though "everything about him was negative. He looked older than his age. He seemed haggard. Quite blind in one eye, his other saw but little. His hands trembled so he could hardly lift his glass of vermouth to his lips from which a cigarette eternally dangled."

Madame Walska may never have even visited her husband's mountain-top laboratory, and indeed, she doesn't mention in her account of her fifth marriage that they even saw each other again after the wedding. They separated legally less than a year later but never did divorce before his death in September 1941. There was no large bequest for Madame Walska in the estate of this husband, however. Grindell-Matthews had poured all his money into his research and died a pauper. The telegram notifying Madame Walska of his heart attack also requested £50 to cover the funeral expenses.

IN THE YEARS before her marriage to Grindell-Matthews, Madame Walska had begun to turn her ambitions from singing to spiritual development. She was forty-four at the time of her divorce from McCormick, and as she wrote in her first memoir, she realized "with a touching sadness that my dreams . . . had not materialized. I realized that youth was already behind me." She explored hypnotism but could not relax enough to be hypnotized. She then became intrigued with Paul Brunton's books, *A Search in Secret India* and *The Secret Path*, but she was disillusioned when she met the author because "he seemed such an ordinary man." She also corresponded with Meher Baba, the Indian avatar who stopped talking in 1925 and communicated by using an alphabet board or hand gestures interpreted by a disciple. Madame had by then reached, as she called it, a level of "serene stability," and realized that her worst enemy had always been her "excessive emotion."

Madame Walska was dividing her time between Paris and New York during those years, and she was back in Manhattan again in late 1939 when a friend invited her to an evening lecture and Yoga demonstration at Theos' recently opened studio at the Pierre Hotel. Written in 1941, before they were married, Ganna's hyperbolic five-hundred-page first memoir, *Always Room at the Top*, concludes with her meeting Theos for the first time. Seventeen pages from the end of the book she describes their meeting as an extraordinary event that occurred just when she was grappling with the question "What next?"

"I could not yet face my tomorrow unless singing held the most predominating place," she wrote. She described Theos at their meeting as "an old soul dwelling in a young Arizona boy," who informed her "that in the East there are still those who have voices developed according to the Great Law and who can by their sounds not only heal any physical illnesses but can even transfer spiritual knowledge to the truth-seeking soul deserving of such illumination."

Theos, she wrote here, was a "prodigy who had brought the purest pearl to my string of knowledge," a master who "unfolded to my soul so much of the Real Knowledge of Divine Law that I have stored up in my inner being enough food to digest and assimilate for the rest of this earthly life."

Ganna bought a copy of Theos' book *Heaven Lies Within Us* and immediately after finishing it sent him a monogrammed note card saying, "I thank Fate for putting this book in my Path! I thank Fate for giving me the privilege to know you! I thank you!"

Theos set out on January 3, 1940, on another cross-country "Penthouse of the Gods" lecture tour. He was gone three and a half months and presented his film and lecture at another forty-five civic clubs, universities, and museums. Returning to New York in mid-April, Theos immediately began another American Institute of Yoga lecture series at the Hotel Pierre and began to lay plans to create an institute for the translation of the Tibetan Buddhist texts he had brought to America.

In his account of getting to know Madame Walska, Theos wrote that on a visit to his studio at the Pierre Hotel, she became intrigued by a large stack of Tibetan manuscripts he was indexing. She visited regularly over the next year to talk about the literature and philosophy of Tibet and to encourage his dream of creating a nonprofit Academy of Tibetan Literature. Theos was trying at the time to raise money to bring Tibetan lamas to America to begin the mammoth project of translating the 5,250 individual texts composing the Tibetan Kangyur and Tengyur, and although other students offered to help, Madame Walska, he said, insisted repeatedly that she underwrite the project entirely by herself.

In the summer of 1940 Ganna went to Los Angeles to study for a time with her voice teacher, who had moved there from New York, and Theos decided to close down the Pierre Health Studio and travel west with her to scout prospective homes in California for the translation institute. Theos had received an offer from one of his Yoga students, the British diplomat Sir Humphrey Clarke, to establish the Academy of Tibetan Literature at his 37-acre estate in Montecito, a wealthy community adjacent to Santa Barbara. Theos visited Clarke at the estate, named Cuesta Linda, and noticed that the 165-acre estate across the road was for sale. Theos called on his background as a lawyer and negotiated the purchase of that property, called Arcady, and another 200-acre mountain lodge at San Marcos Pass in the Santa Ynez Mountains above Santa Barbara, known as El Capitan, from the well-known Santa Barbara developer George Owen Knapp. The two properties were said together to be worth over $1 million, but with America's entry into the war appearing imminent, Theos negotiated a distressed price of $95,000. Ganna had assumed the role of sole sponsor of the Academy of Tibetan Literature, and after seeing the properties she agreed to pay cash for both of them. She put $10,000 into escrow, but then, demonstrating an ominous ambivalence toward the project, changed her mind when it came time to close the deal and wanted her money back. The real estate broker finally sued her for his commission, but rather than go to court, Ganna changed her mind again and concluded the purchase in the summer of 1941.

In the meantime, Sir Humphrey Clarke was summoned by the British government to return to England for the war effort. Regretting that he had to abandon his role in setting up Theos' translation center, he offered to sell Cuesta Linda to Madame Walska "at her price" with the understanding that she would fully fund the operation of the organization. With Theos' help, she then resold Arcady—the property she had just bought across the street—for $125,000. Assuming that "her price" for Cuesta Linda was near the $30,000 figure that represented her profit on the Arcady sale, Madame Walska would have ended up with both the El Capitan mountain lodge and the fully furnished and landscaped Cuesta Linda estate at virtually no net expense. Cuesta Linda would be the public venue for the institute's translation activities and classes, and El Capitan would be Theos' private retreat. Madame Walska agreed that in acknowledgment of Theos' role in negotiating the deals, she would deed ownership of El Capitan to him, but until they could legally organize the entire project, she would hold the property in trust for him.

Cuesta Linda, with its gardens and Mediterranean-style villa, had a reputation as one of the finer estates in Montecito. The main house had six bedrooms and four bathrooms, and there were another five bedrooms and two bathrooms in the servants' quarters. There was also a pavilion separated from the main house by a large patio that had three additional bedrooms, each with its own bathroom, and a large rectangular swimming pool that was flanked by two lily ponds.

Ganna renamed the property Tibetland, and, according to an account Theos wrote of that period, their agreement called for planting about thirty acres of the estate's grounds with citrus trees to provide an income to help support the translation and education programs. Tibetland would house a museum, which Theos would design to display his collection of Tibetan art, and an institute called the Academy of Tibetan Literature, with a comprehensive library of Tibetan texts and a staff of resident Tibetan lama translators. There would also be dormitories for students studying at the academy and an organization to publish the translation projects.

Three months after the deal on the property closed, Theos gathered a group of friends and neighbors in Santa Barbara and delivered a lecture about their plans for the Academy of Tibetan Literature that was as much manifesto as prospectus. He was working to bring the first Tibetan lama to the United States to begin the translation of the Tibetan Kangyur and Tengyur, which he said would be "one of the greatest literary undertakings of this century."

"It is significant," he said, "that there is a country left on this globe where its people are living today much as they did a thousand years ago, working toward the ideal that the purpose of life is for spiritual development." Theos recounted the frequent discussions with a group of *geshes* around Tsarong's dinner table in Lhasa. Rather than argue for their own system, he said, the *geshes* only wanted to know "if our institutions have increased the sum total of human happiness. Have they rid the soul of man of fears, superstitions, hates, jealousy, envy, greed, and lust? Have our universities led to greater knowledge of the perplexities of human existence? Has the church made brotherly love indelible in the human heart? Have our great industrial plants provided leisure for the development of character?"

At the Academy of Tibetan Literature, an initiated core group of students would study and learn "the fundamentals of all the truths of human existence." The curriculum, very similar to what he proposed for the American Institute of Yoga, would focus on Indian and Tibetan philosophy and its application in rites, ceremonies, and logical proof; the operation of karma as described in the Wheel of Life; the subtle body and the chakras; ancient systems of psychology and their explanations of how the mind functions and where our thoughts come from; the science of death and rebirth and what happens in the Bardo; the dynamics of the human body and the effects of the environment and food on the body and mind; and then, only after this comprehensive foundation was laid, would the student take up the practice and theory of Yoga. It would take several years to finish the entire program, but when a student was finished, he would be fully qualified and duty-bound to go out and teach others.

Much of this curriculum existed still only in the Tibetan language, and to begin the greatest literary undertaking of the century, Theos continued working at arrangements to bring the first of what he hoped would be several Tibetan lamas to begin the translation of the comprehensive library he had brought back from Tibet. Nine months before the purchase of Tibetland, Theos had already begun the search for a lama to recruit with a letter to the friend who had helped him so much when he first arrived in Darjeeling, S. K. Jinarosa. At the schoolhouse meeting at which Theos first met Jinarosa, Theos also was introduced to the brilliant but iconoclastic incarnate Tibetan lama Gendun Chopel. Gendun Chopel had helped Jinarosa translate Master Shantideva's fundamental Buddhist text, *Guide to the Bodhisattva's Way of Life,* and Jinarosa now wrote to Theos that Gendun Chopel was the perfect candidate to go to America and help him with his massive translation project. "I must tell you that he is the greatest Tibetan scholar I have ever met with in my life and he is one of the few rare best scholars in Tibet so you must not miss him by all means to help you in your Great Work," Jinarosa wrote to Theos. "If you miss him I doubt very much whether you will again get another man like him. So do not miss him by all means."

Gendun Chopel was in many ways ideally suited to be the first Tibetan Lama to move to the United States. He was fluent in English and had collaborated with Tharchin on writing the Tibetan-English dictionary Tharchin was busy with during the time Theos studied with him in Kalimpong. Gendun Chopel was also fond of debating Tibetan orthodoxy. Once while studying at the Drepung monastery, he took a beating for irrefutably asserting that the enlightened state of Buddhahood can't exist, and in 1938 he wrote an article for Tharchin's *Tibet Mirror* titled "The World Is Round or Spherical." In his article, under the pseudonym "Honest Dharma," Gendun Chopel exhorted Tibetans to apply the same arts of interpretation to the Buddha's assertion that the world is flat that they routinely do to his contradictory statements about the ultimate nature of reality. Tharchin would write of him in *Tibet Mirror:* "Nowadays, if one needed to acquire the learning of the likes of this excellent spiritual friend, even if one spent several hundred thousand coins, it would be difficult for such a scholar to appear."

With such plaudits, Theos was convinced that, along with the perfect place for the Academy, he now had the perfect Tibetan lama for it. Gendun Chopel had recently returned to India from sixteen months in Ceylon, where he collaborated on translating the entire Dhammapada from Pali into Tibetan, and immediately after the purchase of Tibetland, Theos convinced Madame Walska to put Gendun Chopel on a $100-a-month retainer to keep him standing by in Kalimpong while they worked out the details of his visa for the United States. America's entry into the war and the flood of refugee applications from Europe complicated that, and the visa process dragged on through interminable rounds of paperwork that had to be mailed or urgently cabled to India for Gendun Chopel to complete. Ganna sent her New York lawyers twice to Washington, D.C., to expedite the visa application for Gendun Chopel, but even though her chief lawyer was a friend of the secretary of state, he could make no progress—the State Department had a firm policy of leaving visa decisions to the issuing consulate and would not interfere.

By this time there were only a few ships sailing at uncertain dates across the Pacific, and the lawyer pointed out that a primary objection raised by the State Department was that if Gendun Chopel received the visa to visit the United States, there might be no ships available at the expiration of his visa on which to return home. The lawyer reported to Ganna on his months of futile efforts: "A warring country does not welcome outsiders."

Finally, in November 1941, Ganna wrote to her lawyer that she needed to know about the chances of getting a visa for Gendun Chopel because she could not "keep a man without work all my life and I must pay him $100 a month for doing nothing there." The disappointing reply came: "I do not believe we will be able to get the gentleman a permit no matter what we do or how much money we spend."

There was nothing more to be done. Theos realized this was a significant setback to his plans, and reluctantly wrote to Jinarosa that they would have to wait until the war ended to bring Gendun Chopel to the United States.

WITH THE TRANSLATION PROJECT now on hold, Theos took the first tentative steps to opening the Academy of Tibetan Literature to students by broadening its library beyond the thousand volumes of Buddhist scriptures he had brought home from Tibet. Theos ordered hundreds of volumes from the Gateway Bookshop in New York on the esoterica of Vajrayana Buddhism, Taoism, Zen, Vedanta, Sufism, Theosophy, Christian mysticism, astrology, psychic research, magic, hypnotism, Jungian psychology, and psychoanalysis. Ganna would later complain that the library additions alone cost her over $20,000.

When Ganna insisted on fully underwriting the development of the

Academy of Tibetan Literature, as well as paying the expenses for the El Capitan mountain retreat property at San Marcos Pass, she may not have fully understood the scope of Theos' vision for the project. It was a huge financial commitment, even for someone with the resources of Madame Walska, and now with the Nazis occupying Paris, she began to worry about the prospective value of the lavish properties she owned there and felt vulnerable to the same financial disaster befalling many of her aristocratic friends in Europe. She would later write in a second, revisionist memoir that her vision when she purchased Cuesta Linda was to own a small, self-sustaining farm where she could retire to a simple life "independent of all servants" in the event that the worst happened and she lost her fortune.

Ganna poured her money and her passion, however, into a dream for the Tibetland property that was neither a small, self-sustaining farm nor the Academy of Tibetan Literature. Rather than plant thirty acres of citrus groves to support the program's operations, Ganna embarked in the first months after buying Cuesta Linda on an ambitious project for replanting the estate's gardens. She hired the best-known landscape architect in Santa Barbara, Lockwood de Forest, to design and supervise the work, which soon grew to include entire new gardens with exotic succulents and cactus. He also repaired the greenhouse, set statues acquired from a neighboring estate, turned the stable into a music studio, and converted the three-bedroom pavilion into Ganna's living quarters.

The lack of a common vision for their enterprise soon showed up as well in their personal relationship. Although Ganna was twenty-one years older than Theos and love was little in evidence, an awkward romance soon infiltrated their partnership. From the beginning their relationship seemed always to revolve about their complementary but conflicting motives for being together. For Theos, it appears, that the relationship was first and foremost about coaxing the level of financial support for the Academy of Tibetan Literature from Ganna that she had promised. Ganna, it seems, believed she was investing in her personal spiritual attainment, and her view of Theos teetered between exultant deifying highs and abject demonizing lows.

Soon after the purchase of Cuesta Linda, Ganna could blithely write: "What was the value of money when finally I found a companion with whom I could plan the future life according to my heart's desire, with an eye on my spiritual development. Here was lying my long life craving. For the first time I could associate my earthly existence with one whose dreams were parallel of mine, who was looking for God and enlightenment."

Her outlook a few months later had darkened, however. Ganna left Tibetland and returned to New York in November 1941 for the winter season of the Metropolitan Opera and to continue her voice lessons while Theos stayed in Santa Barbara to develop plans for the academy. Ganna's letters that winter began to show the radical mood swings that would characterize their relationship. In January Theos wrote and asked about her progress with her voice lessons. "How is your work? ... I am always waiting to hear what you are doing. . . . To know that your work is progressing always means a great deal to me."

To this she immediately wrote an acerbic and martyred reply: "I was much surprised to read that my work's progress means a great deal to you. Surprised because it is the contrary to what you *always* thought, expressed, told and openly cynically made fun of and in the moment of depression hated more than anything else about me. Still if it was so it would change completely my outlook on our future."

As would become the pattern, Theos replied to her vitriol with a romantic grandiloquence intended to reassure and pacify her. "Let this message remove forever and a day the stones of doubt that lie so heavily upon your heart. As the Spirit is our common source of Life, the Sun our source of Light, the Earth our source of strength, your Work is my source of Happiness."

Ganna's mood soared again at reading that, and she replied that when Theos was ready to join her in New York at her Ninety-fourth Street house, "you are always welcome here. . . . Where your heart wants to be— there is your domain—there is your home, there you have [a] right to be and are entitled to be. Is that clear?"

Both of them would later say that they were placating the other by agreeing to marriage. Theos said that, "I agreed to her every request without question, even to the extent of marriage." She wrote that Theos was apprehensive that she could expel him from Tibetland at some point, or that lawyers would find some way of subverting her will (which left both California properties to him), and that she agreed to marry him because she sensed the issue was interfering with his work. Whichever of them it was that insisted on it, both agreed at any rate that the motive for the marriage was Theos' concern for creating a secure home for the Academy of Tibetan Literature at Tibetland.

Ganna's attorney drew up a prenuptial agreement protecting their separate property in case of divorce and arranged for a ceremony in Las Vegas on July 27, 1942. They decided to keep the wedding a secret, and through the four years of their marriage, the society page editors who had dogged Madame Walska for twenty years were unaware they had wed. Even Madame Walska's friends believed Theos to be only her young lover.

After the wedding Theos returned to New York with Ganna and in the fall of 1942 enrolled at Columbia University for a year to study Sanskrit and rewrite his dissertation to complete his Ph.D. In an indication of just how businesslike their relationship continued to be, Theos moved into a separate floor Ganna reserved for him at her Ninety-fourth Street house. Theos had closed the Pierre Health Studio when he first left New York for California a year and a half earlier, and he now lectured in Ganna's living room every Thursday night on the philosophy of Yoga to a standing-room-only group of his dedicated students happy to welcome him back.

The draft board classified Theos as 4-F, unfit for military service because of his heart condition, so while the rest of the country mobilized for war, Theos continued through the winter to study at Columbia and teach classes in Ganna's living room. They had to contend with wartime rationing and practice blackouts that darkened all of Manhattan, and Theos began one of his Thursday night lectures: "Can't we leave the light on until the whistle blows? Let's see if we can't get some thought under way that will hold our attention during the dark. I don't know which would be more profitable—for me to continue talking during the blackout, or to let you just sit and reflect . . . to find out whether an individual really lives according to his . . . high and noble thoughts. The idea of Yoga is something to be lived, and not something to be talked about."

The six months of living room lectures provided a survey of the philosophy of Tantra, which he described as "an interpretation of all knowledge from the standpoint of universal energy and how this energy manifests itself in life down to the individual." The most important aspect of Tantric teachings, he said, dealt specifically with Yoga, the practice of which was encompassed within Hatha Yoga. "They approach the physical instrument as a machine in the sense that it is an electric dynamo filled with energy moving through its nervous system. The Hatha Yoga instructions focus first on purifying this system, then strengthening it, and then directing the flow of energy through the system to bring on awareness of higher consciousness."

Over the weeks he addressed the function of the chakras and made a frequent topic of Kundalini, which he said is similar to the view of physicists that all matter is a great reservoir of energy, similar to the electricity that makes a lightbulb radiate and which survives undiminished if the lightbulb is broken. A practiced yogi could not only awaken Kundalini, he taught, but also raise it through the central channel of the subtle nervous system to the crown chakra at the top of the head. If he could hold it there for three hours or more, the yogi would experience a great light and his breath would stop. With this kind of control of Kundalini, he said, "a yogi stays awake through death."

Theos also devoted several lectures that winter to Tibetan teachings on the Bardo, the state between death and rebirth. Tibetan Yogis, he said, devoted themselves to Kundalini practices in which they passed through all the experiences of death and developed control of the release of consciousness from the physical body, observing the whole process as it happened.

THEOS TOOK TWO SANSKRIT COURSES at Columbia during the fall semester of 1942 and another in the spring term. He also rewrote the dissertation that had been rejected five years earlier, and changed the title from "Tantric Yoga" to "Hatha Yoga, the Report of a Personal Experience." This time it was accepted and Theos received his Ph.D. in philosophy from Columbia on June 1, 1943.

Ganna contributed the $1,200 to publish the dissertation and file a hundred copies with the philosophy department, and a year after its acceptance, Columbia University Press printed five hundred copies—dedicated to Ganna Walska—in a fine edition that featured a gold embossed Tibetan double *dorje* on the cover and thirty-seven full-page studio photographs of Dr. Bernard in a skimpy brief demonstrating his mastery of the major asanas and mudras he described in the text.

The revised dissertation, although it was accepted this time by his review committee, did nothing to address several of the faults that led to its rejection in 1938, including the needs to identify the gurus he studied under and to "distinguish his experiences from the theories about them." He again described his putative experiences with frequent references to the foundational fifteenth-century text *Hatha Yoga Pradipika*, and in detailed footnotes and long excerpts inserted into his narrative, he quoted extensively from that text and compared its advice on particular practices with sections from two other classic Hatha Yoga texts, *Gheranda Samhita* and *Siva Samhita*.

Aside from the obvious problem of where he actually learned the practices on which he comments with such authority, Theos' *Hatha Yoga* was a groundbreaking technical compendium of the asanas, mudras, and purification and Pranayama practices that lead to the Samadhi of Raja Yoga, the fruit "which destroys death, is the means of obtaining happiness, and gives the Brahman-bliss."

The book was highly appreciated in the small circle in which it circulated. Writing in the *Review of Religion*, Vaman R. Kokatnur called it "the first book to bring to the student the validity of Yoga practices." As he wrote:

Dr. Theos Bernard has placed the western world particularly under a debt of gratitude by bringing to it his personally verified account of Hatha Yoga practices. In this age of science, his approach and study of the subject are to be highly commended. It is probably the first time in the English language that such clear and practical directions have been supplied to the student so that anyone can practice these.

It was this experimental approach—testing the potential of an ancient worldview for spiritual development in the modern mind—that made

Theos Bernard's introduction of Hatha Yoga and Tantra to the West so pioneering. His mastery of the asanas, to which the book's photographs clearly attest; his incisive comments and advice on the Kriyas, Pranayama, and Kundalini practices; and the scope of his lectures and teaching ambitions are all evidence that Theos Bernard was an advanced practitioner and well-qualified teacher of Hatha Yoga. And considering he did not actually have the advantage of the traditional apprenticeship with an Indian guru that he claimed, in a time when there were almost no other Western teachers, the experimental results he reports from his self-directed studies are all the more remarkable.

AFTER THEOS FINALLY GOT HIS PH.D. in June 1943, he and Ganna left New York to spend the summer at Tibetland. Ganna continued to develop the estate's gardens, replacing the traditional landscaping in front of the house with unusual, mature cactus and adding improvements to the lotus pond, lower garden, fuchsia garden, rose garden, palm grove, bamboo garden, and the now famous blue garden—all of which went in the opposite direction of Theos' plan to plant a thirty-acre citrus orchard to help support the Academy.

Theos understood a huge investment would be required to realize his vision for the academy, and he now began to complain that instead of putting money into the museum, dormitories, and citrus orchards, Ganna was creating exotic gardens and making plans to spend even more for a music conservatory at Tibetland with an outdoor theater that would seat three hundred. She told him to leave the management of the properties to her—she had ample experience from managing her French château and Theos should devote his undivided attention to his studies.

All the while, with the expenditures required for the new gardens, the properties began to deteriorate for lack of maintenance. The roof leaked, termites were infesting the floors, the basement flooded, and because Ganna occupied the separate smaller quarters in the pavilion, the large house remained unheated during the damp winter and mildew became a problem.

Theos and Ganna had agreed at the time of its purchase that El Capitan, the two-hundred-acre lodge at San Marcos Pass, would be Theos' private retreat. Theos renamed the property Penthouse of the Gods, and when in California, he spent most of his time there. Theos complained to Ganna that, just as at Tibetland, the lack of a budget for maintenance at Penthouse of the Gods was causing problems. The water system was inadequate for fire protection, which placed the Tibetan manuscripts at risk, and Theos felt that a fireproof vault should be built to prevent disaster. The roof, fireplace, and foundation needed work; plumbing and heating equipment needed repairs; termite damage was spreading; and a bulldozer was needed to maintain the road.

Ganna was back in New York by October 1943 and replied to his appeals for investment in the project by saying that with the pressure of wartime taxes it was impossible to do more than she already was. "As you never realize the value of money I must write this to you in order not to speak about it anymore," she wrote from New York. "My income now is less than $3,000 a month." Half of that was already committed, she said, to fixed expenses, and the remainder had to cover everything from the grocer and butcher to the lawyers and four telephones.

Even though Madame Walska was no longer on the stage, she still enjoyed making an appearance at the opera, and she was happy to pay to bring Theos to New York on the train for the gala diamond jubilee premiere of the Metropolitan Opera season. Theos, in a new tuxedo, top hat, and cane, was noticed by the *New York Times* correspondent to be sitting in Ganna's box in the famous Golden Horseshoe along with a Polish count and countess and the Polish consul general. Although the dashing Dr. Bernard's presence was certain to have been the subject of much gossip, they were able still to keep their marriage a secret.

The awkwardness of their situation—meaning for Ganna the twenty-one-year difference in their ages—was a frequent embarrassment to her. She wrote to Theos that "it looks not right because my dear absent minded of realistic things boy, Americans can not admit without freakish embarrassment that a young man is living on his wife's money."

Even though they managed to keep their marriage under wraps, their relationship was well known, and Theos was, by his association with Madame Walska, lampooned for the first time in his career by tabloid press reports in much the same way his uncle Pierre Arnold Bernard had been years earlier. The December 12, 1943, issue of the Sunday newspaper supplement *American Weekly* (published by the Hearst Corporation with a circulation of fifty million) carried a full-page screened headline "The Disappointed Diva Yodeling Now with a Yogi." Replete with large caricatures and photographs, the article began, "Ganna Walska, the would-be-grand opera star whose vain, 25-year assault on the citadel of musical fame forms one of the most bizarre dramas of modern times has at long last found consolation for her blighted career.... She has found it in Yoga as preached by a fabulous and very handsome young American named Theos Bernard."

The article called Theos "a beneficent sort of Svengali" who taught, it joked, that "one incarnation just leads to another, and so on through the millennia toward some ultimate perfection." Madame Walska could therefore "relax philosophically in expectation of becoming the Jenny Lind of the year 4000."

Earlier in the year, the New York tabloid *Sunday Mirror* magazine section ran a three-page illustrated article with a similar mocking tone. Headlined "Ganna Walska Fabulous Glamor-Glitterer, Who Won and Chucked Multi-Millionaires, Turns from Bad Singing to Weird Cults." The article said that "Under the tutelage of a robed oriental practitioner of the occult Hindu cult of yoga, Mme. Walska has attained through mysticism the thing that neither millions nor hypnotism, nor surgery nor a secret application of the principle of the death-ray could procure for her: the certitude she can sing."

The piece then sketched an imagined scene with Lily Pons singing onstage at the Met while Madame Walska sits watching from her box in the Golden Horseshoe. The piece cites a dictionary definition that Yoga has as its goal the identification of consciousness with its object, resulting in *samadhi*. "Will SAMADHI work? SAMADHI never Fails! 'Identification of consciousness with the object,' is coming through. That is no longer Lily Pons, down there ... But only Walska will ever know that Walska sang."

Until that point the hundreds of articles describing Theos' pilgrimage to Tibet and his development of Hatha Yoga in the United States had all provided glowing publicity for both him and the spiritual pursuits he advocated. He was able to laugh off the new angle the yellow journalists found to ridicule Madame Walska, but the spate of bad press must have given Theos another instance to wonder if Ganna's involvement in his big plans was making them all possible or providing the greatest obstacle to his success.

Theos put his new tuxedo in mothballs and left New York a few days after his appearance with Ganna at the opera and was home in Santa Barbara before December 10, his thirty-fifth birthday. On his way back he made a stop in Berkeley to promote the Tibetan Text Society, as he was now calling the publishing branch of the academy, and talked with anthropologists and Sanskrit scholars at the University of California as well as the director of the university press, who told Theos he was eager to expand the press's Oriental publications division.

Theos wrote about the encouraging prospects in a letter to one of his most ardent students, Helen Graham Park, a forty-year-old New York interior architect. "All without exception or reservation were interested in the project proposed for the Tibetan Text Society," Theos wrote to her in the earliest surviving letter of what was clearly by this time a well-established teacher-student relationship. The letter shows they are thoroughly briefed on the other's projects, and he thanks her for sending *History of Aryan Medical Science* and *The Antiquity of Hindu Medicine* for the library, but tells her, "Remember you are not to rob your library in order to build mine. Only when you happen to have a duplicate or something you want to discard must you indulge me—my influence is always to be one of contribution." He closes the letter with an ambiguous line that hints there may be more to their relationship: "I will be with you again soon—always yours, Theos."

After writing his letter, Theos made a blunder so careless it could have made a defining case study for Freud on the unconscious motivation of behavioral slip-ups. Theos wrote Ganna the same day he wrote Helen and sent the letters off in the wrong envelopes. Ganna promptly returned Helen's letter to him and wrote in the margin of it in her gigantic blue pencil script, "I am sorry you *never* informed me that you have other friends that are sending you books, etc."

Theos also hadn't told her, Ganna wrote in her accompanying letter, that he didn't like to celebrate holidays. Theos had written to Helen thanking her also for the gift of two more Tibetan grammar books and told her to call them his birthday and Christmas gifts. But then in the next phrases he remonstrated: "You know how much I dislike the material acknowl-edgement of those events. The birthday one cannot help, but I am certainly opposed to insulting my intelligence by recognizing the ignorant supersti-tion of Christmas." About that Ganna wrote to Theos in her letter:

> You will get this on your birthday but I will not offend you by silly
> wishes knowing that all those years—contrary to all evidences—you
> disliked any fuss about it. . . . I did not know I was *insulting your*
> *intelligence!!!* I wanted to send you a little birthday present—naturally
> I cannot lower your inner vibration by such superstition. On the other
> hand . . . I do not want you to have good opportunity to write to your
> friends complaining of my . . . stinginess as I do not suppose you told
> them that last year for your birthday and Xmas presents I sold my
> bracelet and earrings! . . . I do not think I will come for Xmas . . . I
> was doing it mostly for your sake. . . . Now I see you do not need it.

That winter, after his Christmas alone, symptoms associated with his heart condition returned for the first time since Theos began practicing Yoga seventeen years earlier in Arizona. His New York cardiologist, Dr. Milton J. Raisbeck, had commented after Theos' examination three years earlier that there was some ventricular enlargement still present, and that overactivity or strain of any kind—even running to catch a train—could be dangerous for his heart.

Thinking the dry desert air would help, Theos went to Arizona in January for some recuperation. Because his mother, Aura, had died three and a half years earlier, and his three half brothers were all away in the war, Ganna was unsure where he was staying in Tucson and sent her let-ters to him in care of general delivery, University Station. She had appar-ently forgiven him for the faux pas with Helen's letter, and wrote that she had received two letters from him with great joy, and hoped he had re-ceived her Valentine's Day card. She hoped that the reason he was now out of touch was that he "had found an Ashram worthy of my boy's high vibrations to live good mind."

Theos returned to Santa Barbara via San Francisco at the end of Feb-ruary without telling Ganna of his plans, and she wrote to him at Tibetland, "Why did you decide to leave Arizona, and how? On foot . . . plane or train? . . . Why not let me know . . . I had no way would it be important to reach you." It appears that the place Theos really fantasized about disappearing to was Tibet, but a trip there was impossible at that time for many reasons, including Theos' commitment at Tibetland and the fact that in 1944, because of the war, there were no planes or ships carrying travelers to Asia. His desire to return to Tibet had apparently been a recent topic of their conversation, and a week after Theos returned to Santa Barbara Ganna wrote him a message urging him "to be in the present and not to live in hope, for instance, of going to India, which is in the worst case *very unreliable* because suppose that the Dalai Lama would not allow you to go there—then what? All your inner life must crumble down?"

Six weeks after Theos returned to Santa Barbara, Ganna arrived to spend the summer. She was in crisis from the beginning and spent those sunny months at Tibetland in the bleak grip of paranoia. Ganna later wrote to Theos that on the days he stayed at Tibetland with her, she locked herself in her room because she was afraid he might choke her to death, and when she felt ill, she suspected he was poisoning her. But, believing that thieves had heard of her reputation for keeping a hoard of valuable jewelry and would break into the house, she was also terrified when he left her alone to go stay at Penthouse of the Gods. "*Fear* uncontrolled fear filled all my being," she wrote to Theos. "With every crack my heart stopped. . . . All those doors could be forced & I have no way to call anyone. I could not phone without light & I could not speak on phone because they could have heard me through the open windows!"

DESPITE THE DRAMA WITH HIS WIFE, the frustratingly slow progress with the Academy, and the cautions about his heart condition, Theos was prolific in 1944. While Columbia University Press was bringing out his book, *Hatha Yoga, the Report of a Personal Experience*, he wrote two more scholarly books, the first a Tibetan grammar and the second a survey of Indian philosophy.

A Simplified Grammar of the Literary Tibetan Language borrowed heavily from three classic but difficult-to-find grammars, the oldest of which was the

1834 Alexander Csoma de Körös volume he had found while studying in Kalimpong. Theos wrote in April 1944 to his literary agent, Carol Hill, that he had finished the first draft of the grammar but was shelving the project because there was no Tibetan type available in this country to print it. They were eventually able to secure the Tibetan type fonts and the grammar text became the first publication of the Tibetan Text Society in 1946.

The second book, an outline of the six classic systems of Hindu philosophy—Nyaya, Vaisheshika, Samkhya, Yoga, Mimamsa, and Vendanta—was published in England before it was published in the United States. Rider and Co. published it with the title *Philosophical Foundations of India* in 1945, but it was another two years before the Philosophical Library in New York brought it out as *Hindu Philosophy*.

This book, like *A Simplified Grammar*, is a synthesis of classics in the field, but in his compelling introduction, Theos explains why these teachings form a scientific approach to philosophy and its application in spiritual development.

> From the beginning of time, teachers have endeavored to bridge the gap between the seen and the unseen and to show cause for the inescapable experiences of sorrow and suffering.... But the questions still remain: What is the nature of Reality? What is the nature of human existence? What is the cause of pleasure and pain? How can Liberation be attained?...
>
> The West refuses to accept the postulate that the world of mind and matter is but an appearance of a deeper reality which lies beyond the perception of our senses, regardless of how magnified these may be by powerful instruments of precision. One of the reasons for this is due to the preconceived notion that man cannot know metaphysical truths by direct experience; therefore, at best, metaphysical truths can only be speculations, inferences, or ungrounded faith.

To arrive at the direct experience of metaphysical truth, Theos wrote, a student moves through the stages of faith to understanding to realization. The practice of Yoga brings the student at the last stage to "become one with the Ultimate Reality," an empirical proof of his metaphysical faith. This empirical approach, Theos wrote, must be the test of any philosophy.

During this prolific period of academic publishing, Theos invited his father, Glen, to come live with him at his Penthouse of the Gods retreat home. Glen provided insights into the relationship of the main Indian schools for the writing of *Hindu Philosophy,* and Theos dedicated the book "to my teacher." Glen had written his own 120-page "Selective Treatise on the Theory and Practice of Yoga," and Theos undoubtedly planned a teaching role for him at the Academy of Tibetan Literature. For Ganna, though, Glen was an unwelcome intrusion, and seeing some benefit again in disguising his identity, Theos first introduced him to her as his "learned friend," La Varnie. Ganna was unconvinced and unmoved by the role, and after knowing Glen for a year, she wrote Theos, "I do not doubt that your mother was a great soul but . . . I cannot imagine your father as a prototype of Goodness. Or Love."

THEOS RETURNED TO NEW YORK for the winter of 1944–45 and was living with Ganna at the Ninety-fourth Street house by the end of November. They soon picked up the running argument about the California properties, and when Theos brought up again the issue of transferring the deed to Penthouse of the Gods into his name, Ganna interpreted that to mean he was impatient for her to die and decided as a consequence to cut him out of her will altogether.

They also argued over the publishing of his books. Ganna had promised when he started the books, Theos said, to underwrite the cost of publishing *Hindu Philosophy* and *A Simplified Grammar of the Literary Tibetan Language,* but changed her mind when he finished them. She now refused, as well, to pay for a second printing of *Hatha Yoga.*

The initial five hundred copies of *Hatha Yoga* had sold well and Theos was now sorting out with Columbia University Press the complications of arranging a second printing. Under the terms of the contract, Theos paid up front the cost of publishing the book—estimated for this run at $1,198—and then received all the profit on sales. Unfortunately, the high cost of production details—among them good paper for the asana photographs and the gold-stamped double *dorje* on the cover—made the book more expensive to produce than they could sell it for, and the sale of the five hundred copies yielded only $875.

"We are sorry that the picture must be so discouraging financially," his editor wrote to him, "particularly on a volume which has been so well received, but of course you are well acquainted with the problem of pricing a volume which is so expensive to manufacture sufficiently low to attract those who would be interested in your work."

Because of wartime shortages, there was paper available only for another five hundred copies. The paper shortages were a problem in England as well, where Rider and Co. was eager to reprint his first two books but was unable to find enough paper.

Ganna explained her view of the situation in a vituperative note to Theos that would have amused her previous husbands: "*Please, please*, understand that when I met you I was rich, now I have nothing but debts. . . . In these conditions I cannot take care of you financially any longer. . . . You must look for somebody else to finance you. I know you love me but your love for luxury is stronger than any love for human beings." Money, however, wasn't the only issue in Ganna's refusal to continue support for Theos' projects. She wrote to Theos after her final refusal to sponsor another five hundred copies of a book still frequently cited as one of the best guides to Hatha Yoga: "Who needs your books, they do not teach goodness. . . . I will not encourage you any more to write because it flatters only your vanity."

With Ganna's refusal to invest any more in his books, Theos had to look elsewhere for support. Columbia University Press needed an immediate reply if the project was going to proceed, and his editor wrote to him, "The paper problem grows steadily worse almost daily, and we would find it difficult to hold the necessary paper for the reprinting very much longer." Theos was soon able to reply that he had obtained the funds from other friends, and although there is no record of it, the second edition of *Hatha Yoga* was in all likelihood sponsored by the member of the inner group so familiar with the many details of his operations, Helen Graham Park.

Theos left New York to return to Santa Barbara again on March 17, 1945. Ganna wrote to him the day after he left that she had wanted to kick him out of the house in December but was afraid there would be "drama, tragedy, or scandal," so she had decided to wait until he left on his own for California. It was only after he was gone, she said, that she felt safe enough to reveal the truth. "Never will I let you in your present condition live in 94th Street anymore!!"

With Theos now in California, Madame Walska unleashed in her outsized, blue-pencil script all the venom of a well-rehearsed operatic shrew. The first of two months of twice-weekly missiles set the tone:

My dear boy. I was waiting till you go away to tell you the following. I do not love you, I never did. My association with you from the beginning was a series of sacrifices of abnegation in order to save you. Not only I did not succeed but contrary to my reasonable expectation I encouraged the monster in you and in spite of your better health your nastiness grows instead of diminishing.

Another proclaimed:

You are a *monster* of selfishness and at the same time *deeply deeply deeply* godless. You who in life are so ugly in everything you do, who crash and break everything that is beautiful or ideal in others around you. . . . even if you would try to better yourself I am not sure it would be possible. You have to change all your *nature*. . . . It is to become a new man, a man with a *soul!!!*

She wrote that being together in New York the previous winter had become so intolerable that she began to think that it would be better for everyone around him if Theos' weak heart gave out and he died. "Who needs those few books that you wrote? They may be even poisonous to some who will follow your steps instead of God's steps."

She tried to convince Theos that he had an inherited psychiatric disorder while admitting that she was nearly disabled by her own anguish. "I am so nervous, so hysterical, can not get hold of myself, in bed again, calming drugs in day time, sleeping pills in the night time and every time I think of you or write to you—I am worse & worse."

Of all the anguish Ganna suffered in the spring of 1945, however, the most searing pain resulted from the loss of her cherished lifelong companion—the delusion she was a singer. And Theos, she felt, was responsible for that as well.

> You knew more than the whole world that my work is the only thing keeping me alive . . . By pointing out that my well known selfishness prevents me from singing—you put my spirit below any hope. When it was convenient to you—you were telling me how great a singer I am . . . and now, when you can afford to be frank you find only ugliness and selfishness in me. Like a drunken man you *tell the Truth*. You see I always *knew* I could not sing. *Please* do not phone again.

Amazingly, in none of the surviving letters from Theos to Ganna does he retaliate or defend himself. Much of his correspondence to her is undated or headed by only the day and month, so the exact time he is writing must be inferred from events he refers to, but in none of the many examples does he lose his yogi's equanimity. Most are affectionate and encouraging and remind her to rest and not work so hard:

> Do know that I never want to be a hindrance, obstacle, or barrier to your spiritual growth and development; that is my deepest desire to do everything possible to help you aspire and attain the goal that destiny has set for you. Please tell me what to do; show me the way to help and not hamper your efforts.

Although Tibetland meant only misery for her, by mid-April 1945 Ganna felt she had run out of options for happiness in New York and wrote, "I need to be *alone, alone*, absolutely alone . . . If I do not go to Santa Barbara where can I go *now*?" She moved back to Tibetland, but Theos and Ganna saw little of each other that summer. Theos stayed at Penthouse of the Gods with Glen and in two months spent only one night at Tibetland. Although Ganna had gone again to Tibetland to be alone, being alone made her miserable as well, and she left Santa Barbara again for New York at the beginning of October 1945 with the declaration that Theos should consider himself free of all marital restraints.

Over the next months Ganna wrote several times to Theos that circumstances could force her to sell Penthouse of the Gods and she would have no regrets about doing so. That admission eliminated the last reason for Theos to stay in the antagonistic marriage, and he saw that ending it might now be the only way to save Penthouse of the Gods. Ganna flew to Los Angeles on May 20, 1946, to move back for the summer into Tibetland, and expected Theos to meet her at the airport in her Cadillac. She was greeted instead by a process server delivering legal notification of her husband's suit for separation from her and his demands for monthly support payments.

The suit stated that that Madame Walska had treated Theos in a cruel and inhuman manner and had told him numerous times that she no longer loved him and would not live with him any longer. It also stated that Madame Walska had "substantial means" and because Theos was in poor bodily health and unable to support himself by his own efforts, she should pay $1,500 a month for his permanent support and maintenance.

Theos also asked that the court restrain Madame Walska from selling Tibetland and Penthouse of the Gods and from removing the books and cultural artifacts that furnished them. In his deposition to the court Theos broadened his demands and stated that since Madame Walska had broken all her contracts, agreements, and promises to finance his Academy of Tibetan Literature, she should be required to turn both Penthouse of the Gods and Tibetland over to him and should pay an amount of money adequate to repair and maintain the properties and to support their educational activities as she had promised.

The news didn't break in the *Los Angeles Times* until July 9, when Madame Walska's attorneys filed their answer and cross-complaint to Theos' petition for a separation. Of course, the first surprising news was that Ganna Walska had married for a sixth time and managed for four years to

keep it secret. But there was much more. Her appearance in court made—
even by Hollywood standards—bizarre and titillating front-page headlines for days.

Ganna took the witness stand "smartly dressed and still attractive," as
one reporter noted, and told the court that before their marriage, Theos
had misled her by convincing her he had been born to specially chosen
parents and possessed "the power to . . . be the spiritual savior of mankind." He also misrepresented himself as "the spiritual and physical reincarnation of Guru Rimpoche, also known as Padma Sambhava, an
ancient Buddhistic Saint of Tibet," and had told her he "had occult powers giving him control over the mind and body of men and women and
over the physical universe as well."

He further declared to her, the cross-complaint stated, that he "was one
with the Universal Consciousness of Life and as such the knower of ultimate
truth" and if she assisted him he "would use his powers . . . to advance and
perfect the spirituality of his own soul, of the soul of this defendant and of
mankind in general." He could not, however, complete his mission, he convinced her, without her "inspiration and help as his wife and helpmate."

And so, she told the court, desiring to do everything within her power
"to advance the spiritual enlightenment and salvation of mankind," she
agreed to marry him, despite her misgivings about the twenty-one-year
difference in their ages. She bought Tibetland and Penthouse of the Gods
to further that mission, but, disappointingly, they had been "misused well
nigh exclusively and totally for the materialistic enjoyment and pleasure of
Dr. Bernard."

Her court filings went on to say that, aided and abetted by his father
under the alias of La Varnie, Theos had sought to glut and enrich himself
and coerced Madame Walska into satisfying his lavish demands by threats
of force and violence. Not only had he "choked and well nigh strangled to
death" Madame Walska, but she regretfully disclosed that he "threatened
her with dire and awful consequences of his use of the Power of Kundalini,"
the power of which, he claimed, he had demonstrated to her by causing the
earthquake that shook Santa Barbara in June 1941.

Madame Walska asked the court to order Theos to leave Penthouse of
the Gods and Tibetland immediately, and, moreover, to leave behind all

the Tibetan documents, manuscripts, art works, artifacts, and library of religious and philosophical works she said she had acquired to further his mission.

In response to those accusations, the *Los Angeles Times* reported that "The handsome, well-built Bernard, looking younger than his 38 years, told highlights of his life story and answered questions by Mme. Walska's attorney with Oriental courtesy and calm." However, his claim for separate maintenance, being based partly on his assertion that his heart condition left him physically handicapped, was undermined when he admitted under cross-examination that he was able to stand on his head for periods totaling three hours a day. When he admitted further that his first wife, Viola, had created a trust fund for him at their divorce now worth $40,000 and that he held $8,500 in war bonds, Theos realized he was left without grounds for his separate maintenance demands and withdrew the complaint.

The following day, the judge granted the divorce request in Madame Walska's cross-complaint on grounds of extreme cruelty. She agreed to give Theos $5,000 for his attorney's fees and a one-time payment of $1,500. Theos agreed to leave Penthouse of the Gods within four days, taking with him only a few books.

With shocking finality, the court's decision put an end to Theos' dream for the Academy of Tibetan Literature in Santa Barbara. Moreover, if it had been his strategy to marry Ganna in order to protect the academy's assets, the gambit backfired completely with the court's decision that all property in Madame Walska's possession at the time of the decree belonged to her. Luckily, Theos had kept some of the most valuable artifacts and the thousand volumes of manuscripts he acquired in Tibet safely off-site in fireproof storage. But it appears that most of the nine hundred or so Tibetan artifacts that remained at Tibetland and Penthouse of the Gods by court order were also pieces he had collected in Tibet and were housed there as part of the museum he envisioned for the Academy. Those were all now the property of Madame Ganna Walska.

All the machinations Theos had devised to give life to his twelve-year-old vision of creating an institute to teach Hatha Yoga and Tibetan Buddhism in the United States had suddenly crumbled. He was bereft of that dream—but left joyfully unencumbered to contemplate his next move.

Chapter 13

GONE TO THE OTHER SIDE

WITHIN DAYS OF HIS EVICTION from Penthouse of the Gods, Theos was at work on a very different plan to develop the Academy of Tibetan Literature: traveling to India with Helen Graham Park. Only six weeks after the divorce decree was issued in Santa Barbara, Theos wrote to Glen from New York that he and Helen had already had their second round of shots, she had received her new passport, and their names were on waiting lists for five different ships to Asia.

The speed with which they were able to chart this new course suggests it had been under consideration for some time. They at least had long-held separate yearnings to go to India. Several of Ganna's letters to Theos criticize his obsessive hopes for a return to India, and three years before his divorce Theos wrote to Helen with advice about some points of her Buddhist studies: "When you are in India and there is free time, the mind can reflect clearly on these problems."

Helen—a petite, pretty, and classy five-foot-two-inch, brown-eyed brunette with an incisive intelligence and courageous will—was five years older than Theos, and like him, had been abandoned by her father shortly after her birth in 1903 in Walla Walla, Washington. Helen's mother, Hallie, moved with her infant daughter to Seattle, where she got a secretarial job in the office of the prominent architect John Graham, and it wasn't long before she married the boss.

Helen enjoyed design work, and although it was rare in the 1920s to find a woman working in the field, she applied after high school to the architecture program at the University of Washington. She was admitted only to humor her famous stepfather and was never expected to graduate, but after she won a design contest as a junior she was encouraged to complete her degree.

Helen then studied fashion and interiors for a couple of years at the Sorbonne in Paris and after her return to the United States married Brock Park, the founder of an international insurance group. The newlyweds immediately moved to Shanghai, where Brock's thriving office focused on maritime insurance, and the couple was quickly absorbed into the stratum of British society that revolved around the polo club and its continual occasions for gowns and dinner jackets.

Helen was less enchanted with those ostentations than was her husband, and during an episode of what was probably malaria, she lay with a high fever in her hospital room and had a vision of a bright light that told her to leave the marriage and radically change her life or she would die. When she recovered, she left Brock and moved to New York, where she set up an interior architecture business. She became fascinated during this period with dream interpretation and began several years of analytical sessions with Carl Jung's early disciple and translator, H. G. Baynes.

No record survives of Theos and Helen's first meeting, but a *New York Times* article in September 1939 lauding Helen for her design work on the renovation of three floors of loft space at 101 Fifth Avenue indicates she was in New York when Theos opened his yoga studio at the Pierre Hotel. Helen kept in her files until her death undated notes on Theos' lectures that included verbatim passages from a lecture he delivered in the first weeks after opening the Pierre Health Studio in October 1939, suggesting that Theos probably met Helen at about the same time he met Ganna. As Theos' letter to her in December 1943 indicates, she was clearly part of his inner circle by that time, which also meant that she was very likely part of the group attending his 1942 series of lectures in Ganna's living room.

However, even though Theos and Helen had probably known each other for six years by the time of his divorce from Ganna, his surviving letters to her—even one from just two months before he filed for a separation from Ganna—betray no conspiracy to run off together. The letters Helen saved are filled with innocent affection, but the predominant tone is of a teacher giving advice in his homey, aphoristic style to a close student on almost every aspect of her life: what and how to study, family situations, her career, and even her love life.

Less than a year before they were getting their shots and visas for their trip to India, Theos wrote to Helen about a big project decorating seventeen floors that she considered taking. She worried that with a commitment of that scale she might miss an opportunity to go to India. "It is a matter of organization," he counseled her. "One must first have an idea— dream a little, work a little, and then leave the rest to the Gods. And with it all, you will still make India—in a big way."

Even in the last letter of the set, dated March 12, 1946, just ten weeks before the separation papers were served to Ganna at the Burbank airport, Theos advised Helen to focus on her business for now. Referring to what seems to be her own independent long-planned trip to India, Theos advises her to be patient and let things happen as they will. "Forget about results, and give your undivided attention to work. As for India and the many other plans that are hidden in your present dream world, they can come to pass . . . without in the slightest way upsetting the overall picture."

It appears that right up until his divorce and eviction, Theos had an intimate but chaste relationship with Helen, but once Theos found himself suddenly single and without a home, it took almost no time for them to make their plans together for a two-year trip to India.

Hoping to make the trip pay for itself, Theos talked with several New York magazine editors who offered between $700 and $1,200 for articles illustrated with color photographs. He also had a $1,500 contract with the Philosophical Library, the American publisher of his most recent book, *Hindu Philosophy*, to solicit and edit a collection of articles from India's leading minds in the arts and sciences that would survey India's contributions to contemporary thought. The book would be titled *Twentieth*

Century India and the publisher supplied Theos with a list of top scholars in all academic disciplines from astronomy to zoology and included letters of introduction to India's two best-known newsmakers, Mahatma Gandhi and Jawaharlal Nehru.

All the preparations for travel, however, proved far easier than actually getting a ticket out of the country. The end of the war released a pent-up flood of travelers that overwhelmed the surviving commercial ships and planes, and then a strike at the ship lines in the summer of 1946 left the airlines as the only alternative.

Much of Helen's design work was commissioned by her close friend Cornelius Vander Starr, a business associate in Shanghai of her ex-husband, Brock Park, and the founder of an insurance company that grew into the behemoth American International Group, which for decades was the world's largest insurance company. Deploying the influence of C. V. Starr, Helen was able at last to book a ticket for Theos on TWA, but the departure date was uncertain. Helen, they decided, would wrap up a project in New York and then complete her design work on C. V. Starr's new house in Hong Kong before joining Theos in India in November.

By this time, the relationship between Theos and Helen had developed beyond that of a teacher and his student. They had a joint bank account, and as Theos wrote to Glen the day before his departure from New York, "This trip is certainly costing a pretty penny, . . . however . . . it is well worth it, for it will definitely bring our two lives very close together and enable us to do many things together in the years ahead."

Theos spent much of his last days in New York getting his financial and legal affairs in order for a long absence. He wrote a new will that left everything to Glen and assigned to him a power of attorney so that Glen could manage his small investment accounts as if they were his own. At last, on September 20, Theos got a flight out of New York for India with connections in Paris; Geneva; Rome; Cairo; Jerusalem; Bara, Iraq; and Dhahran, Saudi Arabia. His baggage was sent by sea, and while he waited for a month in Bombay for it to catch up with him, Theos called on contacts at universities in the area about writing chapters for *Twentieth Century India*.

Immediately upon his arrival in India, it was evident to Theos that this crown jewel of the British Empire was careening toward a pivotal chapter of its own. Britain was at that time conceiving a plan to grant independence to India, but the date had not been set. Most policymakers in London, though, were resigned to the fact that it had to be soon—preferably before the escalating hostilities between Muslims and Hindus raged into communal war. As Theos wrote to his friend John Mock in California, the "police regulations, curfews, political tension and unrest . . . are much worse than it is reported at home."

After his baggage arrived, Theos left Bombay and traveled north to New Delhi, where he was able to land interviews with Nehru and Gandhi. Nehru, at that critical moment of Indian history, said that he didn't have time to write a chapter for the book; however, if things settled down, he would try to write a foreword for it. The seventy-seven-year-old Gandhi, Theos wrote to Mock, said "he has written his last. His greatest desire is to withdraw from the world, but he must do what circumstances demand in regard to these political problems they are trying to solve at the moment." He did give Theos permission, however, to use anything in the book that he had already written. "It was enough for me that I was able to manage interviews," Theos wrote to Glen, "realizing that I am actually arriving at what is probably the most critical time in history for the career of both of these men."

Despite the nationalistic and anticolonial aspirations for which these men were a symbol, Theos observed in his letter to Mock, "the country has gone all out Western . . . The bazaars and shops are crowded with American products, many of which we cannot get at home. It is an entirely different India than the one visited before, and I fear that the India of old has gone forever; so I feel blessed in being able to be here once more before the knowledge for which she has stood down through the centuries has completely disappeared."

After a few days in Delhi Theos went north into the Himalayan hills on a pilgrimage to sacred sites of that ancient spiritual heritage. He visited Dehra Dun, Mussoorie, and then Hardwar, where millions of pilgrims convene every twelve years on the banks of the Ganges for the Kumbha Mela festival. From Hardwar Theos went up the Ganges about thirty miles through a jungle filled with wildlife to Rishikesh, the "Abode of the

Mystic Sages." Theos visited there the ashram of Swami Sivananda Saraswati, the fifty-nine-year-old former physician who had lived on the west bank of the Ganges near Rishikesh since his initiation as a renunciate Sannyasin twenty-two years earlier.

About seventy students lived at the ashram, and with surprised appreciation, Theos found that they had a comprehensive knowledge of all the forms of Yoga, and a few of the students could demonstrate all the various practices that he described in his book *Hatha Yoga*. Theos wrote to Glen— who had searched with him for just such a place on their trip through India ten years earlier—that "it was the first time, that I had ever run on to a place where they had so much general information that seemed to be in order. No one was overly imbued with any sanctimonious attitude, but were all rather clean, sensible individuals."

Theos had tea with Swami Sivananda at sunset overlooking the Ganges—which here near the headwaters was more a rushing stream than a broad river—and the swami described the method he taught, called synthetic Yoga, in which he advocated a balanced life and broad knowledge of a wide range of subjects. "He says that it is impossible for anyone to get anywhere by following or adhering to any one path," Theos wrote to Glen.

Swami Sivananda invited Theos to stay and spend some time with them, and now that Theos had finally found at the Sivananda ashram a true Hatha Yoga master, there was no reason that he couldn't have stayed and undertaken the kind of three-month retreat that he had described in his books. He and Helen had a long stay in India planned, and as Theos told Glen, it would be "a very worth while experience for Helen, especially if she is going to help run a school for Yoga in the United States. It will give her all the necessary background and also a certain amount of esteem among those who come." But just as eleven years earlier when he and Glen had rushed through Ranchi even though at last they had time to stay with the Hindu Tantricas at their jungle camp, it was the lure of continuing his Buddhist studies and the possibility of returning to Tibet that drew Theos north again to Kalimpong.

HELEN GOT AWAY from New York a month after Theos departed and landed in Hong Kong on October 23 to supervise for a couple of weeks work that she had designed for C. V. Starr's new house, a magnificent structure overlooking the sea that he christened Lookout. She finished that and got on to Calcutta by November 10, but left again four days later to tend to some more work for Starr in Ceylon. A few weeks later, probably in Calcutta, she rendezvoused with Theos, who had just finished his pilgrimage to the foothill shrines, and by about the first week of December they moved up to Kalimpong, the village, as he once wrote, that he loved "more than any other place that I have ever lived on this earth."

Theos and Helen would spend the next eight months in Kalimpong, but Theos wasted no time in getting back to his research and language studies with Tharchin. He also sent off letters to the Tibetan government and to J. E. Hopkinson, who had replaced Basil Gould as the British political officer in Sikkim, with a request for permission to visit Lhasa in February for Monlam Chenmo, the two-week prayer festival during which the city was flooded by a hundred thousand pilgrims and monks.

There were a number of Tibetan lamas in Kalimpong for the winter, and from the beginning Theos was ambivalent about whether he should make the trip or stay and study with them. "Whether or not I will go into Tibet proper depends on the outcome of my work here," he wrote to John Mock. "I find that I am getting old enough not to relish the idea of trekking across fourteen thousand foot plateaus and crossing seventeen thousand foot passes, especially in the dead of winter; so I will not go beyond this point unless it is absolutely necessary to further my research work in their philosophical literature."

Theos was fortunate that among the Tibetan lamas in Kalimpong that winter was his friend Geshe Wangyal. He had last seen the widely traveled Geshe Wangyal in the spring of 1937 on the day that Theos left Kalimpong for Tibet and Geshe Wangyal left Kalimpong for London. The difficult decision about whether to stay in Kalimpong and study with Geshe Wangyal or go to Lhasa was made for Theos when in February he received official notification that his application to visit Lhasa had this time been rejected. It was the British, Theos learned, who rejected the application, probably because they saw that Lhasa was on the brink of civil war and considered it too dangerous to allow a foreigner to enter through their border.

The civil unrest in Lhasa was set off by a power struggle provoked by Theos' friend and patron in Lhasa, the regent, Reting Rinpoche. Reting Rinpoche had proven to be a hopelessly venal leader and had used his position mainly to enrich himself. It was also well known (in the government and in the streets of Lhasa) that Reting Rinpoche, who had taken the monk's vow of celibacy, kept both male and female lovers. It was this general knowledge of Reting Rinpoche's lapsed vows that presented the biggest obstacle to his continued reign as regent.

As the young 14th Dalai Lama's senior tutor, the regent would be called upon in early 1942 to fulfill his most important duty by ordaining His Holiness as a novice monk. One of the vital elements of the ceremony is the granting of thirty-six vows, including the vow of celibacy, to the novice. All monks are taught that it is critically important that the master who gives the vows must himself be keeping them well or the vows will not take root in the novice. Consequently, the only way to avoid the disaster of granting debilitated vows to the Dalai Lama was for Reting Rinpoche to resign as senior tutor, which meant he would have to vacate the regency as well—at least temporarily.

Reting chose his own root lama, the old and otherworldly junior tutor of the Dalai Lama, Taktra Rinpoche, as his successor, and resigned under the pretense that there was some imminent danger to his life and he needed to return to his monastery north of Lhasa for several years of prayers and meditation to remove it. Reting assumed that after the danger to his life had been eliminated—and Taktra had ordained the Dalai Lama—he would return to Lhasa and resume power as the regent.

Taktra immediately set out to restore the high level of discipline and morality in the government that had characterized the reign of the 13th Dalai Lama, and when in December 1944 Reting returned again to Lhasa to reclaim the regency, Taktra refused to hand power back to him. Lhasa was riven between factions loyal to the former and current regents, and in February 1947, while Theos waited in Kalimpong for a permit to visit Lhasa, Reting supporters tried twice to assassinate Taktra with hand grenades.

On April 14, 1947, the Kashag received evidence that Reting had requested Nationalist Chinese troops and air strikes on Lhasa to support his coup attempt and had offered in return to accept Chinese control of Tibet and to cede to China disputed territories in Kham. The threat to Tibetan sovereignty finally forced the government to arrest Reting Rinpoche, and when the monks at Sera monastery's Je college—the monastic division where Reting Rinpoche had received his education—heard he was in prison, they took revenge against their own abbot, a known Taktra supporter. A mob of monks marched to the abbot's house in the monastery, caught him as he tried to escape across the rooftops, and brutally murdered him with knives, swords, and an axe.

The murder of the abbot marked the start of a two-week rebellion at Sera monastery's Je college against the government. On the morning of the twenty-ninth, three regiments of government troops supported by machine gun and artillery fire attacked Sera monastery. Between two hundred and three hundred monks were killed in the assault, and after a formal treaty was signed, five ringleaders received life sentences in Shol prison.

The evidence against Reting was overwhelming, and within days after he was confronted with his letters detailing plans to solicit help from China in unseating Taktra, Reting Rinpoche died in prison, probably from poison.

As Theos learned of the violent insurrection from daily reports coming into Tharchin's newspaper office, he was grateful to the British political officer for having rejected his application to visit Lhasa. A week after the Tibetan government's assault on Sera monastery Theos wrote with genuine relief to a friend in New York, "Am I glad that I am not there."

It was almost certainly the explosive political situation that moved the British political officer to deny Theos permission to travel again to Lhasa, but the goodwill and jolly friendship Theos enjoyed with British officials in Tibet had eroded over the years, and they may have felt some satisfaction that circumstances forced them to prevent the trip. The British kept intelligence files on all foreigners who entered Tibet between 1905 and 1950, and the reports on Theos are filled with a certain pique, perhaps at being upstaged by the often sensational publicity that made Theos a celebrity—even in London—after his 1937 trip to Lhasa. British officials were also likely to have been annoyed by the unflattering portraits of their imperial pretensions that they read in the copies of *Penthouse of the Gods* Theos sent to them.

Gould wrote in his assessment for the intelligence file that (even though Theos was actually living on credit from Tsarong) he

> was very well provided with funds, and good company; and he (and his money) went down well enough with the Tibetan Government for him to obtain permission from the Tibetan Government to travel back to India via Shigatse and N. Sikkim. . . .
>
> In Lhasa he seems to have behaved prudently and to have attracted no unfavourable attention. From conversations which I had with him in the spring of 1937, and from his writings, I have reason to think that he is genuinely interested in Tibetan Buddhism.

But Gould was confused by Theos' assertions that he had received initiations and was given the authority as a lama to pass on the teachings, and he believed, mistakenly, that the term *lama* meant that Theos, a married man, had necessarily been ordained as a celibate monk—something he never claimed.

> I conclude that Mr. Bernard is good at giving people what they want. He had apparently given the American public what he thought they would like—sensationalism, padded out with a good deal of obvious fact and Buddhist jargon.

Hugh Richardson focused his report on a polite examination and rebuttal of some points Theos made in a 1939 *Asia* magazine article that Britain had a strategic interest in discouraging Tibetans from developing their abundant natural resources. But it was Norbu Dhondup, the trade agent who went to Lhasa to fill in during Richardson's leave, who filed the most petulant assessment of Theos' accounts of his time in Lhasa. Despite what Norbu might have learned by interviewing any number of Tibetans, he wrote derisively,

At no time was he seen associating with monks or carrying out religious Buddhist ceremonies. . . .

Bernard arranged to have himself quartered with Tsarong Dzasa in preference to accepting the offer of Mr. Richardson to stay with the Mission. . . . He would naturally not be keen to have his actions and movements too closely watched or discussed by those in intelligent contact with the outside world. . . .

Bernard has not seen or witnessed a ceremony of Buddhist worship which has not also been open to the British personnel.

The intelligence file doesn't mention that shortly after London's *Daily Mail* was on the streets with its November 1937 story headlined "Young Explorer Writes the Greatest Adventure Story of the Year," Tharchin was summoned to Gould's office in Gangtok for a grilling. The political officer wanted to know if there was proof that Theos had been initiated by Tri Rinpoche. Tharchin admitted that he had witnessed the open ceremony at Ganden, but Theos had then met Tri Rinpoche alone in his sanctuary for a couple hours, and Tharchin was unable to personally verify those details. They were skeptical as well about Theos' account—told to them by Tsarong—of receiving Tantric initiation and instruction from the hermit at Drag Yerpa. Tharchin told them that in this case he had participated as the interpreter, and Theos had described it exactly as it happened. Apparently unsatisfied with his testimony, and as retribution for his vital role in Theos' trip, Gould barred Tharchin from ever returning to Tibet. He was soon forced to rescind the ban, however, when he needed Tharchin's help on some projects there, and Tharchin had visited Tibet twice again since then.

However convoluted the motives of the British officials may have been, Theos was hardly disappointed by their rejection of his request to visit Lhasa again. "I will undoubtedly do far more by remaining here than by merely trekking in rarefied air," he wrote to Glen. "I feel rather blessed that a stay is being imposed on me, for the trip would only have newspaper value, whereas my work here will serve me to the end of my time." In another letter to Glen, Theos wrote, "I have seen all there is to been seen [in Lhasa]. . . . I feel that we have more than enough. What remains to be done now is to settle down and mature it rather than seek."

It wasn't long after the British rejected his application to visit Lhasa that the Tibetan lamas in Kalimpong presented Theos with a unique opportunity to settle down as he wished and deepen his studies. He received through Geshe Wangyal an invitation to a monthlong teaching on the Lamrim, or Stages of the Path, a comprehensive outline of the journey to enlightenment from beginning to end.

Theos went immediately for an interview about his qualifications with the teacher of the course, twenty-nine-year-old Dhardo Rinpoche, the thirteenth incarnation of the chief abbot of Lhasa's Drepung monastery, the largest monastery in the world. Theos could hardly have found anywhere a more qualified lama to teach him the Lamrim. Dhardo Rinpoche had earned the *hlarampa geshe* degree (the pinnacle of Gelugpa scholastic achievement) and went on to study at the Gyu Me Tantric college. "They search for all these incarnate Lamas as they do for the Dalai Lama," Theos wrote to Glen. "I must say whoever works out these patterns certainly knows how to pick their men, for this chap has an exceptionally strong personality and is obviously brilliant. . . . Even if I were living in Lhasa I would hardly have an opportunity to get in on such an event."

Although they didn't meet at the time, Dhardo Rinpoche had been at Drepung when Theos visited the monastery in 1937, and as a close friend of Tsarong, he had heard all about Theos' studies in Lhasa. The interview turned into a long conversation about mutual friends and the political tension in Lhasa, and afterward Dhardo Rinpoche enthusiastically invited Theos to join the monthlong series of daily teachings.

The teachings began at noon every day and continued from the full moon of March to the full moon of April in the temple of a new monastery on the hill above Kalimpong, a two-and-a-half-mile walk each way from the house where Theos and Helen lived. The sessions continued until six with just a single break after about four hours of sitting, as Theos put it, "to get rid of the tea that has been coming in a constant stream from the time we enter."

Theos was given the cushion next to Geshe Wangyal, who helped him with the chants that were part of each day's ritual ceremonies. Theos was usually able to follow the Tibetan text in front of him and join the recitation in full voice, but when he lost his place on the page, he confidently tried to keep up by reading Geshe Wangyal's lips. When he stumbled and the assembly of monks heard an off tone, even Dhardo Rinpoche broke out in boisterous laughter.

Dhardo Rinpoche started each afternoon by conveying the *lung*, the blessings of the lineage of the teaching, by reciting the day's section from the five-hundred-page root text. The *shelung*, the Lama's explanation of the root text, filled the rest of the afternoon. Before and after the six-hour sessions, Theos conferred with Geshe Wangyal, who had virtually memorized the text as part of his monastic training, to clarify difficult points.

Dhardo Rinpoche used Je Tsongkapa's massive and authoritative *Lamrim Chenmo* as his root text that spring. The source of all Tibetan Lamrims, however, is *Lamp of the Path to Enlightenment*, composed by the great eleventh-century Indian pandita Atisha. Lord Atisha wrote his seminal work while he was in Tibet at the invitation of the king to spearhead a renaissance of Buddhism and settle quarrels between factions about the legitimacy of one another's Buddhist practices.

Lord Atisha synthesized in his seminal Lamrim text the essence of the Hinayana, Mahayana, and Tantra teachings to show that, rather than contradicting one another, the three vehicles were intended by Lord Buddha to be practiced in a progression that culminates with enlightenment. Part of the genius of the Lamrim is its systematic outline of hundreds of topics in that progression, all intended to be realized in meditation as a foundation for the next topic.

Theos wrote, with the help of Geshe Wangyal, a twelve-page paper he titled "Synopsis of Lam-rim" and another of four pages titled "Key to Understanding Tibetan Literature." Together they form what is undoubtedly the first-ever rendering of the Lamrim outline into English, at least eleven years before Geshe Wangyal—the first Tibetan lama to move to the United States—began teaching Lamrim himself at the monastery he founded in Howell, New Jersey.

Theos began his presentation by pointing out that the Lamrim is organized into practices for those with three different motivations: those of lesser, moderate, or great capacity. Those practicing with a lesser capacity are motivated to find happiness within the realm of samsara, the cycle of suffering, hoping mainly to avoid rebirth in the hells and attain a good human rebirth. They do so by attaining direct realizations in meditation on the inevitability of death, the suffering of the lower realms, and how the laws of karma determine whether our actions create suffering or happiness in this and future lives.

Those practicing with a moderate capacity are motivated by the longing to forever end their own suffering and escape altogether from samsara by eliminating all the mental afflictions that bind them to the suffering realm. All mental afflictions depend on our ingrained ignorance that sees the exterior world as existing independently of our minds. Ignorance is defeated by the wisdom that perceives directly the ultimate nature of reality, which is reached by first attaining the single-pointed concentration of *samadhi*. In the Lamrim, the practices of those with lesser and moderate capacity are regarded as the Hinayana branch of Buddhist practice, and nirvana reached as a result of these direct realizations, as Theos noted, "is an exalted state, but is not the ultimate goal."

The ultimate goal of enlightenment, as distinguished from nirvana, is achieved only by those whose practice is motivated by the defining quality of Mahayana Buddhism, bodhicitta, the desire to become fully enlightened in order to benefit all living beings. These are the practitioners of great capacity, the third broad division in the Lamrim outline. Their training focuses on how to think and how to act like a bodhisattva, a warrior seeking enlightenment mind. One approach to learning to think like a bodhisattva employs a series of meditations that lead to the realization that the boundary between "myself" and "others" is only a mental construct, and if "myself" is redefined to include "others," I will naturally cherish "others" with the same obsession I now reserve for "myself." Once a practitioner has learned to think like a bodhisattva, he will naturally desire to act like a bodhisattva by following the Six Perfections: generosity, ethics, patience, joyful effort, concentration, and wisdom.

The Lamrim emphasizes that only with a foundation of renunciation, great compassion, and wisdom is it safe to enter Vajrayana, the path of Tantra. Practicing Tantra without those is as dangerous as a child jumping on a wild horse. But with experiential realizations of these three principal paths, it is possible for one practicing the Unsurpassed Class of Tantra to become enlightened in this very lifetime.

EVEN WITH THE SIX HOURS of Lamrim teachings and the hour walk each way, Theos kept to a strict routine that allowed him to get in three hours of Tibetan language study every morning. He translated a section from the Lamrim dealing with the Twelve Links of Dependent Origination, illustrated in the Wheel of Life, and he thought that perhaps with Geshe Wangyal's help he might undertake the first English translation of Je Tsongkapa's *Lamrim Chenmo*, a project that eventually was undertaken by a committee of fourteen translators in the United States but not completed until 2002.

While Theos was studying and translating Lamrim, Helen spent most of her days in Kalimpong studying the Tibetan language with two teachers of her own. "I must say that she has certainly done a remarkable job," Theos reported proudly to Glen, "and especially so when you consider that she didn't even know that the Tibetans had a language until her arrival here. She definitely has a talent along this line."

By March, after four months of study, she could understand colloquial Tibetan and even join the conversation when Geshe Wangyal stopped in to consult with Theos. She was also beginning to translate and was given the difficult assignment of deciphering a Tibetan medical text for Glen. Few of the technical terms and names of the plant compounds were found in dictionaries (aside from the most general descriptions such as "spicy roots"), and frequent cross-referencing in other medical texts and consultations with Tharchin were necessary to make any progress.

Theos sent her first results to Glen and bragged, "I think it quite remarkable. To watch her work, one would think that she brought me out here to keep her company instead of the other way around. Occasionally she will lend me her ear for a few moments, but never her head, that is always busy trying to figure out the next sentence."

In Helen Theos had at last found the partner to his aspirations that he had tried to create in Viola and Ganna. "We will be a real working team before the year is out," he wrote to Glen, "and in this way we will probably be able to keep our efforts alive for the rest of our life times."

Helen was scheduled to return to Hong Kong in March to finish the interior design for C. V. Starr's seaside home but wired him that she wasn't able to make the trip this time and would take care of the details from Kalimpong. Theos was delighted by the signal. "If we are going to build a world together, it is going to be impossible to be riding two horses," he wrote to Glen, "especially where they are so different as the two worlds represented by her past and the future, and I am sure that she is the one that I have been looking for to further these ambitions."

Every day Theos and Helen talked about what they would do when they got home. They would start by taking a trip with Glen to find the perfect location at which to establish a school, perhaps modeled after the monastic training at Drepung. They might even create a correspondence course. Theos had a vision of creating a Yoga practice text based on the Lamrim that would include material on the chakras, Kundalini, and Pranayama. "It hardly seems the best move to teach Yoga classes alone," Theos wrote to Glen. "Yoga and the like should be used only for those special students who are serious and willing to settle down to the sort of routine and discipline that it requires. But for the public there should be . . . a graduated path so that there is something for everyone and eternal bliss for that one creature that might stumble by in the course of a life time."

But for now they were content in Kalimpong, which in March was a flowering paradise. "Never again in our lives do we ever expect to be blessed with so many things," Theos wrote to Glen. "The only thing that I can find wrong in this place is that one cannot live for ever, in that respect it is like every other spot on earth and that is about the only thing that it has in common with the rest of this terrestrial globe."

As the Lamrim teaches, though, in samsara all pleasures—like Kalimpong's fields of flowers—are temporary blossoms. Just as some important logic texts arrived that Theos was planning to study with Geshe Wangyal, Geshe Wangyal decided to leave town. And then rumors circulated that before Britain pulled out of India, Bhutan would forcibly annex Kalimpong, and Sikkim would use the opportunity take over the Darjeeling area. Guns were being smuggled through the bazaar, and Theos wrote to a friend in New York, "It will not remain healthy here much longer. I am keeping my work up to date so that I can make a run for it at the last moment." And then, on top of everything else, the monsoon arrived, drenching Kalimpong in two months with most of its eighty inches of annual rainfall. Of those soggy weeks Theos wrote, "Never again will I choose it."

On Tharchin's recommendation, Theos and Helen decided they would move farther west along the Himalayas to the Kulu Valley, which gets about half as much rain as Kalimpong and would, they hoped, be more isolated from the political upheavals accompanying imperial Britain's impending departure from India. From the Kulu Valley they could travel across the Himalayan crest to Tharchin's birthplace, Lahoul, and then into Ladakh and Kashmir. The journey to the Kulu Valley required that they travel through Calcutta, and when they arrived there in the first week of August, they eagerly accepted the hospitality of a friend of Helen's, the American executive in charge of C. V. Starr's Calcutta insurance office.

India was a powder keg set to explode, and Theos realized that "once this thing breaks it will be a long time before we could return and carry on our work." Hoping to defuse the charge, Calcutta's beleaguered civil authorities had shut down the city again with one of its frequent curfews, and when Theos and Helen arrived on the train, they had to hire an army truck to take them from the station to the luxurious apartment of their host.

The city was still haunted by the specter of Direct Action Day, the grisly riots staged in Calcutta a year earlier in response to the Moslem League's call to take direct action to prove to Britain and the Hindu Congress Party that the partition of India into separate Hindu and Muslim nations was the only acceptable outcome of independence. The leader of the Moslem League, Mohammed Ali Jinnah, was convinced that in a democracy with three hundred million Hindus, his one hundred million Muslims would remain forever a powerless minority. Only an independent Muslim nation, for which separatists coined the name Pakistan, could prevent that, he believed. But both Britain and the Congress Party (which represented the majority of Hindus) refused to consider partitioning into two separate states the enormous nation cobbled together from hundreds of fiefdoms and kingdoms during 350 years of British rule.

Jinnah staked out his negotiating position: "We shall have India divided, or we shall have India destroyed." In response to his call, on Direct Action Day, August 16, 1946, Muslim mobs burst from their slums wielding clubs, iron bars, or shovels, whatever was at hand, to bludgeon any Hindu skull in their path. Twenty-six thousand Hindus were killed in seventy-two hours, and then, in calculated reprisals, Hindu mobs stormed from their neighborhoods looking for defenseless Muslims. The slaughter left the city's streets littered with corpses for the feasting vultures.

The message that denying India's Muslims a sovereign homeland would result in the bloodiest civil war in Asian history was reluctantly acknowledged by India's recently appointed last viceroy, Lord Louis Mountbatten, and all sides recognized that Britain's speedy transfer of power to the new nations was the only way to stem the escalating atrocities. A plan to partition the nation was formally announced in a radio address by the Congress Party's Jawaharlal Nehru and the Moslem League's Jinnah on June 3, 1947.

The day after Jinnah and Nehru broke the news that India would be partitioned, Lord Mountbatten held a news conference with three hundred journalists from around the world to answer questions about the details. Mountbatten was asked at the very end if he had settled on a final date for the transfer of sovereignty. He had not, but for some reason he could not admit it. The British government had earlier in the year agreed to an independence date in June 1948, but Mountbatten had, since negotiating that agreement, concluded that it was wildly optimistic to believe that the collapsing Indian civil service would survive the year. Now put on the spot by the journalist's question, Mountbatten shocked not only Downing Street and Buckingham Palace but Nehru and Jinnah as well by spontaneously announcing that the transfer of power would take place on August 15, 1947, only seventy-three days away.

In that brief time, two of India's most storied regions, the Punjab in the west and Bengal in the east, would have to be carved into Indian and Pakistani sections. The resulting Muslim nation of Pakistan would have its two territories separated by almost a thousand miles, but it would nonetheless leave fifty million Muslims scattered between East and West Pakistan within the Indian border.

India's population of four hundred million people was at the time one-fifth of the population of the globe, and the division of their public assets required a frenzy of do-or-die negotiations. Pakistan, it was finally agreed, would get 17.5 percent of the cash in the treasury and be required to cover 17.5 percent of India's national debt. All the moveable assets—the chairs, tables, ink pots, umbrella racks, brooms, and typewriters—in the offices of India's vast administrative system were to be divided, with 80 percent to India and 20 percent to Pakistan.

Deciding which of the chairs and ink pots went to each country provoked arguments and even fistfights between once staid bureaucratic office mates. At the public libraries, sets of the *Encyclopaedia Britannica* were split up, with alternate volumes sent to either country. Dictionaries were ripped in half, with *A* through *K* going to India and the rest to Pakistan. Beyond the reasonable men overseeing that vivisection were Muslim extremists who insisted that because the Taj Mahal had been built by their Mughal forebears it should be broken up and shipped to Pakistan, and Hindu extremists who asserted that the Indus River, deep in Pakistani territory, should belong to them because many centuries earlier the Vedas had been written on its banks.

Theos and Helen left the relative safety of Kalimpong and arrived in a tense Calcutta less than two weeks before India and Pakistan were scheduled to receive their independence, but they seemed for the moment blithely unaware of the explosive potential of the epochal events ahead. During the week they were there, they spent their days buying supplies for the several-month trek through remote Ladakh and Kashmir that they planned for autumn, and every evening they visited with their host, the American insurance executive, a different club he belonged to for a final imperial hurrah.

There were also daily visits to the telegraph office. To finance the months ahead, Theos sent instructions to Glen to withdraw another $2,500 from the capital of the trust Viola had set up for him, and also instructed him to deposit a check that his half brother was sending for his share of the royalties on the sale of the family's San Juan mine near Tombstone.

They shipped seven trunks of unneeded items along with eleven boxes of books home to Glen, but just the bare essentials for the varied roads ahead added up to an expedition-style total of thirty trunks to haul with them. They now planned, after leaving India, to go to France, which required they have in their luggage a few suits along with warm clothes for winter in Kashmir and light clothes for the Indian plains. The camera equipment and film alone required three large trunks of their own.

No Hindu in India would set off on such a momentous journey without first consulting an astrologer. The advice of the stars was sought by maharajas and humble villagers alike before undertaking anything from cutting a moustache to arranging their own funerals, and during the week in Calcutta Theos and Helen took the precaution of having their charts done by a famous seer at the city's huge Kali temple.

The thirty-two-page, richly detailed analysis of the cosmic forces shaping his character and the events of his life told Theos: "There is a melancholy in the mind which constantly creates restlessness. . . . There is a strong tendency toward occultism and philosophy. . . . You will be fond of preserving old things and curios and much interested to be associated with the old races of the world. . . . There is a strong fascination for secret affairs of things but you will simply waste your time if you run after all the subjects but one—philosophy."

Considering the accuracy of those assessments, Theos may have been disconcerted enough by the predictions of the chart for the months ahead to dismiss it all as superstition. Under the influence of the planet Budha, or Mercury, and the ascending lunar node Rahu, or the Dragon's Head, he should prepare for "traveling and a voyage—many obstacles—suffering in Health—death of a relative, accident in journey, loss by cheating or theft."

To ensure that Theos and Helen would have someone to practice their colloquial Tibetan with on their travels, Tharchin had sent with them one of his own servants to act as cook, guide, bearer, and bodyguard. Named Senge, Tibetan for "lion," he was a giant of a boy who had never been beyond Kalimpong and spoke no English. On August 8, exactly one week before India and Pakistan were to be granted independence as separate dominions, Theos and Helen made their way to the Calcutta train station with the powerful Senge hauling their piles of trunks. They were glad they left early for the station, for that evening again the streets were cleared by a city-wide curfew. Guarding their luggage on the platform, the massive

Senge, "rigged up in full Tibetan regalia," attracted a crowd of gawking porters. "With these trying conditions," Theos wrote to Glen, "we are happy that we decided to bring him, for his very presence is a guarantee of a certain amount of protection."

They were fortunate to have an express train across the entire breadth of what would remain as the north of India, from Calcutta on the Bengali shores in the east to Amritsar near the new western boundary in the divided Punjab. After two days of travel, the train glided into Amritsar's red-brick railway station and the open windows of their carriage brought them the deafening babble, pungent odors, and swarm of color that coalesced as a mass of Hindu refugees stirring to meet them. Having fled from Pakistan's half of the Punjab, the desperate horde on the platform reflexively surged toward their carriage, shoving and trampling one another, and shrieking with hysterical tears the name of a child they'd been separated from or some missing relative, even though this train had come in from the east.

Senge cleared a spot for them on the platform, and they made a tall pile of their trunks while around them massive Sikh men wearing turbans and long beards patrolled the milling crowd with three-foot sabers hanging from their belts, looking for Muslims trying to escape to Pakistan. "It was rather a dangerous place to be," Theos wrote to Glen, "for no small amount of rioting has and is going on and on numerous occasions they have been dragging people out of the trains and beheading them right there in the station."

From Amritsar Theos and Helen needed to take an eastbound local train and make a transfer to the foothill road head for the Kulu Valley. "All afternoon . . . trains going east came in fairly bulging with humanity," Helen wrote in a diary she began keeping at this time. "On top were hundreds of men mostly Sikhs carrying their villainous looking swords." On every eastbound train that pulled in to the station already jammed with refugees from the Muslim section of Punjab, hundreds more jumped on at the Amritsar platform and clung from every available handhold.

Theos and Helen had a first-class reservation on a train that was already hours late, and they began to think that the only way to get out of Amritsar might be to take one of the nearly empty trains heading west to Lahore, the area the Hindu refugees were fleeing, and then go north to Rawalpindi, where they would rent a car to take them to Kashmir. But before they were forced to risk that decision, the "overloaded flimsy little train" for which they had tickets chugged in. The conductor informed them that the baggage car was already full, so their tremendous pile of trunks and suitcases had to fit in their compartment with them or be left on the platform to be picked over by the refugees.

There was only one first-class compartment on the train, but a 200-rupee bribe, along with their tickets, procured seats in it for them. The only other occupant was a Parsi businessman, and in no time Senge and Theos loaded their bags and trunks through the window. As they settled in for a five-hour crawl to another transfer at Pathankot, only seventy miles away, little did they know, as Helen later wrote, that the havoc they were witnessing was actually "the last day of peace on the plains of Punjab."

IF INDIA WAS THE CROWN JEWEL of the British Empire, Punjab was its treasury. Extending from the Indus River in the northwest to the suburbs of Delhi (an area half the size of France), Punjab was an oasis of abundant wheat fields irrigated with water distributed from the state's five Himalaya-fed rivers through a matrix of British-engineered canals. The abundance had been shared and sustained for generations by mixed communities of Sikhs, Muslims, and Hindus, all of whom now waited anxiously to hear whether their farms and towns would belong to Pakistan or to India. The job of plotting the new international boundary fell on the shoulders of just one man, the brilliant English barrister Sir Cyril Radcliffe, who had never even set foot in India before he arrived to begin his work only five weeks before the handover of power. With only a Royal Engineers map and population and statistics tables to guide him, Radcliffe had to create, on average, thirty miles of boundary a day to make his August 15 deadline. Although the job was technically feasible when viewed on an engineer's map, the spot on which the boundary actually fell across the ground was ruinous for countless peasants in hundreds of villages. In places the boundary line ran right through the center of a village, leaving a farmer's house in Pakistan and his fields and well in India. In larger towns, factories were separated from their freight depots and power plants from their grids.

The greatest tragedy, however, was that the boundary line left five million Sikhs and Hindus in Pakistan's half of the Punjab and five million Muslims in India's half. And although they all spoke a common Punjabi language and had lived peacefully for generations under the British, the memories of the earlier centuries of mutual atrocities could not allow them to live ruled by the other.

The details of the boundary location were kept secret until Independence Day, August 15, but since June, when the decision was announced that the Punjab would be divided between Pakistan and India, the ethnic purges had picked up a remorseless momentum on both sides, creating new religious majorities in formerly mixed communities for the cartographers to consider. Lahore, the "Paris of the Orient," was only thirty-four miles from Amritsar and was well known as a tolerant, cosmopolitan city of five hundred thousand Hindus, one hundred thousand Sikhs, and six hundred thousand Muslims. Everyone knew that the new boundary would have to fall somewhere between the two cities, giving Amritsar to India and Lahore to Pakistan, and in the months before partition, the Moslem League mounted a crusade to drive Hindus and Sikhs out of Lahore. As part of their campaign of intimidation, they stuffed the postboxes of every Hindu and Sikh in the city with postcards graphically portraying rape and murder victims and the message on the back: "This is what has been happening to our Sikh and Hindu brothers and sisters at the hands of the Moslems when they take over. Flee before those savages do this to you."

The motivation for much of the early savagery on both sides of the line, however, was not religious fervor but unbridled avarice. Murder and arson were the means to drive away the owners of neighboring shops and land, which the righteous persecutors were ready to claim as their own. Once it became a matter of honor to avenge the other side's atrocities, people who had lived side by side for generations turned on one another in a frenzy of killing, and with the tribal justice of an eye for an eye, each massacre provoked another. As Dominique Lapierre and Larry Collins put it in their masterful account, *Freedom at Midnight*, "It was not . . . a civil war, not a guerrilla campaign. It was a convulsion, the sudden, shattering collapse of a society."

The enraged communities rivaled one another in savagery. A British officer found in a village raided by Sikhs four Muslim babies roasted on spits. In Sheikhpura, a trading town north of Lahore, the entire Hindu and Sikh population was herded into a warehouse, then massacred by Muslim police with machine guns. There were reports of Muslim mobs dragging Hindu men from their homes and beating them to death in the streets, while up on the roofs the women of the house, knowing they would be raped and mutilated, made a bonfire, threw their babies in it, and then flung themselves into the flames after them.

As August 15 approached and the desperate flight for safety in both directions grew in volume, the swollen refugee trains became prime targets for terrorists on both sides. Trains were assaulted while they stood in stations or were ambushed after being derailed by torn-up tracks or stopped at a spot where an on-board accomplice pulled the emergency brake. For a man, the surest proof that he was Muslim was his circumcised penis. On the India side of the border, Sikhs and Hindus marauded through the stopped train carriages slaughtering every man who was circumcised. On the Pakistan side, Muslims raced through the cars killing every man who was not.

A few days after Theos and Helen got safely away from the Amritsar station, the Number Ten Down Express pulled into the same platform from Pakistan. On this train, however, not a single anxious refugee stood at the open windows or rushed through the doors. Inside were only tangled corpses with throats slit, skulls smashed, and entrails hacked out. In whitewashed letters on the last car was written a greeting to India's new leaders: "This train is our Independence gift to Nehru and Patel."

AT THEIR TRANSFER STATION, Pathankot, Theos and Helen changed to a narrow-gauge train that would take them to the road head at Nagrota. It was 3:00 a.m. and there were no porters around to help with the baggage transfer, but again dutiful Senge and a few rupees as baksheesh for the guard got them seats in the first-class compartment, this time with a woman and her five children. On reaching Nagrota, they realized immediately they would never get all their baggage on an overcrowded local bus, and they hired a ten-ton Chevrolet truck for the trip up the narrow road into the mountains.

"For almost two hundred miles there is not a foot of straight road," Theos wrote to Glen, and "the drivers would put to shame any New York taxi driver." They reached the hidden principality of Mandi that night and got their first sleep in forty-eight hours. They set off early the next morning through the breathtaking foothills for the Kulu Valley—the Valley of the Gods. When they arrived that afternoon they were referred to Tyson's Riverview Inn, a small guesthouse operated by the only Europeans in the village of Katrain. In the entire forty-mile-long valley, with its five small villages, there were said to be fewer than two dozen Europeans, and Theos surmised that the difficulty in getting there was the main reason the valley was "far more native and untouched than the Kalimpong side."

The Beas River tumbled down from its head at 13,326-foot Rohtang Pass through a succession of cataracts and gorges to the broad Kulu Valley. Virgin forests of deodars (Himalayan cedars) ran up its slopes in stands whose oldest trees reached 150 feet in height and 10 feet in diameter, and in the higher villages picturesque four-story wood chalets huddled closely together in little groups on the ledges. Theos wrote to Glen, "We are one hundred percent satisfied with no regrets for having made the move."

Among the small group of Europeans that lived in the valley was the famous Roerich family, who lived just two miles away and across the river from Katrain near the village of Naggar. Theos had been trying to meet Nicholas Roerich, the family patriarch, for more than a decade, and the two kept up an occasional correspondence. The Roerichs had lived in the Kulu Valley for eighteen years on an estate that offered magnificent panoramic vistas from its site fifteen hundred feet above the valley. An American sponsor had purchased the Kulu villa for them as a haven from the cult-like following the Roerichs had attracted for more than two decades. Nicholas and his wife, Helena, were ardent Theosophists, and in seven thousand paintings during his career, Nicholas illustrated mystic scenes that expressed the spiritual quest of heroic characters in settings of sacred beauty. Nicholas regarded his paintings as Theosophical visions transmitted from the mahatmas, great spiritual adepts who telepathically guide the development of civilizations, and believed that through the mahatmas his works were imbued with healing powers. The power of his paintings brought Roerich enormous success, especially in America. In Manhattan, his wealthy patrons built for him a twenty-nine-story tower to house an art school, exhibition center, two libraries, and the Roerich Museum.

But aside from his paintings, it was Roerich's quest to discover in the remote middle of Asia the actual site of the legendary hidden kingdom of Shambhala that attracted such fervent support of his mission. Roerich believed that the king of Shambhala would appear on earth for the final destruction of evil and a purification of creation, and in the fall of 1925 he set off on a three-year, fifteen-thousand-mile expedition through the middle of Asia to find his kingdom.

His American sponsors put up $300,000 to finance the expedition, which included his wife, Helena, and son George, and after two years of trekking across Ladakh, Russia, and Mongolia, they were stopped in early October 1927 at a Tibetan army outpost on the Chang Tang plateau south of Kamrong Pass. The expedition did not have a *lamyik,* and they were forced to halt while they requested a passport to be sent from Lhasa. It took five months before permission came to proceed, and the group was forced to spend the entire winter in summer tents at one of the coldest places in Asia.

During those months at an altitude of fifteen thousand feet, the temperature dropped to −40°F, and they ran out of food, fuel, and fodder for their animals. Ninety of their caravan animals starved and five men died, but the party was forbidden to speak to passing caravans or buy food from the local nomad population. At last, at the beginning of March, the Tibetan authorities allowed the decimated caravan to cross Tibet but by a route that took a wide detour around Lhasa.

Nicolas Roerich was seventy-three years old and in poor health when Theos and Helen arrived in the Kulu Valley, but his wife, Helena, replied to Theos' note with an immediate invitation to visit. Nicholas had had surgery for prostate cancer just two months earlier but with his shaved head, patriarchal beard, and hypnotic gaze, he remained the archetypal image of the mystical artist. Bed rest had been prescribed, but with his remaining strength he continued to paint.

Theos and Nicholas had much to talk about. Having been stranded for a Tibetan winter tying to get permission to visit Lhasa, Nicholas understood better than anyone the singular achievement of Theos' invitation to the Forbidden City ten years earlier. The two bearded Roerich sons, George and Svetoslav, were there as well and also had things in common with Theos. Harvard-educated George, a noted Tibetologist, was working on a Tibetan-English dictionary, and he and Theos rambled on in their colloquial tones about quirks of grammar while Helen listened in and tried to keep up. They also had their mutual friend Gendun Chopel to discuss. Six years earlier, after giving up on receiving a visa to go to work for Theos in Santa Barbara, Gendun Chopel had come to Kulu and lived with the Roerichs while he helped George with the massive project of translating a fifteenth-century volume on the early history of Tibet, *The Blue Annals.* Theos had things in common with the younger brother, Svetoslav, as well. Both had studied at Columbia University, and they enjoyed a humorous reminiscence about the place and the pitfalls of student life in New York.

"I must say, they certainly eat well," Theos wrote to Glen, "in typical Russian pomp and splendor." But what Theos envied most about the Roerichs' life at their Naggar estate was the eighteen years of scenic seclusion that had allowed them all to be so productive in their work. He had been tantalizingly close to having something similar in Santa Barbara, and he wrote to Glen, "We must find such a place at home."

IN THEIR CONVERSATIONS, Theos and the Roerichs expressed no concern about the fact that on the next day, August 14, India and Pakistan would begin their independence celebrations. The official transfer of sovereignty would occur that night at the stroke of midnight—the moment that belonged to neither the fourteenth nor the fifteenth—as a concession to India's astrologers. As soon as the radio announced Mountbatten's transfer date of August 15, astrologers all over India warned that it was an ill-fated day. To begin with, the date fell on Friday, an inauspicious day of the week. Moreover, the moment after midnight on August 15 marked the waxing of the destructive planet Saturn and the malignant influence of the ascending lunar node, Rahu. Also on the fifteenth, Saturn, Jupiter, and Venus would all lie in the accursed ninth house of Karamstahn. As one astrologer implored Mountbatten in a letter to him, "For the love of God, do not give India her independence on 15 August. If floods, drought, famine and massacres follow, it will be because free India was born on a day cursed by the stars."

In the Kulu Valley, the fourteenth was as tranquil as all other days. "Today is India's Independence day," Theos wrote, home early enough that night to type a long letter to Glen. "I suppose in the larger centers they are celebrating the occasion in regal splendor, but here life is little different than the day before except for the fact that everything is closed."

That morning they attended a flag-raising ceremony at which Boy Scouts marched, dignitaries delivered speeches, and the audience sang local anthems. In the evening they attended a dramatic production under the open sky at the school yard. A curtain was hung from two posts of the front porch and the audience sat in the dirt of the play yard, men on one side of a stretched rope and women on the other. Theos and Helen sat with four other Europeans on a bench in the back row and watched village thespians in homemade costumes walk into the amber glow of a gasoline-lantern footlight to play out the beloved story of Rama and Sita from the Ramayana. Between acts, a pair of comic mimes performed a lampoon in which a gullible doctor negotiated a price with a crafty porter to carry his bedroll. By the end, the porter had talked the doctor out of not only the bedroll but all his clothes as well, and had the doctor hauling the load.

That homespun commentary on the Indian character was innocently performed in front of the drawn curtain, on which was painted a large image of Kali in her form as the four-armed and fanged goddess of destruction. With raging red eyes and garlands of snakes and human skulls, she was an ominous emblem below the hand-lettered proclamation "Jai-Hind, Long Live India."

"And so Helen and I saw the birth of a new India," Theos wrote that night to Glen. "We will probably not feel the impact of this change until we begin to move about a bit again on the plains when we will have to travel from Hindustan to Pakistan. Actually I would prefer being here than anyplace I can think of, for tension is high throughout the land."

The rest of the Punjab was, in fact, awash in blood on Independence Day. In Pakistan's Lahore, Muslim celebrants cut the water lines to the Old City, leaving the quarter's nearly one hundred thousand Hindus and Sikhs agonized by thirst in the unbearable summer heat. Roving Muslim mobs stalked the alleys, awaiting with their knives and bludgeons any woman or child who went out to beg a pail of water. Fires raged out of control, and a festive crowd cheered the screams of Sikhs being burned alive in their most famous temple.

Only thirty-four miles away, on the Indian side of the new boundary, as the new civil authorities gave Independence Day speeches at Amritsar's Mughal fortress, enraged Sikhs stormed into a Muslim neighborhood a mile away and slaughtered every male they found. The women were repeatedly raped, then paraded naked and terrified to the Golden Temple to have their throats cut.

That mayhem, or even news of it, had not yet reached the Kulu Valley, and Theos began packing for a three-week trip to visit the Ki monastery in Spiti. The shortcut to Spiti crossed the difficult Hampta Pass, and Theos considered that crux and the rest of the trail as well—with no dak bungalows, its high altitude, and few villages—to be too rugged for Helen's first outing. She would remain with the Tysons at Katrain, resume her Tibetan-language studies, and spend some time riding every afternoon to get in shape. On his return, Theos and Helen would take the main route from the Kulu Valley over the Rohtang Pass, through Tharchin's homeland of Lahoul, and into Ladakh—the same trail Padmasambhava had taken to Tibet, Theos was told.

The day after the Independence Day celebrations, Theos sent Senge to the village of Kulu to buy provisions. "We are heading into the wildest and barrenest section of this part of the Himalayas so every thing must be in order," Theos wrote to Glen. "For the next twenty-one days, at least, I will be sleeping under the open skies unless I can stay in the monastery during the days I am there. I have tried to locate a tent, but there is not one to be had—this was also the case in Calcutta—however I prefer the open skies except in the case of rain and for this we will have enough tarps to get under."

The caste system regulated every aspect of Hindu society in India at that time, and because there were no Hindus in the occupational caste of pack outfitter in the Kulu Valley, the only local outfitter was Muslim. Theos hired five pack ponies and two riding ponies, and arranged for the outfitter's eldest son, Fais Mohammed, along with another young Muslim, and a Lahouli to accompany them as guides and wranglers. With Senge they had a party of five, all of whom could speak Tibetan but, except for Theos, no English. They left Katrain on the morning of August 20 with the plumed and brightly decorated ponies carrying, along with their Spartan gear, more than $5,000 worth of movie and still camera equipment and enough film for three weeks.

The Kulu Valley falls from the south side of the Pir Panjal range, a two-hundred-mile-long mountain chain running through Kashmir to just beyond the Kulu Valley. The central ridge rises sharply from its foothills to peaks of over twenty thousand feet, and crossing the range through Hampta Pass was the highest and most difficult part of the entire journey to the Spiti Valley. Beyond the pass and across the deep valley of the Chandra River lay the even higher, glaciated spine of the West Himalayas, but Theos' route followed the Chandra upstream to another pass, beyond which lay Spiti.

The group began the three-day crossing of Hampta Pass following a shepherds' trail below precipitous cliffs and camped the first two nights in a profusion of wildflowers beside waterfalls of snowmelt. They climbed through verdant pastures where Gujar herders grazed buffalo, Gaddi shepherds grazed sheep, and vistas opened of the high peaks Deo Tibba, Indrasan, and Hanuman Tibba. At eleven thousand feet they reached the timberline, above which only a few silver birches and stunted rhododendrons remained scattered on the hills. Beyond that, across long scree slopes, they ascended early on the third day into the realm of the hanging glaciers, and with a final climb up a steep snowfield that was treacherous for the ponies, they reached the fourteen-thousand-foot Hampta Pass.

Most of the water vapor in monsoon clouds condenses and rains out as it rises against the barrier of the Pir Panjal range, and as Theos and his party descended the leeward side of the pass, they dropped steeply through the barren rock slopes of the rain shadow and reached just before dark their camp on a terrace high above the Chandra River at Chatru.

A dak postal runner came through camp, and they held him up long enough for Theos to write Helen a short letter from the trail. "The first two days out were magnificent beyond description," he wrote to her. But once they crossed the pass into the Chandra Valley, it was "a land of nothing but boulders, boulders and more boulders. If I am not a mountain goat by the time I get back I will never know why." It was the most difficult trail he had encountered on any of his travels, he told her, and he was glad he had not encouraged her to come along. Theos was exposed to more sun and quick altitude change when crossing the pass than he could handle, and by the time they reached camp he was running a fever. Senge bought fresh milk from some shepherds camped nearby and fixed a bowl of rice and milk for him, and then Theos went to bed early under a magnificent star-filled sky.

The trail on the fourth day followed the windswept cobble bed of the Chandra River and then climbed to their camp below the snout of the six-mile-long, one-mile-wide Shigri glacier. They crossed the glacier the next morning and two days later climbed up the side of the Chandra Valley to Kun Zum La, from where they looked past a breathtaking sweep of twenty-one-thousand-foot glaciated peaks into the Spiti Valley. The crest of the pass was marked by a *chorten* and a wall of carved *mani* stones, the familiar Tibetan landmarks that indicated they were stepping again into a Buddhist realm. Since the seventh century, great masters such as Padmasambhava, Shantarakshita, Atisha, Lotsawa Rinchen Zangpo, and Milarepa nourished Buddhism in Spiti. In the tenth century, Spiti was united with Lahoul and adjacent Zanskar as part of the vast western Tibet kingdom of Guge, whose lost capitals at Tholing and Tsaparang were introduced to Western archeologists only in the 1930s by the work of the man who couldn't get past Gyantse while Theos was in Lhasa, the great Tibetologist Giuseppe Tucci.

Beyond the flapping prayer flags at Kun Zum La, Theos peered down into a moonscape of stark splendor painted in hues of purple, pink, and russet. The deep gorges—carved by snow-fed streams through layers of shale laid down as ancient marine sediments—revealed fossils of tightly coiled ammonites that had been extinct for a hundred million years.

Just below Kun Zum La, Theos and his party came to the first village since leaving Katrain, a cluster of whitewashed, flat-roofed mud houses called Lossar. It was a shockingly verdant strip of irrigated fields and willows along the river set in a vast amphitheater of alpine meadows that fattened the villagers' scattered herds of Pashmina goats, horses, and yaks and was flourishing with wild ibex and blue sheep.

From Lossar the party followed the stream-cut terraces and braided gravel channels of the Spiti River for three more days and arrived at their destination, Ki Monastery, probably on August 28. Home to about three hundred monks under the care of the current incarnation of the great translator Lotsawa Rinchen Zangpo, the 950-year-old monastery was Spiti's largest and most important Buddhist center as well as its oldest. Arrayed up the slopes of an isolated conical hill rising just off the river, the accretion of flat-roofed, two- and three-story whitewashed buildings was sacked three times in the nineteenth century by the armies of rival princely states of Kulu, Kashmir, and Punjab, and with each rebuilding its labyrinthine alleys grew more and more to resemble a fortress.

The monastery housed a large collection of scriptures and rare *thangkas* that were well photographed by Tucci on his trip through the area in 1933, but Theos' visit was prompted by Geshe Wangyal's recommendation that he might find there some unique manuscripts on Sipay Khorlo, the Wheel of Life. For more than ten years Theos had been working with Glen on the outline of a book, and in the final letter he wrote his father from Kulu, Theos said he had a title for it: *Tendrel, the Tibetan Book of the Twelve Supporting Causes of Life.*

Apparently the search was successful. The head lama gave Theos some books, and Theos made a donation of 300 rupees to the monastery. After at most three days at Ki monastery, Theos began his return to Kulu over the same route he had come in on, a schedule that should have had him back in Katrain with Helen by the ninth of September.

IN HIS LAST LETTER to Glen before leaving Kulu, Theos mentioned that he had asked Helen to drop his father a line from time to time during his absence to fill him in on the latest and assure him that they were all right. "So do not feel it is presumptuous if you receive a letter from her, for she will be doing it at my suggestion. I regard her as a part of the family and want her to keep you informed as to what we are doing."

A week after Theos left, Helen did write to Glen describing her routine of translation work in the morning and riding in the afternoon to harden up for the five 16,000-foot passes she would be crossing on the way to Ladakh as soon as Theos returned.

She also described for Glen the peculiar local deities of the area, the *devtas*. Each village tucked away in the hills of that area had its own *devta*, who, along with being an object of worship, was the arbiter of all the traditions and conventions governing village life: social, moral, economic, and political.

The village *devta* was represented by a chair covered in a large red blanket on which silver masks of her various aspects were placed. *Devtas*, Helen wrote, liked to visit neighboring *devtas* for consultations, and on sacred days the chair and masks were paraded on the shoulders of two priests down cow paths and through the fields, preceded by the sacred fire and followed by a band of musicians. Sometimes, though, the *devtas* acted up or were lax about performing their duties—for instance, in bringing rain—and were paraded instead to the local jail until they agreed to behave.

The *devtas* were now, it seemed, all willfully misbehaving, for even in the bucolic Kulu Valley, all the traditions and conventions of the villages were unable to keep the hateful poison of the Punjab plains from seeping into even the most remote settlements in the hills.

The large majority of people in the Kulu Valley were Hindu, and as everywhere in the Punjab that fall, the powerful fell upon the powerless with the murderous intent of extirpating them from their communities. Having peacefully shared the lanes, pastures, forests, and markets for generations, on August 24 Hindus in the village of Kulu, just ten miles down the valley from Katrain, burned two Muslim shops and the tiny mosque. The next day, Helen heard reports that Muslim shops up the valley in Manali were burned. Out for a walk that day, Helen encountered the procession of a *devta*. Whether she was being borne to an emergency council with her peers or to jail, Helen couldn't say.

"Heaven only knows when you will receive this," Helen had begun her letter to Glen, "as we seem to be completely isolated in this corner of India. No mail has entered or left the valley since the British turned over India to her own fate on Aug 15th."

None of India's political leaders—Muslim, Hindu, or British—foresaw the magnitude of the cataclysm that dividing the Punjab would bring. And certainly no one expected that the Kulu Valley would be anything but a haven from the short-lived dislocations on the plains. But two weeks after partition, as Helen later recounted, "all hell broke loose with the Hindus leading the native mountaineers into killing and looting and burning of Moslems." Muslims were rounded up and sent to a detention camp in Kulu village, "with the usual destruction of property." And she reported ominously, "we understand it took considerable persuasion to convince the people from the mountain villages that Europeans and Mohammedans were not the same animals."

Realizing that the Muslim outfitters traveling with Theos would be in grave danger if they returned, Helen wrote a letter telling him of the trouble and sent it off with two Spiti men, paying them 40 rupees up front and promising that Theos would give them 20 rupees more when they delivered it. There were now guards posted day and night at Tyson's Riverview Inn, and Helen began to count the days until September 9, when Theos was expected back. He would need, of course, a few days to repack after he returned, but she was glad they already had a plan for leaving north over Rohtang Pass through Lahoul and on to Ladakh, "as there is little chance of getting out of this valley by any other route," she wrote to Glen.

Out for an afternoon walk, Helen met a parade of dozens of Muslim captives being taken, she was told, to Kulu to be executed. The local district commissioner and police chief stopped in at the Riverview Inn for tea and told Helen and the Tysons not to interfere. He warned them that their going down to the road the previous night with their flashlights had hampered proceedings. They would be safe if they heard and saw nothing. He detailed where the mob would be going that night, but if they remained inside, their house was not on the program.

There were rumors, the police chief said, that escaped Muslims were massing to attack Kulu, and he had deployed his small force to guard the police station; he couldn't spare any men to guard the Muslim internees in the detention camp from the threatened attack of a Hindu mob. A few days after that conversation, Helen jotted in her notes that lorries piled with corpses dumped their loads behind the schoolhouse, and from there the bodies were thrown into the Beas River. The account of a well-known Pakistani artist who was there at the time wrote that of thirty-five thousand Muslims who lived in the larger district around the Kulu Valley, only nine thousand managed to escape to Pakistan, and "the Beas was littered with dead bodies and a foul odour was in the air for weeks after the massacres."

On September 16, a small detachment of the Tenth Gurkha Rifles, a fragment of the fifty-five-thousand-man Punjab Boundary Force, finally arrived in Kulu. The units of the Boundary Force had been specially selected from the Indian army for their discipline or an ethnicity that would keep them above the communal passions they would be sent to police, but their number was quickly overwhelmed once the carnage started. Captain R. Wilson, the commander of the unit dispatched to the Kulu Valley, announced on his arrival that he would evacuate any Europeans who wished to leave as soon as a truck and gasoline became available.

It was actually rare during those tempestuous months for the British to be molested. Even during the worst week in Lahore, an orchestra played every night at Faletti's Hotel for English gentlemen and ladies sipping cocktails at dinner only blocks from a burning Hindu neighborhood. In the Kulu Valley, in fact, one of the British (named only as Macdonald by Helen in her diary) killed five Hindus as he defended his household's Muslims against a mob, and then a week later, after the staff was gone, surrendered the house to be looted without a shot. He himself, though, was not harmed or marked for vengeance.

Gangs of Hindu *goondas*, Helen heard, had gone over Rohtang Pass into Lahoul to cut off the escape of Muslims fleeing the Kulu Valley north into Ladakh. By September 16, the date of Captain Wilson's arrival, Theos was already a full week overdue, and Helen noted in her diary, "Besharis had seen Dr. Bernard. Trouble at border—news brought by Roerichs." "It was a very vague rumor," she added in a letter a week later, "and from sources who were terrified for their lives and households for having breathed this much."

Helen reported what she knew to the Kulu police, who were sympathetic but regretted that they already had their hands full and were unable to investigate rumors. On the seventeenth the authorities sent a letter of inquiry, but Helen noted there was "no news—except through innuendo." On the eighteenth, Helen met the so-called raja of Manali, Major Henry Banon, on the road. Of the conversation she noted only, "Bad news."

Fearing what the convergence of rumors might mean, Helen sent for Captain Wilson to discuss the situation. He wished to take a squad over the pass immediately to investigate, but under the new chain of command, the captain took his orders from the Indian government and needed a directive from Kulu's civil authorities.

On the nineteenth, the local police sent an officer toward Hampta Pass, and he reported that even houses up high had been looted. That day also, Helen dispatched a group of porters with food and supplies over Hampta Pass for Chatru in case Theos was still camped there and his provisions had been stolen. By the twenty-first, Helen recognized that she would have to make an international incident out of Theos' delayed return in order to get any real action, and she sent a telegram to the American embassy in Delhi: "Dr. Theos Bernard recently visiting monasteries in Spiti is rumored to be in serious trouble at border on returning to Kulu. Please request immediate official investigation." Unsure of how far down the telegraph lines the message might have reached, she followed up with a letter, but was uncertain how far that would get either.

By the twenty-fifth, however, Captain Wilson received the necessary orders and set off with twenty men in three trucks for the trailhead at Manali. From there they would trek over Rohtang Pass to Koksar, the first village on the other side, to investigate the rumors.

Even as they left, more rumors kept arriving, including one that Theos was in Koksar and would arrive in Manali the next day. But as it turned out, there would be no traffic in either direction for a while. The afternoon Captain Wilson headed up the valley with his convoy, sudden torrential rains brought flash floods. As Helen described in her diary: "Sound of river terrifying—trees falling like matches...roar of rocks from hillsides—crops destroyed." Within hours that afternoon, all the bridges over the Beas River were washed away, and Captain Wilson was stranded with his detachment at Manali.

As the astrologers had forecast, it appeared there would be no end to the afflictions in the ill-starred Punjab that fall. The police had always said that the most effective method of riot control in India was a lashing sheet of rain, but that summer India's normal monsoon rains failed to arrive and the prayers of farmers and policemen alike were mocked day after day by clear skies and a maddeningly hot sun. Then in late September, just as it should normally be ending, the monsoon came with a fury not witnessed in half a century. The five great rivers of the Punjab flooded in foaming torrents off the mountains through riverbeds that had dried to a trickle. Helen described the devastation up in the Beas River's Kulu Valley headwaters to be "equally as terrifying as the recent man-made holocaust we have just been through." But farther down the Beas on the Punjab plain it got worse. A wall of water as high as a house swept down the empty channels and in moments drowned tens of thousands of refugees who had staggered with their last hopes to camp on its banks.

It was five days before the Beas dropped enough at Manali so that a temporary bridge could be built for Captain Wilson to cross, this time with just three of his men and a local subinspector of police who had previously been stationed in Lahoul and knew the district. The heavy rains had fallen as snow in the higher elevations, and the party had a difficult crossing of Rohtang Pass. Reaching Koksar, the village on the banks of the Chandra River on the Lahoul side of the pass, they questioned everyone including the village Lama, but even under the influence of the local liquor, no one confessed to having seen Theos in the area. There was no evidence of an angry mob having formed there and none of Theos' property was found for sale in the market. The investigators could carry only a limited supply of rations, and with the weather continuing to worsen, they recrossed the pass just before it was snowed in for the winter. They learned nothing definite about Theos' whereabouts and returned convinced, as the final report said, "that whatever happened did not happen where it was said to have happened."

Captain Wilson briefed Helen on his futile investigation when he returned, and within two days of hearing that discouraging news, Helen decided she must take the opportunity to join a party of her friends leaving the valley the following week for Simla. Helen was advised by an official that it would be at least another month before things settled down in the Kulu Valley, and she eagerly packed to join the evacuation party orga-

nized by Major and Mrs. R. E. Hotz. She had little choice; the encouragement of the authorities for Europeans to leave had apparently become an
evacuation order, with fines of 5 rupees per day levied against those who
stayed. And then, as if intended to prevent anyone from changing their
mind, the news spread that the raja of Kulu had consulted his *devta* and she
indicated that still worse things were in store for the valley. "So far she has
only used a little stick," Helen wrote in her diary, "but a big one will be
coming . . . floods & earthquakes."

The little stick had already brought down all the bridges and left most
of the roads under water, meaning that for Helen and her refugee party,
the only way to escape the valley and get to Simla, 126 miles away, was the
same as it was for millions of Punjabis seeking refuge in those weeks:
on foot.

DOWN ON THE PLAINS, the scale of the flight of Sikhs and Hindus to
India and Muslims to Pakistan exceeded everyone's bleakest projections.
Their families had lived on the same plot for generations, but now these
refugees carried on their heads or on their backs whatever possessions they
could salvage or thought most essential for starting over—a wooden plow,
a shovel, a sack of seed grain, or heirloom sacred books. All across the
Punjab they staggered toward safety—depending on their religion—in
either the rising or setting sun. Down dirt paths, across unharvested fields,
or over the asphalt of the Trunk Highway, they plodded numbly, tortured
by hunger and thirst. Sensing safety in vast numbers, they swarmed into
miles-long refugee columns—one estimated to be of eight hundred thousand people.

It was the greatest uprooting of a population in the history of the
world, with ten and a half million people conceding their ancestral homes
to their enemies and groping at survival by moving to a new nation of their
imagined kin. Many died along the way, and the thirty-four-mile road
between Amritsar and Lahore was lined with their corpses, a feast so plentiful the wild dogs ate only livers and the vultures grew so bloated their
flapping wings could not lift them off the ground.

The day before Helen left the Kulu Valley with her party of evacuees, she got a note from a friend saying the native rumors now had it that Theos had returned to Spiti and would try to get through to Leh, the capital of Ladakh. Helen was cheered by the thought that if Theos had returned to Spiti, he would from there be more likely to head south to India than north to Ladakh, and if he did, he would eventually come out on the main trade route of the Hindustan-Tibet road and take it to Simla, having, perhaps, an easier time getting there than she would face.

On October 13, a brass band prepared to send the group off from Katrain, but the scheduled trucks never arrived and the group spent the first day marching ten miles downstream to Kulu village. The next day Captain Wilson was able to round up army trucks to take them eighteen miles to Largi, and from there they set out on their six-day trek over a rugged back route to Simla, the picturesque hill station and summer capital of the former British Raj.

Helen noted little of the terrain or her companions in her telegraphically styled diary except that they walked up to sixteen miles a day and climbed across passes more than nine thousand feet high to drop in the same day to valleys at two thousand feet. Their arrival in Simla on October 20 was coordinated to catch a special train evacuating British nationals with an escort of British troops. There was no news of Theos in Simla, not even a fresh rumor to deliberate, so Helen boarded the train to Delhi. She arrived the next morning, and immediately after checking in at the Hotel Cecil, Helen visited the American embassy. The American consul did what he could at this point to assist a lone U.S. national missing behind a snowed-in pass, which amounted to making inquiries of dazed Indian bureaucrats in a government that was still forming and understandably preoccupied.

The collapse of the Punjab civil administration was so complete that it was impossible to know even how many people died along the roads, were hacked to pieces and thrown into wells, or were cremated in the flames of their own homes, but the most reliable estimates range between a quarter and a half million. By the end of October, though, vigilante frenzy in the Punjab finally fatigued and some degree of order returned. The armies of both nations were beginning to protect trains and refugee columns, and an intelligence report stated blackly: "The practice of throwing Moslems from train windows, is on the decline."

In the event that Theos did make it to Ladakh, Helen sent a telegram to him in care of the postmaster at the capital, Leh: "Leaving for Calcutta. Please contact Donovan American Embassy Delhi for information. Love Helen." She sent telegrams to Tharchin and the Macdonalds in Kalimpong and got a reply: "Wire Hopkinson and Tsarong. We also taking immediate action."

Helen asked their friend Howard Donovan, the chargé d'affaires at the American embassy, to make the contact with Hopkinson, the British political officer in Sikkim, stating, "I strongly feel that any communications with him should come through more official channels as the British . . . are very reluctant to further friendly relations between Dr. Bernard and Lhasa."

Donovan also wired Lhasa and got a reply from the Tibetan Foreign Bureau: "Received your telegram. We have not heard news of Theos Bernard's arrival in Tibet. Will assist him if he comes." India's Department of External Affairs informed the embassy that it had made inquiries at Leh but there was no indication that Dr. Bernard had attempted to make his way there.

To give herself greater standing in her dealings with them, Helen had presented herself to the staff at the American embassy as Mrs. Bernard, and now, after six days in Delhi and with no miracle in evidence from her attempts, Helen released the story to newsmen that her husband, Dr. Theos Bernard, was missing and feared dead. On October 31, newspapers all over America carried his familiar picture and reported that Dr. Bernard had been missing since mid-September on a trip to a Tibetan monastery and shepherds reported seeing his party attacked by Lahouli tribesmen. Helen acknowledged to the press that he could be dead, but until that was proven she chose to be optimistic. "He may be snowed in," she told the Associated Press. "If he is, I know he would be delighted to spend the winter in a Tibetan monastery."

Having done everything she could in Delhi, Helen stored a suitcase of clean clothes for Theos at the Hotel Cecil and left for Calcutta, where at least she had some friends with whom she could await new developments.

On arrival in Calcutta, however, Helen was informed by the new Indian Security Control that her visa would under no condition be extended beyond November 30. She had one month to wrap up her business in India, which included trying diligently to pull together the articles that academics were still finishing for the book Theos had been editing on India's contributions to modern culture, the suddenly outdated *Twentieth Century India*. She wrote to his publisher, Dr. Dagobert Runes at the Philosophical Library Press in New York, that she had fifteen of the articles in hand and was trying to get the others as quickly as possible. She began her letter to Runes with an explanation for the unavoidable delay in the delivery of the manuscript:

> No doubt you have read in the newspapers by now that Dr. Bernard met with difficulties in attempting to return to the Kulu Valley from Spiti where he had gone to visit the famous Ki Monastery. As there is no means of communication with that part of the world other than by foot over passes which are now snowed up we will have to wait to learn what happened. According to all the rumors from the mountain people living in the Kulu Valley he is unharmed though his baggage was looted, etc. It's quite likely that he will turn up with a darned good story one of these days—we hope.

Those wishful lines from Helen resulted in the *New York Times* headline "Theos Bernard Reported Alive." The short article stated that his publisher in New York had received a letter from Mrs. Bernard stating "her husband was safe. She said that the marauding tribesmen had attacked her husband's expedition and slain most of the carriers but that he had escaped. His present whereabouts are unknown, she added."

She had to explain the confusion to the American embassy in Delhi, which was still pushing its inquiries. "Let me hasten to assure you that I have heard no more from Theos than I had when I saw you in Delhi. Obviously the New York publisher had an eye towards the sales on Theos' new book when he released that bulletin after carefully omitting the all-important word . . . 'Hope.' After all, I can still do that without causing a furor I'm sure."

As an expression of her enduring hope, Helen left two suitcases of clothes for Theos at C. V. Starr's insurance headquarters in Calcutta and an envelope in the office safe with $900 in traveler's checks and a passbook giving access to another $200 in a bank account. Helen left for Hong Kong on November 13 and spent three months in China, as she told Runes, "in order to be close at hand to finish this book and also to do all possible to locate Dr. Bernard." The week before leaving China for home she wrote two letters to Howard Donovan at the American embassy in Delhi. The first letter requested the embassy's advice on how to arrange for someone to "make the trip to Spiti next summer and ascertain the facts of the events which took place involving Dr. Bernard.... After all, there is always the possibility that he was wounded and incapacitated in someway which would prevent him from returning particularly since he is presumably without funds."

The second letter was a personal message to Donovan telling him that she was back in Hong Kong after going for a time to Shanghai. "Actually I'm pretty fed up with this whole Oriental business. Shanghai is a seething mass of fear and unrest and may shortly repeat the Indian situation.... I'd just prefer not to be around when the balloon goes up as I've had all I care for this year." If there were any developments, she could always be reached, she told him, care of Glen Bernard at his home address in Northridge, California, or at his cable address—SAHIB.

THE BODY OF THEOS BERNARD never materialized as proof of his death, which allowed Helen and Glen to cling to the hope that he was still alive, perhaps living in a cave or in a remote monastery in Ladakh or Tibet. He might even be in one of the caves in which Padmasambhava had left his handprints impressed in the rock, preferring to stay there in retreat the rest of his life rather than return to "the world of affairs," as he had so often called it. The possibility, at least, was a final point of intersection in Theos Bernard's modern sequel to the life of Padmasambhava.

Tibetan lamas and high officials repeatedly told Theos that the reason he had come to Tibet was because of his past life as a spiritual teacher there, but nowhere do his daily journal entries or his long letters to Viola document his assertion that they recognized him specifically as the incarnation of Padmasambhava. Theos may have chosen to believe that it was Padmasambhava they were referring to simply because he felt a powerful and compelling connection with him. Beginning even before he went to Tibet, Theos chose Padmasambhava's biography as his first translation project, and after the jongpen of Gyantse presented him with an heirloom *thangka* of Padmasambhava with the hope that he would spread the master's teachings in the West, Theos seemed to cultivate that connection at every opportunity.

One aspect of the Tantric practices Theos was initiated into by the Ganden Tripa in Lhasa revolve around the premise that identifying powerfully with a saint or Tantric deity—and trying to act, think, and speak like them—plants powerful seeds that ripen in time in becoming oneself divine. The Tibetan teacher Chögyam Trungpa told a group of his Western students in 1972: "In talking about Padmasambhava, we are not referring purely to a historical person. If we were doing that, we would just be having a history lesson. Instead, what we are trying to point to here is that Padmasambhava is our experience." To illustrate his point, Trungpa told this story:

> There was a great Tibetan siddha called the Madman of Tsang. My guru told us that he asked the Madman of Tsang, "How should we go about uniting ourselves with Padmasambhava?" The madman told him the following. "When I was a young student and a very devout Buddhist, full of faith, I used to want my body to become one with Padmasambhava's body. I did countless recitations, thousands and millions of mantras and invocations. I used to shout myself half to death reciting mantras. I called and called and called to Padmasambhava, trying to make my body one with his. But then suddenly I just realized: I am—my body is—Padmasambhava. So I decided not to call on him any more. Then I found that Padmasambhava was calling on me."

The many biographies that attempt to recount the life of the historical Padmasambhava do not agree even on how long he stayed in Tibet, and accounts range from three months to 120 years. An explanation for the discrepancy is offered in an introduction to one of those biographies, *Oasis of Liberation*, which states that Padmasambhava's "definitive biography is told by each person who perceives him. In this way Guru Padmasambhava has countless unimaginable biographies, one biography for each being."

Most accounts, though, say that when Padmasambhava did leave Tibet it was on an emergency mission to subjugate a race of cannibal savages who were massing to invade South Asia and murder all humans for their meat—a situation not so unlike the communal slaughter rampant in the Punjab in the fall of 1947. In the moments before he left them, Padmasambhava gave some final advice to the despairing Tibetans on defeating ignorance and the disturbing emotions, and then he mounted a beam of sunlight and flew away into the sky, disappearing without a trace.

As with the life of Padmasambhava, every person Theos Bernard appeared to at the climax of his life had a different story to tell about it. The first rumors to reach the Roerichs in the Kulu Valley were carried by Bashahri herb collectors and shepherds who had come from the direction of the Chandra Valley about September 15 saying that Theos and Senge, his Tibetan servant, had been seen some days before at Chatru, the camp on the Chandra River below Hampta Pass.

Another shepherd reported that at Chatru on September 14, Theos and Senge bought some *atta*, the stone-ground wheat flour used for making chapattis. They were camping at Chatru and had with them a pile of baggage but no riding or pack ponies, and according to this account, Theos offered to pay 10 rupees each for ten porters to carry his equipment over the Hampta Pass and back to Katrain in the Kulu Valley.

Others said Theos and Senge were seen three days before that, on his return from Ki monastery, leading four of the original five pack ponies, but there were no Muslim pony attendants with them. Beyond that, there were some who swore that a band of fierce Khampas—who would have been months from their home in eastern Tibet—had rescued Theos and Senge, but it was unknown where they went.

The self-styled "raja of Manali," Major Henry Banon, told Helen that he had received a message from Theos and had sent food to him while he waited for porters to take him from his camp at Chatru to Kulu. Helen regarded the man as a notorious confabulator, but still, his account was another of the species in circulation that kept Helen's hopes alive.

However, another, more dire version of events had, as Svetoslav Roerich told the American consul in Bombay, become "a matter of such common knowledge in the Kulu Valley, that they explained beyond a reasonable doubt Dr. Bernard's disappearance." According to this explanation, Theos began his return from Ki monastery with the manuscripts he was given just as the atrocities in the Kulu Valley reached a crescendo during the first week of September. Helen noted in her diary about this time that squads of Hindu *goondas* had gone over Rohtang Pass to Lahoul to cut off the escape of any Muslims trying to flee toward Ladakh, and the *goondas* were inciting the local hill tribesmen to join their roving bands and take advantage of the lawless conditions to plunder any Muslims they could find.

It is unknown whether the note Helen sent to Theos warning that it was unsafe for his Muslim outfitters to return to Kulu actually reached him, but the group no doubt would have heard the grisly news in the gossip of shepherds and from travelers they encountered on the trail. The Muslims in Theos' party likely would have decided to escape toward Ladakh, but Fais Mohammed, the outfitter's son, apparently wished not to leave Theos completely stranded and sold him four pack ponies, with which Theos and Senge continued their trip down the Chandra River to the camp at Chatru. Here the pair would have faced the decision of whether to return to the Kulu Valley over Hampta Pass, the route by which they had come, or take the longer but easier major trade route over Rohtang Pass, which they would pick up one more day downstream at the village of Koksar.

The rains that were finally beginning to fall in Kulu left fresh snow on Hampta Pass, and Theos undoubtedly would have considered that, even with experienced guides leading the way, it was the most difficult trail he had ever been on and the snowfields at the top had been especially treacherous for the ponies. Given that, it would have been an easy decision to choose Rohtang—which means "the land of death"—for the crossing.

According to Roerich's "common knowledge," Theos and Senge set off from Chatru and followed the racing Chandra River down the twelve-mile trail to Koksar. Along the way they found the trail blocked by an armed mob of two hundred Lahouli Hindus whose blood lust would have spiked when they saw approaching them on the trail four ponies with decorations on their rigging that clearly marked them as belonging to Muslims. As the bearded American confidently approached the mob, he raised his hand in a gesture of peace. But before he could speak a single word, one enraged Hindu in the vanguard raised his gun and fired.

The yogic experience of death was a common theme in Theos' lectures and writing. Helen would say later that Theos had often described his death to her, and it was very likely she who transcribed the Thursday night lecture Theos gave in Ganna Walska's Manhattan living room on the evening of December 3, 1942, which now seems so eerily prescient. As his blood drenched the stony ground on the banks of the Chandra River, the words of his teaching to his Manhattan students five years before may have returned as a script for the next leg of his journey.

We have this individual and a shot is fired and the individual falls. What has happened; we say he is dead, he becomes lifeless, the body is cold. Something has changed. Now everything is there except this power of animation. . . . Kundalini has become *awake*. When Kundalini has become awake it removes our consciousness from our external organs back into its original center.

Immediately after Theos was shot, according to Roerich's account, two men stepped out of the mob. One took his ankles, the other his wrists, and they carried him off the trail to the edge of the flooding Chandra River. Developing momentum with well-practiced swings, they flung the inert body with its still-living mind from the high bank, and watched it bob along on the waves while the horrified Senge wrestled with his captors.

The experience of death, Theos told his students that Thursday in New York, follows a universal pattern. In the final moment of this life,

there is something that we will all experience. It is impossible to be killed so quickly that all of these experiences will not take place in all of their detail.

When we pass out we will all see a light. That light is Kundalini. . . .
For the general run of mankind, this flash of light will be so rapid
that we will not see it except as a sudden flash. But immediately afterwards comes a reflection. This is first a brilliant shining light and
right after it comes an afterglow that we'll see and linger in it for a
while, a few seconds, a few minutes. . . . He is not yet dead. . . . They
tell us that for the average individual it will be a day, or two days, or
three days. An individual who has great power, an individual that we
refer to as a Yogi, will tell you it stays there a week.

Describing the course of the Chandra River in an 1871 geography
survey, A. F. E. Harcourt wrote: "The river Chandra passes through a totally barren land where there are no signs of life, the solemn mountains
clad in eternal snow lying on its either flanks. No villages adorn its banks,
no attempts at cultivation, no human life is met with and nothing greets
the eye but the never ending monotonous cliffs, which are lapped by the
fierce stream as it rushes in wild fury against its banks."

From the spot where Theos was said to have been flung into the river,
the current would have borne him along in a northwesterly direction for
about thirty miles to where the Chandra joins the Bhaga. From there it
was not far until he would have entered Kashmir, where the stream is renamed the Chenab, one of the five sacred rivers of the Punjab. Though
flowing in September 1947 from two separate, bleeding nations, the waters of all five sacred rivers—and their freight of unknown thousands of
corpses—mingled and coalesced into one great river, the Indus, before
continuing their run to the Arabian Sea. How far the body of Theos
might have traveled toward that destination during the week that his consciousness could have remained in it is anyone's guess, but somewhere
along the journey, as he told his students, the most subtle mind leaves the
body and enters the dream-like state of the Bardo, the consciousness between death and rebirth.

The soul is going to leave the body and wake up in the same way that
we go to sleep and wake up every day of our lives. When it wakes up,
the principle of intelligence will manifest as a great light, a brilliant,

powerful, white light. . . . It is possible to gain liberation if you can grab on to that light . . . to look at yourself and realize that the whole thing is an illusion.

If the Bardo being who was Theos Bernard did not seize the opportunity for liberation before the end of its forty-nine-day life in the Bardo, the Wheel of Life would have continued to turn with another of its countless rebirths in the realms of samsaric suffering. Karmic seeds that Theos planted with virtuous and nonvirtuous actions during the thirty-eight years of his just-finished life and seeds remaining from his previous lives would determine whether he was fortunate enough to be reborn again as a human, the qualities of his mental and physical endowments, and the propensities that would shape the story of his next life.

However it began, the point of his next life would remain the same as it was in all his previous lives. "The whole purpose of our destiny on this plane is to escape," Theos said in one of his first lectures after returning from Tibet. All the possessions we slave during life to accumulate, the fame we achieve, everyone we love, all will be left again at death.

As if giving testimony for the point Theos was making there, the American consul in Bombay concluded his report on Theos Bernard's disappearance by noting: "Apparently nothing is known as to the disposition of Dr. Bernard's luggage, which included some valuable items. It is Roerich's theory, however, that the enterprising Lahoulis would not destroy them and that eventually they will show up in some northern Indian market."

EPILOGUE

SUMMER CAME LATE to the Kulu Valley in 1948. Mountain passes normally crossable by the beginning of May were still snowed in by the third week of June when Tom Tyson wrote to Helen from Katrain to say that a Sikh subinspector of the police had been dispatched to make an inquiry about the disappearance of Dr. Bernard.

The letter reached Helen in Northridge, California, where she rented a place near Glen's house. They set up a room for Theos, and as the summer dragged on with no news, Glen watched over and over again with a deepening despair the films Theos had shot in Tibet. After a few more months in California, Helen moved back to New York and immersed herself in her design business.

At the end of February 1949 she wrote to Howard Donovan at the American embassy in New Delhi, "I have not yet reached the point where I feel we should take up this question [of proof of death] with the American courts. At the present I am waiting until such time as Dr. Bernard's father thinks this step should be taken. . . . In the meantime we are being very quiet and going about our business of letting time heal the wounds and indicate what is to happen next."

In December 1950, the Indian Ministry of External Affairs filed a report with the American embassy stating that despite a three-year police investigation of the case, "all efforts to trace the whereabouts of Dr. Bernard have proved in vain. . . . In the absence of definite information in the matter, it is regretted, it is not possible to unearth the mystery surrounding the disappearance of Dr. Bernard."

IT WAS MORE THAN SIX YEARS after Theos disappeared before Glen filed a petition with the Los Angeles Superior Court for a certificate of death so that he could begin executing the last will and testament Theos had prepared just days before his final journey to India. A delayed certificate of death was granted on November 27, 1953, listing the cause of death as "shot by bandits." Glen was sole heir to the estate, but it was another three years before the legalities finally concluded with the release of $41,000 remaining in Theos' New York trusts.

Helen signed an affidavit for the court that although she had presented herself as Mrs. Bernard to the press and the American embassy, she and Theos had never wed. Theos did remain, however—as Helen told her niece decades later—the love of her life, and she never remarried.

Once back in New York, Helen went back to work for C. V. Starr, who had moved the headquarters of his insurance business to New York City after the Communist Party took power in China. He re-formed the company as AIG, which would become the world's largest insurance company, and he kept Helen busy designing interiors for new office buildings in Kuala Lumpur, Manila, Karachi, Dhaka, Penang, Bangkok, Beirut, Guyana, Hong Kong, and Singapore. Helen also decorated the lavish homes Starr scattered around the world and the penthouses he included in his office buildings and kept staffed for his occasional visits. As the distinguished architect I. M. Pei said of Starr, "He was a perfectionist. He wanted both utility and beauty."

Starr's fifteen-year marriage ended in 1952, and Helen was for the rest of his life an affectionate companion. She kept a residence at Morefar, Starr's five-hundred-acre country estate north of New York City, as did a few top AIG officers who had houses on adjacent lots. She decorated many of the dozen buildings at Morefar with Asian accents and chose the twenty-five bronze sculptures displayed around the estate's private eighteen-hole golf course, among them a boy and girl rolling a ball to each other that is set in a sand trap beside the fifth-hole green.

Starr died in 1968, and Helen retired the following year. Over the next twelve years she moved from New York to Coral Gables, Santa Barbara, Corpus Christi, and finally Austin, Texas, where she died in 1993, a few weeks before her ninetieth birthday.

Viola also never remarried and kept the Bernard name through the rest of a ninety-one-year life that was devoted to her distinguished career in psychiatry. She maintained a large private clinical practice, but Viola was best known as a founder of the emerging field of community psychiatry. She established the country's first low-fee clinic at Columbia University to provide psychoanalytic services to the poor and minorities, and was the founder and director of Columbia's Division of Community and Social Psychiatry, which trained hundreds of psychiatrists and public health specialists in the field. She published more than a hundred scientific articles, the last a month before her death in 1998, and the American Psychiatric Association awarded her in 1996 a Presidential Commendation in recognition of her "compassion, creativity, and courageous intervention in human pain."

Ganna Walska also continued to dazzle her admirers into her nineties—dying at age ninety-one or ninety-six, depending on which of her birthdates you believe—though even she gave up marriage after her divorce from Theos. Tibetland was renamed Lotusland, and Ganna spent the rest of her life and fortune creating there a stunning collection of gardens connected by labyrinthine pathways. There is a Japanese Garden, Bromeliad Garden, Water Garden, Aloe Garden, Theater Garden, and Cactus Garden, but Lotusland's greatest jewel is the Cycad Garden, in which flourish about 170 of the 230 known varieties of the palm-like prehistoric cycads. It is one of the best collections in the world, and one for which Madame Walska, then in her eighties, sold her tiaras to create. Before her death in 1984, she established the Ganna Walska Lotusland Foundation, which continues to maintain this horticultural wonderland and offer limited public tours.

Glen was already seventy-three by the time the paperwork giving him possession of Theos' estate was concluded, and he invited a housekeeper, Gertrude Eleanore Murray, known as Eleanore, to move in with him to help manage the hundreds of boxes of texts and art objects that Theos had collected in Tibet. Eleanore had seen Theos present his "Penthouse of the Gods" lecture and was inspired to read *Heaven Lies Within Us.* She eventually wrote to Theos for spiritual advice, and her letter was forwarded to Glen, whose reply with the news of his son's tragic disappearance started a regular correspondence between them. She was forty-six and living in West Virginia when she paid a visit to Glen in Northridge and then decided to stay. Over the years, Eleanore's role expanded to being secretary, care provider, companion, and disciple of Glen. He gave her the name Kamala, the name by which she was known to her friends at the Hollywood Self-Realization Fellowship center, where Glen taught.

With the estate finally settled, the aging Glen concentrated on trying to find a new home for Theos' Tibetan collection. Eleanore wrote letters to collectors in the United States and Europe (among them Eleanor Roosevelt and Nelson Rockefeller) hoping to sell major parts of the collection as a group. She focused first on offering the long Tibetan horns and the rare Tantric bone dress and accoutrements, then solicited interest in some of the valuable sculptures and *thangkas.* Considering today's acknowledged value of the pieces, she offered tantalizingly low prices, but apparently never sold any of the art objects.

Eleanore had more success in negotiating the sale of the Tibetan books, the raw material for the massive translation project Theos had envisioned in Santa Barbara. In March 1958 she concluded the sale of the 316 volumes of the Derge Kangyur and Tengyur that Tsarong had sacrificed. It went to the Harvard-Yenching Institute for $8,000.

The pair of hundred-volume Lhasa editions of the Kangyur Theos brought home (the first being the set he bought from the Panchen Lama's envoy, Ngagchen Rinpoche, in Calcutta and the second being the deal he couldn't refuse when he was packing to leave Lhasa) were bought by Westdeutsche Bibliothek, Marburg, a postwar successor to the former Prussian State Library in Berlin. After lengthy negotiations, Eleanore concluded that deal in November 1962, getting $8,250 for both sets.

Those two sales of the Tibetan canon moved more than three hundred thousand folio sides of block-printed scriptures, but the most significant part of the collection was sold in different installments over seven years to the Beinecke Rare Book and Manuscript Library at Yale University, with the last of the books being shipped in 1964. Eleanore negotiated the sale with Wesley Needham, an advisor to the Beinecke who, as a Theosophist, had written to Theos about a past-life experience in Tibet. He later learned to read Tibetan using only the simplified grammar of literary Tibetan that Theos had published and sent to him.

The collection the Beinecke bought from Glen is estimated to contain four thousand separate titles, and even in 1964, Needham knew from the cursory handlist Eleanore had compiled that it was a remarkable collection. In it were the collected works of four Dalai Lamas and five Panchen Lamas as well as the biographies of twelve Dalai Lamas. But that was just the start. There was a sixty-three-volume encyclopedic collection of Nyingma texts from the time of Padmasambhava along with *termas* discovered in the thirteenth century that had been printed especially for Theos in Lhasa and was only the second set known to exist in the West. There were also eighteen volumes of the collected works of the illustrious founder of the Gelugpa School, Je Tsongkapa, and another twenty volumes of the collected works of his preeminent disciples Khedrubje and Gyaltsabje. There were biographies of Marpa, Milarepa, and Atisha; seventeen volumes of medical texts; Nagarjuna's six sets of Madhyamika principles; *Pramanavarttika* by Dharmakirti; *Bodhisattvacharyavatara* by Shantideva; monastic textbooks; volumes on monastic discipline; and more.

But just how remarkable a collection Theos hauled out of Lhasa on muleback is still being discovered. Forty-five years after the Beinecke acquired it, only two-thirds of the collection has yet been cataloged in even the most basic way. Tibet scholar Paul A. Draghi wrote in his 1994 report for the Beinecke on its Tibet holdings that the Bernard Collection is "an extremely select group of important and rare editions," and "although several libraries in the west contain duplicates of some of the books in the Bernard Collection, none possesses a set of equal comprehensiveness and scholarly authority."

"It is no exaggeration to say," Draghi wrote, "that a survey of Tibetan Buddhist Literature could be written depending solely on the contents of the Bernard Collection. . . . No other collection of Tibetan books in the west could honestly make the same statement."

The comprehensive scope of the Bernard Collection, Draghi pointed out, results from "the undeniable connoisseurship and reputed religious eminence of Mr. Bernard." Other scholars and museum collectors who visited Tibet in the nineteenth and twentieth centuries tended to buy large numbers of mediocre-quality books and paintings and were able to figure out what they had only after they got home. Theos, however, followed a carefully laid plan for acquiring the most authoritative versions of the major works of all the schools of Tibetan Buddhism, and was assisted in that by the regent of Tibet himself, who unlocked government vaults where some of those editions were stored. The patronage of the most power- ful people in Tibet also allowed him to acquire texts that were forbidden even to most Tibetan lamas, such as the four volumes of Nyingma writ- ings compiled by the 5th Dalai Lama, who, although he was the head of the Gelugpa School of Tibetan Buddhism, studied with lamas of the rival Nyingma sect and wrote extensively on their history and doctrine. In Tibet, those volumes were sealed and available only to Gelugpa monks with special permission. The set given to Theos is the only set of the original block prints known in the West.

The fact that Theos employed highly educated lamas while packing at Tsarong House to check each page of each book for completeness and leg- ibility before crating them up also enhances the collection's scholarly au- thority, Draghi stated. The unbound folios of Tibetan books were usually printed by illiterate workmen and sometimes from worn or inaccurately carved woodblocks, so many of the Tibetan books in Western collections are illegible, contain spelling mistakes, or have pages that are out of order or missing.

Gene Smith, a Tibet scholar who since the 1960s has probably done more than anyone to bring Tibetan texts to the West, said in a lecture at the Beinecke Library in 2006 that the collection deserves to be better used. To his knowledge only one person has to date ever made significant use of this irreplaceable collection, now stored in 386 acid-free cases in the high-security, climate-controlled stacks of the Beinecke Rare Book and Manuscript Library at Yale University.

GLEN BERNARD DIED in a San Bernardino nursing home in 1976 at age ninety-two. In his will he wrote of his intention still to marry Gertrude Eleanore Murray and named her as heir to the large remaining collection of Theos' papers, photography, and collection of Tibetan art objects.

By 1990, at the age of eighty, Eleanore was, in the words of a friend, "in very poor health 'physically' and has an awful time seeing, walking and getting around. She is far far over-burdened with the property she has had to keep up since Glen Bernard's death." Another visitor wrote that "her entire house was stuffed with manuscripts, rotting animal trophies, oriental brassware, thangkas, statues, and dust from fifty years of collecting. In fact, her entire house is something of a shrine to Theos Bernard."

Gertrude Eleanore Murray died in 1998, and one of the first jobs for the court-appointed conservator for the estate was to establish the value of this shrine to Theos Bernard in order to determine the size of the estate's tax deduction when it was donated to some yet-to-be-selected institution.

Along with all the dusty art in her house, experts were called in to appraise the contents of 119 boxes and 18 large trunks and packing crates in four self-storage units in Upland, California. What they found piled inside was a staggering trove. Along with Theos' personal library of three thousand books on Tibet, Buddhism, and Yoga were found thirty shelf-feet of his papers: typescripts of his lectures, book drafts, the exhaustive journals of his trip to Tibet, hundreds of letters, news clippings, financial records, and legal papers. Those boxes comprise a rich archive of Theos Bernard's life, but the other boxes held what was in essence a time capsule of Tibetan culture at its zenith. Thousands of Theos' photographs, many with negatives, and several dozen steel cans with thousands of feet of motion picture film—what had been described in 1937 as the best photographic record of Tibet in existence—had ended up in cardboard boxes and forgotten in California storage units. There also were piles of other boxes holding a treasury of more than 750 major artifacts from Tibet.

Those included 22 bronze images of Buddhist deities, 40 *thangka* paintings, 23 Tibetan rugs, 25 large painted mandalas, more than 100 large cloth wood-block prints of historical figures and deities, 79 volumes of Tibetan texts, and a large number of Tibetan textiles, religious robes, hats, ritual implements, and household items.

The same connoisseurship and high connections that allowed Theos to find the best-quality Tibetan texts also showed in the collection of the art objects he brought home. Fifteen items were valued at $10,000 and three were valued at $50,000 or more. Among some of the most valuable were an illuminated manuscript with gold ink on black paper, an Amitayus gilt-copper statue from the thirteenth or fourteenth century, a magnificent wood and lacquer *phurbu* (magic dagger) from perhaps the twelfth century, and a fifteenth-century Mahakala *thangka* on black silk herringbone that may be one of the earliest examples of that style.

Dr. Richard Kohn, a specialist in Tibetan art and artifacts, wrote in his introduction to the appraisal, "The collection . . . is both important and wide-ranging." "Two comparisons come to mind," he continued, "the original bequest of Robert Shelton that formed the basis of the Newark Museum's Tibetan collection and the original gift of Avery Brundage that formed the nucleus of the Tibetan holdings at the Asian Art Museum of San Francisco. Over the decades, these gifts have been expanded into two of the greatest collections of Tibetan art in the United States."

He goes on to speak of "the synergy between the art and artifacts and the other parts of the Bernard collection: the films, photos, and field notes. Together they form a priceless resource." He concludes that the "collection is unique in that it represents a slice of Tibetan culture at its peak . . . Any institution lucky enough to receive it, would at a stroke, be provided with a rare and irreplaceable resource as well as a major collection of Tibetan art and ethnography."

The University of California, Berkeley, was the lucky institution selected in April 2000 as the recipient of the Theos C. Bernard–G. Eleanore Murray Collection and Archive. The university wrote in its winning proposal, "Your gift would ensure that the varied materials of the Bernard Collection would receive proper care and archiving [and] be made accessible to the scholarly and general communities. . . . Placing the Bernard collection at Berkeley would also do much to return Theos Bernard to his rightful place in the history of Tibetan studies." But despite the persuasive intentions, budget shortfalls have made for slow progress in carrying out that pledge. By the end of 2003 the collection had been inventoried but was still being fumigated and divided between four different campus institutions to be curated. Theos' papers were sent to the Bancroft Library. The *thangkas*, mandalas, and sculpture were sent to the Berkeley Art Museum. The motion picture film was given to the Pacific Film Archive. And the Hearst Museum of Anthropology received the still photography, ritual implements, textiles, costumes, and other ethnographic items.

Since then, the Berkeley Art Museum in 2004 exhibited four of the *thangkas* and a few of the photos as parts of larger exhibitions, and the Bancroft Library in 2007 completed a detailed finding aid for the thirty shelf-feet of Theos' papers, opening a rich source of biographical information. However, even by the end of 2008 only about three thousand of the eleven thousand still photographs Theos shot in Tibet had been cataloged at the Hearst Museum, and little progress had been made on the costly process of preserving the ten thousand feet of movie film from Tibet. The film curator at the Pacific Film Archive said the footage was shrunken and fragile when it arrived and almost all the color film was faded, and wrote, "I am afraid it will be quite a while before footage can be made accessible."

As with the bulk of most museums' collections, the fantastic assortment of Tibetan art and ritual objects that Theos returned with from Tibet is being safely stored from public view until some future exhibition when a few pieces will be called upon to represent the group. Perhaps the best hope of glimpsing the unique synergy between the art, photographs, and stories that Theos Bernard collected on his historic visit to Lhasa is the possibility, as one of the Berkeley curators said, of a "collaborative exhibition by the various campus units which received parts of the Bernard-Murray collection, but frankly," she wrote, "this seems years away."

THE FIFTY MULELOADS of Buddhist scriptures and art objects that Tibetans sent home in 1937 with Theos Bernard, their emissary to the West, are artifacts of Tibet's medieval culture in full bloom and in one of its final summers before Mao's revolution flooded across the border. Hardly three decades after the first Western pilgrim visited Lhasa, the culture he chronicled was all but destroyed in its homeland.

Immediately after the Communist Party took power in China in 1949, it began asserting its claim that Tibet was part of Chinese territory and that its people were crying out for liberation from the "reactionary feudal regime in Lhasa." Forty thousand troops of the People's Liberation Army entered eastern Tibet on October 7, 1950, and by the spring of 1956 the PLA had deployed a hundred thousand troops to suppress a growing rebellion against forced land redistribution. The brutality of PLA reprisals for Khampa skirmishes escalated, and monasteries were bombed and pillaged; captured resistance fighters were starved and forced to watch the rape of their wives; monks and nuns were compelled to renounce their celibacy vows, then copulate with one another before being summarily executed.

By the spring of 1959, thirty thousand PLA troops kept a wary eye on the rising tensions in Lhasa. When rumors spread of a purported Chinese plan to abduct the Dalai Lama and spirit him off to Beijing for the upcoming Chinese National Assembly, three hundred thousand Tibetans surrounded the Norbulingka palace to protect him. After consulting the Nechung oracle, His Holiness decided he must make an escape, and on the night of March 17, the 14th Dalai Lama slipped through the Chinese lines dressed in a soldier's uniform with a gun slung over his shoulder.

Two days later fierce fighting broke out in Lhasa, and the National Assembly convened at government offices below the Potala to debate a resolution to negotiate with the Chinese. Theos' host in Lhasa, the seventy-one-year-old onetime commander in chief of the Tibetan army, Dasang Damdul Tsarong, volunteered to organize a guerrilla campaign based from the southern forests while assistance from foreign countries was sought. Others loudly objected to that approach, but before a negotiating position could be ratified, shells started falling on the Potala. PLA troops stormed the meeting and arrested the entire National Assembly—Tsarong included—and marched them to Chinese army headquarters, where they were imprisoned.

Over the next weeks, the prisoners were taken one by one to face a group of Tibetans recruited from the ranks of criminals, malcontents, or those known to have a personal grudge against the former noble to face a session of choreographed public humiliation in which liberated retainers were urged to beat and spit on their former masters, and put bits in their mouths and mount their backs.

Tsarong spent three months in prison, his legs chained, in a cell with three other prisoners except for the occasions they were summoned to join work parties around the camp. The night before Tsarong was scheduled for his parade of humiliation, the authorities allowed the prisoners to have visitors while they watched a film. Tsarong watched with a niece in his lap and gave away his last cigarette to another prisoner. He then went off to sleep and died quietly in his bed.

Theos' cosmopolitan friend Jigme Taring accompanied His Holiness the Dalai Lama and his party as it fled south to the Indian border. They crossed Khenzimana Pass two weeks after escaping Norbulingka, and on April 3 Jawaharlal Nehru announced that the government of India had granted them asylum. Jigme's wife, Mary Taring, was not with him, however. They were separated by the chaos before the battles broke out, and she fled by a different route with a single servant through deep snow to Bhutan, unable even to say good-bye to their three grown children and eight grandchildren, who all remained behind in Lhasa.

Jigme and Mary were eventually reunited and relocated to a Tibetan refugee village in Mussoorie, India, where they directed children's homes and a Tibetan school. For twenty years they had no news of the fate of their own children and grandchildren until in 1979 they heard the voice of their grandson, Jigme Wangchuk, telling them via shortwave radio from Lhasa that they were all alive and well. Mary Taring wrote near the conclusion of her autobiography, *Daughter of Tibet*, "When people die the next generation replaces them, but when a whole culture is destroyed it can never be replaced."

The total extirpation of traditional culture was exactly what Mao had in mind, and beginning in 1966, Tibet, like China, was caught up in the politics of the Cultural Revolution. From that point any display of religious devotion was seen as support of the Four Olds: old ideas, old culture, old customs, and old habits. Chairman Mao's aphorisms of revolutionary class struggle declared that the new could be created only by

smashing the old, and the cult and worship of Mao was meant to irrevocably replace that of the Buddhas and bodhisattvas. His portrait hung in
every house and workplace, and in every village the people were mobilized
to rid their homes and their society of the last vestiges of the traditional
culture that Theos Bernard had only thirty years earlier so thoroughly
sampled.

After the death of Mao in 1976, Beijing's policy toward Tibet softened
considerably. But as shown by the lethal protest demonstrations in Lhasa
on October 1, 1987, and in the weeks before the Beijing Olympics, there is
still much discontent among Tibetans. Police repression continues to
check dissent, and it appears that Beijing has succeeded in making Tibet a
Chinese province through the simple strategy of outnumbering Tibetans
with Chinese immigrants.

Government relocation incentives have turned Lhasa into a boomtown
that has mushroomed from a population of about thirty thousand when the
Chinese took control fifty years ago to around six hundred thousand today,
with most Western analysts estimating at least 60 percent of those to be
Han Chinese. Lhasa is now a modern city with grids of square concrete
apartment blocks and uniform boulevards lined with fine hotels and
glass-fronted offices buildings. The Qinghai-Tibet railway, which opened
in 2006, connects Lhasa across the Tibetan Plateau to the rest of the Chinese rail network, and the 5.8 million Chinese tourists who in 2010 visited the once forbidden city arrived to a welter of mostly Chinese-owned
video arcades, all-night karaoke bars, and massage parlors.

Although Theos Bernard predicted in 1939 that Tibet's militarist
neighbors threatened "far reaching changes, little short of cataclysmic,"
and that Lhasa the forbidden, the mysterious, was about to be turned into
"the Chicago of Asia," the point of his collecting was not to acquire
museum archives of a vanished culture. His goal was to establish vital
institutions in the West devoted to the spiritual technologies of Tibetan
Buddhism and Hatha Yoga. The World Buddhist Directory now lists
eighteen hundred Tibetan Buddhist centers in Europe and the United
States, and market research indicates that almost sixteen million Americans practice some form of Yoga. With both having succeeded so spec-
tacularly in the West during recent decades, it is hard now to comprehend

that when Theos sailed home on the *Queen Mary* in 1937, the general public knew little of either Tibetan Buddhism or Yoga beyond their caricatures as Shangri-La or Pierre Bernard's love cults.

Had Theos Bernard lived another fifty-one years, to the age of ninety—as did his father, Glen; his first wife, Viola; his second wife, Ganna; and his prospective third wife, Helen—this charismatic pioneer undoubtedly would have been well known today not only for his contributions to Yoga but also for his founding of the field of Tibetan studies in America. After the U.S. State Department denied a visa to Gendun Chopel in 1941—thereby scuttling Theos' plan to bring Tibetan lamas to Santa Barbara—it was another fourteen years before the first lama moved to the United States. That lama was none other than Theos' mentor in Kalimpong, Geshe Wangyal, who arrived in Freewood Acres, New Jersey, in 1955 to minister to a community of Kalmyks (ethnically Mongolian Tibetan Buddhists) who immigrated as political refugees after the Second World War. Aspiring Buddhists in Manhattan and Boston eventually began to make the trip to study with Geshe Wangyal, among them the now-eminent Tibet scholars Robert Thurman and Jeffrey Hopkins, who both left Harvard in 1963 to live at Geshe Wangyal's Lamaist Buddhist Monastery of America. The effect of Geshe Wangyal through his students on the current state of Buddhist studies in the United States is, as Tibet scholar Donald Lopez writes, "difficult to overstate." Jeffrey Hopkins would go on to found the highly regarded Tibetan studies program at the University of Virginia, where he taught for thirty years and wrote thirty-four books. Thurman has, since 1988, been the Jey Tsong Khapa Professor of Buddhist Studies at Columbia University. One of the jobs of that position is to oversee the translation into English of the more than thirty-six hundred texts of the Tibetan Tengyur, a project started in 1972 by the American Institute of Buddhist Studies at the behest of Geshe Wangyal.

The description of the translation project on the institute's website is illustrated by a picture of a bearded Theos Bernard sitting in his Tibetan silk gown at a low table filled with stacks of Tibetan folios. It credits him with being the first to dream of undertaking that mammoth translation project. Just how ambitious the vision Theos dreamed for himself and Gendun Chopel at Tibetland really was is illustrated by the fact that even with the fanfare generated by having a celebrity scholar such as Robert Thurman as editor in chief, and even with ten members on its editorial board, the American Institute of Buddhist Studies has so far been able to translate only eleven of the canon's thirty-six hundred titles in twenty years.

Tibet scholars still speculate about what influence Gendun Chopel might have had on the development of Tibetan studies in the West if Theos had been able to get a visa for him. The writings of the brilliant and iconoclastic scholar have been rediscovered in such volumes as the work Jeffrey Hopkins translated and published in 1992 as *Tibetan Arts of Love: Sex, Orgasm, and Spiritual Healing.* Robert W. Clark, a Stanford University professor who spent more than eight years in a Buddhist monastery in the 1960s and 1970s and has worked as a translator for the Dalai Lama, wrote in an introductory piece to the Bernard Collection at Berkeley, "Had Theos lived to bring Geshe Chopel to America . . . the influence of this brilliant, English speaking Lama on the development of Buddhism in the West would have been enormous, especially if combined with a long lived Theos Bernard." Donald Lopez concurs with that opinion in his biography of Gendun Chopel, *The Madman's Middle Way*: "One can only imagine how the landscape of Tibetan studies and Tibetan Buddhism in the West may have been transformed had he come to America."

THEOS HOPED that his establishment in 1939 of the American Institute of Yoga would found a new lineage in America through which the fragmented Yoga lineages of India could be practiced with a scientific approach and promise the same results in modern lives as attained by realized masters in the threatened cultures that produced them. His lineage, however, still didn't have a successor, and the American Institute of Yoga couldn't survive his untimely death. It seems clear from his last letters to Glen that if Theos had returned to teach again, his new approach to Yoga would have included the practices and philosophies of both Tibetan Buddhism and Hatha Yoga, lineages with common Tantric ancestors that were decimated eight hundred years ago with the Mughal conquest of northern India. Again, Theos was a generation ahead of his time, as that sort of synthesis has only recently begun appearing in Yoga studios, notably through the programs of the Yoga Studies Institute, which bases its course series on new translations of classic Sanskrit and Tibetan texts by Geshe Michael Roach and Lama Christie McNally.

Because he disappeared before his thirteen years of groundwork could be preserved in the enduring institutions he dreamed of, Theos Bernard's greatest legacy to this generation of yogis in the West lies in the detailed accounts of the experiments he conducted on himself with the nearly extinct techniques of Hatha Yoga. His books *Heaven Lies Within Us* and *Hatha Yoga* are both still commonly cited on Yoga websites and blogs as being among the best available resources, and, amazingly, all of his books except the Tibetan grammar are still available as small-press reprints.

Theos would have been thrilled to know not only that Hatha Yoga survived its near extinction in India but also that well-trained teachers in authentic lineages are now comparatively easy to find in the West. Today in major American cities one can find classes for the distinct forms of the Iyengar, Ashtanga, Sivananda, Kripalu, Integral, Ananda, Jivamukti, Anusara, Vini, Kundalini, Hidden Language, Somatic, Tri, White Lotus, Ishta, and Bikram Yoga lineages; all are descended from a handful of Indian teachers who were virtually unknown in the West during the time of Theos Bernard.

But Yoga's millennia-old traditions—rooted in virtue, contentment, discipline, and wisdom—have never before been forced to adapt as radically as they have in the last decades in the West. Especially in America, where philosophy has always been decidedly pragmatic, the booming popularity of Yoga can be traced to the marketing of its tangible health benefits. Since 1990, when Dr. Dean Ornish published the first of his studies in the *Lancet* suggesting that the combination of a low-fat diet and Yoga could stabilize and even reverse the arterial blockage associated with heart disease, Yoga has been recommended for almost any health need, from weight management, back pain, and stress reduction to speeding recovery from heart attacks and cancer. Clinics have even developed Yoga regimens more narrowly targeted for carpal tunnel syndrome, lupus, fibromyalgia, asthma, diabetes, insomnia, headaches, obsessive-compulsive disorder, postmenopausal symptoms, and substance abuse.

But Yoga in the West does much more than make sick people well; it makes people who are merely well beautiful. Celebrity endorsements from

Madonna, Sting, and a dozen others with whom pop culture is on a first-name basis have created a halo of chic around Yoga to which Gucci responded with an $850 Yoga mat and a $350 matching leather carrying case.

The sixteen million people in America who practice some form of Yoga spent $5.7 billion on classes and products in 2008, an annual revenue that if reported by a single corporation would put it on the Fortune 500 list. Major retailers have come up with their own Yoga fashion lines, and marketing campaigns that present Yoga as a lifestyle accessory employ airbrushed models balanced in graceful asanas to pitch everything from automobiles to vodka. Their target is a demographic group in which 44 percent of yoga practitioners in America report household incomes greater than $75,000 and 71 percent have college degrees—not bad for a tradition that teaches renunciation as a cardinal virtue. One of the most pressing questions debated by Yoga devotees today is whether the Yoga that narrowly avoided extinction in India can survive the good life in the West.

One can be cynical about the proliferation, but every point of access could be a portal to Yoga's goals of self-transcendence, self-transformation, and self-realization. Theos Bernard was one of the first popularizers of Hatha Yoga, and it is instructive to recall what he told his audience of three million housewives about that very issue. In the fourth of his articles in *Family Circle* in 1939 he told his interviewer, "The conception of Yoga in the public mind is about 99% erroneous. . . . However, if a man comes to me for a knowledge of Yoga to help him make more money or make him stronger, or to get him better grades in his college classes, I will take him as a pupil and trust to his intelligence that ultimately he will grow curious about the spiritual idea behind the simpler forms of Yoga."

That spiritual idea, he said, is expressed as a progressive path; "the asanas are merely preparation." When the body is strengthened and the mind quieted, the student should move on to Pranayama and use its practices of breath control to move *prana* to crucial points in the subtle nervous system. This leads, Theos wrote in his book *Hatha Yoga*, to the *samadhi* of Raja Yoga, the fruit "which destroys death, is the means of obtaining happiness, and gives the Brahman-bliss."

The way to accomplish this audacious goal, the destruction of death itself is, he wrote, to awaken the Divine Energy, Kundalini, with the practice of Pranayama and bring it to rise through the Sushumna, the central channel of the subtle nerve network. "When the Prana flows in the Sushumna and the mind has entered sunya, then the Yogi is free from the effect of Karmas," he quotes from the *Hatha Yoga Pradipika.* "Other practices are simply futile for the Yogi."

The asana training—the preparation, as Theos called it—of the path of Yoga is now easily available at studios, gyms, and clinics throughout the Western world, and for most practitioners, the physical benefits are all that motivates them to practice. But along with the great breadth of the forms of Yoga in the West there is also, in places, great depth, and perhaps never in its millennia of history has the complete and authentic path of Yoga been so easily available from fully qualified teachers in India, the West, Singapore, Japan, Australia, China, and any number of other countries. Yoga centers and individual teachers capable of instructing and inspiring students in all of Yoga's potential are, of course, few relative to the many millions practicing worldwide, but they are certainly much easier to find now all over the world than when Theos searched India for a fully qualified master in the 1930s. Even in Tibet and India before their collisions with the modern world, those who dedicated their lives to attaining the fruit that destroys death and gives the Brahman-bliss were, as Theos discovered, always a small number.

No one can say whether Theos himself attained that final liberation from the world of suffering before his body floated to the Arabian Sea, but it is clear that if he had returned to America and had a chance to chart a course for the practice of Yoga in the West, his curriculum would have provided a comprehensive model that included the wisdom and practices of Tibetan Buddhism, Hatha Yoga, and Western science in a graduated path that offered, as he said, "something for everyone and eternal bliss for that one creature that might stumble by in the course of a life time."

For Theos Bernard, the transcendent goal of Yoga remained the same as the one Padmasambhava described to Tibetans before he mounted a sunbeam and disappeared from them in the eighth century: "Realize the wisdom of pure awareness," he told them. "That is how you truly obtain the name yogi. . . . Tibetan Yogis of future generations, keep this in your hearts."

NOTES

AHS Arizona Historical Society, Theos Casimir Bernard Collection MS 1060 Tucson, AZ. AHS F. (File Number)

VWBP Viola Wertheim Bernard Papers, 1918–2000, Columbia University Health Sciences Library, Archives & Special Collections. New York, NY. VWBP X:X (Box:Folder). Finding Aid online: http://library.cpmc.columbia.edu/hsl/archives/findingaids/bernard.html

BANC The Bancroft Library, University of California, Berkeley, Theos Bernard Papers, BANC MSS 2005/161 z. BANC X:X (Carton:Folder) Finding Aid online: http://oac.cdlib.org/findaid/ark:/13030/kt967nd5pw

ACSS Archives of Charles Scribner's Sons, 1786–2003 (bulk 1880s–1970s) Princeton University Library, Department of Rare Books and Special Collections, Manuscripts Division, C0101. Author Files and Manufacturing Records. ACSS X:X (Carton:Folder). Finding Aid online: http://diglib.princeton.edu/ead/getEad?eadid=C0101

HGPF Helen Graham Park Foundation, Miami Shores, FL. HGPF F. (Folder Number in Preliminary Finding Aid).

INTRODUCTION

I there are more than eighteen hundred Tibetan Buddhist centers in Europe and the United States: The figure on the number of Tibetan Buddhist centers in the West comes from the *World Buddhist Directory*, a project of the online site Buddhanet. The figure on the number of people doing Yoga in North America comes from the *Yoga Journal* 2008 "Yoga in America" Market Study (15.8 million in the United States) and a 2005 study from *PMB (Print Measurement Bureau)* cited by NAMASTA (North American Studio Alliance) in the report "Canadian Yoga Statistics" (1.4 million in Canada). These are the most current metrics available, and considering their age and the trajectory of growth in Yoga, rounding up to nearly eighteen million seems conservative.

2 a London newspaper proclaimed: "Young Explorer Writes the Greatest Adventure Story of the Year," *Daily Mail*, November 12, 1937, 13–16.

2 the first Westerner in the six-hundred-year history of Tibet's Sera Mey monastery to earn the *geshe* degree: Michael Roach was ordained as a Buddhist monk in 1983, and in 1995, after approximately 20 years of daily intensive study with his teacher, Sermey Khensur Geshe Lobsang Tharchin, in New Jersey and at Sera Mey monastery in southern India, he received the *geshe* degree, which is frequently described as being similar to a doctorate of divinity.

4 Hemingway himself asked Perkins for advance copies: Michael S. Reynolds, *Hemingway's Reading 1910–1940: An Inventory* (Princeton: Princeton University Press, 1981).

CHAPTER 1: OUT OF A CLEAR SKY

7 "Somebody named Aura with a son named Theos": Letter from Viola Bernard to biographical researchers J. M. Mahar and Carol Lingham, 1982, AHS. Theos Casimir Bernard Collection, MS 1060 F.17.

8 "Men killed every few days": Cited in Lynn R. Bailey, *Tombstone, Arizona, "Too Tough to Die": The Rise, Fall, and Resurrection of a Silver Camp; 1878 to 1990* (Tucson: Western Lore Press, 2004), 121.

9 Her father, when he was young, had spent several years in India: Aura Gordon, letter to Viola Bernard, n.d. [1937], AHS F.20.

9   "She used to give me a book review once in a while": Mahar and Lingham, inter-
     view with Mary Price, Tucson, 1983, AHS F.37.

9   "Aura was a good writer and was almost daily asked to pen letters": J. M. Mahar,
     draft of biographical article on Theos Bernard, AHS F.9.

10   The only surviving letter, written by Aura to Glen: Aura Bernard, letter to
     Glen Bernard, n.d. [1910 or 1911], BANC.

10   Tombstone would have become another of Arizona's ghost towns: Bailey, Tomb-
     stone, 255.

11   American entry into the war in the spring of 1917: Ibid., 269–70.

11   Gordon was described by a grandson: Carol Lingham, notes on meeting with
     Theos' nephew, Gregory A. Gordon, 1984, AHS MS1060.

11   One of Theos' school friends: Mahar and Lingham, interview with Tombstone
     residents Daniel Hughes, Mary Price, and Burton Devere, 1983, AHS F.36–38.

12   the house was an occasional "battlefield of debate": Mahar and Lingham, inter-
     view with Theos' half brother, Dugald Gordon, 1982, AHS F.35.

12   "without even a cowboy saddle for a pillow": "Religious Wealth in Tibet's Wil-
     derness Seen by Bernard," Arizona Daily Star, November 7, 1937.

12   promised with fingers crossed behind their backs: Ian Gordon, letter of applica-
     tion to Black Mountain College, 1936, AHS F.22.

13   to descend a cliff face to reach their favorite swimming hole: Mahar and Ling-
     ham, interview with Dugald and Gretchen Gordon, Tombstone, 1982, AHS
     F.35.

13   "Theos didn't go to church that much": Lingham, interview with Daniel and
     Emma Hughes, Tombstone, 1983, AHS F.36.

13   even nine-year-old Dugald pitched in: Mahar and Lingham, interview with
     Dugald and Gretchen Gordon, Tombstone, 1982, AHS F. 35.

14   "He will not live": Theos Bernard, Heaven Lies Within Us (New York: Charles

Scribner's Sons, 1939), I. The account of Theos' convalescence at the mine and discovery of Yoga in his mother's library is his account from this book.

16   "He seldom lived in a room alone": Lingham, interview with Daniel and Emma Hughes, Tombstone, 1983, AHS F.36.

16   Theos got B's in three classes: University of Arizona, transcript of student record, AHS MS 1060 F.4.

16   had "a great deal to do with deflecting his path from law": Viola Bernard, letter to Carol Lingham, September 12, 1983, AHS F.21.

17   He had been married to a hairdresser for a time: Information on Glen's occupation, brief marriage, and residence come from the 1920 and 1930 U.S. federal census record.

17   Perry began an intensive course of Vedic studies: Stephanie Syman, *The Subtle Body: The Story of Yoga in America* (New York: Farrar, Straus and Giroux, 2010), 83–84.

18   by purchasing from the swami a large, full-headed tiger skin: Julian Don Alexander, letter to Roy Eugene Davis, Center for Spiritual Awareness, Lakemont, Georgia, Nov. 12, 1993. Copy provided by Alexander.

18   the pseudonym Arthur Avalon—under which Woodroffe published: See Kathleen Taylor, "Arthur Avalon: The Creation of a Legendary Orientalist," in Julia Leslie, ed., *Myth and Mythmaking* (Richmond: Curzon, 1996).

19   "a language more fit for the expression of spiritual ideas than English": Atal Behari Ghosh, letter to Glen Bernard, January 11, 1928, BANC MSS 2005/161 z.

19   "Reasonableness will dawn before you as you progress": Ibid.

20   "out of a clear sky, I was summoned by one who had just arrived from India": Bernard, *Heaven Lies Within Us*, 9.

22   Theos maintained a steady correspondence with his guru: The account of the instruction Theos received from his guru and his initial practices are from Bernard, *Heaven Lies Within Us*, 20–44.

25 headstand on the back of one of their placid mining camp burros: AHS F.35.

25 even his good friend Daniel Hughes knew nothing about it: Mahar and Lingham, interview with Daniel Hughes, AHS F.36.

26 "Theos loved girls": Mahar and Lingham, interview with Dr. William Wharton in Tucson, 1982, AHS F.39.

26 "Dr. Pierre A. Bernard no longer wears the robes": "Off the Record: Evolution," *Fortune*, July 1933, 4.

CHAPTER 2: THE PHILOSOPHER'S DANCE

28 "a play-time pursuit of the deepest philosophies of life": *Life at the Clarkstown Country Club* (Nyack, NY: privately published, c. 1935). The description of the CCC amenities are also from this small book.

29 called the finest collection of Sanskrit manuscripts and translations: Richard S. Stringer-Hye, "The Library of Pierre Arnold Bernard," http://www.vanderbilt .edu/~stringer/library.htm.

29 "as well-versed in the ways of the world as of the spirit": Alan Watts, *In My Own Way: An Autobiography 1915–1965* (New York: Pantheon, 1972), 127.

29 vast range of topics such as the comparison of Shankara Vedic philosophy: "Off the Record: Evolution."

30 Performing under the club's big top: Charles Boswell, "The Great Fuss and Fume over the Omnipotent Oom," *True: The Man's Magazine*, January 1965.

30 work alongside the elephants in building a 3,500-seat stadium: Stringer-Hye, "The Library of Pierre Arnold Bernard."

31 Tantra groups branded a "national danger": "Country Club Specializes in Sex Worship: Initiates, Known As Tantrik Yoga, Hold Wild Orgies in Nyack New York," *San Francisco Chronicle*, October 1, 1922. See Robert Love, *The Great Oom: The Improbable Birth of Yoga in America* (New York: Viking, 2010) for a full discussion of the press coverage of the early years of P. A. Bernard's career and the development of the CCC.

31   parents divorced when he was three, and Perry, . . . , lived with his grandparents: 1880 and 1900 federal census records.

31   he never traveled to India: See Syman: *The Subtle Body*, 80–115, for a full discussion of P. A. Bernard and his importance in the introduction of Yoga to America. Also Love, *The Great Oom.*

32   probably the first group of Western students of Tantra ever organized: *The Encyclopaedia of American Religions*, ed., J. Gordon Melton, 3rd ed. (Tarrytown, NY: Triumph, 1989).

32   "one of the greatest souls not only of India but of the whole world": K. K. Khullar, "Swami Ram Tirath: The Unfettered Thinker," http://www.atributetohinduism .com/articles_hinduism/82.htm.

32   Tantrik Order had adapted Tantra perfectly for Americans: *Vira Sadhana: International Journal of the Tantrik Order* V, I (1906): 95.

33   the worst of which survived in the perverse rituals of the Tantras: Hugh B. Urban, *The Omnipotent Oom: Tantra and Its Impact on Modern Western Esotericism*, Ohio State University, http://www.esoteric.msu.edu/VolumeIII/HTML/ Oom.html.

34   "I may perform the duties of a Yogi and reveal true religion": "Omnipotent Oom Held as Kidnapper," *New York Times*, May 4, 1910, 7.

34   "What my wife and I have seen through the windows of that place is scandalous": "Night Revels Held in Sanskrit College," *New York Times*, December 15, 1911, 22.

35   "Country Club Specializes in Sex Worship": *San Francisco Chronicle*, October I, 1922.

35   New York State Police arrived on horseback one evening: Boswell, "The Great Fuss and Fume over the Omnipotent Oom."

36   "This ain't no love cult here": Stringer-Hye, "The Library of Pierre Arnold Bernard."

36   "Some folk like to spout a lot of Sanskrit terms": Ibid.

36 successive years at Smith College, Barnard, and then Johns Hopkins: Biographical information from the Viola Wertheim Bernard Papers, 1918–2000, VWBP.

37 profits should be split among employees: *Tobacco Trade Journal*, November 18, 1920.

38 they were so completely sure of themselves: Viola Wertheim, letter to her brother Maurice, July 23, 1934, VWBP 9:2.

38 "She just turned over $25,000 to him": Theos Bernard, letter to Glen Bernard, July 20, 1934, BANC.

41 voyage back to New York through the Panama Canal: Theos Bernard, letter to Glen Bernard, July 22, 1934, BANC.

42 found on drugstore shelves as well as at university bookstores: Peter Watson, *The Modern Mind: An Intellectual History of the 20th Century* (New York: Perennial, 2001), 281.

42 "What is much needed at the present time": Theos C. Bernard, "Introduction to Tantrik Ritual," master's thesis, Columbia University, May 15, 1936, 18.

43 "what I have to go through in getting the degree": Theos Bernard, letter to Viola Bernard, August 15, 1935, VWBP 9:6.

43 "What we know as Yoga in the West is so vulgarized": Glen Bernard, letter to Viola Bernard, February 11, 1935, VWBP 11:11.

44 "It is a great mistake to think that the Indian is born an inevitable savage": excerpted from a paper read by Capt. Richard C. Pratt at the Nineteenth Annual Conference of Charities and Correction, Denver, Colorado, 1892, http://socrates.bmcc.cuny.edu/bfriedheim/pratt.htm.

44 "a model that must be preserved for human rejuvenation": "'A Bill of Rights for the Indians': John Collier Envisions an Indian New Deal," History Matters online history course, http://historymatters.gmu.edu/d/5059.

45 getting advice on how to preserve their fathers' way of life: All the letters cited between Theos and Viola Bernard while he is in New Mexico were dated June 12 to September 15, 1935, VWBP 9:6–7.

48   "India is a lousy place with good stuff so scarce": Glen Bernard, letter to Viola Bernard, December 5, 1935, VWBP 11:11.

49   Evans-Wentz suggested that Theos use his anthropological skills: Glen Bernard, letter to Viola Bernard, December 29, 1935, VWBP 11:11.

49   Glen spent almost three months with the Tantricas: Glen Bernard, letter to Viola Bernard, March 14, 1936, VWBP 11:11.

49   visited for Tantric research in earlier decades: Kathleen Taylor, *Sir John Woodroffe, Tantra and Bengal: An Indian Soul in a European* (New York: Routledge, 2001), 96.

50   most famous of all alchemical compounds: Steven A. Feite, Alchemy Forum 0901-0950, http://www.levity.com/alchemy/frm0950.html. For a comprehensive discussion of the practice of alchemy in Hatha Yoga, see David Gordon White, *The Alchemical Body: Siddha Traditions in Medieval India* (Chicago: University of Chicago Press, 1996).

51   "Yoga can better be practiced in the Southwest": Viola Bernard, notes on letters from Glen Bernard, VWBP 11:12

51   "With them goes this knowledge": Bernard, "Introduction to Tantrik Ritual."

52   its radically new approach to spiritual practice: George Feuerstein, *The Yoga Tradition: Its History, Literature, Philosophy and Practice* (Prescott, AZ: Hohm Press, 2001), 64.

52   As Theos put it: Theos Bernard, *Philosophical Foundations of India* (New York: Philosophical Library, 1947), 136.

52   In the human body, Theos wrote: Theos Bernard, "Introduction to Tantrik Ritual," 53.

54   if it was true he could levitate: J. M. Mahar, draft of biographical article on Theos Bernard, AHS 10:25.

55   "I do love you ever so much": Theos Bernard, letter to Viola Bernard, July 1936, VWBP 10:7.

CHAPTER 3: THE PAGEANT OF INDIA

56   they flew from Shanghai to Peking: Theos did not keep a journal of his travels with Viola in India. Most of the information about where they traveled and who they met on specific dates come from Viola's travel diary, VWBP 9:9. Theos described some of the major events of their travels together in later book and magazine accounts.

57   dozens of letters of introduction she carried: Viola thanks Dr. Joshi for the letters and describes how they made use of them in her letter to him, December 4, 1936, VWBP 9:16.

60   They all agreed Theos should return in November: Entry dated September 20, 1936 in typescript copy of Viola's travel diary, VWBP 9:9.

61   "waiting crocodiles below the town": Stewart Robertson, "India Forever Foul, Forever Fair," *Family Circle*, November 18, 1938, 12, VWBP: 11:24.

63   "dinner engagements could not be made": Viola Bernard, letter to Dr. Joshi, December 4, 1936, VWBP 9:16.

63   able to walk on water: Entry dated October 16, 1936, in typescript copy of Viola's travel diary, VWBP 9:9.

64   "tottering trees of prejudice": Bernard, *Heaven Lies Within Us*, 144.

65   The interior of Theos and Viola's tent: Robertson, "India Forever Foul, Forever Fair," 12.

66   dress uniforms and all their medals: Much of the colorful details of the Durbar are from Bernard, *Heaven Lies Within Us*, 137–41, and Robertson, "India Forever Foul, Forever Fair." The details of the schedule are from Viola's diary.

68   "even a Yogi needs a 'white tie'": Bernard, *Heaven Lies Within Us*, 141.

68   Krishnamacharya innovated a series: Linda Sparrowe, "The History of Yoga," *Yoga* (Berkeley, CA: Yoga Journal Books, 2008).

69   no one could say where he had gone: Bernard, *Heaven Lies Within Us*, 145.

69 "Only remnants of true Yoga are accessible today": Ibid., 57.

70 "It was easy enough to find": Ibid., 144.

CHAPTER 4: KALIMPONG

72 one who is clean within: Bernard, *Heaven Lies Within Us*, 146.

72 sitting rather than walking on water: Theos Bernard, letter to Viola Bernard, January 1937, VWBP 10:8.

73 so unjust as to deny the poor man: Theos Bernard, letter to Viola Bernard, November 30, 1936, VWBP 10:8. From this point in the story until Theos leaves India for Tibet and begins keeping a journal, his long, frequent letters to Viola become the major source of documentary evidence.

73 nine-foot-tall elephant: Theos Bernard, letter to Viola Bernard, November 18, 1936, VWBP 10:8.

73 "a couple other Tantric retreats": Theos Bernard, letter to Viola Bernard, November 25, 1936, VWBP, 10:8.

74 Tibetan kings made a concerted effort: See David Snellgrove and Hugh Richardson, *A Cultural History of Tibet* (Boston: Shambhala, 1995), 66–80, and Giuseppe Tucci, *The Religions of Tibet* (Berkeley: University of California Press, 1988), 1–28, for full discussions of the introduction of Buddhism from India to Tibet.

74 "the north was my goal": Stewart Robertson, "White Lama—Part One," *Family Circle*, April 22, 1938, 10, VWBP 11:24.

75 "you want to run, fly, jump": Theos Bernard, letter to Viola Bernard, December 9, 1936, VWBP 10:8.

75 "say he can kill men at a distance": Alexandra David-Neel, *Magic and Mystery in Tibet* (New York: Dover Publications, 1971), 41.

75 "send petitions to him with huge gifts": William Montgomery McGovern, *To Lhasa in Disguise* (New York: Grosset & Dunlap, 1924), 95.

76   was poisoned by his stepmother: Barbara and Michael Foster, *The Secret Lives of Alexandra David-Neel*, rev. ed. (Woodstock, NY: Overlook Press, 1998), 68–70, 112–14.

77   "These holy men need not move": The account of his stay in Gangtok and trip to Lachen are from several letters Theos wrote to Viola Bernard, between December 17, 1936, and January 10, 1937, VWBP 10:8.

80   At Kalimpong the loads were transferred: Snellgrove and Richardson, *A Cultural History of Tibet*, 235.

81   "more than any other place that I have ever lived": Theos Bernard, letter to Vera Macdonald, 1938, BANC.

81   Macdonald served as the British trade agent: See David Macdonald, *Twenty Years in Tibet* (New Delhi: Gyan Publishing House, 2002).

82   "He was exceptionally competent": Theos Bernard, *Penthouse of the Gods* (New York: Charles Scribner's Sons, 1939), 36.

82   *Mirror of the New Vicissitudes:* From an article in the *Detroit News*, Sunday, October 3, 1937, which the reporter based on a dispatch from Tharchin in Tibet.

82   the 13th Dalai Lama had a subscription: *Tibetan Bulletin* (Dharamsala, India) 3, no. 1 (January–February 1999).

82   learned about the fast-changing world: "G. Tharchin: Pioneer and Patriot," *Tibetan Review*, December 1975, 18–20.

82   current events, such as the Olympics: Jamyang Norbu, "Newspeak & New Tibet: Part III: The Myth of China's Modernization of Tibet and the Tibetan Language," http://www.tibetwrites.org/articles/jamyang_norbu/jamyang_norbu14.html.

82   advocate of progressive reform: "G. Tharchin: Pioneer and Patriot."

82   a salon for Tibetan nationalists: Thubten Samphel, "Virtual Tibet: The Media: The Effect of Media and the Internet on Tibetan Attitudes," http://www.tibetwrites.org/articles/thubten_samphel/samphel03.html.

83   The disciplined schedule paid off: Details of Theos' daily schedule from his letters to Viola on January 11, January 24, and February 1, 1937, VWBP 10:8.

83   "If he met one in his dreams": Excerpts from several letters Theos wrote to Viola Bernard, between November 18, 1936, and February 8, 1937, VWBP 10:8.

85   Theos met Geshe Wangyal at Tharchin's house: Theos Bernard, letter to Viola Bernard, February 13, 1937, VWBP 10:8.

86   "a Yogi who is a Yogi": Theos Bernard, letter to Viola Bernard, February 20, 1937, VWBP 10:8.

87   "are not able to lead others": Theos Bernard, letter to Viola Bernard, March 28, 1937, VWBP 10:8.

87   "if I am going to win my invitation": Theos Bernard, letter to Viola Bernard, February 27, 1937, VWBP 10:10.

88   "would flower as divine": Younghusband quoted in Marcus Braybrooke, *A Wider Vision: A History of the World Congress of Faiths* (Oxford: One World, 1996), 32.

88   "Joy had begotten love": Braybrooke, *A Wider Vision*, 22.

88   feud actually dated back more than thirty years: Melvyn C. Goldstein, *A History of Modern Tibet, 1913–1951, The Demise of the Lamaist State* (Berkeley: University of California Press, 1989), 62.

89   slipped out of the country with his entourage: Ibid., 113.

90   simultaneously witness an epic event: A. Scott Berg, *Lindbergh* (New York: G. P. Putnam's Sons, 1998), 3–6.

91   ten thousand soldiers and sailors: Ibid., 156.

91   "It is amazing his interest": Theos Bernard, letter to Viola Bernard, March 1, 1937, VWBP 10:10.

92   private interviews with Ngagchen Rinpoche: These accounts of dealings with Ngagchen Rinpoche are drawn from letters Theos wrote to Viola Bernard, March 3 to March 6, 1937, VWBP 10:10.

93   Basil Gould, had just returned home: Gould replaced Williamson, who the

previous fall, as Sikkim political officer, had arrived in Lhasa to lead the mission but died while there. Gould arrived in Lhasa in February 1936.

94 "puts some showmanship and imagination into it": The account of the trip to Calcutta with Chapman comes from three letters Theos wrote to Viola Bernard, March 10 to March 16, 1937, VWBP 10:10.

94 "all time high of conscious feeling": Account of return to Kalimpong from four letters Theos wrote to Viola Bernard, March 16 to April 18, 1937, VWBP 10:10.

95 Theos' routine now had him rising: Theos Bernard, letter to Viola Bernard, April [22], 1937, page 62.54, VWBP 10:10.

95 memorize thirty-five new words in an hour: Account of Theos' language studies and translation activities from six letters Theos wrote to Viola Bernard, from December 1936 to April 27, 1937, VWBP 10:10.

96 "tasted of enough to prove to me": Account of his Yoga practice from six letters Theos wrote to Viola Bernard, January 24 to May 1, 1937, VWBP 10:10.

97 "for the good of posterity": His future plans with Viola from five letters Theos wrote to Viola Bernard, January 24 to April 19, 1937, VWBP 10:10.

98 "too damn busy and perhaps discouraged": Viola Bernard, letter to Theos Bernard, n.d. [1937], BANC 3:48.

98 "he has a perfect set up": Situation at the CCC and plans for World's Fair from five letters Theos wrote to Viola Bernard, January 30 to April 27, 1937, VWBP 10:10.

99 focus on getting permission to enter Tibet: Account of plans for getting to Tibet and meeting Tibetan nobles in Kalimpong from seven letters Theos wrote to Viola Bernard, March 20 to May 6, 1937, VWBP 10:10.

100 a response to his request from Gould: Account of his meeting with Gould from two letters Theos wrote to Viola Bernard, May 1 and May 4, 1937, VWBP 10:10.

101 before Theos' departure were filled with orchestrating: Account of the last days of preparation from three letters Theos wrote to Viola Bernard, May 1 to May 6, 1937, VWBP 10:10.

103 Frank rapped on the door: Theos Bernard, Journal of Travels in Tibet, Part I, May 11, 1937. VWBP 10:2.

104 amusing contrast to his preparations: The account of his stay with Gould in Gangtok is from letter Theos wrote to Viola Bernard, May 13, 1937, VWBP 10:10, and Bernard, "Journal of Trip to Tibet," May 12–13, 1937, VWBP 10:2.

CHAPTER 5: GYANTSE

106 woke at 4:00 a.m. with the queasy symptoms: The account of his crossing of Natu La comes from letter Theos wrote to Viola Bernard, May 17, 1937, VWBP 10:11; also Bernard, Penthouse of the Gods, 36–39; Bernard, Journal of Travels in Tibet, Part I, Natu La, May 15, 1937, 10–17, VWBP 10:2.

108 emphasizes different Tantric practices: John Powers, Introduction to Tibetan Buddhism (Ithaca, NY: Snow Lion Publications, 1995), 314. The Kagyu school traces its lineage back to the Indian Tantric sage Tilopa (988–1069) and his illustrious student Naropa (1016–1100). An important collection of Tantric practices for Kagyus is called the Six Yogas of Naropa, and Theos had heard that the head lama of this Chumbi Valley monastery was a master of them.

108 left the bungalow in darkness: The account of his visit to the Kagyu monastery comes from Bernard, Penthouse of the Gods, 41–43; Bernard, Journal of Travels in Tibet, Part I, May 16, 1937, Chumpi Tang, 17–20.

110 "bleeding at both ends": Bernard, Journal of Travels in Tibet, Part I, May 16, 1937, Chumpi Tang, 20; Bernard, Penthouse of the Gods, 44.

110 historian Melvyn Goldstein notes: Goldstein, A History of Modern Tibet, 4.

111 "they call this the top of the world": The account of his travels across the Tibetan Plateau to Dochen Lake from letter Theos wrote to Viola Bernard, May 19, 1937, VWBP 10:11; Bernard, Penthouse of the Gods, 50; Bernard, Journal of Travels in Tibet, Part I, May 20–21, 1937, 34–41.

111 seduce the pack mules: "A Caravan Journey from Kumbum to Lhasa," as told by Thubten Jigme Norbu to Heinrich Harrer (originally published in 1960), in Tibet Is My Country, http://www.iras.ucalgary.ca/~volk/sylvia/Caravan.htm.

112 Lhare's mother had died: The account of breaking the news to Lhare and Tibetan funeral customs from Bernard, *Penthouse of the Gods*, 53–54; Bernard, Journal of Travels in Tibet, Part I, May 22, 1937, Khangma, 51–52.

114 the vast Gyantse Plain: The account of his final stage to Gyantse from Bernard,
Journal of Travels in Tibet, Part I, May 24, 1937, Gyantse, 56–61; Theos Bernard, letter to Viola Bernard, May 26, 1937, VWBP 10:11.

115 containing several million repetitions: Macdonald, *Twenty Years in Tibet*, 131.

115 powerful blessing for the practice of a path: Each school has a different explanation of the mantra. H.H. the 14th Dalai Lama's definition: "Thus the six syllables,
om mani padme hum, mean that in dependence on the practice of a path which is an
indivisible union of method and wisdom, you can transform your impure body,
speech, and mind into the pure exalted body, speech, and mind of a Buddha."
Method here is the altruistic intention to become enlightened in order to all
lead others to enlightenment; wisdom here means recognizing the ultimate nature of all things. From a lecture given by His Holiness The Dalai Lama of
Tibet at the Kalmuck Mongolian Buddhist Center, New Jersey, http://www
.circle-of-light.com/Mantras/om-mantra.html.

115 The abbot greeted them: The account of the day's visit to Palkor Chode from
Bernard, Journal of Travels in Tibet, Part I, May 25, 1937, Gyantse, 67–75;
Theos Bernard, letter to Viola Bernard, May 26, 1937, VWBP 10:11.

118 biggest dance performance of the year: The account of the day's dance performance from letter Theos wrote to Viola Bernard, May 26, 1937, VWBP 10:11,
Bernard, Journal of Travels in Tibet, Part I, May 26, 1937, Gyantse, 76–81.

119 Rinchen Dolma and Jigme Taring had just arrived: Bernard, Journal of Travels
in Tibet, Part I, May 26, 1937, Gyantse, 82–86; Bernard, *Penthouse of the Gods*, 72.

119 Mary and Jigme: Bernard, *Penthouse of the Gods*, 72.

120 hanging of the Kigu Banner: Bernard, *Penthouse of the Gods*, 72.

120 Taring Raja could have succeeded: Rinchen Dolma Taring, *Daughter of Tibet: The
Autobiography of Rinchen Dolma Taring* (London: Wisdom Publications, 1986), 106.

120 nuances of Tibetan etiquette: Account of Taring luncheon from Bernard, Journal

of Travels in Tibet, Part I, May 27, 1937, Gyantse, 88–94; Bernard, *Penthouse of the Gods,* 75.

122 Theos thought he might use the photos: Theos Bernard, Journal of Travels in Tibet, Part I, May 27, 1937, Gyantse, 88.

122 more than a hundred different ensembles: Dundul Namgyal Tsarong, *In the Service of His Country: The Biography of Dasang Damdul Tsarong, Commander General of Tibet* (Ithaca, NY: Snow Lion Publications, 2000), 48.

122 must be a gift from heaven: Bernard, Journal of Travels in Tibet, Part I, May 29, 1937, Gyantse, 99.

122 responsible for maintaining law and order: Taring, *Daughter of Tibet,* 21.

123 eager to cultivate the friendship: Account of polo matches with Captain Cable from Bernard, *Penthouse of the Gods,* 79; Bernard, Journal of Travels in Tibet, Part I, May 27, 1937, Gyantse, 91, 102, 112; Theos Bernard, letter to Viola Bernard, June 12, 1937, Gyantse, Tibet, VWBP 10:11.

124 Theos addressed 125 cards: Bernard, Journal of Travels in Tibet, Part I, May 31, 1937, Gyantse, 115; Theos Bernard, letter to Viola Bernard, June 6, 1937, Gyantse, Tibet, VWBP 10:11.

124 early start was required for the *jongpen's* party: Bernard, Journal of Travels in Tibet, Part I, May 30, 1937, Gyantse, 104–9; Bernard, *Penthouse of the Gods,* 83.

126 eight-hour game of cricket: Bernard, Journal of Travels in Tibet, Part I, June 3, 1937, Gyantse, 137.

126 worked according to the feudal arrangement: Taring, *Daughter of Tibet,* 22.

126 two-thirds of the arable land: Goldstein, *A History of Modern Tibet,* 3.

126 The rest was held by the nobility: Taring, *Daughter of Tibet,* 21.

126 result in confiscation: Ibid., 21.

126 lord generally contributed seed: Goldstein, *A History of Modern Tibet,* 3.

127 ranked in four divisions of nobility: Dorje Yudon Yuthok, *House of the Turquoise Roof* (Ithaca, NY: Snow Lion Publications, 1990), 30.

127 Gyantse district, there were fifteen *gerpa:* Ibid., Appendix I, 308.

127 elaborate code of Tibetan etiquette: Bernard, Journal of Travels in Tibet, Part I, June 1, 1937, Gyantse 118–22; Bernard, *Penthouse of the Gods,* 88–89.

129 sent to Gyantse for military training: Macdonald, *Twenty Years in Tibet,* 223.

129 the matter of gifts to send: Bernard, Journal of Travels in Tibet, Part I, June 3, 1937, Gyantse, 137–51.

130 would like to come over that evening: The account of the *jongpen*'s presenting the *thangka* from Bernard, Journal of Travels in Tibet, Part I, June 5, 1937, Gyantse, 142, 154–55; Bernard, *Penthouse of the Gods,* 95–96; Theos Bernard, letters to Viola Bernard, May 26 and June 6, 1937, Gyantse, Tibet, VWBP 10:11.

132 ambitious project of creating an index: Bernard, Journal of Travels in Tibet, Part I, June 6, 1937, Gyantse, 160–63.

133 intensity of his polo diplomacy: The account of the colonel's visit and race day from Bernard, Journal of Travels in Tibet, Part I, June 9, 1937, Gyantse, 179–99; Bernard, *Penthouse of the Gods,* 107–11.

133 "I would much rather talk about": Bernard, Journal of Travels in Tibet, Part I, June 11, 1937, Gyantse, 192.

134 While Theos was being saturated: Bernard, Journal of Travels in Tibet, Part I, June 11, 1937, Gyantse, 194.

134 three other Westerners had been caught: Bernard, Journal of Travels in Tibet, Part I, June 11, 1937, Gyantse, 193–97; Bernard, *Penthouse of the Gods,* 112.

135 YOUR MUCH RELIGIONSHIP MAY VISIT LHASA: Bernard, *Penthouse of the Gods,* 120.

136 remaining days were filled with sorting: Ibid., 119–23; Bernard, Journal of Travels in Tibet, Part I, May 26 and June 9, 1937, Gyantse, 82, 177.

NOTES

CHAPTER 6: GATES OF THE FORBIDDEN CITY

138   "do not show that sense of inferiority": Bernard, *Penthouse of the Gods*, 127.

139   godless and devil-ridden Tibetans: John MacGregor, *Tibet: A Chronicle of Exploration* (New York: Praeger Publishers, 1970), 86.

139   The friars even built a church: Ibid., 86.

139   won only thirteen souls: Orville Shell, *Virtual Tibet: Searching for Shangri-La from the Himalayas to Hollywood* (New York: Metropolitan Books, 2000), 130.

139   adopted the xenophobia of the Chinese: "Tibet," originally published "Littell's Living Age/Volume 137/Issue 1775/Tibet" (1938), Wikisource, The Free Library, http://en.wikisource.org/w/index.php?title=Littell%27s_Living_Age/Volume_137/Issue_1775/Tibet&oldid=492642 (accessed November 30, 2007).

140   "manners of a well-educated, princely child": MacGregor, *Tibet*, 222.

140   would not compromise with the heathens: Ibid., 227.

140   "they will spellbind you": Ibid., 246.

141   thrown into the river to drown: Macdonald, *Twenty Years in Tibet*, 137.

141   4,500 yaks, 5,000 bullocks: Karl E. Meyer and Shareen Blair Brysac, *Tournament of Shadows: The Great Game and the Race for Empire in Central Asia* (Washington, D.C.: Counterpoint, 1999), 299.

142   "The Dalai Lama, they say, will die": Cited in Schell, *Virtual Tibet*, 193.

142   British suffered twelve wounded: Meyer and Brysac, *Tournament of Shadows*, 299.

142   They didn't cower or run for cover: Cited in Peter Bishop, *The Myth of Shangri-La: Tibet, Travel Writing and the Western Creation of Sacred Landscape* (London: Athlone Press, 1989), 173.

143   "there are no real mysteries": Ibid., 171–72.

143 "We found the city squalid": Cited in Peter Hopkirk, *Trespassers on the Roof of the World: The Secret Exploration of Tibet* (New York: Kodansha International, 1995), 184.

143 where was the "inner power": Cited in Bishop, *The Myth of Shangri-La*, 172.

143 "actual meaning they trouble themselves but little": Cited in Donald Lopez, *Prisoners of Shangri-La: Tibetan Buddhism and the West* (Chicago: University of Chicago Press, 1998), 37.

144 rife with ritual and superstition: Ibid., 35–36.

144 "dissipate the dense mists of ignorance": L. Austine Waddell, *Lhasa and Its Mysteries with a Record of the British Tibetan Expedition of 1903–1904* (New York: Dover, 1988), 446.

144 Victorian Buddhologists reigned unchallenged: Lopez, *Prisoners of Shangri-La*, 42.

144 *Egyptian Book of the Dead*: Ibid., 52.

145 ranging from Anaïs Nin to Carl Jung: Ibid., 57–58; Bishop, *The Myth of Shangri-La*, 237–38.

145 discovered the original *terma*: "Transitions to the Other World: The Tibetan Books of the Dead," University of Virginia library online exhibition, http://www.lib.virginia.edu/small/exhibits/dead/otherworld.html.

145 "the apex of the pyramid": Cited in Rick Fields, *How the Swans Came to the Lake, A Narrative History of Buddhism in America* (Boulder, CO: Shambhala), 287.

146 serialized in the *Daily Telegraph*: Hopkirk, *Trespassers on the Roof of the World*, 227–29.

147 weakened by influenza, wasted to skin and bones: Foster and Foster, *The Secret Lives of Alexandra David-Neel*, 220.

147 "viewpoint of a poor pilgrim": Ibid., 7.

147 "gain by experience an estimate of the truth": Bernard, *Introduction to Tantrik Ritual*, 20.

148 wiped it with his grimy sleeve: The account of his travels between Gyantse and the gates of Lhasa is from Bernard, *Penthouse of the Gods*, 128–51; Bernard, Journal of Travels in Tibet, Part II, June 24, 1937, Lhasa, 84a-86b; Theos Bernard, letter to Viola Bernard, July 4, 1937, VWBP 10:11.

CHAPTER 7: THE PILGRIM'S WELCOME

152 the city's first glass windows: Dundul Namgyal Tsarong, *In the Service of His Country: The Biography of Dasang Damdul Tsarong, Commander General of Tibet* (Ithaca, NY: Snow Lion Publications, 2000), 73.

152 "chubby ball of enthusiastic fire": The account of his arrival at Tsarong House is from Bernard, Journal of Travels in Tibet, Part II, June 24, 1937, Lhasa, 86b–87a.

153 modernizers received encouragement: Goldstein, *A History of Modern Tibet*, 121.

153 change would mainly bring problems: Bernard, *Penthouse of the Gods*, 154.

154 present himself at the British mission: Bernard, Journal of Travels in Tibet, Part II, June 24, 1937, Lhasa, 87b–88b.

155 born with the name Chensal Namgang: Tsarong, *In the Service of His Country*, 13.

155 the 13th Dalai Lama noticed an uncommon air of confidence: Ibid., 13.

155 Chinese reacted to the Dalai Lama's flight: Goldstein, *A History of Modern Tibet*, 47–53.

156 Chinese cavalrymen in close pursuit: Tsarong, *In the Service of His Country*, 26.

156 he conceived a new vision of Tibet: Goldstein, *A History of Modern Tibet*, 54.

156 mutinied and killed their commanders: Goldstein, *A History of Modern Tibet*, 58–59.

157 due to the success of his diplomacy: Tsarong, *In the Service of His Country*, 35.

157 executed on the same spot: Ibid.

157 marry the widow of the murdered son: Taring, *Daughter of Tibet*, 40.

157 to preserve the blood lineage: Ibid.

157 customary welcoming load of gifts: Bernard, Journal of Travels in Tibet, Part II, June 25, 1937, Lhasa, 89a–b; Bernard, *Penthouse of the Gods*, 159.

158 three life-size, gilded copper images: Tsarong, *In the Service of His Country*, 72.

159 lost consciousness and never spoke another word: Goldstein, *A History of Modern Tibet*, 141.

159 a five-month power struggle: Ibid., 147, 165.

159 small but exquisitely appointed palace: The account of his first meeting with the regent from Bernard, Journal of Travels in Tibet, Part II, June 26, 1937, Lhasa, 90b–91a; Bernard, *Penthouse of the Gods*, 164–67.

161 an appointment to call on the *lonchen:* The account of his first visits to the *shapes* from Bernard, Journal of Travels in Tibet, Part II, June 26, 1937, Lhasa, 91b; Bernard, *Penthouse of the Gods*, 166–67.

161 the home of Langcunga Shape: Theos calls him Nangchunnga Shape, undoubt-edly referring to the *shape* called Langcunga by Goldstein and British sources.

161 visit Kalon Lama Shape: Goldstein identifies the monk *shape* as Tregang; how-ever, photos from the archive of the British mission to Lhasa identified him as well as Kalon Shape, http://tibet.prm.ox.ac.uk/photo_1998.131.461.html.

162 Kalon Lama offered a guide: The account of his first visit to the Potala from Bernard, *Penthouse of the Gods*, 171; Bernard, Journal of Travels in Tibet, Part II, June 27, 1937, 93b–94b.

163 covered with one ton of solid gold: Spencer Chapman, *Lhasa: The Holy City* (London: Chatto & Windus, 1938).

164 Lungshar had for decades advocated: Goldstein, *A History of Modern Tibet*, 204–11.

164 only one eye popped out: Ibid., 208.

165 government's most charming personalities: Bernard, *Penthouse of the Gods,* 176.

165 would not serve foreign scholars: Bernard, Journal of Travels in Tibet, Part II, June 29, 1937, 98b; Theos Bernard, letter to Viola Bernard, July 10, 1937, VWBP 10:11.

166 had hopes that after the death of the 13th Dalai Lama: Goldstein, *A History of Modern Tibet,* 265.

166 hand grenades, and ammunition: Ibid., 278.

166 five hundred well-armed Chinese soldiers: Ibid., 291–93.

166 visit to Bhondong Shape: Bernard, *Penthouse of the Gods,* 176. Theos calls the *shape* Pondrong Shape, Chapman and the British call him Bhondong Shape, and Goldstein identifies him as Bonsho.

167 the perfect justification: Bernard, Journal of Travels in Tibet, Part II, June 29, 1937, 98a–102a.

168 returned with Tsarong's garden shears: Bernard, Journal of Travels in Tibet, Part II, July 4, 1937, 108a.

168 second visit to the regent: Bernard, *Penthouse of the Gods,* 193; Bernard, Journal of Travels in Tibet, Part II, July 4, 1937, Lhasa, 108b–109a.

169 a 1,176-page volume illustrated: Description from University of California Berkeley initial catalog of Bernard collection. The item (temporary number BQ-68) was almost certainly the one presented to Theos by Reting Rinpoche on their second meeting. The catalog description reads, "This large zylographic text is a sutra on the Golden Eon, in which 1000 Buddhas appear. The current Buddha, Shakyamuni, is the fourth of the 1000. This text provides iconographic prints of all 1000 Buddhas, each with their names inscribed below their image. It also gives the portraits and names of 72 Lamas, Bodhisattvas, Lamas, Yidams, and sacred symbols. These pictures are on each folio, one on either side, bracketing the text. Each portrait is brilliantly clear, and is labeled with the name of the deity. This type of labeling is very rare. Most Buddhist iconography confronts the viewer with baffling arrays of Buddhas and tantric divinities whose identity must be inferred by way of subtle differences in mudras, clothing or attributes, etc. All this can make the identification of Buddhas and deities very difficult."

169 they had refused to meet each other: Bernard, Journal of Travels in Tibet, Part II, July 1, 1937, 103a.

169 Chiang Kai-shek saw an opportunity: Goldstein, *A History of Modern Tibet*, 223–246.

170 "Chinese Government began to make regular payments": Hugh E. Richardson, *Tibet and Its History*, (Boston: Shambhala, 1984), 143.

170 The British sent a delegation to Lhasa: Ibid., 144–47; Goldstein, *A History of Modern Tibet*, 269–78.

171 "neutral soil of friendship": The account of his tea for the British and Chinese is from Bernard, Journal of Travels in Tibet, Part II, July 1 to July 4, 1937, 103b–109b; Bernard, *Penthouse of the Gods*, 195.

171 Tibet's most sacred temple, the Jokhang: The account of the ceremony at the Jokhang is from Bernard, Journal of Travels in Tibet, Part II, July 8, 1937, Lhasa, 114a–115b; Bernard, *Penthouse of the Gods*, 178, 202, 204–13.

172 "They could not quite figure out...": Bernard, Journal of Travels in Tibet, Part II, July 7 and July 8, 1937, 114a.

173 appointed after competitive examinations: Alexander Berzin, "A Brief History of Ganden Monastery," 1991, expanded with Tsenshap Serkong Rinpoche II, September 2003, Berzin archives, http://www.berzinarchives.com/web/en/archives/study/history_buddhism/gelug/brief_history_ganden_monastery.html.

175 a party at the home of Tethong Shape: Bernard, Journal of Travels in Tibet, Part II, July 10, 1937, 118a–119b; Bernard, *Penthouse of the Gods*, 218–20.

176 giant firecracker at each of the four corners: McGovern, *To Lhasa in Disguise*, 358–59.

177 left when they wanted, but with an entourage: Bernard, Journal of Travels in Tibet, Part II, August 25, 1937, 221a.

177 of the Lhasa movie: Bernard, Journal of Travels in Tibet, Part II, July 7, 1937, 113d.

177 Screenings typically ran over four hours: Chapman, *Lhasa: The Holy City,* 247–55.

CHAPTER 8: LIVING RITUAL

178 "propitiate" Dorje Jikje: The account of his Ramoche initiation is from Bernard, Journal of Travels in Tibet, Part II, July 15, 1937, 128a–129b; Bernard, *Penthouse of the Gods,* 239–40.

180 Days now began at five for Theos: Bernard, Journal of Travels in Tibet, Part II, July 11, 1937, page 120a.

180 sessions with a well-known Nyingma lama: Theos Bernard, letter to Viola Bernard, July 16, 1937, Lhasa, VWBP 10:11.

180 a small image of Padmasambhava: Theos Bernard, letter to Viola Bernard, July 16, 1937, Lhasa, VWBP 10:11; Bernard, *Penthouse of the Gods,* 247; Bernard, Journal of Travels in Tibet, Part II, July 11, 1937, 120b–121a.

181 he had received a letter from Giuseppe Tucci: Theos Bernard, letter to Viola Bernard, July 28, 1937, VWBP 10:11.

181 problems that the renowned Tucci: Tucci's plight also highlights the fact that Theos Bernard's invitation to Lhasa did *not* indicate that the Kashag had reversed Tibet's centuries-old policy and decided that the moment was right to open Tibet's borders to foreign scholars. If that had been the case, Theos Bernard's visit would have been notable still because he was the first of them admitted, but the exclusion of foreigners remained the official policy of Tibet until limited numbers of tourists were first allowed by the Chinese in 1980.

182 "what leaves me speechless": Bernard, Journal of Travels in Tibet, Part II, July 17, 1937, 133b.

182 "hardly bright enough to attract the bugs": Ibid., August 15, 1937, 200b.

183 "indulge in a few of the juvenile pleasures": Ibid., July 27, 1937, 157b.

183 "It is my contention that": Ibid., July 19, 1937, 136b.

184   next morning to leave for Drepung: The account of his visit to Drepung is from Bernard, Journal of Travels in Tibet, Part II, July 19 and July 21, 1937, 137b–141b; Bernard, *Penthouse of the Gods*, 260; Theos Bernard, letter to Viola Bernard, July 20, 1937, VWBP 10:11.

184   Drepung (founded in 1419) was the largest: Goldstein, *A History of Modern Tibet*, 24.

184   a fifth of all males in Tibet were monks: Ibid., 5.

184   said to control 185 estates: Ibid., 34.

185   develop a list of texts to acquire: The account of his strategy for collecting and the obstacles are from Bernard, Journal of Travels in Tibet, Part II, July 27, 1937, 156b; Theos Bernard, letter to Viola Bernard, July 14, 1937, VWBP 10:11.

186   several sheets were pasted together: Bernard, Journal of Travels in Tibet, Part II, July 12, 1937, 122b.

186   under lock and key in a government warehouse: Bernard, Journal of Travels in Tibet, Part II, July 27, 1937, 156b.

186   Theos was low on cash: Viola Bernard, letter to Theos Bernard, August 3, 1937, BANC 3:48; Theos Bernard, letter to Viola Bernard, July 28, 1937, VWBP 10:11.

187   unable to find a copy of the Tengyur: Bernard, Journal of Travels in Tibet, Part II, July 11 and 12, 1937, 120b, 122b; Theos Bernard, letter to Viola Bernard, July 14, 1937, VWBP 10:11.

187   wanted corroboration from Tsarong: Bernard, Journal of Travels in Tibet, Part II, July 28, 1937, 158b.

188   invited to the Potala for a Tantric *puja:* The account of the oracle and Yamantaka *puja* at the Potala from Bernard, Journal of Travels in Tibet, Part II, July 23, 1937, 146a–148b; Bernard, *Penthouse of the Gods*, 269–72.

188   so cumbersome he could hardly walk: H.H. the 14th Dalai Lama in his autobiography, *Freedom in Exile*, cited in "Nechung—The State Oracle of Tibet," http://www.tibet.com/Buddhism/nechung_hh.html.

189 "a sign of favor conferring the blessing": "Young Explorer Writes Greatest Adventure Story of the Year," *Daily Mail*, November 12, 1937, 13.

189 Yongdzin Ling Dorjechang: Theos identifies him only as the abbot of the Gyuto Tantric college. The identification of the abbot as the illustrious Ling Rinpoche is from his biography, "His Holiness Kyabje Yongdzin Ling Dorjechang 1903–1983," at http://www.fpmt.org/teachers/hhling.asp.

190 second of the Three Seats, Sera monastery: The account of his visit to Sera from Bernard, *Penthouse of the Gods*, 277–280; Bernard, Journal of Travels in Tibet, Part II, July 26, 1937, 153b.

191 songs of the household's workmen: Description of the work songs and fascination with typewriter in Bernard, Journal of Travels in Tibet, Part II, July 25, 1937, 152b; Bernard, *Penthouse of the Gods*, 285; Theos Bernard, letter to Viola Bernard, July 14, 1937, Lhasa, VWBP 10:11.

193 "I am going to fly straight home": Theos Bernard, letter to Viola Bernard, July 21, 1937, VWBP 10:11.

193 on duty for thirty-six hours straight: Viola Bernard, letter to Theos Bernard, June 2, 1937, BANC 3:48.

193 "on the trail of your rainbow": Viola Bernard, letters to Theos Bernard, June 2 and 28, 1937, BANC 3:48.

194 she would be his secretary and manager: Viola Bernard, letter to Theos Bernard, July 27, August 8, 1937, BANC 3:48; Theos Bernard, letter to Viola Bernard, August 11, 1937, VWBP 10:11.

194 spend a few years studying in one of the monasteries: Theos Bernard, letter to Viola Bernard, July 5, 1937, 10:11.

194 "adapt those teachings to our new set of facts": Theos Bernard, Journal of Travels in Tibet, Part II, July 11, 1937, 121b; Viola Bernard, letter to Theos Bernard, n.d. [1937], BANC 3:48; Theos Bernard, letters to Viola Bernard, August 15, 9, and 11, 1937, VWBP 10:11.

195 "remembering a certain August first": Viola Bernard, letter to Theos Bernard, July 27, 1937, BANC 3:48.

CHAPTER 9: THE HERMIT'S BLESSING

196   last of the Three Seats, Ganden monastery: The account of his journey to Ganden from Bernard, Journal of Travels in Tibet, Part II, July 28, 29, and 30, 1937, 158a–162b; Theos Bernard, letter to Viola Bernard, July 11, 1937, VWBP 10:11.

197   escorted to their quarters: The account of his visit to Ganden from Theos Bernard, Journal of Travels in Tibet, Part II, July 30 and 31, 1937, Lhasa, 163b–166b; Bernard, *Penthouse of the Gods*, 3–15.

198   Theos getting hastily from the warm bed: Bernard, Journal of Travels in Tibet, Part II, July 31, August 1, 1937, 164a–167b; Bernard, *Penthouse of the Gods*, 18.

200   typically read and recite only their prayer books: Goldstein, *A History of Modern Tibet*, 24.

202   visit a hermitage high on a ridge: The account of his journey to Drag Yerpa from Bernard, Journal of Travels in Tibet, Part II, August 1, August 2, August 3, 1937, 168a–172b.

203   a hermit living in one of the caves: The account of his initiation by the hermit and return to Lhasa from Bernard, Journal of Travels in Tibet, Part II, August 3, 1937, 175a–177a.

207   "external actions of daily living": Bernard, Journal of Travels in Tibet, Part II, August 10, 1937, 189a–189b.

207   agreed to sell him his for a very reasonable price: Bernard, Journal of Travels in Tibet, Part II, August 5, 9, 14, and 15, 1937; Theos Bernard, letters to Viola Bernard, August 9 and 15, 1937, Lhasa, VWBP 10:11.

208   printer commissioned to find the sixty-four-volume: Details of his collecting in Bernard, Journal of Travels in Tibet, Part II, August 21, 13, and 18, July 17, and August 3, 1937.

209   confiscated in lieu of back taxes: Bernard, Journal of Travels in Tibet, Part II, August 3, 1937, Lhasa, 174b.

209   around the neck of a dog and shooting it: Bernard, Journal of Travels in Tibet, Part III, "On the Road Back," September 23, 1937, 55.

209 the latest about Tucci: Theos Bernard, letters to Viola Bernard, August 5 and July 28, 1937, Lhasa, VWBP 10:11.

210 Tharchin's dedication to the mission: Theos Bernard, letters to Viola Bernard, July 24, August 11, September 6, 1937, VWBP 10:11; Bernard, Journal of Travels in Tibet, Part II, August 4, 1937, 178b.

211 invited Theos to a three-day performance: Bernard, Journal of Travels in Tibet, Part II, August 15, 16, and 17, 1937, 199b–204a; Theos Bernard, letter to Viola Bernard, August 15, 1937, VWBP 10:11; Bernard, *Penthouse of the Gods*, 185.

212 Japanese forces in downtown Shanghai: Theos writes in his journal the news was of the attack of Nanking. However, it was the beginning of the battle of Shanghai that was raging on the date of his journal entry, August 16, 1937. The battle of Nanking began in October 1937.

214 Theos got the reply he had hoped for: Theos Bernard, letter to Viola Bernard, August 18, 1937, VWBP 10:11; Bernard, Journal of Travels in Tibet, Part II, August 20, 1937, 211a.

215 series of eighty-nine *thangkas:* There were said to be eighty-nine; however, no. 24 and nos. 79–89 (eleven in all) were missing. Bernard, Journal of Travels in Tibet, Part II, September 3, 1937.

215 "Never before has anyone ever": Ibid., September 8, 1937, 249b.

215 sacred charm block: Descriptions of charm and bone dress from Bernard, Journal of Travels in Tibet, Part II, August 27, August 26, September 2, 1937, Lhasa.

216 all agreed this was a prize collection: Theos Bernard, Journal of Travels in Tibet, Part II, August 27 and September 1, 1937.

217 Tsarong tried to convince Theos to delay his departure: Theos Bernard, Journal of Travels in Tibet, Part II, September 8, 1937, Lhasa, 248a.

217 insisted on throwing a three-day party: Bernard, Journal of Travels in Tibet, Part II, August 26 and 27, September 10 and 13, August 28; Theos Bernard, letter to Viola Bernard, August 29, 1937, VWBP 10:11.

218   his past lives as a teacher in Tibet: Bernard, Journal of Travels in Tibet, Part II, August 28, 1937, 227a.

218   Cutting began in 1928 cultivating a friendship: Meyer and Brysac, *Tournament of Shadows*, 493–503.

219   the first to welcome Cutting back to Lhasa: Theos Bernard, letters to Viola Bernard, September 6, July 8, and August 18, 1937, VWBP 10:11; Bernard, Journal of Travels in Tibet, Part II, September 4, 5, and 6, 1937.

221   Beginning his last week in Lhasa: Bernard, Journal of Travels in Tibet, Part II, September 11, 6, 9, and 2, 1937.

221   countless details to settle with Tsarong: Bernard, Journal of Travels in Tibet, Part II, September 12, 13, and 6, 1937.

222   gave Theos a thorough razzing: Bernard, Journal of Travels in Tibet, Part II, September 8, 6, and 9, 1937, Lhasa.

223   "asked that I return to Tibet soon": Bernard, Journal of Travels in Tibet, Part II, September 14, 1937, 260a.

223   mobilizing to oppose the heavily armed: Bernard, Journal of Travels in Tibet, Part II, September 12, 1937, 256a.

223   no troops to spare for his escort:. Goldstein, *A History of Modern Tibet*, 296.

224   began at four-thirty in the morning: Bernard, Journal of Travels in Tibet, Part III, September 15 and 16, 1937, 1–2, 11.

224   a final visit with the regent: Bernard, Journal of Travels in Tibet, Part III, September 15, 1937, 3–4; Part II, August 30, 1937, 231b; Theos Bernard, letter to Viola Bernard, September 1, 1937, VWBP 10:11.

225   folded accordion-wise across its length: Robert Warren Clark, "The Bernard-Murray Tibetan Collection at the University of California, Berkeley," April 3, 2003, 29.

225   "To His Excellency the great Mr. Roosevelt": Translation likely by Gegen Tharchin, BANC 4:34.

226 again offered to go to America: Theos Bernard, letter to Viola Bernard, September 1937, Shigatse, VWBP 10:12.

226 already midafternoon: Bernard, Journal of Travels in Tibet, Part III, September 15, 1937, Lhasa, 6.

227 "I damn near cracked right there": Ibid.

CHAPTER 10: THE TREASURE OF PADMASAMBHAVA

228 as swift as the Colorado: Account of his journey from Lhasa to Shigatse from Theos Bernard, letters to Viola Bernard, unknown day in September, October 21, 1937, VWBP 10:12; Bernard, Journal of Travels in Tibet, Part III, September 20 and 22, 1937, 35, 49.

229 The headman was expecting them: Bernard, Journal of Travels in Tibet, Part III, September 22–24 and 27, 1937.

230 an official from Tashilhunpo monastery: Bernard, Journal of Travels in Tibet, Part III, September 24, 28, and 30, 1937; Theos Bernard, letter to Viola Bernard, unknown day, September 1937, Shigatse, VWBP 10:12.

231 "the prize of this Tibetan trip": Bernard, Journal of Travels in Tibet, Part III, October 3, 1937, 114–17; Stewart Robertson, "White Lama—Part One," *Family Circle*, April 22, 1938, 16.

232 keeping other beggars away from parties: Taring, *Daughter of Tibet*, 25.

234 he decided he would make an offer: Bernard, Journal of Travels in Tibet, Part III, October 4, 1937, 121–22.

235 letter of introduction he carried from Tsarong: The account of his stay in Sakya from Bernard, Journal of Travels in Tibet, Part III, October 7–9, 1937.

236 Sakya rule lasted about a hundred years: "Brief History of Tibet," http://www.friends-of-tibet.org.nz/tibet.html.

237 To the Most Illustrious King of America: Translation likely by Gegen Tharchin, BANC 4:34.

238 "Poor old Franklin": Theos Bernard, letter to Viola Bernard, undated, Kalimpong, VWBP 10:12.

238 fastest way to Khampa Jong: Bernard, Journal of Travels in Tibet, Part III, October 9–10, 1937, 154–62.

239 over the somewhat tamer Kongra La: Bernard, Journal of Travels in Tibet, Part III, October 11–12, 166–70.

241 still twelve miles to their destination for the night: Bernard, Journal of Travels in Tibet, Part III, October 12, 1937, 171–73.

242 When the muleteers arrived: Bernard, Journal of Travels in Tibet, Part III, October 13, 1937, 174–75.

242 They got as far as Chungtang: Bernard, Journal of Travels in Tibet, Part III, October 13–15, 178–88.

243 Sitting alone on the porch of the dak bungalow: Bernard, Journal of Travels in Tibet, Part III, October 15, 1937, 189.

245 waited the recent letters from Viola: Theos Bernard, letter to Viola Bernard, undated, Kalimpong, VWBP: 10:12; Viola Bernard, letters to Theos Bernard, September 28, 1937, Nyack, NY, VWBP 11:3; undated, 1937, BANC 3:48.

246 Tharchin was still in Gyantse, sick in bed: Theos Bernard, letter to Viola Bernard, October 24, 1937, Kalimpong, VWBP 10:12.

247 £50 to write a three-thousand-word story: Theos Bernard, letters to Viola Bernard, undated, October 24 and 26, 1937, VWBP 10:12. Historical currency values: £1 = U.S. $5 in 1937, £50 = $3,198 in 2003 (using the Consumer Price Index, the most commonly used comparison), EconomicHistory.Net, http://eh.net/hmit/compare.

248 Her mother had died: Theos Bernard, letter to Viola Bernard, October 24, 1937, Kalimpong, VWBP 10:12.

248 first-ever footage of the sky burial: Theos Bernard, letter to Viola Bernard, October 26, 1937, VWBP 10:12.

249 almost $2,400 in today's currency: In 1937, 2.68 Indian rupees = U.S. $1, 500 rupees = $186 in 1937 = $2,380 in 2003 (using the Consumer Price Index, the most commonly used comparison), EconomicHistory.Net, http://eh.net/hmit/ compare.

249 cost almost $7,000: http://www.imperial-airways.com/Ops_passenger_rates _eng_aust.html.

249 greeted with this banner headline: "Young Explorer Writes the Greatest Adventure Story of the Year," *Daily Mail,* November 12, 1937, 13–16.

251 "including Douglas Fairbanks": Theos Bernard, letter to Viola Bernard, November 19, 1937, VWBP II:1.

251 leader of a Scottish missionary society: *Daily Mail* (Scotch edition), November 17, 1937.

252 "I am sold 100%": Theos Bernard, letter to Viola Bernard, November 18, 1937, London VWBP II:1.

253 "capable of carrying on his work": Theos Bernard, letter to Viola Bernard, August 9, 1937, VWBP 10:11.

253 possibility for developing airfields: Charles Lindbergh, letter to Theos Bernard, September 24, 1937, BANC 4:24.

254 the complications of his reunion with Viola: Theos Bernard, letters to Viola Bernard, n.d., London VWBP II:1.

255 redefined luxury afloat: Uncommon Journeys, http://uncommonjourneys.com/ pages/qmservice.htm.

256 written down in mystical verse: Theos Bernard, 91-page unpublished typescript translation of the life of Padmasambhava, HGPF, 32–35; Yeshe Tsogyal, *The Lotus-Born: The Life Story of Padmasambhava* (Boston: Shambhala, 1993), 34–40, 58.

258 "treasures in their minds": Robert A. F. Thurman, *The Tibetan Book of the the Dead* (New York: Bantam Books, 1994), 84.

259 "my dangers lie in the future": Theos Bernard, letter to Viola Bernard, November 1937, Calcutta, VWBP II:1.

CHAPTER 11: AMBASSADOR OF SHANGRI-LA

260 seven-hundred-word article: "Buddhist Worship in Tibet Pictured," *New York Times*, November 28, 1937, 47.

260 "too much vitality and effort to waste": Theos Bernard, letter to Viola Bernard, September 8, 1937, Nyack, NY, VWBP II:3.

261 Christmas in Arizona with his family: Theos Bernard, letters to Viola Bernard, December 17 and 30, 1937, VWBP II:1.

262 Theos met some of Glen's colleagues: Theos Bernard, letter to Viola Bernard, Los Angeles, January 1938, VWBP II:4.

263 "I could suit myself to your convenience": Letter of Maxwell Perkins to Theos Bernard, January 7, 1938; Maxwell Perkins to Carol Hill, January 25, 1938; Theos Bernard to Maxwell Perkins, January 24, 1938, ACSS, Author Files 12:1.

264 "We will store more memories away": Theos Bernard, letter to Viola Bernard, Tuesday, London VWBP II:1.

264 reporter Stewart Robertson visited Stepping Stones: Stewart Robertson, "White Lama—Part Two," *Family Circle*, April 29, 1938, 22.

264 "alternating between explosive heights": Viola Bernard, letter to Theos Bernard, Charleston, S.C., April (illegible, but probably first week of April) 1937, VWBP II:3.

265 "neither from emotional outburst": Ibid.

266 created a multimillion-dollar industry: Patricia Leigh Brown, "Some in Reno Say Do Not Put Asunder Artifacts of Divorce," *New York Times*, April 22, 2002.

267 joy of life in the strong arms: "New Freedom," *Time*, September 15, 1930.

267 "a sense of humor can feed on": Viola Bernard, letter to Louis S. Weiss, n.d. but in response to his letter of May 12, 1938, Lake Tahoe, VWBP II:18.

267 flung their wedding bands: Brown, "Some in Reno Say Do Not Put Asunder Artifacts of Divorce."

267 elegant Glenbrook Inn: Kimberly Danek Pinkson, "Sons and Daughters of the Pioneers," *Tahoe Quarterly*, http://www.tahoequarterly.com/articles/pioneers.aspx.

267 "suffering did not end": Louis S. Weiss, letter to Viola Bernard, May 12, 1938, VWBP II:18.

268 "absorbed in the breath of the universe": Theos Bernard, letter to Viola Bernard, May 17, 1938, WBBP II:4.

268 "wish Mr. Bernard would get on faster": Maxwell Perkins, letter to Carol Hill, March 3, 1938, ACSS 12:1.

269 the man who made Lawrence of Arabia famous: "Lowell Thomas," Wikipedia, http://en.wikipedia.org/w/index.php?title=Lowell_Thomas&oldid=141525102 (accessed June 30, 2007).

270 two months more after that before a plane arrived: "Richard E. Byrd II, 1888–1957, Byrd Antarctic Expedition 1933–35," http://www.south-pole.com/p0000107.htm.

270 "he felt that I should understand him": Theos Bernard, letter to Viola Bernard, May 29, 1938, VWBP II:4.

270 outside authorities to read "Tantrik Yoga": "Report of the Examining Committee on Mr. Theos C. Bernard's *Tantric Yoga* and Suggestions for Its Revision," n.d., Columbia University Philosophy Dept., BANC I:14.

271 "Mr. Bernard is merely at the thresh-hold": Theos Bernard, letter to Viola Bernard, May 29, 1938, VWBP 114; Clark, "The Bernard-Murray Tibetan Collection," 11.

272 packaging the dissertation with a popular book: Theos Bernard, letter to Maxwell Perkins, January 24, 1938; Maxwell Perkins, letter to Carol Hill, May 12, 1938, ACSS 12:1.

273   reached a circulation of three million: Erwin V. Johanningmeier, "St. James Encyclopedia of Pop Culture," http://findarticles.com/p/articles/mi_g1epc/is _tov/ai_2419100416/pg_3.

273   "Theos Bernard . . . is a Buddhist lama": Robertson, "White Lama—Part One," "White Lama—Part Two."

274   attempts to deliver the letters: Theos Bernard, letter to President Franklin Roosevelt, January 24, 1938; George T. Summerline, Chief, Division of Protocol, Department of State, Washington, letter to Theos Bernard, February 4, 1938; William B. Chamberlain, secretary to Theos Bernard, letter to Frederic A. Delano, April 16, 1938; Frederic A Delano, letter to Theos Bernard, April 9, 1938, BANC.

275   reflects diplomatic calculations: Meyer and Brysac, *Tournament of Shadows*, 504.

276   Thomas offered to help arrange a meeting: Theos Bernard, letter to Carol Hill, February 6, 1940, ACSS 12:1.

277   Viola had the lawyers include a clause: Viola Bernard, letter to Louis S. Weiss, April 5, 1937, VWBP 11:18; Theos Bernard, letter to Viola Bernard, July 19, 1938, VWBP 11:4.

277   preview at Manhattan's exclusive Lotos Club: Theos Bernard, letters to Viola Bernard, July 22 and June 9, 1938, and undated letter from New York to Viola in New York, VWBP 11:4.

278   eight hundred pages of a first draft: Theos Bernard, letters to Viola Bernard, July 22, 1938, July 1938, VWBP 11:4; Maxwell Perkins, letter to Theos Bernard, August 3, 1938, ACSS 12:1.

278   published ten novels of his own: "John Cournos," Wikipedia, http://en .wikipedia.org/w/index.php?title=John_Cournos&oldid=193879050 (accessed April 10, 2008).

278   "Penthouse of the Gods" national lecture tour: Printed itinerary for tour, VWBP 11:10.

278   tour's brochure cover: Lecture Brochure from W. Colston Leigh, Inc., VWBP 11:10; Bernard, "Penthouse of the Gods" lecture script, BANC 2:25.

281 a blockbuster film: *Los Angeles Times*, "Capra Film Reissue to Be Timely," June 17, 1940, p. 12.

281 title cards at the opening of the film: Tim Dirks, review of the film *Lost Horizon*, http://www.filmsite.org/losth.htm.

281 book supplies a number of details: James Hilton, *Lost Horizon* (New York: Perennial, 2004), 139–47.

282 Americans believed Hitler was driven by ambition: "Survey Finds U.S. Fears Nazi Attack," *New York Times*, September 29, 1939, 13.

283 lust for power must perish: Hilton, *Lost Horizon*, 164–65.

283 "Humanity Can Be Saved!": James Hilton, "Humanity Can Be Saved! An Easter Challenge to a Groping World," *Los Angeles Times*, April 17, 1938, 12.

284 "exists in fact as well as in the fancy": "Modern Young American Also Tibetan Lama," *San Francisco Chronicle*, January 5, 1938, 1.

285 "inside story of Lost Horizon": *Reno Gazette*, advertisement, March 21, 1939.

285 "The priests of fabulous Tibet": "White Lama Tells of Old Prophecy, Prediction Made That New Sovereign Will Be Found in West," *Pittsburg Telegraph*, May 14, 1939. There is a similar prophecy attributed to Padmasambha (Guru Rinpoche) that is frequently repeated these days: "When the iron bird flies, and horses run on wheels, the Tibetan people will be scattered like ants across the World, and the Dharma will come to the land of the red-faced people." Although Padmasambhava is always mentioned as the source, I have not found anyone who has been able to trace it back to an authentic text.

286 "very good book at least": Maxwell Perkins, letter to Carol Hill, July 5, 1938, ACSS 12:1.

287 "gained contact with an old soul": Bernard, *Penthouse of the Gods*, 337–38.

288 initial print run of 3,270 copies: Manufacturing Records 1902–1955, ACSS, Box 2, B-Be; Maxwell Perkins, letter to Theos Bernard, April 19, 1940; Maxwell Perkins, letter to Carol Hill, January 29, 1940; ACSS 12:1.

288 book's literary shortcomings: Katherine Woods, "An American in Lhasa's Shrines," *New York Times*, April 2, 1939, 97.

288 at the Los Angeles Public Library: "The Book Parade, What Los Angeles Is Reading, According to the Los Angeles Public Library," *Los Angeles California Express*, July 8, 1939.

289 "the Timeless Spiritual Science": Theos Bernard, letter to Maxwell Perkins, January 26, 1939; Maxwell Perkins, letter to Theos Bernard, January 30, 1939, ACSS 12:1.

289 "odd intervals in the diary": Bernard, Journal of Travels in Tibet, Part II, July 31, 1937, Lhasa, 166b.

291 "The ultimate success of all Yoga": Theos Bernard, *Heaven Lies Within Us* (New York: Charles Scribner's Sons, 1939), 294.

292 could suspend breathing for a full six minutes: Theos Bernard, letters to Viola Bernard, January 24, March 28, and April 27, 1937, Kalimpong; VWBP 10:10.

293 during the first-ever cataloging: John Brady, director, Asian Classics Input Project, New York, interview with author, April 3, 2008. Since their discovery in St. Petersburg the images have been again widely seen as the logo for the Yoga Studies Institute, www.yogastudiesinstitute.org. The title of the text in which the drawings are found is *The Illustrated Asanas of Naropa (Naro Trulkor Peri) from: A Collection of Alphabets and Assorted Illustrations from India, China, Russia, Kashmir, Nepal, and Mongolia (Peri Namdrang)*. The text is written by the Tibetan lama Ngawang Lobsang Tenpay Gyeltsen, the Changlung Pandita (1770–1846). The title and description are found in *Tibetan Heart Yoga, Working Manual 5: The Guru Bliss Series*, by Geshe Michael Roach and Lama Christie McNally.

294 reprinted in small-press, paperback editions: A small South African publisher has in recent decades kept it circulating by reprinting *Heaven Lies Within Us* as a paperback, and some Yoga websites selling books still have it on their list of recommended texts for teachers.

294 "registering a deeper consciousness": Pierre Health Studio brochure draft, 1939, BANC 3:38.

295 "not dealing with a religion": Theos Bernard, lecture notes, Pierre Health Studio Yoga class, October 19, 1939, BANC 2:27.

295 ranged in age from nineteen to seventy: Stewart Robertson, "The White Lama on Yoga," *Family Circle*, August 25, 1939, 15.

296 "laws pertaining to the coming and going": Pierre Health Studio brochure draft, 1939, BANC 3:38.

296 Lord Buddha personally directed: Theos Bernard, "The Tibetan Wheel of Life," *Review of Religion*, May 1939.

297 "antidote to ignorance is wisdom": Theos Bernard, lecture notes, Pierre Health Studio Yoga classes, October 31, 1939, November 14, 1939, BANC 2:27.

297 "So many readers have written to the *Family Circle*": Robertson, "The White Lama on Yoga."

298 "beneficial for this and the next life": Tsarong, letters to Theos Bernard, June 4, 1938, BANC 4:15.

299 "changes, little short of cataclysmic": Theos Bernard, "The Peril of Tibet," *Asia*, September 1939, 500.

299 working title of *Tibetan Pilgrimage*: Maxwell Perkins, letter to Carol Hill, January 25, 1938; Maxwell Perkins, letters to Theos Bernard, February 28 and April 19, 1940; Theos Bernard, letter to Carol Hill, February 6, 1940, ACSS 12:1.

CHAPTER 12: TIBETLAND

301 into a hostel for refugees: Viola's Life Chronology from VWBP 4:1.

302 Hanna decided to divorce him: Sharon Crawford, *Ganna Walska Lotusland: The Garden and Its Creators* (San Rafael, CA: Companion Press, 2006), 7.

302 The divorce financed her move in 1914 to Paris: Ibid. *Lotusland.*

302 performance name Ganna Walska: Ibid., 8.

302 on her second visit to his office: "Cochran's Alimony to Walska Fixed," *New York Times*, May 2, 1922.

302 audience pelted the stage: Jay Robert Nash, *Makers and Breakers of Chicago* (Chicago: Academy Chicago, 1985), 184–87.

303 "received enlightenment by the hours": Ganna Walska, *Always Room at the Top* (New York: Richard R. Smith, 1943), 36.

303 Madame Walska had a voice the world had to hear: Nash, *Makers and Breakers of Chicago*, 184–87.

303 $500,000 in cash: Theodore Roosevelt Gardner II, *Lotusland: A Photographic Odyssey* (Santa Barbara: Allen A. Knoll, 1995), 114.

303 McCormick had fallen in love: "Harold McCormick Divorces Walska," *New York Times*, October 11, 1931, 24.

304 "the richest bachelor in the world": "Cochran's Alimony to Walska Fixed," *New York Times*, May 2, 1922; Crawford, *Ganna Walska Lotusland*, 10–12; Gardner, *Lotusland*, 115–16.

305 "please sing in your natural voice": Nash, *Makers and Breakers of Chicago*, 184–87.

305 "amicable financial arrangement": "Cochran's Alimony to Walska Fixed," *New York Times*, May 2, 1922; "Harold McCormick Divorces Walska," *New York Times*, October 11, 1931, 24.

305 *Citizen Kane* was inspired: "Citizen Kane," Wikipedia, http://en.wikipedia.org/w/index.php?title=Citizen_Kane&oldid=150825350 (accessed August 13, 2007).

306 "laughter broke across the stalls": "Audience Titters at Walska's Gilda, Opera Hopes Are Dimmed," *New York Times*, June 27, 1923.

306 she must not appear again: "Ganna Walska Fails As Butterfly," *New York Times*, January 29, 1925; "May Let Walska Sing, but Mayor of Nice Wants 50,000-Franc Guarantee Against Loss," *New York Times*, March 8, 1925, 27.

306 "courteous but unencouraging silence": "Mme. Ganna Walska Sings for New

York; Analysis of a Serious Effort by an Artist Who Has Striven Long and Ardently," *New York Times*, February 13, 1929, 21.

307   charged Madame Walska with desertion: "Chicago Report That McCormick Plans to Sue Ganna Walska for Divorce," *New York Times*, November 13, 1927.

307   "One may overtake me at any time": "Notes Here and Afield," *New York Times*, June 24, 1934.

307   a reclusive British electrical research scientist: "British Mentor of Death Ray Dies," *New York Times*, September 12, 1941, 21.

307   announcement of the London wedding: "Ganna Walska Bride of British Inventor," *New York Times*, January 26, 1938, 25.

308   government officials pleaded: Quoted in Crawford, *Ganna Walska Lotusland*, 16.

308   "everything about him was negative": Quoted in Gardner, *Lotusland*, 117.

308   "with a touching sadness": Quoted in Crawford, *Ganna Walska Lotusland*, 13–16.

309   friend invited her to an evening lecture: Crawford, *Ganna Walska Lotusland*, 17.

309   "could not yet face my tomorrow": Walska, *Always Room at the Top*, 488–92.

309   "I thank Fate": Ganna Walska, letter to Theos Bernard, undated, BANC 4:1.

310   insisted repeatedly that she underwrite the project: Theos Bernard, draft statement prepared for deposition during hearings for divorce from Ganna Walska, Santa Barbara, May 1946, BANC 4:13.

310   Theos negotiated a distressed price: Account of the real estate transactions in Ibid.

311   one of the finer estates in Montecito: Crawford, *Ganna Walska Lotusland*, 25–27.

311   "greatest literary undertakings of this century": Theos Bernard, "Lecture on the Value of Translating Tibetan Literature," Santa Barbara, CA, September 29, 1941, BANC 2: 29.

312 "the fundamentals of all the truths of human existence": Theos Bernard, Academy organizing papers, BANC 3:42.

312 iconoclastic incarnate Tibetan lama Gendun Chopel: S. K. Jinorasa, letter to Theos Bernard, December 24, 1941, BANC 4:38.

313 ideally suited to be the first Tibetan Lama: Jeffrey Hopkins, *Sex, Orgasm, and the Mind of Clear Light: The Sixty-four Arts of Gay Male Love* (Berkeley, CA: North Atlantic Books, 1998), ix; Donald S. Lopez Jr., *The Madman's Middle Way: Reflection on Reality of the Tibetan Monk Gendun Chopel* (Chicago: University of Chicago Press, 2006), 15.

314 Theos ordered hundreds of volumes: Alan Watts, *In My Own Way* (New York: Pantheon, 1972), 169.

315 "independent of all servants": Crawford, *Ganna Walska Lotusland*, 18.

315 replanting the estate's gardens: Ibid., 19.

316 "finally I found a companion": Quoted in Ibid., 18.

316 Theos wrote and asked about her progress: Theos Bernard, letters to Ganna Walska, January 23 and 17, 1942; Ganna Walska, letter to Theos Bernard, January 20, 1942; Theos Bernard, letter to Ganna Walska, January 24, 1942; Ganna Walska, letter to Theos Bernard, February 4, 1942, BANC 4:1.

316 placating the other: Theos Bernard, draft statement prepared for deposition during divorce hearings, May 1946, BANC 4:13; Crawford, *Ganna Walska Lotusland*, 19.

317 attorney drew up a prenuptial agreement: Crawford, *Ganna Walska Lotusland*, 19.

317 classified Theos as 4-F: Theos Bernard, lecture notes, October 23, 1942, February 18, 1943, BANC 2:31.

317 six months of living room lectures: Theos Bernard, lecture transcripts, January 7, 1943, February, 1943, October 29, 1942, November 12, 1942, December 3, 1942, BANC 2:30–31.

319 "which destroys death": Theos Bernard, *Hatha Yoga: The Report of a Personal Experience* (New York: Columbia University Press, 1944), 45.

319 "personally verified account of Hatha Yoga": Vaman R. Kokatnur, "Review of Hatha Yoga, The Report of a Personal Experience," *Review of Religion*, March 1945.

320 continued to develop the estate's gardens: Crawford, *Ganna Walska Lotusland*, 29.

320 properties began to deteriorate: Bernard, draft deposition for divorce.

321 "you never realize the value of money": Ganna Walska, letter to Theos Bernard, October 1, 1943, BANC 4:2.

321 Ganna's box in the famous Golden Horseshoe: "Brilliant Throng at Opera Opening," *New York Times*, November 23, 1943, 18.

321 "dear absent minded of realistic things boy": Ganna Walska, letter to Theos Bernard, November 4, 1945, BANC 4:4–8.

321 lampooned for the first time in his career: "The Disappointed Diva Yodeling Now with a Yogi," *American Weekly*, December 12, 1943, 5; "Ganna Walska Fabulous Glamor-Glitterer, Who Won and Chucked Multi-Millionaires, Turns from Bad Singing to Weird Cults," *Sunday Mirror* magazine section, January 10, 1943, B–D.

323 "you are not to rob your library": Theos Bernard, letter to Helen Graham Park, probably about December 1, 1943, BANC 4:2. It is marked as Thursday, but otherwise undated. Ganna Walska returned it to Theos (mistakenly sent to her on December 6) but with no year noted. Theos refers to finishing a draft of the Tibetan grammar book by the end of the year, and the following spring, 1944, he tells his agent he has finished that book, so the year must be 1943.

323 "*never* informed me that you have other friends": Ganna Walska, handwritten letter inserted with letter Theos Bernard wrote to Helen Graham Park, BANC 4:2.

324 could be dangerous for his heart: Cardiological Examination of Mr. Theos C. Bernard, Hotel Pierre, Fifth Avenue, New York, by Milton J. Raisbeck, M.D., January 11 and 17, 1941, VWBP 11:19.

324 Ganna was unsure where he was staying: Ganna Walska, letters to Theos Bernard, February 14 and 18, March 1 and 5, 1944, BANC 4:3.

325 bleak grip of paranoia: Ganna Walska, letters to Theos Bernard, March 18 and April 17, 1945, BANC 4:4–8.

326 "bridge the gap between the seen and the unseen": Theos Bernard, *Hindu Philosophy* (New York: Philosophical Library, 1947), 2–3.

327 Glen had written his own 120-page: Glen Bernard, "Selective Treatise on the Theory and Practice of Yoga," BANC 7:9–23.

327 "do not doubt that your mother": Ganna Walska, letter to Theos Bernard, April 22, 1945, New York, BANC 4:4–8β.

327 cut him out of her will: Ganna Walska, letter to Theos Bernard, March 18, 1945, BANC 4:4–8.

327 complications of arranging a second printing: Columbia University Press, letter to Theos Bernard, March 21, 1945; Rider and Co., letter to Columbia University Press, May 24, 1945, BANC.

328 Ganna explained her view: Ganna Walska, letters to Theos Bernard, March 17 and 18, 1945, BANC 4:4–8.

328 "The paper problem grows steadily worse": Columbia University Press, letter to Theos Bernard, April 14, 1945, BANC.

329 felt safe enough to reveal the truth: Ganna Walska, letters to Theos Bernard, March 18, April 17 and 11, 1945, BANC 4:4–8.

330 does he lose his yogi's equanimity: Theos Bernard, letter to Ganna Walska, n.d. [1944], BANC 4:1.

330 "I need to be *alone*": Ganna Walska, letters to Theos Bernard, April 17, 1945, May 11, 1946, New York, BANC 4: 4–10.

331 greeted instead by a process server: "Divorce Decree Granted to Mme. Ganna Walska," *Los Angeles Times*, July 14, 1946.

331   asked that the court restrain Madame Walska from selling: Theos Bernard, draft deposition for divorce hearings, BANC 4:13.

331   attorneys filed their answer and cross-complaint: "Ganna Walska Fights Mate's Support Suit," *Los Angeles Times*, July 9, 1946, A1; "Walska's Husband Will Accept $1500 Monthly," July 13, 1946, 8; "Divorce Decree Granted to Mme. Ganna Walska," July 14, 1946; Answer of Ganna Walska to Complaint for Separate Maintenance of Theos Bernard in California Superior Court, July 8, 1946, BANC 4:13.

333   all now the property of Madame Ganna Walska: In 1996, fifty years after the divorce, a museum-quality collection of about five hundred devotional objects, shrines, Buddhas, bodhisattvas, incense vessels, *phurbas*, paintings, and sculptures, described in the catalog as having been collected as tribute by the maharaja of Kashmir from passing high lamas and purchased by Dr. Theos Bernard, were sold at auction by a New York art gallery. The collection was being liquidated by a Buddhist group that had received it as part of a bequest at the death of Madame Ganna Walska.

CHAPTER 13: GONE TO THE OTHER SIDE

334   on waiting lists for five different ships: Theos Bernard, letter to Glen Bernard, August 26, 1946, BANC 3:47.

334   "When you are in India and there is free time": Theos Bernard, letter to Helen Graham Park, probably about December 1, 1943, BANC 4:2.

334   abandoned by her father shortly after her birth: Biographical information about Helen Graham Park from notes of interview with Helen's niece, Barbara Graham, on April 1, 2004. Helen's younger half brother, John junior, also studied architecture and took over his father's firm. He is best known for designing the world's first shopping center and was a principal designer of Seattle's iconic Space Needle, built for the 1962 World's Fair.

336   betray no conspiracy to run off together: Excerpts of letters from Theos Bernard to Helen Graham Park, 1945, HGPF, "HGP—Notes," F.9.

336   Hoping to make the trip pay for itself: Theos Bernard, letter to Glen Bernard, August 26, 1946, BANC 3:47.

337 relationship between Theos and Helen had developed: Theos Bernard, letter to Glen Bernard, September 14 and 19, August 26, 1946, BANC 3:47; Theos Bernard, letter to John Mock, September 19, 1947, BANC 4:65.

338 "much worse than it is reported at home": Theos Bernard, letter to Glen Bernard, Almora, India, undated except for "the 20th, I think," BANC 3:47; Theos Bernard, letter to John Mock, January 26, 1947, BANC 4:65.

339 visited there the ashram of Swami Sivananda: Theos Bernard, letter to Glen Bernard, undated except for "the 20th, I think," BANC 3:47.

340 loved "more than any other place": Theos Bernard, letter to Vera McDonald, June 27, 1939, BANC.

340 Tibetan lamas in Kalimpong for the winter: Theos Bernard, letter to John Mock, January 26, 1947, BANC 4:65; Theos Bernard, letter to Glen Bernard, February 15, 1947, BANC 3:47.

341 civil unrest in Lhasa was set off by a power struggle: Goldstein, *A History of Modern Tibet*, 359, 437, 488–510.

342 "Am I glad that I am not there": Theos Bernard, letter to Ashbel R. Welch, May 6, 1947, BANC 4:47.

342 satisfaction that circumstances forced them: Theos Bernard, letter to Glen Bernard, June 27, 1947, BANC 3:47.

342 British kept intelligence files on all foreigners: A file with the curious title "Travelers: Theos Bernard, an American 'Imposter' Nov 1937–Feb 1941" contained reports from Basil Gould, Hugh Richardson, and Norbu Dhondup. British Library, India Office Records: Political and Secret Department Records, Political (External) Collection 36: Tibet, FILE–Coll 36/31 Exploration by Mr Theos Bernard.

344 Tharchin was summoned to Gould's office: Theos Bernard, letter to Glen Bernard, June 27, 1947, BANC 3:47.

344 "will serve me to the end of my time": Theos Bernard, letters to Glen Bernard, February 15 and June 27, 1947, BANC 3:47.

345 twenty-nine-year-old Dhardo Rinpoche: Theos doesn't name the lama but from

his description it must have been Dhardo Rinpoche. "Dhardo Rimpoche," Wikipedia, http://en.wikipedia.org/w/index.php?title=Dhardo_Rimpoche& oldid=157131793 (accessed October 26, 2007).

345 "Even if I were living in Lhasa": Theos Bernard, letter to Glen Bernard, March 14, 1947, BANC 3:47.

346 great eleventh-century Indian pandita Atisha: See Pabongka Rinpoche, *Liberation in Our Hands, Part I,* transl. Sermey Khensur Lobsang Tharchin and Artemus B. Engle (Howell, NJ: Mahayana Sutra and Tantra Press, 1990), 30–65.

346 the first-ever rendering of the Lamrim outline: Theos Bernard, "Key to Understanding Tibetan Literature," HGPF F.4.

347 learning to think like a bodhisattva: See Pabongka Rinpoche, *Liberation in Our Hands, Part III,* transl. Sermey Khensur Lobsang Tharchin and Artemus B. Engle (Howell, NJ: Mahayana Sutra and Tantra Press, 2001), 208.

347 as dangerous as a child jumping on a wild horse: Ibid., 303.

348 Theos kept to a strict routine: Theos Bernard, letters to Glen Bernard, March 14, June 27, February 15, March 10, 1947, and undated letter fragment, Kalimpong, BANC 3:47.

348 cross-referencing in other medical texts: The drafts of Helen Graham Park's medical translations, archived in HGPF F.6.

349 Just as some important logic texts arrived: Theos Bernard, letters to Glen Bernard, March 10, August 7, 1947, undated letter fragment, Kalimpong, BANC 3:47; Theos Bernard, letter to Ashbel R. Welch, Kalimpong, May 6, 1947, BANC 4:47.

350 haunted by the specter of Direct Action Day: Dominique Lapierre and Larry Collins, *Freedom at Midnight* (New Delhi: Vikas Publishing, 1997), 32–35, 137, 209–11. Read this masterly work cover to cover for an unparalleled account of the partition of India.

352 spent their days buying supplies: Theos Bernard, letter to Glen Bernard, Calcutta, August 7, 1947, BANC 3:47.

353 advice of the stars was sought by maharajas: Lapierre and Collins, *Freedom at Midnight*, 209.

353 richly detailed analysis of the cosmic forces: Theos Bernard, Hindu Horoscope, HGPF F.2.

353 sent with them one of his own servants: Hisao Kimura as told to Scott Berry, *Japanese Agent in Tibet* (London: Serindia Publications, 1990), 154.

353 made their way to the Calcutta train station: Theos Bernard, letter to Glen Bernard, August 14, 1947, BANC 3:47.

354 glided into Amritsar's redbrick railway station: Ibid.; diary notes of Helen Graham Park, "Kulu Notes," 10–11, HGPF F.12.

355 plotting the new international boundary: Lapierre and Collins, *Freedom at Midnight*, 244, 266, 270, 343, 358–62, 378.

358 the Valley of the Gods: Helen Graham Park, "Kulu Notes," 12, HGPF F.12; Theos Bernard, letter to Glen Bernard, August 14, 1947, BANC 3:47.

358 the famous Roerich family: Theos Bernard, letter to Glen Bernard, August 14, 1947, BANC 3:47; Meyer and Brysac, *Tournament of Shadows*, 470–71.

359 forced to spend the entire winter: Meyer and Brysac, *Tournament of Shadows*, 469.

360 official transfer of sovereignty would occur that night: Theos Bernard, letter to Glen Bernard, August 14, 1947, BANC 3:47; Lapierre and Collins, *Freedom at Midnight*, 210–11, 309, 341.

362 Theos began packing for a three-week trip: Theos Bernard, letter to Glen Bernard, August 14, 1947, BANC 3:47; "A Preliminary Presumptive Report of Death, Note on the Disappearance of Dr. Theos Bernard 1947," American embassy, New Delhi, India, mailed to Helen Graham Park on March 1, 1950, BANC 4:68; Helen Graham Park, letter to American consul, New Delhi, September 24, 1947, BANC 4:68.

363 A dak postal runner came through camp: Helen Graham Park, letter to Glen Bernard, August 27, 1947, BANC 4:68.

366 Helen did write to Glen describing her routine: Helen Graham Park, letter to Glen Bernard, August 27, 1947, BANC 4:68.

366 the arbiter of all the traditions and conventions: Molu Ram Thakur, *Myths, Rituals and Beliefs in Himachal Pradesh* (New Delhi: Indus Publishing, 1997), 68.

367 None of India's political leaders: The best proof of that was the fact that still joining Helen for afternoon tea was the Austrian-born wife of one of the Moslem League's—and the new nation of Pakistan's—most important leaders. She was the beautiful, twenty-seven-year-old Vickie Noon, wife of Sir Feroz Khan Noon, the Oxford-educated, former Indian high commissioner in England who was soon to be appointed by Jinnah as Pakistan's special envoy to the world's major powers. Feroz Khan Noon owned a villa near Katrain, and nothing could be more telling about how blithely the leadership undertook the division of Punjab than the fact that one of Pakistan's most important officials sent his wife to their vacation home deep within Hindu territory to rest from her work as a high-level organizer for the Moslem League. She was forced to escape the Kulu Valley in disguise.

367 "Hindus leading the native mountaineers into killing and looting": Helen Graham Park, letter to Theos Bernard's half brother Marvene Gordon, February 28, 1949; Helen Graham Park, letter to American consul, New Delhi, September 24, 1947, BANC 4:68.

367 outfitters traveling with Theos would be in grave danger: "Note on the Disappearance of Dr. Theos Bernard 1947," American embassy, New Delhi, BANC 4:68; Helen Graham Park, letter to Glen Bernard, August 27, 1947, BANC 4:68.

367 Helen met a parade of dozens of Muslim captives: Helen Graham Park, "Kulu Notes," 12, 19, HGPF F.12.

368 "the Beas was littered with dead bodies": Ishtiaq Ahmed, "Forced Migration and Ethnic Cleansing in Lahore in 1947: Some First Person Accounts," Department of Political Science, Stockholm University, June 15, 2004, 23.

368 Boundary Force had been specially selected: Lapierre and Collins, *Freedom at Midnight*, 272.

368 for the British to be molested: Ibid., 412; Helen Graham Park, "Kulu Notes," 12, HGPF F.12.

368 "Trouble at border": Ibid.; Helen Graham Park, letter to American consul, New Delhi, September 24, 1947, BANC 4:68.

369 no end to the afflictions: Lapierre and Collins, *Freedom at Midnight*, 271, 429–30.

370 for Captain Wilson to cross: Helen Graham Park, "Kulu Notes," HGPF F.12; "Note on the Disappearance of Dr. Theos Bernard 1947," American embassy, New Delhi, BANC 4:68.

370 she eagerly packed to join the evacuation: Helen Graham Park, "Kulu Notes," HGPF F.12; Helen Graham Park, letter to Marvene Gordon, February 28, 1949, BANC 4:68.

371 "So far she has only used a little stick": Helen Graham Park, "Kulu Notes," F.12; Helen Graham Park, letter to Marvene Gordon, February 28, 1949, BANC 4:68.

371 scale of the flight of Sikhs and Hindus: Lapierre and Collins, *Freedom at Midnight*, 370–71, 402.

372 collapse of the Punjab civil administration: Lapierre and Collins, *Freedom at Midnight*, 429, 431.

373 Helen sent a telegram to him: Helen Graham Park, letter to Henry F. Grady, American ambassador, New Delhi, November 10, 1947; Howard Donovan, counselor of embassy, American embassy, New Delhi, India, letter to Helen Graham Park, December 5, 1947, BANC 4:68.

374 began her letter to Dr. Runes with an explanation: Helen Graham Park, letter to Dr. Dagobert Runes, November 5, 1947, BANC 4:68.

374 publisher in New York had received a letter: "Theos Bernard Reported Alive," *New York Times*, November 17, 1947; Helen Bernard, letter to Howard Donovan, February 10, 1948, BANC 4:68.

375 wrote two letters to Howard Donovan: Helen Bernard, letter to Howard Donovan, February 10, 1948, BANC 4:68.

376 "we are not referring purely to a historical person": Chogyam Trungpa, *Crazy Wisdom* (Boston and London: Shambala, 1991), 99–101.

377   "definitive biography is told by each person": "Oasis of Liberation," (1999, Ngagyur Nyingma Institute, India) published on Internet by Muktinath Foundation International, http://www.muktinath.org/buddhism/padmasambhava1 .htm.

377   had a different story to tell about it: Helen Graham Park, letter to American consul, New Delhi, September 24, 1947; Helen Graham Park, letter to Howard Donovan, November 14, 1948, BANC 4:68.

378   "explained beyond a reasonable doubt": Charles O. Thompson, letter to Howard Donovan, October 14, 1948; "Note on the Disappearance of Dr. Theos Bernard, 1947," BANC 4:68. Nicol Smith, an American writer who was in the area at the time, told the *New York Times*, just days after the story of Theos' disappearance broke, that he had heard repeatedly the same story. An Indian army officer as well reported that he heard a corroborating account from more than one source in Lahoul when he was stationed there the spring after Theos disappeared. And His Royal Highness Prince Peter of Denmark and Greece, after returning from doing archeological work in the area a year later, reported to the Explorer's Club in New York that he had heard there the same story.

379   Theos had often described his death to her: Notes of author's interview with Barbara Graham, April 1, 2004.

379   "We have this individual and a shot is fired": Theos Bernard, lecture transcript, December 3, 1942, BANC 2:30.

380   "Chandra passes through a totally barren": Quoted in "Chandra River," http://library.thinkquest.org/10131/lahaul_chandrariver.html.

EPILOGUE

382   a Sikh subinspector of the police: Tom Tyson, letter to Helen Bernard, June 21, 1948, BANC 4:68.

382   They set up a room for Theos: Viola Bernard, notes of visit with G. Eleanore Murray, VWBP 11:17.

382   "I have not yet reached the point": Helen Graham Park, letter to Howard Donovan, February 28, 1949, BANC 4:68.

383 "not possible to unearth the mystery": Government of India, Ministry of External Affairs, New Delhi, letter to American Embassy, Delhi, December 14, 1950.

383 legalities finally concluded with the release: Law Office of Henshey & Beeman, letters to Glen Bernard, June 12 and 24, 1957, BANC 8:4.

383 the love of her life: Notes of author's interview with Barbara Graham, April 1, 2004.

383 designing interiors for new office buildings: Ron Shelp, *Fallen Giant: The Amazing Story of Hank Greenberg and the History of AIG* (New York: Wiley, 2007), 73–74.

383 "He was a perfectionist": Ibid., 150.

384 she died in 1993: Notes of author's interview with Barbara Graham, April 1, 2004.

384 devoted to her distinguished career in psychiatry: Biographical Note to Archive Finding Aid, VWBP, http://library.cpmc.columbia.edu/hsl/archives/findingaids/bernard.html.

384 sold her tiaras to create: Sean K. MacPherson, "Enemy of the Average," *New York Times Magazine*, April 14, 2002, 80.

385 he invited a housekeeper, Gertrude Eleanore Murray: Clark, "The Bernard-Murray Tibetan Collection," 37.

385 Eleanore wrote letters to collectors: Ibid., 37–40.

385 bought by Westdeutsche Bibliothek: Letter from Westdeutsche Bibliothek, Marburg/Lahn, to G. Eleanore Murray, November 27, 1962, BANC 8:24–25.

386 had written to Theos about a past-life experience: Gene Smith, lecture at the Beinecke Library, Yale University, October 12, 2006, notes taken by Jessica Kung.

386 estimated to contain four thousand separate titles: Paul A. Draghi, "A Report on the Tibetan Books and Materials in the Beinecke Rare Book and Manuscript Library," June 1994, 4–6, 14–16.

387 deserves to be better used: Gene Smith, lecture at the Beinecke Library, Yale University, October 12, 2006, notes taken by Jessica Kung.

388 Glen Bernard died in a San Bernardino nursing home in 1976: Julian Don Alexander II, letter to Gilah Yelin Hirsch, June 19, 1990, from the collection of Mr. Alexander.

388 and named her as heir to the large remaining collection: Goldsmid & Allen, Book and Manuscript Appraisers, "Appraisal of Archive and Library of Theos C. Bernard & Related," May 26, 1998, 1.

388 "far over-burdened with the property": Julian Don Alexander II, letter to Gilah Yelin Hirsch, June 19,1990; Ken Winkler (biographer of Lama Govinda and Evans-Wentz), letter to Julian Don Alexander II, May 6, 1992, from the collection of Mr. Alexander.

388 experts were called in to appraise: Clark, "The Bernard-Murray Tibetan Collection," 4.

388 There also were piles of other boxes holding a treasury of more than 750 major artifacts from Tibet: Ibid.

389 Fifteen items were valued at $10,000: Ibid. Valuations cited are from the 1998 appraisal of art and artifacts by Dr. Richard Kohn, a specialist in Tibetan art and artifacts. The books, Bernard's field notes, files, manuscripts, typescripts, and photographs were appraised by Dr. Charles Goldsmid and Dr. Robert Allen.

389 "Placing the Bernard collection at Berkeley": "A Proposal to G. Eleanore Murray for the Theos Bernard Collection at the University of California, Berkeley," 9.

390 "quite awhile before footage can be made accessible": Mona Nagai, Film Collection Curator, University of California, Berkeley Art Museum and Pacific Film Archive, correspondence with the author, January 19, 2005 and November 18, 2008.

390 "this seems years away": Ibid., January 19, 2005.

391 Forty thousand troops of the People's Liberation Army: Tsering Shakya, *The*

Dragon in the Land of the Snows: A History of Modern Tibet Since 1947 (New York: Columbia University Press, 1999), 43.

391 suppress a growing rebellion against forced land: Ibid., 140–41; John Kenneth Knaus, *Orphans of the Cold War: America and the Tibetan Struggle for Survival* (New York: Public Affairs, 1999), 134.

391 His Holiness decided he must make an escape: Shakya, *The Dragon in the Land of the Snows*, 185–211.

391 Tsarong, volunteered to organize: Tsarong, *In the Service of His Country*, 144–46.

392 "When people die": Taring, *Daughter of Tibet*, 243, 307–11.

392 caught up in the politics of the Cultural Revolution: Shakya, *The Dragon in the Land of the Snows*, 320–24.

393 turned Lhasa into a boomtown: Ronald David Schwatz, *Circle of Protest: Political Ritual in the Tibetan Uprising* (New York: Columbia University Press, 1994), 203–4; Schwartz quoted in Tim Johnson, "Tibetans see 'Han Invasion' as Spurring Violence," McClatchy Newspapers, March 28, 2008, http://www.mcclatchydc.com/2008/03/28/31913/tibetans-see-han-invasion-as-spurring.html.

393 "the Chicago of Asia": Bernard, "The Peril of Tibet," 500.

393 eighteen hundred Tibetan Buddhist centers: World Buddhist Directory, http://www.buddhanet.info/wbd/search.php?keyword=Tibetan&search=Begin+Search&type_id%5B%5D=1&country_id=0&province_id=0&offset=1825.

393 sixteen million Americans practice some form of Yoga: "Yoga in America" Market Study, *Yoga Journal* press release, February 26, 2008, http://www.yogajournal.com/advertise/press_releases/10.

394 who both left Harvard in 1963: Lopez, *Prisoners of Shangri-La*, 163.

394 oversee the translation into English: "History," American Institute of Buddhist Studies, http://www.aibs.columbia.edu/history.shtml.

394 description of the translation project: Ibid. The American Institute of Buddhist

Studies was founded in 1972 at the behest of Geshe Wangyal to create the framework for the long-term project of translating the Tibetan Tengyur.

395 "the influence of this brilliant, English speaking Lama": Clark, "The Bernard-Murray Tibetan Collection," 13; Lopez, *The Madman's Middle Way*, 31.

396 descended from a handful of Indian teachers: Georg Feuerstein, "Styles of Hatha-Yoga," adapted from *The Deeper Dimension of Yoga: Theory and Practice*, http://www.shambhala.com/html/learn/features/yoga/basics/styles.cfm.

397 target is a demographic group: "Yoga in America" Market Study, 2008.

397 "the public mind is about 99% erroneous": Robertson, "The White Lama on Yoga," 14.

397 the fruit "which destroys death": Bernard, *Hatha Yoga*, 45.

398 "Other practices are simply futile for the Yogi": *Hatha Yoga Pardipika*, Chapter 4, lines 16–21, cited in Bernard, *Hatha Yoga*, 45.

398 "might stumble by in the course of a life time": Theos Bernard, letter fragment to Glen Bernard, n.d., Kalimpong, BANC: 3:47.

398 "Realize the wisdom of pure awareness": Yeshe Tsogyal, *The Lotus-Born: The Life Story of Padmasambhava* (Boston: Shambhala, 1993), 170–71.

ACKNOWLEDGMENTS

Writing seems such a solitary experience until the time comes to list some of the people who were indispensable in this book's creation. Without the direct and insistent early involvement of Geshe Michael Roach and Lama Christie McNally this book would never have been conceived. They gave me the idea, told me I would write a book, and then introduced me to their editor. Beyond that they taught me how to understand and approach the practices of Hatha Yoga and Tibetan Buddhism that Theos Bernard helped introduce to the West. For their love and wisdom and continued involvement I will always be grateful. I am grateful also to Winston Mc-Cullough, who gave me the solid foundation in these teachings and encouraged the critical acumen with which to explore further. Any errors about Yoga or Buddhism that I have allowed into this book are mine, not my teachers'.

Once I accepted the inevitability of writing this book, my agent, Ellen Levine at Trident Media Group, and editors Trace Murphy, Gary Jansen, and John Burke at Harmony Books guided me through the process and helped shape a sprawling manuscript. To them I am deeply appreciative for their patience and insight throughout.

Early in my research I discovered that others were working on parallel projects. Julian Don Alexander II had been researching Theos Bernard for a decade and generously sent me everything he had uncovered to jump-start my own project. Stefanie Syman, Robert Love, and Paul Hackett were all writing about other aspects of Theos Bernard's story and the development of Yoga in the United States, and my thanks goes to them for the helpful conversations and fine work they produced that together create a more comprehensive picture of that seminal period.

My own research was conducted over the course of seven years at archives in five states. I am especially grateful to Stephen Novak and Henry Blanco for their help in the Viola Wertheim Bernard collection at the Augustus C. Long Health Sciences Library at Columbia University, and Anthony Bliss for help with the Theos Bernard collection at the Bancroft Library at the University of California, Berkeley. Alicja Egbert, Media Collections Manager at the Phoebe A. Hearst Museum of Anthropology in Berkeley, spent hours finding and preparing photos for me from the Theos Bernard collection, and I am most appreciative of her good work and tolerance of my deadline rushes. Barbara Graham was most gracious and generous with her help finding and preparing documents at the Helen Graham Park Foundation archive in Miami Shores, Florida, and Deanna Hatch and Linda Gluck were equally gracious with their assistance in the archive at Ganna Walska Lotusland in Montecito, California. My research assistant, Jessica Kung, uncovered many valuable documents, especially at the Beinecke Rare Book and Manuscript Library at Yale.

This project took much longer to complete than anyone imagined when I first embarked on it. For support and encouragement over the last seven years I am grateful to my coconspirators Kimberley Theresa, John and Kristi Roadhouse, James Connor and Lisette Garcia, John Brady, Lama Sumati Marut, Darcy Jones, and Reema Datta. I also appreciate the patience and support of my colleagues in our Dorje and Vajra study groups. The long and frequent absences from my other obligations over the years would not have been possible without the joyful bearing of the loads I dumped on my colleagues at Diamond Mountain. My sincere thanks to Steve Yochum, Bert Scott, David Stumpf, John E. Oyzon, Matt Gallup, and Jarret Levine.

And going further back, I would like to thank Mary Moseley, with whom I made my first romps in the Himalayas, and Leahe Swayze and Greg Knott, who taught me in igloos and snow pits how to appreciate a long story well told.

If any of you had not showed up at the right time, this whole thing would either not have happened or been much more difficult. Thank you.

INDEX